International Advertising

Communicating
Across
Cultures

Recent Titles
from the Wadsworth
Series in Advertising
and Public Relations

**Advertising and Marketing
to the New Majority:
A Case Study Approach**
by Gail Baker Woods

Creative Strategy in Advertising
5th Edition
by A. Jerome Jewler

Public Relations Cases
3rd Edition
by Jerry A. Hendrix

**Public Relations Writing:
Form and Style**
5th Edition
by Doug Newsom and Bob Carrell

**This Is PR:
The Realities of Public Relations**
6th Edition
*by Doug Newsom, Judy VanSlyke Turk,
and Dean Kruckeberg*

International Advertising

Communicating
Across
Cultures

Barbara Mueller

San Diego State University

Wadsworth Publishing Company

I(T)P^RM An International Thomson Publishing Company

Belmont ▪ Albany ▪ Bonn ▪ Boston ▪ Cincinnati ▪ Detroit ▪ London ▪ Madrid ▪ Melbourne
Mexico City ▪ New York ▪ Paris ▪ San Francisco ▪ Singapore ▪ Tokyo ▪ Toronto ▪ Washington

Advertising Editor: Todd R. Armstrong
Editorial Assistant: Laura Murray
Production Editor: Jerilyn Emori
Managing Designer: Carolyn Deacy
Designer: Bruce Kortebein
Print Buyer: Karen Hunt
Permissions Editor: Robert Kauser

Art Editor: Nancy Spellman
Copy Editor: Thomas Briggs
Illustrator: Precision Graphics
Cover: Bruce Kortebein
Cover Photo (bottom): Digital Equipment Corp.
Compositor: Thompson Type
Printer: Quebecor Printing / Fairfield

*This book is printed on
acid-free recycled paper*

Printed in the United States of America
1 2 3 4 5 6 7 8 9 10—01 00 99 98 97 96

For more information, contact Wadsworth Publishing Company:

Wadsworth Publishing Company
10 Davis Drive
Belmont, California 94002, USA

International Thomson Publishing Europe
Berkshire House 168-173
High Holborn
London, WC1V 7AA, England

Thomas Nelson Australia
102 Dodds Street
South Melbourne 3205
Victoria, Australia

Nelson Canada
1120 Birchmount Road
Scarborough, Ontario
Canada M1K 5G4

International Thomson Editores
Campos Eliseos 385, Piso 7
Col. Polanco
11560 México D.F. México

International Thomson Publishing GmbH
Königswinterer Strasse 418
53227 Bonn, Germany

International Thomson Publishing Asia
221 Henderson Road
#05-10 Henderson Building
Singapore 0315

International Thomson Publishing Japan
Hirakawacho Kyowa Building, 3F
2-2-1 Hirakawacho
Chiyoda-ku, Tokyo 102, Japan

Library of Congress Cataloging-in-Publication Data

Mueller, Barbara
    International Advertising : communicating across cultures /
Barbara Mueller.
        p.   cm.
    Includes index.
    ISBN 0-534-19278-5
    1. Advertising.   2. Export marketing.   3. Intercultural
communication.   4. Advertising media planning.   I. Title.
HF5823.M83   1995
659.1—dc20   95-17905

Contents

CHAPTER 3

The International Marketing and Advertising Environment

CHAPTER 4

The Cultural Environment

CHAPTER 5

Coordinating and Controlling International Advertising

CHAPTER 6   **Creative Strategy and Execution**   138

CHAPTER 7   **Advertising Media in the International Arena**   163

CHAPTER 8   **Research in the International Arena**   195

CHAPTER 9

Advertising Regulatory Considerations in the International Arena

CHAPTER 10

Social Responsibility and Ethics in the Global Marketplace

Preface

INTERNATIONAL ADVERTISING: COMMUNICATING ACROSS CULTURES serves four purposes. First, it is an appropriate textbook for undergraduate and graduate students in specialized courses dealing with international advertising or marketing. Second, it is an effective supplemental text for introductory advertising, marketing, or mass communications courses, in that it provides expanded coverage of the international dimension to the curriculum. Third, it should also prove useful to practitioners of international advertising—be they on the client side or within the advertising agency. Finally, researchers of international advertising and marketing will find it a valuable resource.

This book introduces the student, practitioner, and researcher to the challenges and difficulties in developing and implementing communications programs for foreign markets. While advertising is the major focus, the author recognizes that an integrated marketing communications approach is critical to competing successfully in the international setting. In order to communicate effectively with audiences around the globe, marketers must coordinate not only advertising, direct marketing, sales promotions, personal selling, and public relations efforts but the other aspects of the marketing mix as well. Therefore, the basics of international marketing are briefly reviewed in the first several chapters of this text. The remainder of the book explores international advertising.

Every attempt has been made to provide a balance of theoretical and practical perspectives. For example, the issues of centralization versus decentralization and standardization versus localization or specialization are addressed as they apply to the organization of international advertising programs, development and execution of creative strategy, media planning and buying, and advertising research. Readers will find that these are not black-and-white issues. Instead, they can be viewed as a continuum. Some marketing and advertising decisions can be centralized while others may be decentralized. Similarly, depending on the product to be advertised and the target audience to be communicated with, some elements of the marketing and advertising mix may be standardized while others will be specialized.

This text comprises a total of eleven chapters. In Chapter 1 factors influencing the growth of international advertising are examined. Chapter 2 highlights the role that product, price, distribution, and promotion play in selling abroad. Domestic advertising and international advertising differ not so much in concept as in environment; the international marketing and advertising environment is outlined in Chapter 3. Chapter 4 is devoted to developing a sensitivity to the various cultural factors that impact international marketing efforts. Chapter 5 addresses the coordination and control of international advertising. Chapter 6 deals with creative strategies and executions for foreign audiences. Chapters 7–9 explore media decisions in the global marketplace, international advertising research and methods for obtaining the information necessary for making international advertising decisions, and, finally, regulatory considerations. Chapter 10 focuses on the social responsibility of international advertising agencies and multinational corporations in foreign markets. While this text is not intended to provide a country-by-country analysis of the global marketplace (a futile effort, given how quickly our world changes), several marketing frontiers are highlighted in Chapter 11: the European Union, the new Commonwealth of Independent States, China and the Pacific Rim, and Latin America.

I am indebted to a great many individuals for the successful completion of this project. Dozens of advertisements, charts, diagrams, and tables were employed to illustrate various points in this text. Inclusion of these materials would not have been possible without the permission granted by advertisers, their agencies, various publications, and other advertising-related organizations. A number of colleagues provided detailed reviews of several versions of this manuscript. The author wishes to thank the reviewers for their invaluable comments and ideas: Tom Duncan, University of Colorado at Boulder; Katherine Frith, Pennsylvania State University; Hower Hsia, Texas Technical University (retired); Wei-Na Lee, University of Texas at Austin; Yorgo Pasedeos, University of Alabama; Jyotika Ramaprasad, Southern Illinois University; and Fred Zandpour, California State University at Fullerton. In addition, I would like to acknowledge the folks at Wadsworth Publishing for supporting the idea of a textbook on international advertising. In particular, my appreciation goes to Kris Clerkin for encouraging me to begin this project, and to Todd Armstrong, who saw it to completion. Thanks also go to Tom Briggs, who did a wonderful job editing the manuscript, and to Jerilyn Emori, who held my hand during the production process. On a personal note, I am grateful to my parents, Heinz and Johanna, who instilled in me an appreciation for education. Without my husband, Juergen, there would be no manuscript, for he gave me the confidence to write this book and stood by me through the several years it took to bring it to fruition.

CHAPTER 1

The Growth of International Business and Advertising

Two major phenomena are currently impacting consumers worldwide. The first is the extraordinary growth in the number of businesses operating internationally. Today, consumers around the world smoke Marlboro cigarettes and write with Bic pens, watch Sony television sets and drive Toyota autos. Shoppers can stop in for a McDonald's burger in Paris or Beijing, and German and Japanese citizens alike increasingly make their purchases with the American Express Card. The growth and expansion of firms operating internationally have led to the rise of the second phenomenon—the growth in international advertising. U.S. agencies are increasingly looking abroad for clients. At the same time, foreign agencies are rapidly expanding around the globe, even taking control of some of the most prestigious U.S. agencies. Advertising expertise is no longer an American monopoly. Madison Avenue faces stiff competition from London, Madrid, and Tokyo. This chapter outlines the growth of international business and advertising.

Growth of International Business

Historical Overview

Historically, the vastness of the U.S. marketplace offered sufficient opportunities for corporate expansion at home, and as a result, U.S. firms were not forced to look abroad. An additional deterrent was the sheer distance to foreign markets—with the exception of Canada and Mexico. Yet, during the late 1800s, a number of firms recognized the importance of foreign expansion, and by the early 1900s, firms such as Ford Motor, Singer, Gillette, National Cash Register, Otis, and Western Electric had commanding world market shares.

> Driving this first wave of modern globalization were rising production scale economies due to advancements in technology that outpaced the growth of the world economy. Product needs also became more homogenized in different countries as knowledge and industrialization diffused. Transport improved, first through the railroad and steamships and later in trucking. Communication became easier with the telegraph then the telephone. At the same time, trade barriers were either modest or overwhelmed by the advantages of the new large-scale firm.[1]

The trend to globalization slowed between 1920 and the late 1940s. These decades were marked by a world economic crisis as well as a second world war, which resulted in a period of strong nationalism. Countries attempted to salvage and strengthen their own economies by imposing high tariffs and quotas so as to keep out foreign goods and protect domestic employment. It was not until after the Second World War that the number of U.S. firms operating internationally again began to grow significantly. In 1950 U.S. foreign direct investment stood at $12 billion. By 1965 it had risen to $50 billion, and by the late 1970s to approximately $150 billion.[2] And in 1991 (the most recent year for which figures are available) foreign direct investment had swelled to over $450 billion.[3]

International tensions—whether in the form of cold war or open conflict—tend to discourage international marketing. However, since 1945, the world has been, for the most part, relatively peaceful. This, paired with the creation of the International Monetary Fund (IMF) and the General Agreement on Tariffs and Trade (GATT) at the close of World War II, facilitated the growth of international trade and investment. Indeed, during this period tariffs among the industrialized nations fell from about 40 percent in 1947 to roughly 5 percent in 1991. As a consequence, according to a 1994 *Fortune* magazine survey, the top 50 multinational companies alone generated almost $2.25 trillion in sales in 1993. The United States led all countries with 159 companies on the list; Japan ranked second (135 companies), and Britain

TABLE 1.1	The World's Twenty-five Biggest Companies by Industry, 1993 (in million $)		
INDUSTRY	**COMPANY**	**COUNTRY**	**SALES**
Aerospace	Boeing	U.S.	$25,285
Apparel	Levi Strauss	U.S.	5,892
Beverages	PepsiCo	U.S.	25,021
Building materials	Saint-Gobain	France	12,630
Chemicals	Du Pont	U.S.	32,621
Computers	IBM	U.S.	62,716
Electronics	Hitachi	Japan	68,582
Food	Philip Morris	U.S.	50,621
Forest/paper goods	International Paper	U.S.	13,685
Industrial/farm equipment	Mitsubishi Heavy Industries	Japan	25,804
Jewelry/silverware	Citizen Watch	Japan	3,501
Metal products	Pechiney	France	11,127
Metals	IRI	Italy	50,488
Mining, crude oil production	Ruhrkohle	Germany	14,155
Motor vehicles	General Motors	U.S.	133,622
Petroleum refining	Exxon	U.S.	97,825
Pharmaceutical	Johnson & Johnson	U.S.	14,138
Publishing/printing	Bertelsmann	Germany	10,957
Rubber/plastic products	Bridgestone	Japan	14,377
Scientific and photo equipment	Eastman Kodak	U.S.	20,059
Soaps/cosmetics	Procter & Gamble	U.S.	30,433
Textiles	Toray Industries	Japan	8,196
Tobacco	RJR Nabisco	U.S.	15,104
Toys/sporting goods	Nintendo	Japan	4,500
Transportation equipment	Hyundai Heavy Industries	Japan	6,735

SOURCE: "Fortune's Global 500," *Fortune*, July 25, 1994, pp. 137–196.

third (41). As outlined in Table 1.1, U.S. firms are ranked No. 1 in 13 of the top 25 industries on the list.[4]

In addition to these large corporations, thousands of smaller U.S. firms are engaging in international marketing. Indeed, the majority of U.S. exporters have fewer than 100 employees. Southern Gold Honey Co., a small honey producer in Vidor, Texas, provides an excellent example. Almost overnight in 1985, the fifteen-year-old company's domestic market turned sour and sales tumbled due to imports of less expensive honey. When the firm realized it could no longer compete on U.S. soil, its owners looked overseas. Within four years sales quadrupled—due solely to major exports to the Middle East.[5]

International business continues to expand for other reasons as well. Corporations may look abroad for the very same reasons they seek to expand their markets at home. Where economies of scale are feasible, a large market is essential. However, if a single market is not large enough to absorb the entire output, a firm may look to other markets. If production equipment is not fully utilized in meeting the demands of one market, additional markets may be tapped. Seasonal fluctuations in demand in a particular market may also be evened out by sales in another. During economic downturns in one market, corporations may turn to new markets to absorb excess output. Firms may also find that a product's life cycle can be extended if the product is introduced in different markets—products already considered obsolete by one group may well be sold successfully to another. In addition to the reasons noted, significant changes in the United States and around the globe have helped fuel this phenomenal growth in international business.

Saturated Domestic Markets

The slowing U.S. population growth rate has directly impacted U.S. firms. Between 1970 and 1980, the number of households increased at a rate of 27 percent; however, between 1980 and 1990, the rate of increase slipped to little over 15 percent. Further, in 1960 the average household contained 3.3 persons; by the early 1990s that number had dropped to 2.63. And this downward trend in both size and growth rate is expected to continue. As a result, many firms must cultivate new markets if they are to continue to prosper. For example, Tambrands, with $700 million in sales worldwide, has led the U.S. feminine hygiene products market since 1936. While domestic sales of its products have been rising by less than 10 percent annually, the company's overseas sales are increasing at over 15 percent per year. Tambrands has built plants in China and the former Soviet Union to gain access to faster-growing markets. Sales in these two regions alone could more than double to $42 million by 1995.[6] Likewise, in 1984 Toys 'R' Us, anticipating the day when it would saturate its domestic market, began looking abroad. Today, the toy company has retail outlets in Canada, Europe, Hong Kong, Singapore, and, most recently, Japan. With more than $6 billion in annual sales, Japan is the world's No. 2 toy market after the United States.[7]

Higher Profit Margins in Foreign Markets

According to *Business Week*, "American manufacturers with factories or sales subsidiaries overseas are outperforming their domestic counterparts. A study of more than 1,500 companies reported that U.S. multinationals during the 1980s posted faster growth than domestics in 19 out of 20 major industry groups, and higher earnings in 17."[8] The typical U.S. industrial company today rings up 25 percent of its sales overseas, compared with only 15 percent in 1980.[9] For example, firms such as General Motors, ITT, and Philip Morris generate over a quarter of total sales from exports. More internationally oriented firms such as Ford Motor, Johnson & Johnson, Eastman Kodak, and Procter & Gamble generate 35–50 percent of their total revenues from foreign sales. And for an increasing number of businesses, international sales represent over 50 percent of total sales—for example, for Coca-Cola 64 percent of sales, and for Exxon 75 percent.[10]

Increased Foreign Competition in Domestic Markets

Even as American products are increasingly sold abroad, foreign products are playing a more significant role in the United States. Although the phonograph, color TV, video- and audiotape recorder, telephone, and integrated circuit all were invented in the United States, domestic producers account for only a small percentage of the U.S. market for most of these products today—and an even smaller share of the world market. For example, in 1970 U.S. producers' share of the domestic market for color TVs stood at nearly 90 percent. By 1990 it had dropped to little more than 10 percent. The decline in sales of U.S.-produced stereo components is even more serious—from 90 percent of domestic sales to little more than 1 percent during the same time span.[11] Brand names such as Sony and Panasonic have become household words for most American consumers. In 1992 Japan-based automakers alone held a 23 percent market share in U.S. sales.[12] The fact that imports are taking an increasingly larger share of the domestic market for many products—consumer as well as industrial—is an additional incentive for U.S. firms to adopt an international marketing orientation.

As Rachel McCulloch notes, "After decades as the leading source country for outward direct investment, by the mid 1980s, the U.S. had replaced Canada as the world's number one host country in total value of foreign controlled business activity."[13] As a consequence of the investment boom of the 1980s, foreign companies now play a prominent part in the daily lives of Americans. When a U.S. consumer buys new tires, shops for the latest bestseller, or purchases cat food, chances are increasingly good that the supplier will be a local subsidiary of a company based in Japan, Europe, or Canada. For example, both Firestone Rubber and CBS Records were acquired by Japanese firms; Macmillan Publishing and Pillsbury are now owned by British firms; and Carnation (makers of Coffee-mate and Friskies pet food) was acquired by a Swiss company.

Since the 1980s there has been a significant slowdown. Foreign direct investment in the United States fell 47 percent in 1992, the fourth consecutive annual drop.[14] The current investment slowdown in the United States

TABLE 1.2 Direct Foreign Investments in the United States (in U.S. billion $)

COUNTRY	KEY INDUSTRY	INDUSTRY AMOUNT	TOTAL INVESTMENT
Japan	Trade	$31.7	$ 86.6
Britain	Manufacturing	50.1	106.0
Netherlands	Petroleum	12.2	63.8
Canada	Finance and insurance	9.7	30.0
Germany	Manufacturing	16.5	28.1
Switzerland	Manufacturing	9.7	17.9

SOURCE: U.S. Department of Commerce, Bureau of the Census. *1993 Statistical Abstracts of the United States* (113th ed.) (Washington, DC: GPO, 1993), p. 798.

reflects fewer new investment opportunities as well as competing opportunities elsewhere in the world. Despite this slowdown, however, claims *Fortune* magazine, foreigners still appear to want things American: "Their tastes for the tangible extend across the map, from Kentucky racehorses and Texas refineries to New England factories and Sonoma Valley vineyards. They own farmland in all but one state (Rhode Island so far has eluded them) and sizable hunks of Wall Street, both in real estate and the investment banking business. They sign paychecks for three million Americans, including employees of 19 Fortune 500 companies."[15] This "selling of America" has caused a good deal of concern among the business community as well as the general public. Table 1.2 outlines direct foreign investments in the United States by country and by industry.[16]

Increased foreign competition on domestic soil is not unique to the United States, but rather is occurring in both other developed countries and emerging economies. *Fortune* magazine summarizes the globe's rapidly changing economic landscape: "The mature economies still account for most foreign direct investment. The flow into Britain mainly reflects heavy spending by the Japanese companies entering the European Community. But the emerging countries—which barely figured in the international investment equations a decade ago—will augment their own savings with an ever growing share of the world's market."[17] Table 1.3 shows foreign direct investment inflows for both developed and emerging markets.

The Trade Deficit

Exports have accounted for an ever increasing proportion of the U.S. gross national product—more than 10 percent in recent years. In 1993 the United States exported an estimated $464 billion of goods and services. However,

TABLE 1.3 Foreign Direct Investment Inflows (in U.S. billion $)

DEVELOPED MARKETS	AMOUNT	EMERGING MARKETS	AMOUNT
Britain	$21.1	Mexico	$4.8
France	15.2	Singapore	3.6
United States	11.5	Malaysia	3.5
Spain	10.5	Thailand	2.0
Belgium/Luxembourg	9.4	Venezuela	1.9
Germany	6.6	Indonesia	1.5
Sweden	6.4	Hungary	1.5
Australia	4.7	South Korea	1.1
Canada	4.5	Brazil	0.9
Netherlands	4.1	Chile	0.6

SOURCE: "Fortune's Global 500," *Fortune,* July 26, 1993, pp. 188–231.

imports during that same year totaled almost $603 billion, resulting in a balance-of-trade deficit of over $138 billion.[18] Exports are considered a central contributor to economic growth and well-being for a country. For example, every $1 billion in merchandise exports supports approximately 19,000 U.S. jobs. The current trade deficit has made it a matter of vital national interest to increase exports.

The Emergence of New Markets

European Union The emergence of new markets has stimulated interest in international business. On December 31, 1992, many physical, fiscal, and technical barriers to trade among the twelve-nation European Union (EU) began to disappear—giving birth to something akin to the United States of Europe. This single market consists of 460 million consumers—44 percent more than in the United States—making it the world's largest industrialized market. The original "European 12" (Belgium, Denmark, France, Germany, Greece, Ireland, Italy, Luxembourg, the Netherlands, Portugal, Spain, and the United Kingdom), now joined by Sweden, Norway, and Austria, constitute the world's greatest trading area monetarily—accounting for well over 20 percent of the world's trade. Many companies are already making plans to approach Europe as a single market—rather than as a group of distinct countries—by realigning their product lines and developing strategies that can be employed throughout the EU. For example, Gillette Europe recently scrapped its country-by-country marketing strategy for the Blue II disposable razor blade and replaced it with a pan-European approach.

Commonwealth of Independent States With the failed coup of August 1991, the subsequent resignation of President Mikhail Gorbachev, and the relegation of the former Soviet Union to official oblivion, trade and investment opportunities in the newly formed Commonwealth of Independent States (CIS) are expected to increase dramatically in the coming years. Corporations around the globe are eying the CIS, with its population of over 200 million, as the next marketing frontier. Procter & Gamble signed a joint venture agreement in August 1991 with Leningrad State University to begin marketing and distributing consumer products, such as Wash & Go shampoo (the European name for Pert Plus) throughout the Ukraine and Baltics. Philip Morris signed agreements with the Soviet government and the Russian republic to supply more than 20 billion cigarettes—the largest order in the company's history—but still only 5 percent of the market for cigarettes in the CIS. And, in late 1991, Visa became the first credit card available to the general public in the CIS. However, only a small percentage of citizens holding non-CIS currency will be able to obtain the cards, which expire every six months. As with many other goods being introduced to the new commonwealth, firms are looking toward future sales rather than immediate profits.

Pacific Rim As recently as 1977, the total volume of two-way trade between the People's Republic of China and the United States was under $400 million. Less than two years later, China began to experiment with open markets and continued to liberalize trade laws. In 1979 Coca-Cola became the first American product available in China when the company was awarded the sole privilege of selling soft drinks to the Chinese market. That same year, for the first time, Chinese authorities permitted domestic product advertising in newspapers. By 1988 total two-way trade between the United States and China had jumped to almost $17 billion. Despite the events in Tiananmen Square in June 1989, U.S. businesses continue to knock on China's door. In 1992, for example, in a joint venture with a Chinese state-owned company, McDonald's opened a restaurant in Beijing that executives hope will be the flagship of a growing presence in China. The restaurant—with its 700 seats and 29 cash registers—is the biggest McDonald's in the world, slightly bigger than the one that opened in Moscow in early 1990. At the close of the first day of business, the restaurant had registered 13,214 transactions—representing approximately 40,000 customers—setting a new one-day sales record for any McDonald's in the world. Beijing is also home to four Kentucky Fried Chicken outlets, two Pizza Huts, three Holiday Inns, and innumerable other foreign-managed hotels and restaurants.

In addition to China, the Pacific Rim economies of Hong Kong, Thailand, Malaysia, Singapore, South Korea, Taiwan, Indonesia, the Philippines, and Australia are expected to be the centers of global growth and the hottest markets worldwide in the coming decade. Luis Kraar comments:

> While the West's economy remains sluggish, their [Pacific Rim's] demand for fast food, paint, semi-conductors, life insurance, and much else remains strong. By the decade's end, the Asia-Pacific region (population 1.8 billion) could wield more buying power than the European Community. Asia is so vast, and its wealth rising so quickly, that for many companies it will be more than just another attractive market. It could become one of the largest contributors of revenues and profits within the decade.[19]

Analysts note that despite this potential, few U.S. companies have a long-term strategy for the region. The region also poses special challenges for marketers because it is significantly less homogenous than North America or even Europe.

Canada/Mexico Negotiations between President Clinton, Mexican President Carlos Salinas de Gortari, and Canadian Prime Minister Brian Mulroney have resulted in the signing of a North American Free-Trade Agreement (NAFTA). This pact creates a market of 360 million consumers with a gross national product of over $6 trillion—representing a formidable competitor to the fifteen-nation EU. NAFTA has generated a great deal of debate, and the pact is likely to produce both winners and losers in each country. For example, some jobs in each country are likely to be lost as manufacturers move both north and south across the borders. On the other hand, goods are expected to become cheaper as tariffs on thousands of products are removed, and shoppers are likely to have a greater variety of products to choose from.

World Trade

In the past twenty years alone, world trade has expanded from $200 billion to over $4 trillion. The United States was once considered the "hub" of world trade. While it remains a major player, U.S. participation in world trade measured as a portion of world market share has declined drastically. Whereas in 1950 the United States accounted for nearly 25 percent of the world trade flow, its current share is less than 10 percent. It is not that U.S. exports have actually dropped during this period; rather, these figures reflect the entrance of other trading partners into the picture. In 1980 twenty-three American companies made *Fortune*'s top 50, compared with only five Japanese firms. Today only fifteen American companies rank among the top 50, while the number of Japanese companies has increased to thirteen. Competition for world markets comes not only from other industrialized countries but from newly industrialized countries as well. Two of the largest corporations on *Fortune*'s list—Samsung (No. 14) and Daewoo (No. 33)—are South Korean. A Mexican petroleum-producing firm also ranks among the top 100 companies. American corporations have come to realize that the United States is no longer an isolated, self-sufficient national economy, but rather simply another player in the global marketplace.

Growth in Advertising Expenditures Worldwide

Patterns in the growth of international advertising mirror those of international business. At the end of World War II, the bulk of advertising activity was domestic, and 75 percent of recorded advertising expenditures worldwide was concentrated in the United States. Since then, the growth in advertising expenditure worldwide has been phenomenal. In 1950 estimated advertising expenditure totaled $7.4 billion worldwide, including $5.7 billion in the United States alone. By the late 1970s the advertising expenditure had swelled to nearly $72 billion worldwide, including $38 billion in the United States. And today, total advertising expenditures worldwide stand at $312 billion.[20]

The role of advertising varies significantly from country to country, as the figures in Table 1.4 suggest. Table 1.4 lists countries with over $1 billion in advertising expenditures in 1993. Countries spending the most on advertising are primarily the rich industrialized nations, such as the United States, which spent as much on advertising as the next six countries combined. The United States has traditionally been the world leader in total advertising expenditure—contributing over 50 percent of the total figure year after year. However, in 1989 advertising growth rates outside the United States outstripped U.S. growth for the first time.

For the most part, the developing countries in Asia, Africa, and the Middle East appear to be light advertisers. However, economic development is not the sole predictor of advertising expenditure. Some relatively rich countries, such as Austria, are not even on this list, while countries such as Brazil and South Korea are. This suggests that other variables, such as culture, must be considered in attempting to understand the role of advertising in a particular country. Nor do the figures in the table reflect the relative costs of media time/space in each of the countries. It should be noted that media costs in many developing countries tend to be rather low, and this factor should be taken into consideration when making comparisons.

TABLE 1.4   1993 Total Advertising Expenditures (in U.S. million $)

COUNTRY	AMOUNT	COUNTRY	AMOUNT
United States	$84,872.0	Mexico	$2,914.8
Japan	34,003.3	Netherlands	2,584.4
Germany	15,984.9	Switzerland	2,306.8
United Kingdom	14,119.0	Sweden	1,659.2
Italy	8,811.9	Belgium	1,446.5
France	8,573.9	Hong Kong	1,347.0
Spain	8,029.3	Venezuela	1,195.9
South Korea	4,688.3	Austria	1,142.8
Australia	3,651.1	Denmark	1,103.8
Taiwan	3,215.1	Finland	1,013.1

NOTE: Total expenditures include major media only and exclude direct mail.
SOURCE: International Advertising Association Worldwide Summary, 1994.

The leading advertising spenders outside the United States, by both U.S. and foreign firms, are listed in Table 1.5. Overall, the top 50 spent $18.9 billion outside the United States in 1993, up only 0.4 percent over 1992. Spending by the sixteen companies based in Asia rose only 2.3 percent, while the twenty-one companies based in Europe, suffering from a lingering recession, cut back by 1.7 percent. The remaining thirteen, all U.S.-based, stepped up spending by 3.4 percent.[21]

The Trend Toward International Agencies

Around the turn of the century, in order to better service clients who were beginning to market their products internationally, advertising agencies also moved abroad. The first American agency to establish itself overseas was J. Walter Thompson, which opened an office in London in 1899 to meet the needs of its client, General Motors. By the early 1920s both J. Walter Thompson and McCann-Erickson had large overseas networks with offices in Europe, India, and Latin America. Overall, however, agency movement to foreign soil was rather slow prior to 1960.

A study of fifteen large American multinational agencies revealed that in the forty-five years between 1915 and 1959, these agencies had opened or

TABLE 1.5 Top 50 Advertising Spenders Outside the United States (in U.S. million $)

RANK				AD SPENDING OUTSIDE THE U.S.		
1993	1992	COMPANY	HEADQUARTERS	1993	1992	% Change
1	1	**Procter & Gamble**	Cincinnati	**$1,901.0**	$1,866.0	1.9%
2	2	**Unilever**	Rotterdam/London	**1,888.0**	1,850.4	2.0
3	3	**Nestlé**	Vevey, Switzerland	**1,122.7**	1,154.3	−2.7
4	4	**Philip Morris**	New York	**713.2**	706.7	0.9
5	6	**Volkswagen**	Wolfsburg, Germany	**706.6**	624.4	13.2
6	5	**PSA Peugeot-Citroen**	Paris	**701.4**	676.6	3.7
7	8	**General Motors**	Detroit	**600.6**	583.4	3.0
8	11	**Ford Motor**	Dearborn, Mich.	**534.2**	528.6	1.1
9	9	**L'Oreal**	Paris	**526.8**	529.5	−0.5
10	12	**Mars**	McLean, Va.	**517.6**	515.8	0.4
11	7	**Fiat**	Turin, Italy	**503.5**	603.1	−16.5
12	10	**Renault**	Paris	**462.0**	529.1	−12.7
13	14	**Coca-Cola**	Atlanta	**448.2**	437.3	2.5
14	17	**Kao**	Tokyo	**435.6**	412.2	5.7
15	13	**Toyota Motor**	Toyota City, Japan	**422.2**	439.8	−4.0
16	15	**Henkel Group**	Düsseldorf	**415.0**	429.7	−3.4
17	19	**Nissan Motor**	Tokyo	**411.5**	379.8	8.3
18	16	**Colgate-Palmolive**	New York	**407.3**	413.0	−1.4
19	18	**Danone**	Levallois-Perret, France	**362.5**	404.6	−10.4
20	20	**Kellogg**	Battle Creek, Mich.	**362.1**	355.5	1.8
21	21	**Ferrero**	Perugia, Italy	**361.8**	327.6	10.4
22	22	**PepsiCo**	Purchase, N.Y.	**344.8**	316.6	8.9
23	27	**Suntory**	Tokyo	**314.3**	268.2	17.2
24	28	**McDonald's**	Oak Brook, Ill.	**298.0**	261.0	14.2
25	23	**Philips**	Eindhoven, The Netherlands	**280.7**	301.5	−6.9
26	29	**Honda Motor**	Tokyo	**273.3**	251.3	8.8
27	24	**Mitsubishi Motor**	Tokyo	**270.4**	285.8	−5.4
28	25	**Matsushita Electric Industrial**	Osaka	**261.2**	272.2	−4.0
29	26	**Sony**	Tokyo	**244.7**	270.4	−9.5
30	30	**Shiseido**	Tokyo	**236.5**	248.0	−4.6
31	33	**Johnson & Johnson**	New Brunswick, N.J.	**207.5**	182.3	13.8
32	31	**C&A Breninkmeyer**	Amsterdam	**202.0**	240.6	−16.1
33	32	**Daimler-Benz**	Stuttgart	**187.5**	185.1	1.3

U.S. AD SPENDING		WORLDWIDE AD SPENDING			REGIONAL 1993 AD SPENDING				
1993	1992	1993	1992	% Change	Asia	Europe	Latin America	Mideast	Canada
$2,397.5	$2,164.3	$4,298.5	$4,030.3	6.7%	$341.6	$1,319.8	$154.7	$18.4	$66.5
738.2	690.4	2,626.2	2,540.8	3.4	269.2	1,308.1	249.3	33.7	27.7
793.7	731.1	1,916.4	1,885.4	1.6	243.3	729.5	114.7	8.1	27.0
1,844.3	1,977.5	2,557.5	2,684.2	−4.7	80.9	499.4	91.5	12.9	28.6
85.5	82.6	792.1	707.0	12.0	29.1	638.3	22.3	7.5	9.4
0.0	0.0	701.4	676.6	3.7	1.0	681.6	16.8	2.0	0.0
1,539.2	1,345.2	2,139.8	1,928.6	11.0	22.8	417.3	66.2	5.4	89.0
958.3	794.8	1,492.5	1,323.4	12.8	40.1	421.8	36.9	9.2	26.2
NA	NA	526.8	529.5	−0.5	0.9	504.6	19.9	1.4	0.0
337.6	320.4	855.2	836.2	2.3	70.3	438.2	0.0	0.0	9.1
1.0	0.2	504.5	603.3	−16.4	0.0	481.2	21.7	0.6	0.0
0.0	0.0	462.0	529.1	−12.7	0.6	450.5	9.4	1.5	0.0
341.3	392.0	789.5	829.3	−4.8	130.0	170.5	111.2	18.6	18.0
14.8	18.4	450.3	430.6	4.6	427.0	8.5	0.0	0.0	0.0
690.4	648.9	1,112.6	1,088.7	2.2	254.2	132.6	0.0	19.5	15.9
0.2	0.0	415.2	429.7	−3.4	0.0	415.0	0.0	0.0	0.0
413.1	370.7	824.6	750.5	9.9	198.5	176.2	13.4	10.6	12.7
287.4	315.5	694.7	728.5	−4.6	71.2	211.7	108.2	8.7	7.5
33.8	24.4	396.3	429.0	−7.6	0.6	352.6	9.3	0.0	0.0
627.1	630.3	989.2	985.8	0.3	41.8	234.0	54.1	6.0	26.1
9.1	7.3	370.9	334.9	10.8	3.5	358.4	0.0	0.0	0.0
1,038.9	929.6	1,383.7	1,246.2	11.0	82.4	40.9	174.7	19.2	27.7
2.8	2.6	317.1	270.8	17.1	314.3	0.0	0.0	0.0	0.0
736.6	743.6	1,034.6	1,004.6	3.0	90.3	166.1	13.4	0.2	27.9
158.3	161.6	439.0	463.1	−5.2	11.7	226.1	42.4	0.5	0.0
354.4	349.1	627.7	600.4	4.6	160.5	92.6	0.0	2.1	18.2
113.4	109.2	383.8	395.0	−2.8	232.9	35.5	0.0	2.0	0.0
385.1	312.0	646.3	584.2	10.6	241.7	16.0	0.0	1.8	1.8
589.0	517.0	833.7	787.4	5.9	128.5	93.5	6.4	1.7	14.6
1.7	1.6	238.3	249.6	−4.5	224.3	12.2	0.0	0.0	0.0
762.5	717.4	970.0	899.7	7.8	70.5	90.1	31.9	0.3	14.7
0.0	0.0	202.0	240.6	−16.1	0.0	192.5	9.5	0.0	0.0
116.6	100.8	304.1	285.9	6.4	35.2	141.3	3.4	4.0	3.6

(continued)

13

TABLE 1.5   (continued)

RANK				AD SPENDING OUTSIDE THE U.S.		
1993	1992	COMPANY	HEADQUARTERS	1993	1992	% Change
34	34	Toshiba	Tokyo	$180.4	$181.6	−0.6%
35	37	Ajinomoto	Tokyo	158.0	140.9	12.1
36	36	B.A.T. Industries	London	148.5	144.6	2.7
37	35	Volvo	Goteborg, Sweden	145.3	160.3	−9.3
38	40	Beiersdorf	Hamburg	141.1	127.4	10.7
39	42	Lotte Group	Seoul	131.7	120.7	9.2
40	38	BMW	Munich	121.8	130.8	−6.8
41	39	Time Warner	New York	119.8	130.0	−7.8
42	47	RJR Nabisco	Winston-Salem, N.C.	105.9	110.1	−3.9
43	48	Hitachi	Tokyo	105.3	106.3	−0.9
44	58	Daewoo Group	Seoul	97.3	67.4	44.3
45	56	Lucky Goldstar	Seoul	95.8	76.1	25.9
46	44	Mazda Motor	Hiroshima, Japan	95.6	116.2	−17.7
47	45	NEC	Tokyo	94.5	110.3	−14.4
48	46	Bayer	Leverkusen, Germany	94.2	110.2	−14.6
49	49	Cadbury Schweppes	London	92.6	101.6	−8.9
50	55	British Aerospace	London	90.6	77.0	17.6

SOURCE: *Advertising Age,* November 21, 1994, p. I4. Reprinted by permission.

acquired only 50 overseas branch offices. Yet, in the subsequent twelve-year period, 210 overseas branch offices were opened or acquired—a fourfold increase.[22]

When firms began to expand to foreign markets, their advertising agencies were faced with the following options: (1) allow a local agency abroad to handle the account, (2) allow a U.S. agency with an established international network to service their client, or (3) open or acquire an overseas branch. Initially, when multinational clients were the exception rather than the rule, the second alternative was the most common practice. However, allowing another agency to handle a client's international business became rather risky. For example, when D'Arcy, the agency handling advertising for Coca-Cola, was unable to provide service to Coca-Cola's overseas branches, the client turned to McCann-Erickson to handle its international account. Shortly thereafter, Coca-Cola dropped D'Arcy altogether, giving McCann-Erickson both its international and domestic accounts.[23]

The 1960s were characterized by rampant expansion abroad by U.S. advertising agencies. Agencies began to see many advantages to joining their

U.S. AD SPENDING		WORLDWIDE AD SPENDING			REGIONAL 1993 AD SPENDING				
1993	1992	1993	1992	% Change	Asia	Europe	Latin America	Mideast	Canada
$ 10.5	$ 14.1	$190.9	$195.7	−2.4%	$172.3	$ 1.1	$ 6.4	$0.6	$ 0.0
0.0	0.0	158.0	140.9	12.1	150.0	0.0	8.0	0.0	0.0
116.9	73.7	265.4	218.3	21.6	30.7	54.7	60.3	2.9	0.0
99.8	67.0	245.1	227.3	7.9	18.1	123.0	0.0	0.9	3.3
14.1	7.1	155.2	134.5	15.4	0.0	131.7	8.2	1.2	0.0
1.3	1.4	133.0	122.1	9.0	131.7	0.0	0.0	0.0	0.0
97.3	108.8	219.1	239.6	−8.5	25.9	92.1	0.0	1.0	2.8
695.1	637.9	814.9	767.9	6.1	34.0	62.2	7.7	4.8	11.1
499.4	496.2	605.3	606.3	−0.2	15.8	19.1	59.6	3.3	8.1
16.1	20.6	121.4	126.9	−4.3	97.0	0.0	8.1	0.1	0.0
0.2	0.6	97.5	68.0	43.4	93.6	0.0	3.3	0.5	0.0
0.9	0.7	96.7	76.8	26.0	95.7	0.0	0.0	0.1	0.0
228.0	215.4	323.6	331.6	−2.4	9.1	61.0	0.0	7.6	17.9
16.7	11.9	111.2	122.2	−9.0	93.5	1.0	0.0	0.0	0.0
145.3	125.9	239.5	236.1	1.4	0.0	71.0	22.9	0.3	0.0
22.0	15.3	114.6	116.9	−2.0	23.7	54.9	8.3	0.2	5.4
6.6	5.8	97.2	82.8	17.4	15.3	75.3	0.0	0.0	0.0

clients in foreign markets. By moving abroad, these agencies could not only service their domestic clients but also compete for the foreign accounts of other American-based multinational firms and for the accounts of local foreign firms. Thus, as domestic advertising volume began to taper off, foreign markets looked increasingly appealing. In addition, there was the attraction of potentially higher profits. Overseas salaries of advertising staff members in the 1960s were as much as 70 percent lower than in the United States, while average agency profits were often twice that of what they were in the United States.[24] Setting up offices overseas had the additional benefit of freeing U.S. agencies from a total dependency on the performance of the American economy as a whole. For example, during the 1970 recession, domestic advertising agency billings declined 1 percent while the foreign billings of multinational agencies increased 13 percent.[25]

In contrast to the 1960s, the 1970s was a period of consolidation and retrenchment for many U.S. advertising agencies. While the combined annual billings of multinational agencies continued to increase, many smaller multinational agencies with a limited presence overseas were forced to withdraw

TABLE 1.6   The World's Top 50 Advertising Agencies (in U.S. million $)

RANK		
1993	**1992**	**ADVERTISING ORGANIZATION, HEADQUARTERS**
1	1	**WPP Group,** London
2	2	**Interpublic Group of Cos.,** New York
3	3	**Omnicom Group,** New York
4	5	**Dentsu,** Tokyo
5	4	**Saatchi & Saatchi,** London/New York
6	6	**Young & Rubicam,** New York
7	7	**Euro RSCG Worldwide,** Neuilly, France
8	8	**Grey Advertising,** New York
9	12	**Hakuhodo,** Tokyo
10	9	**Foote, Cone & Belding Communications,** Chicago
11	10	**Leo Burnett,** Chicago
12	11	**Publicis Communication/Publicis-FCB,** Paris
13	13	**D'Arcy Masius Benton & Bowles,** New York
14	14	**BDDP Group,** Boulogne, France
15	15	**Bozell Worldwide,** New York

U.S.-BASED AGENCY BRANDS INCLUDED	WORLDWIDE GROSS INCOME		
	1993	1992	% Change
Ogilvy & Mather Worldwide: Cole & Weber; Ogilvy & Mather Direct; A. Eicoff & Co.; Morton Goldberg Associates; **J. Walter Thompson Co.:** Brouillard Communications; J. Walter Thompson Direct; Deltakos; Thompson Recruitment; **other U.S. units:** Einson Freeman; Ferguson Communications Group; Mendoza, Dillon & Asociados	$2,633.6	$2,592.6	1.6%
Lintas Worldwide: Dailey & Associates; Fahlgren; Del Rivero Messianu Lintas; Long, Haymes & Carr; Lintas Marketing Communications; **Lowe Group:** Lowe & Partners/SMS; Lowe Direct; LCF&L; The Martin Agency; Stenrich Group; **McCann-Erickson Worldwide:** McCann Direct; McCann Healthcare; McCann Universal Group	2,078.5	2,054.5	1.2
BBDO Worldwide: Baxter, Gurian & Mazzel; Frank J. Corbett Inc.; Doremus & Co.; Harrison, Star, Weiner & Beitler; Lavey/Wolff/Swift; **DDB Needham Worldwide:** Bernard Hodes Group; Kallir, Philips, Ross; Puskar Gibbons Chapin; **other units:** TBWA Advertising; Alcone Sims O'Brien; Altschiller Reitzfeld; Goodby, Berlin & Silverstein; Merkley Newman Harty; Rainoldi Kerzner Radcliffe; Rapp Collins Worldwide	1,876.0	1,820.5	3.1
Dentsu of America	1,403.2	1,387.6	1.1
Saatchi & Saatchi Advertising: Saatchi & Saatchi/CMS; Saatchi & Saatchi Direct; Team One; Conill Advertising; Cliff Freeman & Partners; Klemtner Advertising; Rumrill-Hoyt; **Backer Spielvogel Bates Worldwide:** BSB/Dryden & Petisi; AC&R Advertising; Kobs & Draft; **CME KHBB**	1,355.1	1,397.4	−3.0
Young & Rubicam; Chapman Direct; CMF&Z; Muldoon Agency; Sive/Young & Rubicam; Sudler & Hennessey; Wunderman Cato Johnson Worldwide	1,008.9	1,058.7	−4.7
Robert A. Becker; Cohn & Wells; Hadley Group; Lally, McFarland & Pantello; Messner Vetere Berger McNamee Schmetterer; Stranger & Associates; Tatham Euro RSCG	864.8	932.1	−7.2
Grey Advertising; Beaumont Bennett Group; Font & Vaamonde; Grey Direct Marketing Group; Gross Townsend Frank Hoffman	765.7	728.1	5.2
Hakuhodo Advertising America	667.8	608.7	9.7
Foote, Cone & Belding Communications; FCB Direct; Borders, Perrin & Norrander; IMPACT; Vicom/FCB; Wahlstom	633.7	661.5	−4.2
Leo Burnett Co.	622.4	643.8	−3.3
Publicis/Bloom	572.0	623.0	−8.2
D'Arcy Masius Benton & Bowles; Clarion Marketing & Communications; Medicus Intercon International	553.6	558.4	−0.9
McCracken Brooks Communications; Wells Rich Greene BDDP	278.8	293.0	−4.8
Bozell Worldwide; Poppe Tyson; Temerlin McClain	269.9	247.3	9.1

(continued)

17

TABLE 1.6 (continued)

RANK		
1993	**1992**	**ADVERTISING ORGANIZATION, HEADQUARTERS**
16	16	**Tokyu Agency,** Tokyo
17	17	**Daiko Advertising,** Osaka, Japan
18	18	**Asatsu,** Tokyo
19	20	**Ketchum Communications,** Pittsburgh
20	19	**Dai-Ichi Kikaku,** Tokyo
21	21	**Dentsu, Y&R Partnerships,** New York/Tokyo
22	22	**Chiat/Day,** Los Angeles
23	23	**N W Ayer,** New York
24	28	**Yomiko Advertising,** Tokyo
25	26	**Cheil Communications,** Seoul
26	24	**I&S,** Tokyo
27	29	**Gold Greenlees Trott,** London
28	25	**Ayer Europe,** London
29	31	**TMP Worldwide,** New York
30	30	**Asahi Advertising,** Tokyo
31	27	**Lopex,** London
32	33	**Man Nen Sha,** Osaka, Japan
33	32	**Ross Roy Communications,** Bloomfield Hills, Mich.
34	35	**Gage Marketing Group,** Minneapolis
35	36	**Oricom,** Tokyo
36	38	**DIMAC Direct,** Bridgeton, Mo.
37	39	**Clemenger/BBDO,** Melbourne
38	34	**Armando Testa International,** Milan, Italy
39	40	**Sogel,** Tokyo
40	41	**Kyodo Advertising,** Tokyo
41	50	**Hal Riney & Partners,** San Francisco
42	45	**Earle Palmer Brown,** Bethesda, Md.
43	43	**Chuo Senko Advertising,** Tokyo
44	47	**Oricom,** Seoul
45	44	**W. B. Doner,** Southfield, Mich./Baltimore
46	46	**Ally & Gargano,** New York
47	49	**Jordan, McGrath, Case & Taylor,** New York
48	48	**Bronner Slosberg Humphrey,** Boston
49	NA	**Duallibi Petit Zaragoza,** São Paulo, Brazil
50	NA	**Springer & Jacoby,** Hamburg, Germany

NOTE: The U.S.-based agencies in boldface, present only among multitiered holding companies, are major divisions.
SOURCE: *Advertising Age,* April 14, 1994, p. 12. Reprinted by permission.

U.S.-BASED AGENCY BRANDS INCLUDED	WORLDWIDE GROSS INCOME		
	1993	1992	% Change
NA	$ 181.8	$ 185.6	−2.0%
NA	181.5	175.9	3.2
Asatsu America	171.3	165.9	3.3
Ketchum Advertising; Botto, Roessner, Horne & Messinger; DiFranza Williamson	140.4	132.8	5.7
Kresser/Craig DIK	135.3	151.4	−10.7
Lord, Dentsu & Partners	124.5	132.3	−5.9
NA	122.1	118.8	2.8
N W Ayer; GBF/Ayer	108.5	117.6	−7.7
NA	108.1	101.3	6.7
NA	106.6	103.5	3.0
NA	105.0	115.0	−8.7
GSD&M; Martin-Williams; Joey Reiman Agency	100.3	100.7	−0.4
NA	96.0	113.4	−15.3
TMP Worldwide	92.0	88.0	4.6
NA	91.6	93.9	−2.5
Chapman/Warwick; Warwick Baker & Fiore	90.0	103.4	−13.0
NA	83.6	79.4	5.3
Ross Roy Communications	81.0	80.7	0.4
Gage Marketing Group	78.8	67.1	17.4
NA	73.6	62.6	17.4
DIMAC Direct	63.5	57.7	10.1
NA	61.7	57.3	7.7
NA	61.1	73.9	−17.3
NA	59.2	54.8	8.0
NA	54.5	53.8	1.3
Hal Riney & Partners	53.1	43.8	21.4
Earle Palmer Brown Cos.	53.1	48.3	9.9
NA	51.9	50.4	3.0
NA	49.7	47.6	4.4
W. B. Doner & Co.	49.2	49.8	−1.1
Ally & Gargano; Dugan/Farley Communications	47.9	47.6	0.6
Jordan, McGrath, Case & Taylor	46.5	44.8	3.7
Bronner Slosberg Humphrey	45.8	45.1	1.4
NA	43.6	NA	NA
NA	43.2	NA	NA

from foreign markets. Many realized that in order to compete successfully, they had to maintain offices in almost all of the important countries of Europe, Latin America, and the Far East—a commitment that only the largest multinational agencies were prepared to make. In 1970 *Advertising Age* listed fifty-eight agencies that had international billings; by 1977 that number had dropped to just thirty-six.

In the 1980s the profile of the industry changed substantially. On Madison Avenue, foreign accents were increasingly heard. London-based Saatchi & Saatchi purchased three American agencies in 1986: Dancer, Fitzgerald, Sample; Backer & Spielvogel; and Ted Bates. In 1989 the British WWP Group brought two of American advertising's most glamorous names—J. Walter Thompson and the Ogilvy Group—into its "family" via hostile takeovers. Madison Avenue, it was said, was being invaded by an army speaking the Queen's English.[26] French agencies, too, have looked to U.S. soil. In 1988, Publicis Group formed the first big Franco-American alliance with Chicago-based Foote, Cone & Belding Communications. In 1989, Della Femina became a subsidiary of Eurocom, France's top agency. And, in 1990, Paris-based Boulet Dru Dupuy Petit bought 40 percent of Wells, Rich, Green. More recently, in 1994, Publicis Group acquired Bloom FCA, with offices in New York and Dallas.[27] Two Japanese agencies, Dentsu (Japan's largest agency) and Hakuhodo, also opened offices in the United States. As part of Dentsu's plan to establish majority-owned advertising and sales promotion networks in the world's major markets, the agency has opened Nova Promotion Group in New York. European offices are likely to follow.[28]

The United States has lost its long-unchallenged grip on hucksterism not only at home but abroad as well. European, Japanese, Australian, and Brazilian agencies have expanded or merged operations with agencies in other countries in order to meet the needs of their clients. And many of the largest multinational agencies have regrouped into multimillion- and multibillion-dollar multiservice transnational holding companies. Table 1.6 (page 16) lists the world's top 50 advertising agencies. While five of the top ten agencies have their headquarters in the United States, the top agency is British-based and, as noted, achieved its ranking via acquisitions.

Summary

The growth of international business has been paralleled by the growth of international advertising. Before turning our attention to the development of effective advertising programs for foreign markets, it is essential to understand the role that advertising plays in the international marketing mix and the challenges posed by the international marketing environment. These topics are the subject of Chapters 2 and 3.

Additional Readings

Foster, Lawrence W., and Lisa Tosi. (May/June 1990). "Business in China: A Year After Tiananmen." *Journal of Business Strategy,* pp. 22–27.

"Going Global." *Business Week* (October 20, 1989), pp. 9–18.

Harris, Greg. (1984). "The Globalization of Advertising." *International Journal of Advertising,* 3, pp. 223–234.

Levitt, Theodore. (May/June, 1983). "The Globalization of Markets." *Harvard Business Review,* pp. 92–102.

Wirklund, Erik. (1987). *International Marketing Strategies.* New York: McGraw-Hill.

Wolfe, Alan. (1991). "The Single European Market: National or Euro-Brands?" *International Journal of Advertising,* 10, pp. 49–59.

Worthy, Ford S. (1990). "A New Mass Market Emerges." *Fortune,* 122(8), pp. 55–59.

Notes

1. Porter, Michael E., "Changing Patterns of International Competition," *California Management Review,* 28(2), 1986, pp. 9–40.

2. U.S. Bureau of the Census, *Statistical History of the United States* (New York: Basic Books), p. 870.

3. U.S. Department of Commerce, Bureau of the Census, *1993 Statistical Abstract of the United States* (113th ed.) (Washington, DC: GPO, 1993), p. 801.

4. "Fortune's Global 500," *Fortune,* July 25, 1994, pp. 137–196.

5. Heineman-Wolfe, Bonnie, "Finding an International Niche: A How To for American Small Business," *Business Horizons,* 34(2), 1991, pp. 13–17.

6. "Go for Global Profits with America's Best-known Brands," *Money,* August 1991, pp. 43–44+.

7. "Guess Who's Selling Barbies in Japan Now?" *Business Week,* December 9, 1991, pp. 72–76.

8. "For Manufacturers, the Grass Is Far Greener Overseas," *Business Week,* December 23, 1991, p. 20.

9. "25 Companies with the Largest Non-U.S. Sales," *Hoover's Handbook of World Business,* 1993, p. 109.

10. *Fortune,* "Overseas Sales Take Off at Last," July 16, 1990, pp. 76–77.

11. "Back to Basics," *Business Week,* June 16, 1989 (Special Issue), pp. 14–18.

12. Horton, Cleveland, and Raymond Serafin, "Recovery Is Good News for U.S. Auto Marketers," *Advertising Age,* June 22, 1992, p. 3.

13. McCulloch, Rachel, "Foreign Direct Investment in the U.S.," *Finance and Development,* March 1993, pp. 13–15.

14. Shaughnessy, Rick, and Diane Lindquist, "Foreign Investment in U.S. Drops 47%," *San Diego Union-Tribune,* June 9, 1993, p. C2.

15. "The Selling of America (cont'd)," *Fortune,* May 23, 1988, pp. 54–64.

16. U.S. Department of Commerce, *1993 Statistical Abstract of the United States,* p. 798.

17. "Fortune's Global 500," *Fortune,* July 26, 1993, pp. 188–231.

18. International Monetary Fund, *Direction of Trade Statistics Quarterly*, June 1994, p. 200.

19. Kraar, Luis, "How Americans Win in Asia," *Fortune*, October 7, 1991, pp. 133–140.

20. International Advertising Association Worldwide Summary, 1994.

21. "Unilever Leads with $1.6 Billion," *Advertising Age*, November 21, 1994, p. I13.

22. Weinstein, Arnold K., "The International Expansion of U.S. Multinational Advertising Agencies," *MSU Business Topics*, 22(3), 1974, pp. 29–35.

23. Tyler, Ralph, "Agencies Abroad: New Horizons for U.S. Advertising," in John K. Ryans Jr. and J. C. Baker (eds.), *World Marketing*, New York: Wiley, 1967, pp. 366–380.

24. "Madison Avenue Goes Multinational," *Business Week*, September 12, 1970, pp. 48–51.

25. "International Agencies," *The International Advertiser*, 12(3), 1971, p. 44.

26. Rothenberg, Randall, "Brits Buying Up the Ad Business," *New York Times Magazine*, July 2, 1989, pp. 14–38.

27. Toy, Stewart, and Mark Landler, "And Now, Reu de Madison," *Business Week*, May 21, 1990, pp. 74–75.

28. Kilburn, David, "Dentsu Opening U.S. Promo Shop," *Advertising Age*, July 8, 1991, pp. 3, 34.

CHAPTER 2

The International Marketing Mix

he primary focus of this text is international advertising. However, because an advertising campaign is part of an overall marketing strategy and must be coordinated with other marketing activities, the role of the other marketing mix elements will be reviewed. Companies operating in one or more foreign markets must decide whether to adapt their *marketing mix* to local conditions; and if so, to what degree. The concept of a marketing mix, popularized by Jerome McCarthy in *Basic Marketing*,[1] includes the following four Ps:

1. *Product:* includes a product's design and development, as well as branding and packaging
2. *Place* (or *distribution*): includes the channels used in moving the product from manufacturer to consumer
3. *Price:* includes the price at which the product or service is offered for sale and establishes the level of profitability
4. *Promotion:* includes advertising, personal selling, sales promotions, direct marketing, and publicity

23

Standardization Versus Specialization of the Marketing Mix

Experts disagree over the degree to which firms should standardize their marketing programs across markets. At one extreme are companies that support the use of a fully standardized approach. Marshall McLuhan coined the term *global village* to describe an emerging world tightly linked through telecommunications. Many marketers believe that these advances in telecommunications, along with cheaper air transportation and the resulting increase in international travel, have created increasingly international consumers, making the world ripe for global marketing—at least for selected products.

This concept is not new. Debates regarding the viability of global marketing surfaced as far back as the late 1960s.[2] However, the concept was popularized by Harvard marketing professor Theodore Levitt, who suggested that people everywhere want goods of the best quality and reliability at the lowest price; and that differences in cultural preferences, tastes, and standards are vestiges of the past, because the world is becoming increasingly homogenized.[3] With a global approach to the marketing mix, a firm utilizes a common marketing plan for all the countries in which it operates—essentially selling the same product in the same way everywhere in the world. Major benefits associated with such standardization include lower production, distribution, management, and promotion costs. Yet, the number of firms with the potential to standardize the majority of their marketing mix elements are indeed few.

Coca-Cola, which operates in over 170 countries around the world, provides the classic example of a standardized global marketer. Notes Thomas Floyd, vice president of Global Market Research for Coca-Cola: "Today there are more similarities than differences. A Coca-Cola Classic tastes the same in Australia as it does in Brazil. The imagery of a cold, refreshing Coke is the same in Kyoto as it is in Calgary. Our target audience in Mexico City loves Fanta Orange for the same reasons as our audience in Boothbay Harbor, Maine."[4] Floyd notes that because of such similarities, more and more global marketing plans are quickly moving from concept to reality. Coca-Cola experiences very real benefits from its marketing approach; on commercial production alone, the company saves millions of dollars—savings that are plowed back into the marketing plan.

At the other extreme are companies committed to specialization. They argue that because consumers and marketing environments in different countries vary so greatly, it is necessary to tailor the marketing mix elements to each foreign market. Although such a customized approach typically results in higher costs, marketers hope that these costs will be offset by greater returns and a larger market share.

The Campbell Soup Company serves as an excellent example of the specialized approach. Sales of Campbell's soups had hit a ceiling in the United States and were losing ground to fresh and frozen foods—products more appealing to today's health-conscious consumers. As a result, the firm had little choice but to try and take the company global. Currently, less than 26 percent of Campbell's revenues, which approached $6.2 billion in 1992, come from outside the United States, but the firm's goal is to generate half of its revenues from foreign sales. Toward that end, Campbell's is creating new products that appeal to distinctly regional tastes. Taste-testing with consumers from around the world has resulted in the development of duck gizzard soup for Chinese consumers, creama de chile poblano soup for Mexicans, and flaki (a peppery tripe soup) for Poles.[5]

A great deal of confusion surrounds the issue of standardization versus specialization in part because of the various terms employed. Marketing standardization has also been called globalization, while marketing specialization has been referred to as localization as well as customization. Regardless of the terminology, too often the issue of standardization versus specialization of international marketing is perceived as an either/or proposition. In fact, standardization versus specialization of the marketing mix may be seen as the end points on a continuum, with many possible approaches between these two extremes. A company may choose to standardize one element, while customizing another. For example, Unilever, the world's largest advertiser outside the United States, sells an identical product to consumers all over Europe but modifies the advertising message content. In launching Impulse, a perfumed spray deodorant, Unilever maintained the same concept (women wear Impulse, causing men to act impulsively) but gave special attention to tailoring the couples' body language in each advertisement to suit regional courtship mores.[6]

The issue of marketing standardization versus specialization, as it pertains to product, price, and distribution, will be addressed in this chapter. Globalization versus localization of advertising will be discussed in detail in Chapters 5 and 6.

Product

The American Marketing Association defines a product as "anything that can be offered to a market for attention, acquisition, use, or consumption that might satisfy a want or need."[7] A product can be thought of in terms of three levels. These three levels, as outlined by Philip Kotler and Gary Armstrong,[8] are illustrated in Exhibit 2.1.

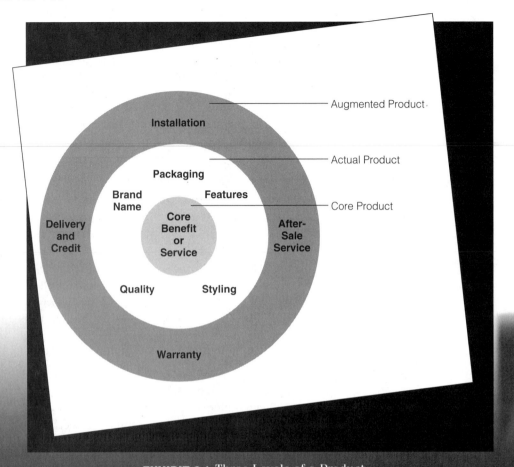

EXHIBIT 2.1 Three Levels of a Product

SOURCE: From Philip Kotler and Gary Armstrong. *Marketing: An Introduction,* 3rd Edition, © 1993, p. 221. Reprinted by permission of Prentice-Hall, Englewood Cliffs, NJ.

The *core product* refers to the bundle of benefits the consumer expects to receive from purchasing the item. These benefits can be functional, psychological, social, and/or economic in nature. For example, a consumer may purchase an automobile for purposes of transportation (functional benefit), select a specific style because it is currently in fashion among his group of friends (social benefit), opt for a stick shift over an automatic because it provides better mileage (economic benefit), and choose the color red because it's his favorite (psychological benefit).

The *actual product* includes the specific features and styling of the product, its quality, the brand name, and its packaging. Finally, the *augmented product* refers to product installation, delivery and credit provided to consumers, warranty, and postpurchase servicing.

Most products can be classified as durable goods, nondurable goods, or services. *Durable goods* are major products, often high-ticket items that tend to last for an extended period of time and, as a result, are purchased rather infrequently. Automobiles, appliances, and furniture are examples of durable goods. *Nondurable goods* are typically lower in price, consumed in a relatively short period of time, and thus purchased frequently. Examples of nondurable goods include food products and personal care items such as shampoos and toothpaste. *Services* are defined as activities or benefits offered by one party to another that are essentially intangible and do not result in the transfer of ownership of any kind. Obtaining health insurance, getting a haircut, or having an auto repaired are examples of services that consumers may purchase.

Products can be further distinguished between consumer goods and industrial goods. *Consumer goods* are items purchased by the end consumer for personal consumption. In contrast, *industrial goods* are items a firm purchases so that it may engage in business. Industrial goods include raw materials that actually become part of the end product (for example, in the garment industry, textiles purchased by a garment manufacturer that become part of its line of clothing), goods such as equipment and machinery used in the manufacturing process itself (for instance, industrial-quality sewing machines purchased to enable the creation of the fashions) and supplies and services (such as photocopier paper and long distance telephone service).

Product planning in the international setting requires that marketers explore the needs and wants of consumers in different markets and determine how those needs and wants might be satisfied by the firm's products. In addition to deciding which products should be offered, the international marketer must determine whether product modifications are necessary.

Product Standardization

One option available to the international marketer is to sell exactly the same product abroad as is sold in the home market—what is known as *product standardization.* The advantages to this strategy are numerous. Selling an identical product in a number of markets eliminates duplication of costs related to research and development, product design, and package design. In 1982, for example, Black & Decker operated twenty-five plants in thirteen countries on six continents, which led to considerable duplication of efforts. Indeed, Black & Decker produced 260 different motor sizes before it undertook global restructuring of its operations. Employing the same raw materials, equipment, plants, and processes typically leads to manufacturing economies of scale. A standardized product also increases the potential for economies of scale related to promotional efforts. Coca-Cola, Kellogg's corn flakes, Perrier bottled water, Pond's cold cream, Mitsubishi autos, Gillette razor blades, Birkenstock sandals, and Colgate toothpaste are examples of products that are available in the same form in markets around the globe.

Studies have revealed that the feasibility of product standardization may depend on the specific product category. Among consumer goods, nondurables generally are believed to require greater customization than durable goods because they appeal more directly to tastes, habits, and customs, which tend to be country-specific.[9,10] Some research has indicated that industrial products are more amenable to standardization than are consumer goods.[11,12] Product standardization also may be effective for markets with highly similar target audiences.[13,14] For example, the youth market around the world is said to be surprisingly similar. Marketers of jeans, records, and soft drinks find that they can sell essentially identical products to teens in Peoria and Paris. And marketers of "global village products"—essentially goods and services targeted to international travelers, such as hotels and rental cars—also find similarities in their target audience. Teresa Domzal and Lynette Unger propose that product standardization appears most feasible when products approach either end of the "high-tech/high-touch" spectrum:

> Consumers around the world who are interested in high-tech products share a common language, in bytes or other technical features, which enable global strategies to be successful. The hypothesized success of global marketing of "high-touch" products is more difficult to explain beyond the fact that products such as fragrance, fashion, or jewelry, for example, simply touch on universal emotional themes or needs. The high-tech/high-touch hypothesis appears to be borne out in the recent success of certain global products. High-tech products such as personal computers, video and stereo equipment and automobiles, and high-touch categories such as health food, fitness clothing, mineral water and fragrances are popular the world over.[15]

Product Adaption

Although product standardization is the less costly approach, the international marketer may choose to engage in *product adaption* for a variety of reasons. Marketing environments vary from country to country, and as a result, a product designed and developed for consumers in one market may not match needs in another.

Mandatory Product Adaption Mandatory adaption refers to situations in which the international firm adapts its products because it literally has no other choice than to do so. Differing levels of technical sophistication may necessitate product simplification. For example, frozen foods cannot be marketed in countries where retailers do not have freezer storage facilities. Likewise, if consumers in these markets typically do not own refrigerators, demand for frozen foods is likely to be quite limited. Variations in electrical systems from one country to the next (and even within countries) must also be considered when marketing consumer or industrial electrical appliances. A television designed for the U.S. market simply will not run in Mexico or Germany because of differences in both the frequency and voltage of the electrical power supply and the broadcast standards in these countries. In addition, the United States still relies on the American/British measurement system, while almost every other country has converted to the metric system. Any American firm attempting to sell a product abroad for which measurement is an important variable must go metric. For example, as Louis Kraar recounts, Hewlett-Packard had little choice—and lots of incentive— but to modify one of its products for the Asian market: "The firm just introduced its first Japanese-language computer printer. The Japanese version of the popular DeskJet 500 machine is being followed by similar models with built-in software to print in Chinese characters and the Hankul alphabet of Korea. Localizing products is well worth the trouble and considerable expense. Hewlett-Packard's sales of $2 billion in Asia and the Pacific last year represent 16 percent of the corporate total."[16]

Governmental regulations often present formidable barriers to product standardization. These regulations relate to product standards as well as testing and approval procedures. Each country has different product requirements designed to protect its citizens and its environment. The German government, for example, has strict guidelines regarding the purity of beers sold in that country—sufficient to prevent many brands from entering the market. Similarly, the United States has very specific safety restrictions on auto emissions that must be met by both foreign and domestic automobiles sold in this country. If such government-mandated standards force international firms to spend additional time and money modifying products, they can function as a nontariff barrier and, in discouraging imports, help protect domestic manufacturers.

Discretionary Product Adaption When faced with technical differences or governmental restrictions, the international firm has little choice but to adapt its product. In other instances the decision to standardize or adapt is not nearly so clear-cut. In these cases the international marketer must explore differences in consumption patterns, such as whether the product is purchased by relatively the same consumer income group from one country to another, whether most consumers use the product or service for the same purpose, and whether the method of preparation is the same for all target countries. In addition, the marketer must consider the psychosocial characteristics of consumers, such as whether the same basic psychological, social, and economic factors motivate the purchase and use of the product in all target countries; and whether the advantages and disadvantages of the product or service in the minds of consumers are basically the same from one country to another. Finally, the marketer must take into account more general cultural criteria, such as whether some stigma is attached to the product or service, or whether the product or service interferes with tradition in one or more of the targeted markets.[17]

Campbell Soup has clearly learned valuable lessons from their early mistakes. The firm would have benefitted from a more in-depth analysis of both consumption and psychosocial factors when they initially moved overseas in the late 1950s. During the decade that followed, the company recorded some $30 million in losses in its overseas operations. The firm's difficulties stemmed mainly from its failure to adapt its product to suit local preferences.[18,19] England comprised Campbell's most important foreign market. A primary mistake was the failure to explain to the English housewife how to prepare the soup. The English were accustomed to the ready-to-eat Heinz soups but were unfamiliar with the concept of condensed soups and thus were unable to justify the cost of the smaller Campbell's soup can compared to the larger Heinz soup can. It took two years for Campbell to provide the necessary explanations and to promote the idea of condensed soups. Failure to adapt the taste of their soups to local palates was another problem. The taste of established local varieties of tomato soup so differed from Campbell's that it was not until Campbell made significant changes in its flavors that sales picked up. As noted earlier, today Campbell is dedicated to tailoring soups to appeal to local tastes.

Regardless of the source of pressure for product modification, the international marketer must attempt to measure the costs and revenues associated with marketing a standardized product and compare them with the costs and revenues expected in a product adaption strategy. Further complicating the decision to standardize or adapt is the fact that this formula may vary on a market-by-market basis. As a case in point, two years after Mattel allowed its Japanese affiliate to "Japanize" Barbie Doll's features, sales blossomed from near zero to 2 million units. Interestingly, Barbie sold well without modification in sixty other countries.[20]

New Product Development

A recent study showed that 80 percent of all exports require at least one change and that most require at least four or five.[21] Too often marketers have attempted to export products that, while appropriate to the home market, were not particularly well suited to the needs of consumers in less industrialized nations without significant modifications. In other instances product modifications may be so extensive that it is no longer profitable to market the item. Here marketers may find that creating a completely new product is the best way to meet the needs of a foreign market. For example, Heinz developed a special line of rice-based baby foods for the Chinese market, and a fruit-based drink for children called Frutsi for the Mexican market. Similarly, Coca-Cola has developed a number of products specifically for the Japanese market—including "Georgia," a highly successful canned cold coffee drink, and Real Gold, an isotonic drink.[22]

Country-of-Origin Effect

Consumers evaluate products on a variety of criteria, including the country in which the product is produced. Marlboro is an American cigarette, Chanel No. 5 is a French perfume, Buitoni is an Italian pasta, and Johnny Walker is a Scotch whiskey—each of these brands has national credentials. Anyone attempting to market worldwide a Scottish pasta or an Italian whiskey likely would have serious credibility problems due to this *country-of-origin effect*.[23] Some countries have particularly positive associations with specific product categories. For example, Germany and Japan are stereotypically seen as producing high-quality autos while France is typically associated with fine wines and perfumes. A plausible national base or home market appears to be an important characteristic of the overall product and may influence perceptions of the product's quality. Exhibit 2.2 shows an example of an advertisement highlighting the country of origin.

Bozell Worldwide, a major advertising agency, recently commissioned a study to determine how consumers in twenty countries rate the quality of goods from some major exporting nations. At the top of the list was Japan, with 38.5 percent of respondents rating manufactured goods "excellent" or "very good." Germany came in second (36.0 percent), the United States third (34.3 percent), and Britain fourth (21.9 percent). At the bottom of the list were Spain (10.3 percent), China (9.2 percent), and Taiwan (9.0 percent).[24] In response to Taiwan's last-place ranking, the China External Trade Development Association is planning a $4.2 million campaign to improve the image of Taiwan's products in major world markets. The campaign addresses the widespread misconception that most of Taiwan's products are either knockoffs or of questionable quality, with the advertisements highlighting a long and growing list of products that are among the best of their kind.[25] For example, Exhibit 2.3 shows an ad for a Taiwan-produced tennis racquet that qualified for a new Symbol of Excellence.

In some instances a firm may wish to downplay a product's country of origin. For example, one Puerto Rican shoe manufacturer shipped its entire

EXHIBIT 2.2 Japanese Advertisement for Evian Highlighting the Country of Origin

inventory to New York City and then back to Puerto Rico in order to advertise the shoes as being from New York. Experience had convinced the manufacturer that Puerto Ricans would buy the shoes more readily if they were perceived as made in New York rather than in Puerto Rico.[26]

The tendency for consumers to evaluate goods manufactured in some countries more favorably may encourage a marketer to highlight the country of origin when promoting those goods. The use of "made in" appeals in advertising fall into three categories:[27]

1. Appeals to the patriotism or national pride of consumers to motivate the purchase of products manufactured in the home country. For instance, Chevrolet long used the advertising slogan "Baseball, apple pie and Chevrolet." "Buy American" themes also surface regularly in U.S. advertising messages.

2. Appeals that highlight for the audience positive and usually stereotypic attributes of another country and then imbue the product or service originating from that country with those image-enhancing qualities. For example, the Marlboro cigarette campaign portrays the image of the American cowboy and the freedom of the west to consumers all around the world.

3. Appeals that allude to a particular expertise that is associated with the country and that, if promoted in advertising messages, might

EXHIBIT 2.3 Image Boosting for Taiwan-made Items

instill confidence in the product. Advertisements for watches that communicate that the manufacturer is Swiss would be an example of this category.

Given the increasingly multinational corporate world, it is often difficult to determine exactly where a product comes from. Because they build their products all over the world, companies like IBM, Mitsubishi, and Siemens AG are in fact American, Japanese, and German in name only. For example, IBM manufactures products in twelve countries, and their IBM PS-1 personal computer—stamped "Made in U.S.A."—might be assembled in Raleigh, North Carolina, yet contain a floppy disk drive from IBM's Japanese plants, a monitor from Korea, and a mixture of imported and domestic computer chips.[28] "Almost any one product weighing more than 10 pounds and costing more than $10 these days is a global composite, combining parts or services from many different nations," notes Robert B. Reich, Harvard political economist and current secretary of labor.[29]

Branding and Trademark Decisions

Branding decisions are an important part of international product marketing strategy. A *brand* is any name, term, sign, symbol, or design—or combination of these—intended to differentiate the goods or services of one seller from those of another. A *trademark* is a brand or part of a brand that is given legal protection. Registering a trademark protects the seller's exclusive rights to the use of that brand name. From the consumer's perspective, trademarks help to identify the origin of the product and provide a guarantee of consistent quality.

Protection of successful and well-known trademarks is challenging in the home market, and doubly so internationally. Marketers may protect their trademarks in each nation in which they operate as well as internationally. Most countries offer some system of trademark registration and protection for both foreign and national firms. There are two basic systems of trademark registration:

1. *Priority in registration:* In Europe and elsewhere the first firm to register a trademark is considered the rightful owner of that trademark.

2. *Priority in use:* In the United States and England, rights to a trademark are established and maintained through use. In order for a brand to be protected, it must both be registered and have, in fact, been sold in that particular country. "Use" is defined legally and varies from one country to the next. In some countries the export sale of several cases of a product is sufficient to be defined as use; in others the product might have to be manufactured locally.

The Madrid Arrangement for International Registration of Trademarks allows the marketer to obtain international protection of a trademark. Twenty-six countries adhere to this accord, including most of the European nations and China. Currently the United States is not a member, although a U.S. firm's subsidiary in a member country can qualify for its benefits. A trademark registered by the Madrid Arrangement permits a registration in one member country to qualify for registration in all other member countries. This makes the registration of trademarks significantly more convenient.

In some countries the international marketer is required to periodically renew registration rights and pay a renewal fee. Registration fees typically are modest, but the associated legal fees can raise costs significantly. Given the costs and efforts required to register trademarks, the international marketer must carefully evaluate each market in order to determine whether to seek protection. The marketer must also continually monitor the foreign markets in which it operates to ensure that trademark infringement does not become a problem. For example, Xerox is one of 13,000 legally registered foreign trademarks in the Commonwealth of Independent States (CIS). With the disintegration of the Soviet Union, however, protection of these trademarks has become problematic. Manufacturers of other copy machines, such as Canon, often use the Xerox name to advertise their machines. As a result, consumers in the CIS are apparently confusing the name *Xerox* with the generic term. Therefore Xerox has undertaken a yearlong TV and radio advertising campaign to combat the problem.[30]

The international marketer must also decide whether to promote a single product brand worldwide—commonly referred to as a *global brand*—or to promote different brands for different regions or even individual markets. Certain advantages are associated with registering a single brand in all countries in which the firm operates. There is often a certain level of prestige associated with an international brand. A recent survey of 10,000 people in eight European countries plus the United States and Japan found that internationally recognized brands command a major position in most developed countries. The top 10 brands in the world, according to this study, are Coca-Cola, Sony, Mercedes Benz, Kodak, Disney, Nestlé, Toyota, McDonald's, IBM, and Pepsi-Cola. The United States fared quite well in the survey, with American brands capturing six of the top 10 positions.[31]

It is clearly less costly to prepare advertising campaigns and promotional literature for a single brand than for several. A single brand also allows the marketer to utilize international media and reap the benefits where media spill over national borders, such as is the case in Europe. With increasing international travel a single trademark will ensure that consumers recognize a firm's products, thereby eliminating brand confusion.

However, certain factors may necessitate modification of the brand name or trademark. For one thing, brand names sometimes do not translate well. When Coca-Cola entered the Chinese market, for example, the company selected characters that phonetically sounded like the English words *Coca-Cola*. Unfortunately, Chinese consumers were confronted with a soft drink named "bite the wax tadpole"; the characters were quickly modified to read "can be delicious and joyous." For another thing, different countries often prefer different types of brand names. For example, there is a pronounced difference in the names Americans and Japanese give to their cars. Whereas the Japanese lean toward pastoral names or names of girls—Bluebird, Bluebonnet, Sunny, Violet, Gloria—American cars have names such as Mustang, Cougar, Thunderbird, and Cutlass. The first sports car Nissan sent to the United States was named the Datsun Fair Lady. Nissan's head of sales for all western United States was so convinced that such a name would not sell cars in this country that he replaced it with one using the company's internal name for the car, the 240Z. The auto went on to become a big seller for Nissan.[32]

Governmental restrictions may prohibit the use of a brand name. For example, in marketing Diet Coca-Cola to a number of countries, including Germany and Spain, the Coca-Cola company encountered restrictions regarding use of the word "diet." As shown in Exhibit 2.4, Coca-Cola solved the problem by changing the product name to Coca-Cola Light.

Target audience preferences may also influence the brand name selected. The *Coca-Cola Light* name was also used for the Japanese market because Japanese consumers tend not to be overweight and do not like to admit they are dieting by purchasing products labeled as dietetic. Accompanying this new brand name was a shift in promotional strategy, which emphasized "figure maintenance" rather than "weight loss."

Brand Piracy

A problem that many well-known brands face in foreign markets is brand piracy. There are three distinct forms of piracy: imitation, faking, and preemption. Imitation basically involves copying an established brand. For instance, LaCoste, manufacturer of the popular jerseys with the alligator logo, must combat knockoffs of its product sold in numerous countries. Faking refers to identifying the fraudulent product with a symbol, logo, or brand name that is very similar to the famous brand. For example, preference for foreign brands in Vietnam has led to knockoffs such as Volgate toothpaste and Lix soap. Coca-Cola, which manufactures the soft drink Sprite, has asked a South Korean court to ban the production and sale in South Korea of Sprint, which was introduced recently with a name, logo, and taste much like Sprite's.

Beba
Coca-Cola
light

MARCA REG.

EXHIBIT 2.4 Diet Coca-Cola Renamed Coca-Cola Light for the Spanish Market

SOURCE: The Coca-Cola Company is the owner of the copyright for this ad. Coca-Cola Light and the Dynamic Ribbon Device are Registered Trademarks of the Coca-Cola Company.

Preemption of brand names occurs in those countries where the law permits wholesale registration of brand names. In such countries a person may register in his or her name a large number of well-known brand names and then sell these names either to those interested in counterfeiting or, better still, to the multinational when it is ready to move into that country.

Packaging and Labeling Decisions

Packaging refers to the design and production of product containers or wrappings. Packaging includes the immediate container (for example, the plastic container surrounding Sure deodorant), a secondary package that is discarded after purchase (the cardboard box that a container of Sure is sold in), and any packaging necessary to ship the product to retailers (such as a cardboard carton containing dozens of packages of Sure deodorant). *Labeling* is also considered part of the packaging and consists of printed information appearing on or along with the packaging.

Packaging has both protective and promotional aspects. In determining whether the same packaging can be used for foreign markets, marketers must consider a variety of marketplace conditions. Packaging must allow the product to reach its destination without damage. Markets with long, slow, or poor distribution channels may require sturdier packaging. Climatic extremes may necessitate packaging modifications. For example, Quaker Oats adopted special vacuum-sealed tins to protect its products in hot and humid climates.

Consumption rates directly influence storage time and may vary from one market to the next. In addition, packaging size is often determined by the income level of a market. Lower per capita income usually translates into lower usage rates and smaller purchase amounts, and it might even suggest that products such as razor blades, chewing gum, and cigarettes be individually packaged, so that consumers with limited incomes can afford them. Smaller sizes also may be more appropriate for countries where consumers shop daily or have smaller homes and thus fewer storage facilities. For example, superconcentrated versions of laundry detergents (Fab Ultra and Wisk Power Scoop) recently introduced to the U.S. marketplace have sold well for over a decade in Europe and Japan, where space in both the supermarket and the home is at a premium. Larger packages are appropriate for markets where shopping is conducted on a weekly basis and storage space is ample.

The type of retail outlet in which the product is sold may further influence the packaging. Self-service retailing, which plays an increasingly important role in most developed countries, dictates that packaging perform a multitude of promotional functions as well—from attracting the consumer's attention, to describing product features, to making the ultimate sale. In markets with predominantly small retail outlets, with limited floor and/or shelf space, it may be appropriate to modify the packaging. In terms of legal restrictions, some countries do not allow the promotional tactics commonly employed in other markets.

Customer preferences—often shaped by culture—may influence whether packaging is persuasive to consumers in various markets. Utilizing the same or similar packaging employed in the home market may cause problems. Even the color of a product's packaging may prove problematic for a marketer. For example, while white connotes purity and cleanliness in many regions and cultures, in the Far East it is also associated with mourning. Likewise, red is a positive color in Denmark as well as many Asian countries, but it represents witchcraft and death in a number of African nations. Using the colors of the national flag may be perceived as patriotic in some countries, yet disallowed in others.

In many countries—both developing and developed—the usefulness of the packaging plays a greater role. Often the package will be kept and reused as a container. Lego, the Danish toy manufacturer, has employed a standardized marketing philosophy in over a hundred countries in selling its building blocks. In recent years, however, Lego has encountered stiff competition from look-alike and lower-priced rival products from Japan, the United States, and elsewhere. The *Harvard Business Review* describes Lego's dilemma—and its response:

> In the United States, where the competition has been the fiercest, Tyco, a leading competitor, began putting its toys in plastic buckets that could be used for storage after each play. This utilitarian approach contrasted with Lego's elegant see-through cartons standardized worldwide. But American parents seemed to prefer the functional toys-in-a-bucket idea over cartons. Seeing a potential for serious damage, Lego's alarmed U.S. management sought permission from Denmark to package Lego toys in buckets. The head office flatly refused the request. The denial was based on seemingly sound arguments. The bucket idea could cheapen Lego's reputation for high quality. Moreover, the Lego bucket would rightly be seen as a "me too" defensive reaction from a renowned innovator. Finally, and perhaps most important, buckets would be a radical deviation from the company's policy of standardized marketing everywhere. Even U.S. consumer survey results comparing buckets favorably with cartons weren't considered a good enough reason for change from the global concept. Two years later, however, headquarters in Billund reversed itself. The impetus was a massive loss of U.S. market share to competitive goods sold in buckets. Soon after, the American subsidiary began marketing some of its toys in a newly designed bucket of its own. Now to the delight of many in Billund, the buckets are outselling the cartons, and the share erosion

has reassuringly halted. Recently, the bucket was introduced worldwide and was a smashing success.[33]

Ecological concerns are an additional variable that must be considered in evaluating product packaging. In some countries certain forms of packaging are either banned or not condoned by consumers or there is a market preference for specific packaging materials, such as glass instead of aluminum or tin, or paper rather than plastic. In Denmark, for instance, soft drinks may be sold only in glass bottles with refundable deposits, and in the United States consumers have been critical of styrofoam packaging used by fast food outlets. Many deodorant manufacturers are considering doing away with the secondary cardboard packaging to cut down on unnecessary packaging material. And consumers in many foreign markets are not accustomed to the elaborate packaging so commonly used in the United States, and consider it quite wasteful. In many European countries, for example, shoppers bring their canvas or string totes to the grocery store in order to carry home purchases.

Labeling laws in many foreign countries are even more stringent than those in the United States. Governmental regulations may affect labeling with regards to a product's origin, name of the producer, weight, description of contents and ingredients, use of additives and preservatives, and dietetic information. David Ricks notes: "Coca-Cola, for example, aroused the anger of the Italians when it printed the mandatory list of ingredients on the bottle cap. Local courts ruled that the cap was easily tossed away and, therefore, did not serve as an acceptable location for this list. Coca-Cola, of course, quickly modified its package and listed the ingredients on the bottles themselves, but the incident was not without its costs."[34]

Regardless of governmental restrictions, the label must be written in a language that local consumers will understand—and this typically means different labels for different markets. Marketers may attempt to get around this by printing multilingual labels. For products sold in the European Union, labels might be printed in German, French, and Italian. In some instances, bilinguality is legally mandated. For instance, products destined for Canada must carry product information in both English and French, while firms marketing products in Belgium and Finland must incorporate dual language labels.

Differing levels of literacy may necessitate greater use of visuals rather than extensive copy. This commonplace practice proved to be quite perplexing for one major marketer. As David Ricks explains, the firm attempted to sell baby food to the indigenous peoples of one developing country by using its regular label showing a baby and stating the type of baby food in the jar. "Unfortunately, the local population took one look at the labels and interpreted them to mean the jars contained ground-up babies. Sales, of course, were terrible."[35]

Place (Distribution)

Once foreign markets have been selected, the international marketer must determine the appropriate channels of distribution. These channels essentially connect the producer of the goods with the end consumer. Firms operating internationally must determine appropriate *channels between nations*—commonly called market entry channels—which involve movement of the product to the borders of foreign countries—as well as *channels within nations*—those that move the product from the foreign entry point to the final consumer. Channels between nations include indirect export, direct export, and manufacture abroad (which includes licensing, franchising, management contracting, foreign assembly, joint ventures, and direct investment). Channels within nations involve decisions regarding wholesalers and retailers.

Channels Between Nations: Indirect Export

Exporting is the most common as well as the simplest means of foreign market entry. Firms lacking the resources to build or acquire factories abroad can penetrate foreign markets via this method. Here all goods are produced in the home market, and the international marketer may or may not choose to modify the product for consumers abroad. In *indirect export* the firm works with independent international marketing middlemen who are responsible for the distribution process. Because a wide variety of middlemen providing these services exists, only the most common methods of indirect exporting will be discussed.

Firms unwilling or unable to establish their own export departments may opt to enter foreign markets with the assistance of domestic sales organizations, better known as *export management companies (EMCs)*. EMCs produce no goods of their own; instead, they act as export departments for several manufacturers of unrelated products. They may operate in one of two ways: (1) functioning as a distributor for the manufacturer or (2) serving as an agent of the domestic firm. As a distributor the EMC actually purchases products (takes title) from the domestic firm and then operates abroad on its own behalf. In an agency capacity the EMC's role is limited to establishing foreign contacts and developing foreign marketing strategies. As a distributor the EMC assumes greater risk but also has the opportunity to reap greater profits than it does acting as an agent. Because EMCs service a variety of clients, their mode of operation may vary from one domestic client to the next. Payment for services is made through commission, salary, or retainer plus commission. EMCs often specialize in a particular geographic area, enabling them to offer expertise to domestic corporations. More than 1,000 such firms currently operate in the United States.

Firms planning to conduct business abroad may also deal with *international trading companies*, which buy, sell, transport, and distribute goods. They may also provide financing, assist in the development of joint ventures, provide technical assistance, and even produce goods. They are typically the major suppliers of goods to the markets which they serve. Trading companies hail from a number of different countries, including Japan, the United States, and even the CIS. Some of these trading companies were designed primarily for export, while others were originally developed to supply import services. Among the most famous export trading companies are the *sogo shosha* of Japan. Contrary to what most Americans believe, these firms actually import more into Japan from the United States than they export from Japan into the United States. Mitsui and Mitsubishi alone account for well over half of all Japan's imports. Some trading companies are region-specific, handling commodities produced in only one geographic area. Others are product-specific, handling only a limited variety of goods. Still others are industry-oriented, handling only goods specific to a particular industry, such as pharmaceuticals or chemicals.

There are certain advantages associated with utilizing the services of independent middlemen. A firm commits neither time nor money to set up an overseas salesforce, and it can rely on the established contacts and marketing know-how of the middlemen operating within foreign markets. And because the indirect approach involves a good deal less investment on the part of the exporting company, it faces considerably less risk. On the downside, the exporter typically has little or no control over the distribution process. Should a product more profitable to the marketing middleman come along, the manufacturer's product may simply be dropped. Also, should sales in a market expand significantly, the exporting firm may find itself without the services of an EMC.

Channels Between Nations: Direct Export

In contrast to indirect export, when a firm engages in *direct export* it does so without the assistance of intermediaries. The manufacturer is responsible for conducting any necessary market research; identifying, evaluating, and selecting foreign markets as well as agents or distributors to represent the firm in those markets; setting product prices; handling international shipping and insurance and preparing export documentation; and coordinating international promotional activities. While both the investment and the risk involved in direct export are greater, the marketer also has more control over the distribution process, which typically results in increased sales and higher profits.

Channels Between Nations: Manufacture Abroad

A variety of circumstances may prevent the international marketer from engaging in direct export. For example, tariffs or quotas may prevent a firm from selling its products in specific countries, or transportation costs may make products noncompetitive. Positive factors may also encourage a firm to produce its goods abroad. For instance, the size of some markets may justify setting up a plant in a foreign country, or local manufacture may allow the marketer to better respond to local market needs, or manufacturing costs may be lower in foreign markets. Foreign production can take the form of licensing, management contracting, foreign assembly, contract manufacturing, joint ownership, and direct investment.

Licensing One method of market entry is *licensing,* in which a company offers a licensee in the foreign market rights to a trademark or patent, the use of a manufacturing process, technical advice, or marketing skills. In exchange for the rights or know-how provided by the licensor, the licensee produces and markets the product and pays the licensor a fee or royalty, typically related to the sales volume of the product. *Franchising* is a particular type of licensing agreement in which the franchisee typically operates under the name of the franchisor, who provides the franchisee with not only trademarks and know-how but also management and financial assistance. Athlete's Foot, Hardee's hamburger chain, and Mailboxes Etc., for example, all offer franchises in Mexico.

A number of advantages are associated with licensing. It offers a quick and easy means of entry into foreign markets. It requires neither capital investment nor an in-depth understanding of the foreign market. In some instances licensing permits entry into markets that might otherwise be closed to imports or direct foreign investments. It can negate high transportation costs, which may make exports noncompetitive. Finally, it offers an alternate means to enter markets with high duty rates or import quotas. For many firms, licensing serves as an intermediate step in the road toward internationalization by providing a means to test foreign markets without an actual outlay of capital or management time.

However, licensing also entails potential disadvantages. The manufacturer has little control over the licensee or its production, distribution, or marketing of the product. From a revenue standpoint licensing is unlikely to be as profitable as the returns that could be generated from a firm's own operations, as license fees are typically only a small percentage of sales—generally 3–5 percent. Licensing in no way guarantees a basis for future expansion into a market. In fact, when a licensing agreement expires, a firm may find it has created a competitor not only in the markets for which agreements were made but possibly in other markets as well. Firms intending to engage in licensing agreements also need to be aware that licensing regulations vary dramatically from country to country. Finally, there may be variations in restrictions regarding registration requirements, royalty and fee payments, and applicable taxes.

Management Contracting A firm may choose to enter a foreign market via *management contracting.* Here the domestic firm supplies the management know-how to a foreign firm willing to invest the capital. The domestic firm is compensated via management fees, a share of the profits, and sometimes the option to buy some share in the managed firm at a later date. Management contracting is a low-risk means of market entry that requires no capital investment, capitalizes on the domestic firm's management skills, and assures a quick return. Here, the local investor has a greater say in how the investment is managed. Profits, however, are not likely to be as great as if the firm were to undertake the entire venture. Management contracting is most commonly used in the following sectors: public utilities, tourism (hotels, for example), and agriculture in developing countries.

Foreign Assembly In *foreign assembly* a firm produces all or most of the product's components or ingredients domestically and then ships them to foreign markets for final assembly. Many products may be more easily shipped broken down, and transportation costs may also be lower as a result. In some instances tariffs prevent a firm from shipping a fully assembled product. By forcing assembly in the local markets, foreign governments increase local employment.

Contract Manufacturing Another option is *contract manufacturing,* which involves the actual production of a firm's product in a foreign market by another producer. Typically, the company placing the contract retains full control over both distribution and marketing of the goods. Benefits associated with contract manufacturing include limited local investment, potentially cheaper local labor, and the positive image associated with being locally produced. On the downside, it may prove difficult to locate a foreign firm with the capability of manufacturing the product to the domestic firm's specifications. Extensive technical training of the subcontractor may be necessary, and even then, the firm has limited control over product quality. Here, too, at the end of a contract, the subcontractor may become a competitor. Types of products generally involved in such arrangements include electronics, textiles, and clothing.

Joint Ownership When two or more firms, in different countries, join forces to create a local business in which they share ownership and control of management, manufacturing, and marketing, they have *joint ownership.* An international firm may purchase interest in a foreign company, or the two parties may form an entirely new business venture. In some joint ventures each partner holds an equal share; in others, one partner holds the majority share. Equity can range anywhere between 10 and 90 percent.

Joint ownership offers the potential for greater profits as compared to contract manufacturing or licensing and may also afford the international marketer greater control over production, distribution, and marketing activities. The national partner in a joint venture can offer the international marketer valuable knowledge about the local marketplace. The joint venture may also lead to better relationships with local organizations—government, local authorities, or labor unions. Finally, it may be the preferred option if 100 percent foreign equity ownership is not permitted by foreign governments. Mexico and India have been particularly restrictive about foreign firms owning more than 50 percent of any venture in their countries. In instances where political or other uncertainties call for some limitation of investment risks, joint ventures may be an appropriate entry method.

General Motors, which has long preferred solo operations abroad, has entered several joint ventures around the world, including one with Toyota in the United States. General Motors is not alone, as the rest of the American auto manufacturers have expanded internationally as well. Likewise, Coors recently formed a joint venture with Jinro, Korea's largest producer of alcoholic beverages, to build a 1.8-million-barrel brewery in Seoul to produce Coors beer. The plant, Coors' first outside the United States, marks the beginning of the firm's international expansion plans. With beer sales a relatively flat 2 percent in the United States, Korea's beer market, which is expanding at a rate of 15 percent per year, appears lucrative.[36]

Certain drawbacks are associated with joint ownership. When compared with contract manufacturing or licensing, there is a greater investment of capital and management resources, as well as an increased level of risk. And, as with any partnership, the potential for conflict of interest always exists. The two parties may disagree about any or all of the marketing mix elements, as well as management style, research and development, personnel requirements, and the accumulation and distribution of profits. What is good for the national firms may not always be beneficial to the international company, and vice versa.

Direct Investment The greatest commitment a firm can make to a foreign market is *direct investment,* which involves entering a foreign market by developing foreign-based manufacturing facilities. The international firm has the option of obtaining foreign production facilities by acquiring an existing foreign producer or by establishing its own facilities. Acquisition is typically a quicker way for a firm to move into a new market, and it also offers the firm benefits such as built-in political know-how and expertise. For example, when Procter & Gamble first entered the Japanese market by absorbing a soap company, it also acquired a well-trained Japanese sales staff. Because it had, in fact, saved the Japanese firm from bankruptcy, P&G immediately established good relations with not only the staff but also the Japanese government. However, establishing a new facility may be preferable if the international firm is unable to find a national company willing to sell or if the national government prohibits the sale of domestic companies. Establishing a new facility also allows the international firm to incorporate the most up-to-date technology and equipment.

Regardless of how acquired, foreign production facilities offer numerous advantages. Complete ownership means that 100 percent of the profits goes directly to the international firm. The firm keeps full control over its investment, and there is no possibility for conflict with a national partner. Foreign direct investment also allows corporations to sidestep trade barriers or tariffs and operate abroad as a domestic firm. Nationalism may also lead foreign customers to prefer locally produced goods and services. And, while some governments limit foreign investments, others actually offer incentives to international firms. For example, many governments are under increasing pressure to provide jobs for their citizens. As compared to direct or indirect exporting, the international firm may benefit from lower costs or increased availability in terms of natural or human resources. Mineral or agricultural resources may be more available in some foreign markets, and/or their costs may be lower than they are domestically. Similarly, a skilled work force may be more readily available and/or less costly.

The major disadvantage associated with direct investment is that it requires substantial investments in terms of capital and management resources. This factor typically prevents smaller firms from engaging in this mode of market entry. The international firm also faces increased risks, such as devalued currencies or even expropriation, which is more likely to happen to wholly owned firms. The international environment is growing increasingly hostile toward full ownership by multinational companies. A major concern is equitable profit repatriation. Therefore, many govern-ments insist that foreign firms engage in licensing or even joint ventures as a means of sharing in the profits obtained in the local market.

Channels Within Nations: Distribution to Consumers

The particular market entry strategy a firm selects will impact its decisions about distribution channels within nations. On the one hand, firms that make their products available in foreign markets via indirect exporting and some forms of direct exporting must rely on the distribution channels selected by their intermediaries. Firms engaging in joint ventures or direct investments, on the other hand, will be responsible for evaluating and selecting from among the available channels of distribution within those nations. The spe-cific distribution channels a firm selects within a particular country will im-pact many of the other marketing elements. For example, product prices will need to reflect markups allowed to middlemen; where and how the product is available to the end user will impact promotional tactics. Channel decisions also involve long-term commitments to foreign organizations that are often difficult to change.

In some instances the international marketer will be faced with distri-bution channels that are a good deal more complex than those in the home market. For example, a U.S. company marketing in Japan will need to deal with a frustrating maze of middlemen. Larry Rosenberg explains that, his-torically, Japan has been a country of numerous small retailers, typically lo-cated in residential areas and near train stations where local people could shop daily for food and other necessities. Dependency relationships devel-oped between consumers and retailers, and patronage was rewarded by guar-antees of a constant supply of high-quality products and good service. Each retailer obtained goods from a long chain of middlemen, who in turn assured retailers of personalized service in exchange for continued patronage. Thus, dependency relationships developed along the entire chain from producer to consumer. The number of wholesalers and retailers is five times greater than in the United States. The sheer number of middlemen, in addition to the dependency relationships that have developed among them, makes it very difficult for foreigners to distribute goods in Japan.[37]

At the other extreme, an international marketer operating in a less de-veloped country may well find that channels taken for granted in the home market simply do not exist. Or channels may have already been contracted on an exclusive basis to competitors. Under such circumstances the foreign investor may choose to lure away distributors by offering extra-high mar-gins or other financial incentives. Other options include buying out local distributors or even building up parallel distribution channels from scratch. Finally, an international marketer may be forced to develop original methods of distribution.

Within-country channels of distribution—both wholesaling and retailing—vary greatly from one market to the next. These channels have typically evolved over many years and reflect differences not only in economic development but in culture as well. Each country poses a unique situation, and no general rules can be applied. The international marketer must carefully analyze the established distribution systems in order to uncover differences in the number, size, and types of middlemen as well as the services they provide.

Channels Within Nations: Wholesaling Abroad

Wholesaling patterns are typically reflective of the cultures and economies in which they operate. As a general rule, industrialized countries have many large-scale wholesaling organizations serving a large number of retailers. In contrast, in developing countries wholesaling is likely to be far more fragmented—smaller firms with fewer employees serving a limited number of retailers.

The spectrum of services offered by wholesalers typically relates to the size of their operations: the larger the wholesaler, the greater the variety of services it can provide. Larger wholesalers also generally have larger staffs available to assist the international firm. If it is necessary to utilize the services of a smaller wholesaler, this typically translates into greater responsibility for the international firm. Smaller wholesalers tend to carry less inventory, are less likely to provide adequate promotional efforts, and offer more limited geographic coverage than their larger counterparts.

Channels Within Nations: Retailing Abroad

Differences in retailing from one international market to the next are at least as extensive as those in wholesaling. Here, too, the international marketer must carefully analyze each country to assess retailing opportunities as well as constraints. As with wholesaling, there is great variation in the number and size of retail operations in foreign markets and in the services they provide. Overall, the more developed the country, the more likely it is to have larger retail outlets. For example, supermarkets and department stores are the norm in the United States, while hypermarkets—huge facilities stocked with thousands of products—are popular in many European countries. Carrefour, a French retailer that once had plans to open ten such hypermarkets in the

United States, recently closed two of its stores. Apparently, the seven-acre hypermarket that sells everything from groceries to auto supplies to refrigerators is just too large for U.S. consumers. Carrefour is not the only retailer to pull back from the concept in this country; both Wal-Mart and Kmart experimented with and then abandoned hypermarkets.[38]

Typically, the number of retail outlets per capita in developed countries is limited. However, even here there is variation. The United States and Germany both have approximately 6 shops per 1,000 people, while France has about 11 and Japan has 13. Developing countries have a much larger number of overall outlets, but these tend to be significantly smaller in size. Mom-and-pop outlets, open-air markets, or peddlers may be the norm. For example, retail outlets in many African countries may consist of no more than 200 square feet of selling space.[39] Exhibit 2.5 shows some sample data on retail outlets as well as grocery stores, auto dealerships, and eateries in various countries. These charts demonstrate the significant variation in retailing from market to market.

In most developed countries, international firms can expect to receive the following services from retailers: stocking the product, displaying and promoting the merchandise, extending credit to customers, providing service, and gathering market information. Because retail outlets are significantly smaller in developing countries, they typically carry very limited inventories. This may mean that the international firm cannot sell its full range of products, that adequate display of products may be a challenge, and that the use of point-of-purchase displays will be limited. The smaller the retailer, the less likely it is to be able to offer customers credit or to service the product.

An ever increasing number of retailers are operating at an international level. Although Woolworth's and Sears are considered the "old-timers" of international retailing, in recent years J. C. Penney, Kmart, Safeway, and Target have also ventured overseas. In addition, fast food outlets such as McDonald's, Pizza Hut, Kentucky Fried Chicken, and Dairy Queen have found foreign markets to be profitable. McDonald's, for example, operates restaurants in over thirty countries around the world. Foreign retailers are also exploring U.S. soil, as American consumer familiarity with brands like Benneton, Laura Ashley, and Ikea indicates. The success of these international retailers suggests that this trend likely will continue.

Distribution Standardization Versus Specialization

An international marketer will need to determine whether factors favor the utilization of uniform distribution patterns in foreign markets or whether a more specialized approach will be more profitable. A standardized approach may offer certain economies of scale. For example, if markets are sufficiently

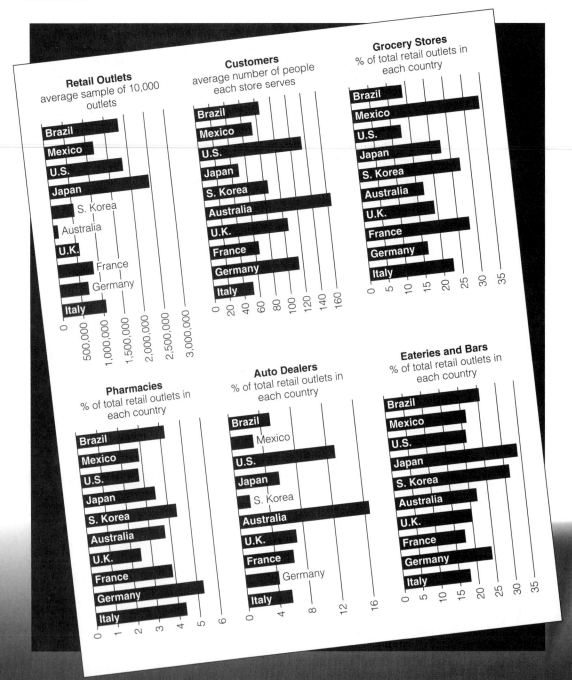

EXHIBIT 2.5 Sample Global Retail Distribution Patterns

SOURCE: "Ad Age International and Audits & Surveys Examine Retail Distribution Patterns Around the World," *Advertising Age*, June 12, 1992; p. I-12. Reprinted by permission.

similar, the international marketing manager's skills in one market may be transferred to another. However, given the variation in the number, size, and nature of wholesalers and retailers described previously, a specialized approach may be the only viable option. And, if the market entry approaches vary from one market to another, the international marketer may have little choice but to adapt distribution efforts. For example, Kentucky Fried Chicken was the first fast food outlet to enter the Japanese market. KFC and Mitsubishi established a 50-50 joint venture and opened the first KFC in 1970 at the Osaka Exposition; several additional restaurants were opened shortly thereafter. However, within a year after opening its doors, the local chain almost went bankrupt. KFC had made the mistake of locating its outlets in the suburbs and on highways, mimicking the U.S. model, only to learn that few Japanese had cars at the time. Only after putting aside the American distribution approach and beginning to open downtown outlets did KFC experience steady growth.

Price

In pricing products, international marketers must determine whether to standardize prices in markets worldwide or to differentiate prices among countries. In setting a *standard worldwide price,* a firm establishes a uniform price for its product all around the world. However, that price may be too high for consumers in less developed countries. For example, Masterfoods just introduced several different brands of pet food to the Russian market. This country, known for chronic food shortages and long lines, had no familiarity with packaged pet foods. Nevertheless, Masterfoods saw a market potential among consumers who often pamper their pets by preparing special meals for them. Yet, price was bound to be a problem. A 40-pound sack of Pedigree Pal dog food costs about $27.70, well above the current Russian average monthly salary of $22.29.[40] It remains to be seen how successful the product is.

At other times the price may not be high enough for consumers in wealthier countries with higher levels of income. Here a marketer may opt to use a *differentiated pricing strategy* in which price is based on a number of factors and not determined in isolation from the other marketing mix elements. One study found that over two-thirds of consumer-nondurables marketers and almost 50 percent of industrial products manufacturers among U.S. multinational corporations adapted pricing to local conditions.[41] This adaptation is justified on the grounds that local market considerations play such a significant role in setting product prices. Among the factors influencing pricing are corporate objectives, competition, consumer demand, and governmental and regulatory considerations.

Pricing Objectives and Strategies

International marketers may adjust pricing objectives based on the specific conditions of the markets they enter. Typical pricing objectives include profit maximization, return on an investment, and increases in total sales volume or market share. In pursuing pricing objectives, a firm may select from a variety of pricing strategies. The pricing strategy adopted will, in turn, impact the other marketing factors. A firm might engage in a *market penetration* strategy, which entails establishing a relatively low price with the goal of stimulating consumer interest. The firm accepts a lower per unit return in hopes of capturing a large share of the market and discouraging competition. Once a satisfactory level of market share is obtained, the firm typically raises prices to increase profitability. Penetration pricing is commonly employed with low-cost consumer products and tends to be most effective with price-sensitive consumers and in countries with significant manufacturing economies of scale.

In a situation in which either no or very few competitors exist or in which consumers are willing to pay a high price, perhaps because a product is unique or innovative, marketers may opt to "skim the cream" from the market. The aim of a *market skimming* strategy is to obtain a premium price for a product—at least initially. This approach allows marketers to recoup research and development costs quickly as well as generate profits. Prices are typically reduced once competitors enter the market or in order to attract more price-conscious consumers.

If a number of competitors already exist in a given market or if a product is essentially undistinguishable from the competition, a firm may engage in *competitive pricing*. Here a manufacturer sets product prices at or just below those of competitors. This approach requires constant monitoring of competitors' prices so the marketer can prominently display a lower price in promotional messages. In contrast, with a *prestige pricing* strategy, product prices are set high and remain high. Promotional messages are aimed at a select clientele who can afford to pay the higher prices, and product quality and service are highlighted.

Clearly, the actual cost involved in manufacturing, distributing, and promoting a product will play a role in the price charged. The actual costs may vary from country to country. If specific markets require product modifications, these will need to be calculated into the price of the product. The manufacturer will also need to calculate into the price any additional operational costs related to the export operation, such as transportation and insurance costs. Further, costs incurred in entering the foreign market—including taxes, duties, and tariffs—must also be taken into account. Finally, wholesaler and retailer markups must be considered.

The number and nature of competitors manufacturing similar products or providing similar services will influence pricing decisions. The fewer the competitors, the greater the pricing flexibility. The intensity of demand for a certain product also impacts its price. Higher prices may be charged where demand is buoyant, and lower prices charged where demand is weak—even if production costs are the same in both instances. Total demand for a product is the net result of the combination of (1) consumer satisfaction derived from the product's "bundle of benefits," (2) the size of the market, and (3) the market's ability to purchase the product. Consumers must not only be willing to purchase a product but also be able to.

Governmental Influences on Pricing

Pricing is often one of the most heavily regulated areas in international marketing. Host countries have a variety of means to influence pricing. International marketers frequently encounter specified price markups, price ceilings, price freezes, restrictions on price changes, restrictions on acceptable profit margins, and government subsidies. The international marketer may also encounter governmental monopolies that control all international selling and buying. Further, tariffs and other government-controlled barriers force prices up for selected goods.

Export Pricing

When U.S. firms export products to international markets, costs associated with freight and shipping, insurance, tariffs, taxes, storage fees, documentation costs, and middleman margins must all be added to the domestic price of the product. These costs typically inflate the final price to a level significantly higher than the price charged in domestic markets for the same product, in what is commonly known as *price escalation.* This higher price for the product may mean that it is out of line with domestically available substitutes—which, in turn, may have a negative impact on consumer demand. In some instances this may be offset by the fact that the foreign goods are perceived as exclusive. For example, U.S. consumers generally pay more for French perfumes, German beers, and Italian leather shoes than for their domestic counterparts, yet demand still remains high.

On the other hand, a variety of factors may lead to a situation in which the imported product costs less than domestic goods. As noted previously, a desire to price products competitively may result in lower prices. In some instances overproduction may necessitate moving product inventories; storage space may not be available or products may be perishable. This may result in a price lower than that charged in the home market.

Numerous international firms also have been accused of dumping goods on foreign markets. *Dumping* refers to the selling of goods in foreign markets for less than they are sold for in the home market or to setting the product price below the cost of production. In some cases this may be unintentional on the part of the international marketer. Some firms, however, intentionally sell at a loss in foreign markets in order to increase their market share. In many countries—including the United States—domestic firms may petition their governments to impose antidumping duties on imports alleged to be dumped. For example, General Motors, Ford, and Chrysler sought an investigation regarding prices charged for Japanese minivans imported into this country. American auto manufacturers claimed that a number of Japanese minivans were being sold at improperly low prices—including Mazda's at 12.7 percent and Toyota's at 6.75 percent below their fair value.[42] While lower prices may be seen as a plus for consumers, dumping tends to have a devastating effect on domestic industries. When low-priced foreign goods flood a market, consumers purchase the imports and neglect domestic products. As a result, domestic manufacturers may be driven out of business, so that the home country loses a supplier in addition to jobs and tax revenues.

Pricing and Manufacture Abroad

When goods are both produced and distributed within the foreign country, the various marketing objectives and strategies discussed previously apply as well. The marketer must take into account consumer demand and the competitive environment. However, firms must take additional factors into consideration in pricing goods. When goods are manufactured abroad, foreign labor and material costs may be lower or higher than those in the home market, directly affecting overall production costs and ultimately product price.

Foreign governments in both developed and developing countries may impose price controls on goods produced within their borders. Should a firm wish to raise product prices, it typically must apply for a price increase and provide documentation supporting the request, which may or may not be granted. Such price controls can jeopardize not only the financial well-being but even the survival of a company. For example, Gerber began operations in Venezuela in the 1960s. Unprofitable operations forced the firm to close its doors in 1979. Gerber blamed price controls for its failure in the market— some of Gerber's products were still being sold at prices set more than ten years earlier because the Venezuelan government had refused repeated requests for price increases.

Inflation rates around the world vary dramatically. In many foreign countries the rate is similar to that in the United States—or perhaps even lower.

However, in other countries double- or even triple-figure inflation rates are not uncommon. Firms operating in such markets face a definite challenge in terms of pricing products. In countries with no price controls, pricing strategy involves raising prices frequently enough to keep pace with inflation. The situation becomes even more problematic when price controls are also imposed.

Promotion

Promotion is the fourth and final component in the marketing mix. Promotion includes advertising, personal selling, sales promotion, direct marketing, and public relations and publicity.

Advertising

Advertising, according to the Definitions Committee of the American Marketing Association, "is any paid form of nonpersonal presentation and promotion of ideas, goods or services by an identified sponsor."[43] Several aspects of this definition deserve further explication. The "paid" aspect refers to the fact that the advertiser must purchase time and space for the message. "Nonpersonal" indicates that the message appears in the mass media, which means there is little opportunity for feedback from the message receiver. Because of this, advertisers utilize research to determine how a specific target audience might interpret and respond to a message prior to its distribution. Finally, the "identified" aspect refers to the fact that the media require sponsors to identify themselves.

The role that advertising plays in a society differs from one market to the next. In Chapter 1 we examined countries in terms of their total advertising expenditures. In comparing the role of advertising in various nations, it is also useful to examine per capita advertising expenditures. Table 2.1 presents this measure for 1991—the most recent year for which data were collected. These figures demonstrate the significant variation from one country to the next. Advertising expenditures per capita range from a high of $328 for Switzerland and $324 for the United States to a low of 80 cents per person in India and a mere 40 cents per person in the People's Republic of China.

As with the other marketing mix elements, advertising can be standardized (whereby the same advertising theme is employed for each foreign market) or specialized (in which case the messages are adapted for local markets). Agencies and advertisers alike are divided over the issue. While

TABLE 2.1   1991 per Capita Advertising Expenditures (in U.S. $)

COUNTRY	AMOUNT	COUNTRY	AMOUNT
Australia	$211.2	Malaysia	$ 20.8
Austria	128.7	Mexico	18.1
Belgium	132.0	Netherlands	172.6
Canada	233.0	New Zealand	180.9
Chile	21.4	Norway	192.3
China, People's Republic	0.4	Philippines	3.0
Colombia	16.3	Portugal	57.1
Denmark	204.8	Puerto Rico	165.1
Finland	206.8	Singapore	136.3
France	153.6	South Africa	23.7
Germany	220.8	Spain	194.1
Greece	58.7	Sweden	196.0
Hong Kong	169.2	Switzerland	328.0
India	0.8	Taiwan	99.9
Indonesia	2.4	Thailand	11.6
Ireland	92.2	Turkey	10.2
Italy	130.2	United Kingdom	235.3
Japan	258.9	United States	324.8
Korea, South	73.4	Venezuela	26.7

SOURCE: International Advertising Association, Worldwide Summary 1994.

some agencies have jumped on the "globalization bandwagon," others remain committed to localization. Both Saatchi & Saatchi and BBD&O are believers in the global approach. Grey Advertising, on the other hand, suggests that each world business challenge is unique and, as a result, espouses "global vision with a local touch." A recent survey of 100 advertisers revealed mixed reviews regarding the effectiveness and practicality of the global approach to marketing messages.[44] Exxon's "Put a tiger in your tank" theme, employed in many different markets, provided the firm with a uniform positioning across markets. Marlboro cigarettes are also advertised in much the same fashion around the globe. Other marketers, due to a variety of constraints, opt to modify their advertising campaigns. Often, themes or appeals used in the home market may not be appropriate for specific foreign audiences. In a classic example, Pepsodent attempted to sell its toothpaste in a remote area of Southeast Asia via a message that stressed how the toothpaste helped whiten teeth. Unfortunately, this campaign had little effect, as this was an area where many local people deliberately chewed betel nut in order to achieve darkly stained teeth—a sign of prestige. A variety of other factors may also limit the feasibility of standardized campaigns. The issue of standardization versus specialization of advertising will be dealt with in greater detail in Chapters 5 and 6. It should be noted here, however, that of all the elements of the marketing mix, advertising is generally acknowledged to be the most difficult to standardize.[45]

In addition to strategic decisions, such as whether to standardize or specialize campaigns, the international marketer must decide on the appropriate message content. Advertising is effective only if it is able to both gain the attention of the target audience and communicate the product benefits clearly. Creative considerations will be addressed in Chapter 6. If the target audience is to receive the advertising message, it must appear in the appropriate medium. Media decisions include whether to employ local or international media. Advertising media will be discussed in Chapter 7. Research guides both whom the advertising should be targeted to and what the content of the message should be. Creative appeals may be evaluated prior to dissemination to help predict whether the message appeals to the correct audience. Research is also undertaken after a campaign has run to determine whether objectives have been met. Research in the international setting is the focus of Chapter 8.

Personal Selling

Personal selling involves individual, personal contact with the customer, with the intent of either making an immediate sale or developing a long-term relationship that will eventually result in a sale. Personal selling can take a variety of forms, including sales calls at a customer's place of business or a consumer's home or customer assistance at a retail outlet. In addition to such face-to-face contact, personal selling may also include contact through some form of telecommunication, such as telephone sales. This form of selling generally involves a greater degree of feedback than advertising, as the impact of the sales presentation often can be assessed directly through consumers' reactions. This provides a sales representative with the opportunity to tailor the presentation.

Personnel selling often plays a greater role in foreign than in domestic markets. Government restrictions on advertising, limitations in available media, and low literacy rates may cause marketers to turn to personal selling as a means of communicating with foreign customers. Lower wages in many developing countries may make personal selling a more cost-efficient method of selling as well.

The international marketer may choose to utilize a traveling sales force based at the company headquarters or perhaps to manage a team of expatriates based abroad. However, this approach tends to be quite expensive and often difficult to coordinate. Because it typically involves both communication and personal contact, personal selling is closely linked to national or even regional cultural characteristics. As a result, personal selling activities are typically conducted on a national basis. Most companies, regardless of their size, prefer to use sales representatives from the host country to staff their sales force. Even in the European Union, personal selling is slow to cross national borders. With few exceptions a German salesperson will not be particularly effective in Holland, nor will a French salesperson have much luck persuading a Swiss consumer. Nationals are quite simply more readily accepted than foreigners, and they also are more familiar with their country. The challenge in utilizing a national sales force lies in recruitment and training, as well as in adapting personal selling activities to fit the local market.

Sales Promotion

Sales promotion consists of a variety of techniques designed to support and complement both advertising and personal selling. The goal of sales promotion is to stimulate immediate consumer purchasing and/or dealer effectiveness. Cents-off coupons, premiums, samples, and point-of-purchase displays may induce trial purchase of products as well as maintain consumer loyalty. Sweepstakes and contests can create interest in and excitement about a company's product or service and increase the likelihood that its advertising campaigns will receive attention. Price deals, trade shows, and contests are typical trade promotion activities that may be directed at wholesalers, distributors, and retailers. The overall use of sales promotion efforts appears to be on the increase worldwide.[46]

While many companies effectively utilize sales promotion tools to help sell their products in foreign markets, marketers must be aware of potential pitfalls. Because of cultural differences among consumers, promotional incentives that have proven successful in the home market may not be as effective in foreign markets. Several years ago, for example, Lego attempted to use the same style promotions for its building blocks that it had employed in the United States in Japan as well. Lego had measurably improved its penetration of U.S. households by employing "bonus-packs" and gift promotions. Encouraged by that success, it decided to transfer these tactics unaltered to other markets, including Japan, where penetration had stalled. But these lures left Japanese consumers unmoved. Subsequent investigations showed that consumers considered the promotions to be wasteful, expensive, and unappealing. Lego's marketers got their first lesson on the limitations of the global transferability of sales promotions.[47]

Promotional efforts should be adapted to a variety of local conditions. For example, when Procter & Gamble mailed 580,000 free samples of Vidal Sassoon Wash & Go shampoo to consumers in Warsaw, it never expected an adverse reaction. The samples were in such demand that some Poles wrecked mailboxes to steal them. Following what was believed to be the first mass mailing of free samples in Poland, about two thousand mailboxes—mostly in large urban areas—were broken into by people who wanted the samples either to use or to sell. The samples turned up at open markets, selling for 60 cents each. P&G has assured the Polish Post that it will pay for the damages.[48]

Differing legal restrictions and regulations from one country to the next may render some promotional efforts impossible while requiring that others be modified significantly. Such restrictions often mean that marketers must develop separate promotions for each country. For example, free mail-in offers are allowed in the United Kingdom, Ireland, and Spain, where rules tend to be more liberal. However, the same promotion may not be permitted in France, Belgium, and Luxembourg and would definitely be ruled out in Germany.[49] Table 2.2 outlines the variety of restrictions on sales promotions in just five European countries.

The following are perceived to be quite liberal with regards to the regulation of premiums, gifts, and competitions: Australia, Canada, France, Hong Kong, Ireland, Malaysia, New Zealand, the Philippines, Singapore, Spain, Sweden, the United Kingdom, and the United States. In contrast, Austria, Belgium, Denmark, Germany, Italy, Japan, Korea, Mexico, the Netherlands, Switzerland, and Venezuela are seen as significantly more restrictive. Because both industrialized and developing countries appear on each list, any attempt to generalize some meaning is rather useless.[50]

Because distribution channels in foreign markets generally are different from those in the United States, promotions that rely heavily on retailer involvement and cooperation may not be effective. For example, while American retailers commonly handle processing of coupons and the display of point-of-purchase materials, international marketers cannot assume that this level of assistance exists in foreign markets. Also, retailers in many foreign markets may be smaller in size or greater in number, and as a result it may be more difficult to contact them. With regards to promotions directed at both consumers and the trade, international marketers must study each country separately.

Direct Marketing

Traditionally, direct marketing has not been considered an element in the promotions mix. However, because of the increasingly important role direct marketing plays in the communications programs of many different kinds of organizations, it is included here. *Direct marketing* refers to a way of doing business—one in which the marketer attempts to sell goods directly to the consumer without the aid of a wholesaler or retailer. Messages are designed

TABLE 2.2 Sales Promotion Restrictions in Selected European Countries

PROMOTION	U.K.	SPAIN	GERMANY	FRANCE	ITALY
In-pack premiums	●	●	✕	○	●
Multiple-purchase offers	●	●	○	●	●
Extra product	●	●	○	●	●
Free product	●	●	●	●	●
Mail-in offers	●	●	✕	●	●
Purchase-with-purchase	●	●	✕	●	●
Cross-promotions	●	●	✕	●	●
Contests	●	●	○	●	●
Self-liquidating premiums	●	●	●	●	●
Sweepstakes	○	○	✕	○	○
Money-off coupons	●	●	✕	●	○
Next-purchase coupons	●	●	✕	●	○
Cash rebates	●	●	○	●	✕
In-store demos	●	●	●	●	●

● = Permitted   ✕ = Not permitted   ○ = May be permitted

SOURCE: "Europe Remains Mixed Bag," *Advertising Age,* August 7, 1989, p. 45.

to solicit a measurable response and/or transaction from the target audience. Direct marketers may employ a variety of media, placing such messages in magazines and newspapers as well as on radio and television. Direct selling, direct mail, catalog sales, and telemarketing are also commonly employed. Direct marketing is seen as much more personal than advertising because it incorporates a degree of two-way communication.

Avon has found direct marketing to be an effective means of selling its line of products deep in the Brazilian rain forest. Avon's army of more than 60,000 vendors trade Avon lipsticks, perfumes, and facial creams for gold nuggets as well as wood, fruit, and even eggs. Their efforts have turned the Amazon region into a gold mine for the Brazilian subsidiary of the U.S. cosmetics giant. Isabel Vincent writes: "Since it changed its marketing strategy three years ago to boost its sales force in the Amazon outback, Avon has become one of the few Brazilian companies to see sales rocket despite a 10 percent drop in per-capita income. In some isolated gold-mining communities, Avon is even more readily available than Coca-Cola."[51]

Amway, another direct marketer, has found success in the Japanese market and currently has a sales force of some 800,000 as well as yearly sales of 130 billion yen—or about $1.25 billion. In the past five years sales have more than doubled, making the company the second biggest U.S. corporate venture in Japan behind Coca-Cola.[52] While companies such as Avon and Amway, as well as Encyclopaedia Britannica and Tupperware, often rely solely on direct marketing to sell their goods, direct marketing methods, tools, and techniques increasingly are being employed by firms that distribute their products via traditional channels. Indeed, direct marketing is currently growing faster than virtually any other form of promotion.

Public Relations

Public relations involves a variety of efforts to create and maintain a positive image of an organization with its various publics. Organizations may wish to communicate with customers, employees, stockholders, suppliers/distributors, governmental agencies, labor unions, the media, and various activist groups, as well as with the public at large. Public relations often plays a more critical role for a firm operating abroad than it does domestically. Clearly, international marketers face fewer problems if their firm is perceived positively in the country in which it operates.

Publicity, as part of the broader function of public relations, involves seeking favorable comments on the product/service and/or firm itself via news stories, editorials, or announcements in the mass media. In contrast to advertising, publicity is not directly paid for by the company, nor does the company have control over the content or frequency of the coverage. While publicity is an important communication technique employed in public relations, public relations practitioners have a number of additional tools at their disposal, such as newsletters and other publications, news conferences, company-sponsored events, and participation in community activities.

Increasingly, companies involved in international marketing recognize the value in incorporating public relations to support and enhance their promotional efforts. Avon, Du Pont, G. D. Searle (manufacturer of NutraSweet), Johnson & Johnson, Combustion Engineering, and Union Carbide all have enlisted the aid of international public relations specialists. To meet this demand, public relations firms—like advertising agencies—are busy merging with and/or acquiring offices outside the United States.[53] For example, Burson-Marsteller, headquartered in New York City, has offices in twenty-two countries around the globe—including the People's Republic of China. Recently, Ketchum Public Relations, headquartered in Pittsburgh, teamed up with firms based in London, Toronto, and Tokyo to better meet the needs of their clients. A variety of groups, including local governments, local media, and the general public, may feel threatened by the presence of a foreign multinational in their country. Thus, it is the responsibility of public relations personnel to position the firm as a good corporate citizen that is involved with and concerned about the future of the host country.

Integrated Marketing Communications

Until quite recently, most firms planned and managed their marketing and promotions functions separately. Increasingly, however, companies are moving toward integrated marketing communications. The American Association of Advertising Agencies defines *integrated marketing communications (IMC)* as "a concept of marketing communications planning that recognizes the added value of a comprehensive plan that evaluates the strategic roles of a variety of communication disciplines, e.g., general advertising, direct response, sales promotion and public relations—and combines these disciplines to provide clarity, consistency and maximum impact."[54] A major benefit associated with IMC is synergism, "meaning that the individual efforts are mutually reinforced with the resulting effect being greater than if each functional area had selected its own targets, chosen its own message strategy, and set its own media schedule and timing."[55]

However, even this view of IMC is too narrow. Researchers and practitioners alike have noted that the messages consumers receive about a company and its products are not limited to advertisements, direct marketing efforts, publicity, and sales promotions. Rather, claim Don Schultz and colleagues, "Almost everything the marketer does relates to or provides some form of communication to customers and prospects, from the design of the product through the packaging and distribution channel selected. These product contacts communicate something about the value and the person for whom the product was designed."[56]

The kind of customer service that is provided after the product is purchased also sends a message to consumers. Thus, the other elements of the marketing mix—which have typically been isolated from the communication strategy—are, in fact, sources of information for the consumer as well. In addition, the target audience may gather information about a product or service from conversations with friends, relatives, and co-workers. Even retailers and the media have something to say about a manufacturer's product. According to Schultz and colleagues, "The marketer has very limited control over much of the information and data that the consumer receives. . . . That's why it's so critical for marketers to maintain some sort of control over the communication they initiate or influence."[57]

IMC, then, is all about managing the various contacts a firm has with its customers, since each of these contacts potentially influences consumer behavior. In order to better manage these contacts, the firm actively solicits responses from consumers. Response solicitation devices may include a telephone call, a direct mail piece, a purchase warranty card, or some other form through which the consumer can engage in two-way communications with the manufacturer. Response information is then stored in a database (along with demographic and psychographic data), providing the marketer with the necessary feedback to adjust future communications.

Schultz and colleagues note: "In short, marketing in the 1990s is communication and communication is marketing. The two are inseparable. And, for that reason, the proper integration of all marketing messages is that much more important."[58] IMC is an emerging concept being developed in the United States. To date, IMC is predominantly practiced by innovative American firms such as IBM and Eastman Kodak. It is merely a matter of time, however, until these sophisticated firms extend and expand their integrated marketing programs into other countries.

Summary

Although the focus of this text is on advertising, the international marketer must realize that decisions relating to advertising in the international arena cannot be made without regard to other promotions efforts or the remaining elements of the marketing mix. From the international marketer's perspective the elements of the marketing mix are generally seen as the "controllable elements" of the marketing decision. This is the case with both domestic and international marketing. However, international marketers must also deal with a number of elements outside their control when they enter a foreign market. Product, price, distribution, and promotion decisions must be made within a framework of several uncontrollable elements of the specific marketplace—what is commonly known as the marketing environment. Although marketing principles are universally applicable, the environment within which the marketer must implement the marketing plan can and usually does change dramatically from country to country. Thus, we turn our attention to this topic in Chapter 3.

Additional Readings

Chan, Allan K. K. (1990). "Localization in International Branding." *International Journal of Advertising*, 9, pp. 81–91.

Duncan, Thomas R., and Stephen E. Everett. (May/June 1993). "Client Perceptions of Integrated Marketing Communications." *Journal of Advertising Research*, pp. 30–39.

Hill, John, Richard Still, and Unal Boya. (1991). "Managing the Multinational Sales Force." *International Marketing Review*, 8(1), pp. 19–31.

Jain, Subhash C. (January 1989). "Standardization of International Marketing Strategy." *Journal of Marketing*, 53(1), pp. 70–79.

Keegan, Warren J. "Multinational Product Planning: Strategic Alternatives." *Journal of Marketing*, January 1969, pp. 224–231.

Kreutzer, Ralf Thomas. (1988). "Marketing Mix Standardization: An Integrated Approach in Global Marketing." *European Journal of Marketing,* 2(10), pp. 19–30.

Peebles, Dean M., and John K. Ryans. (1984). *Management of International Advertising: A Marketing Approach.* Boston: Allyn & Bacon.

Rosen, Barry. (1989). "Global Products: When Do They Make Strategic Sense?" *Advances in International Marketing,* 4.

Schultz, Don E., Stanley I. Tannenbaum, and Robert E. Lauterborn. (1994). *The New Marketing Paradigm: Integrated Marketing Communications.* Lincolnwood, IL: NTC Business Books.

Walters, Peter. (Summer 1986). "International Marketing Policy: A Discussion of the Standardization Construct and Its Relevance for Corporate Policy." *Journal of International Business Studies,* 17(2), pp. 55–70.

Whitelock, Jeryl M. (1987). "Global Marketing and the Case for International Product Standardization." *European Journal of Marketing,* 21, pp. 32–44.

Young, Stephen, James Hamill, Colin Wheeler, and J. Richard Davies. (1989). *International Market Entry and Development.* Englewood Cliffs, NJ: Prentice-Hall.

Notes

1. McCarthy, Jerome, *Basic Marketing: A Managerial Approach* (Homewood, IL: Irwin, 1960).

2. Buzzell, Robert D., "Can You Standardize Multinational Marketing?" *Harvard Business Review,* 6, November/December 1968.

3. Levitt, Theodore, "The Globalization of Markets," *Harvard Business Review,* May/June 1983, pp. 92–102.

4. "Global Marketing Plan: Moving from Concept to Reality," *The Advertiser,* 2, Spring 1992, pp. 12–16.

5. Weber, Joseph, "Campbell: Now It's M-m Global," *Business Week,* March 15, 1993, pp. 52–56.

6. O'Leary, Noreen, "The Hand on Lever," *ADWEEK,* December 14, 1992, pp. 23–27.

7. "Marketing Definitions: A Glossary of Marketing Terms," compiled by the Committee on Definitions of the American Marketing Association, 1960.

8. Kotler, Philip, and Gary Armstrong, *Marketing: An Introduction* (Englewood Cliffs, NJ: Prentice-Hall, 1990), p. 227.

9. Douglas, Susan P., and Christine D. Urban, "Lifestyle Analysis to Profile Women in International Markets," *Journal of Marketing,* July 1977, pp. 53–54.

10. Hoevell, P. J., and P. G. Walters, "International Marketing Presentations: Some Options," *European Journal of Marketing,* Summer 1972, pp. 69–79.

11. Boddewyn, J. J., Robin Soehl, and Jacques Picard, "Standardization in International Marketing: Is Ted Levitt in Fact Right?" *Business Horizons,* November/December 1986, pp. 69–75.

12. Cahn, Kim, and R. A. Mauborgne, "Cross Cultural Strategies," *Journal of Business Strategy,* 7, Spring 1987, p. 31.

13. Sheth, Hagdish, "Global Markets or Global Competition?" *Journal of Consumer Marketing,* Spring 1986, pp. 9–11.

14. Kale, Sudhir, and D. Sudharshan, "A Strategic Approach to International Segmentation," *International Marketing Review,* Summer 1987, pp. 60–71.

15. Domzal, Teresa, and Lynette Unger, "Emerging Positioning Strategies in Global Marketing," *Journal of Consumer Marketing,* 4(4), Fall 1987, pp. 23–40.

16. Kraar, Louis, "How Americans Win in Asia," *Fortune,* October 7, 1991, pp. 133–140.

17. Britt, Stuart Henderson, "Standardizing Marketing for the International Market," *Columbia Journal of World Business,* 9, Winter 1974, pp. 32–40.

18. Ricks, David A., Marilyn Fu, and Jeffrey S. Arpan, *International Business Blunders* (Columbus, OH: Grid, 1974), p. 16.

19. "The $30 Million Lesson," *Sales Management,* March 1, 1967, pp. 31–38.

20. Kotler, Philip, "Global Standardization—Courting Danger," *The Journal of Consumer Marketing,* 3(2), Spring 1986, pp. 13–15.

21. Ibid.

22. Douglas, Susan P., and C. Samuel Craig, "Evolution of Global Marketing Strategy: Scale, Scope and Synergy," *Columbia Journal of World Business,* 24(3), Fall 1989, pp. 47–59.

23. Shalofsky, Ivor, "Research for Global Brands," *European Research,* May 1987, pp. 88–93.

24. "We're Number 1—At Least We Are in Nicaragua," *ADWEEK,* February 21, 1994, p. 15.

25. Westbrook, John, "Taiwan Made Items Receive Image Boost," *Advertising Age,* January 18, 1993, p. I8.

26. Bilkey, Warren J., and E. Nes, "Country of Origin Effects on Product Evaluation," *Journal of International Business Studies,* 13, Spring/Summer, 1982, pp. 89–99.

27. Head, David. "Ad Slogans and the Made-In Concept," *International Journal of Advertising,* 7, 1988, pp. 237–252.

28. "With Multinational Ties, It's Difficult to Tell Where Products Really Came From," *San Diego Union-Tribune,* February 2, 1992, p. A36.

29. "Made in America Gets Tougher to Determine," *San Diego Union-Tribune,* February 2, 1992, p. A33.

30. McCay, Betsy, "Xerox Fights Trademark Battle," *Advertising Age,* April 27, 1992, p. I39.

31. "Global Brands," *U.S. News & World Report,* September 24, 1990, p. 19.

32. Johnston, Jean, "Japanese Firms in the U.S.: Adapting the Persuasive Message," *The Bulletin for the Association for Business Communications,* 51(3), September 1988, pp. 33–34.

33. Kashani, Kamran, "Beware the Pitfalls of Global Marketing," *Harvard Business Review,* 67(5), September/October 1989, pp. 91–98.

34. Ricks, David, *Big Business Blunders: Mistakes in Multinational Marketing* (Homewood, IL: Dow Jones-Irwin, 1983), p. 34.

35. Ibid., p. 31.

36. "Coors Brews Big Plans for Korea," *Business Week,* December 9, 1991, p. 44.

37. Rosenberg, Larry, "Deciphering the Japanese Cultural Code," *International Marketing Review,* Autumn 1980, pp. 47–57.

38. Denitto, Emily, "Hyper Markets Seem to Be Big Flop in U.S.," *Advertising Age,* October 4, 1993, p. 20.

39. "Ad Age International and Audits & Surveys Examine Retail Distribution Patterns Around the World," *Advertising Age,* June 22, 1992.

40. McKay, Betsy, "How to Sell Pet Food in Russia," *Advertising Age,* May 17, 1993, p. I21.

41. Boddewyn, J. J., "American Marketing in the European Common Market, 1963–1973," in *Multinational Product Management* (Cambridge, MA: Marketing Science Institute, 1976), pp. 1–25.

42. Greenhouse, Steven, "U.S. Rules Toyota, Mazda Are Dumping Minivans," *San Diego Union-Tribune,* May 20, 1992, p. C1.

43. "Report of the Definitions Committee," *Journal of Marketing,* October 12, 1948, p. 202.

44. "Differences, Confusion Slow Marketing Bandwagon," *Marketing News,* January 16, 1987, p. 1.

45. Boddewyn, Soehl, and Picard, "Standardization in International Marketing," pp. 67–75.

46. Boddewyn, Jean, *Premiums, Gifts and Competitions* (New York: IAA, 1986), Chapter 1.

47. Kashani, "Beware the Pitfalls."

48. Gajewski, Maciek, "Samples: A Steal in Poland," *Advertising Age,* November 4, 1991, p. 54.

49. "Europe Remains Mixed Bag," *Advertising Age,* August 7, 1989, p. 45.

50. Boddewyn, *Premiums, Gifts and Competitions,* Chapter 1.

51. Vincent, Isabel, "Deep in the Rain Forest, A Familiar Greeting Is Heard—Avon Calling," *San Diego Union-Tribune,* June 25, 1994, p. A28.

52. Green, Frank, "Japanese Have Yen for Amway," *San Diego Union-Tribune,* March 9, 1994, p. C1.

53. "Foreign Ads Go Farther with PR," *International Advertiser,* December 1986, pp. 30–31.

54. Duncan, Thomas R., and Stephen E. Everett, "Client Perceptions of Integrated Marketing Communications," *Journal of Advertising Research,* May/June 1993, pp. 30–39.

55. Novelli, William D., "One Stop Shopping: Some Thoughts on Integrated Marketing Communications," *Public Relations Quarterly,* 34(4), 1989–1990, pp. 7–9.

56. Schultz, Don E., Stanley I. Tannenbaum, and Robert E. Lauterborn, *The New Marketing Paradigm: Integrated Marketing Communications* (Lincolnwood, IL: NTC Business Books, 1994), p. 45.

57. Ibid., p. 47.

58. Ibid., p. 46.

The International Marketing and Advertising Environment

Demographic and geographic characteristics, economic and political-legal factors all are important not only in evaluating a country's potential as a market but also in designing and implementing the marketing mix for a specific market. Thus, each of these environmental factors will be analyzed in this chapter. The international marketer must consider demographic characteristics (size of the population, rate of population growth, education, population density, and age structure and composition of population), economic factors (GNP per capita, income distribution, and rate of growth of GNP); geographic characteristics (size of the country, topographical characteristics, and climate conditions), and the political-legal environment (political stability, laws and regulations, and the degree of nationalism). Clearly, cultural characteristics also play an influential role. However, this aspect of the international marketing and advertising environment will be dealt with separately in Chapter 4. Exhibit 3.1 shows the relationship of these environmental factors to the marketing mix.

EXHIBIT 3.1 The Relationship of Environmental Factors to the Marketing Mix

The international marketer generally has very limited, if any, control over these environmental factors. The marketer's task is to assess these factors in order to identify potential barriers to doing business. Firms operating in affluent markets are accustomed to having extensive secondary data available, but obtaining similar data in developing markets can prove quite a challenge. Often, data are inaccurate or simply not available. If no insurmountable barriers are detected, the research on these uncontrollable environmental elements will provide information that allows the international marketer to adapt the marketing mix to the specific market.

Demographic Characteristics

Just as the demographic characteristics of various segments within the U.S. population make them more or less appealing to marketers, so, too, do demographic characteristics of foreign countries—such as market size, population growth and distribution, and education—influence a marketer's decision regarding whether and how to enter a market.

Market Size

The current world population is estimated at 5.48 billion—and it is expected to grow by 97 million people each year during the remainder of this decade. How these 5.5 billion or so potential consumers are distributed around the globe is of intense interest to the international marketer. Knowing a market's size is essential in determining whether to enter a market, and a country's population provides one basic indicator of market size. Generally, the larger the population of a market, the greater its potential—all other things being equal. However, population figures alone are usually not a sufficient guide to market size. Population size must typically be combined with many other factors, such as population growth rates, distribution patterns, and available income.

There is enormous variation in the population of countries around the globe, as Table 3.1 shows. The table reveals that well over half the people in the world live in only ten countries and that the world's largest nation has a population approximately ten *thousand* times the population of some of the smallest countries.

Population Growth

Most international marketers are also concerned with population growth rates. The majority of countries experience some population growth. While some countries report relatively high population growth rates—such as Saudi Arabia (4.9 percent), Kenya (3.6 percent), Ethiopia (3.1 percent), and Nigeria (3.0 percent)—other countries' growth rates are more moderate—such as China (1.4 percent), Canada (1.1 percent), and the United States (1.0 percent). Hungary, however, reports a declining growth rate (−0.3 percent).[1] Overall, wealthier countries tend to have more stable populations while developing countries have rapidly expanding populations.

From the perspective of the international marketer, high population growth rates may indicate the formation of new households and therefore

TABLE 3.1 Mid-1992 Population Figures (in millions)

COUNTRY	POPULATION	COUNTRY	POPULATION
People's Republic of China	1,162.2	Greece	10.3
India	883.6	Belgium	10.0
Commonwealth of Independent States	290.0	Portugal	9.8
United States	255.4	Guatemala	9.7
Indonesia	184.3	Sweden	8.7
Brazil	153.9	Zambia	8.3
Japan	124.5	Austria	7.9
Pakistan	119.3	Bolivia	7.5
Mexico	85.0	Dominican Republic	7.3
Germany	80.6	Switzerland	6.9
Philippines	64.3	Hong Kong	5.8
Thailand	58.0	Denmark	5.2
Italy	57.8	Israel	5.1
United Kingdom	57.8	Finland	5.0
France	57.4	Norway	4.3
Egypt	54.7	Jordan	3.9
South Korea	43.7	Puerto Rico	3.6
South Africa	39.8	Ireland	3.5
Spain	39.1	Lebanon	3.5
Colombia	33.4	New Zealand	3.4
Argentina	33.1	Costa Rica	3.2
Canada	27.4	Singapore	2.8
Kenya	25.7	Panama	2.5
Venezuela	20.2	United Arab Emirates	1.7
Malaysia	18.6	Oman	1.6
Australia	17.5	Kuwait	1.3
Sri Lanka	17.4	Trinidad & Tobago	1.2
Saudi Arabia	16.8	Cyprus	0.62
Netherlands	15.2	Malta	0.36
Yemen	13.0	Bahrain	0.34
Ecuador	11.0	Qatar	0.23
Zimbabwe	10.4		

SOURCES: World Bank, *World Development Report 1994* (New York: Oxford University Press, 1994), pp. 162–164; U.S. Department of Commerce, Bureau of the Census, *1993 Statistical Abstracts of the United States* (113th ed.) (Washington, DC: GPO, 1993), pp. 840–842.

increased demand for a variety of consumer goods. However, rapidly expanding populations also may have a negative effect on per capita income, translating into more limited purchasing power. Even in countries with stagnant or declining population growth rates, potential exists for the international marketer. For example, although Hungary shows a declining growth rate, in 1991 it received $1.5 billion in direct foreign investment from international firms hoping to tap this market.[2]

Population Distribution

Along with population growth rates, the international marketer will need to evaluate the distribution of the population. Three important population distribution characteristics are density, age and age structure, and household size.

Density As with population size, there is a great deal of variation in population density among nations. In 1993, for example, the United States had a population density of 73 persons per square mile, as contrasted to the 8 persons per square mile in Canada. Note, however, that most Canadians live within 150 miles of the U.S. border and that the population density is actually much lower in the predominantly uninhabited Yukon and Northwest territories. On the high end of the scale, Singapore has an almost unbelievable 11,731 persons per square mile, and Hong Kong a staggering 14,542 persons per square mile.[3]

Age One important aspect of age is the average life expectancy of consumers in various markets. In most Western countries, the average life expectancy is quite similar (for example, 76 for the United States, 77 for Canada, 78 for France, and 79 for Japan). In contrast, most people living in developing nations have a relatively short life expectancy (for example, only 53 in Bangladesh, 51 in Ethiopia, 49 in Nigeria, and 44 in Angola).[4]

Markets also vary in their age structure. Markets with varying age groupings reflect consumers with both differing needs and differing levels of purchasing power. The lower life expectancy in many countries also means their populations are comparatively young. As Table 3.2 shows, a significantly larger percentage of the population in many lower-income countries falls into the 0–14 age grouping than in the higher-income ones. However, even within these groupings variation exists.

Although approximately one-third of China's population is currently under 14 years of age, marketers must keep an eye to the future. In fifteen to twenty years, almost 30 percent of Chinese will be in their late 20s to late 30s, the prime earning and spending years. On the other hand, in the developed nations, an ever increasing percentage of the population is in the over-65 grouping. These older consumer segments, whose numbers are increasing in countries such as the United States and Germany, tend to be more affluent—having reached the peak of their earning potential—and as a result have greater amounts of disposable income available.

TABLE 3.2 Economic Development and Age Structure (percentage between 0–14 years)			
LOW-INCOME ECONOMIES—35.5%		**UPPER-MIDDLE-INCOME ECONOMIES—33.4%**	
Uganda	49.5%	Venezuela	36.5%
Kenya	48.6	Brazil	33.5
India	35.6	Portugal	19.2
China	26.9	Hungary	18.7
LOWER-MIDDLE-INCOME ECONOMIES—37.9%		**HIGH-INCOME ECONOMIES—20.5%**	
Algeria	41.8%	United States	21.5%
Peru	36.3	France	19.2
Thailand	30.0	Japan	17.0
Poland	24.0	Germany	16.3

SOURCE: World Bank, *World Development Report 1994* (New York: Oxford University Press, 1994), pp. 210–211.

Household Size A *household* refers to all persons, both related and unrelated, who occupy a housing unit.[5] The term means very different things in different countries. A household in Thailand typically consists of an extended family, with grandparents and grandchildren, aunts and uncles, and cousins all living under one roof. The typical household in the United States, in contrast, is generally limited to the nuclear family. Also, in many parts of the world, households pool their incomes, which slightly distorts per capita income figures. While population figures in many developed countries remain stable, the number of households has increased while the average household size has decreased. This can be attributed to two factors: increases in the divorce rate and in the number of sole-survivor households. Smaller-sized households have direct implications for the marketers of consumer goods. For example, package sizes may need to be smaller or prepackaged for single servings. This, in turn, impacts advertising message content.

Education

Another demographic variable of interest to international marketers is education. The education information available is largely limited to the national enrollments in the various levels of education—primary, secondary, and university or college. A fairly close relationship seems to exist between economic development and educational attainment, with individuals in the more developed countries generally completing more years of education. As one

TABLE 3.3   Illiteracy Rates by Country (as of September 1992)

COUNTRY	RATE	COUNTRY	RATE
Afghanistan	81.8%	Venezuela	15.3%
Sierra Leone	79.3	Costa Rica	7.4
Uganda	51.7	Argentina	6.1
Guatemala	44.9	Spain	4.2
Malaysia	30.4	Italy	3.5
Hong Kong	22.7	Commonwealth of Independent States	2.0
Brazil	22.2		
Zimbabwe	22.2	Poland	1.2
Mexico	17.0	Hungary	1.1
Philippines	16.7	United States	0.5

SOURCE: United Nations Statistical Office, *Statistical Yearbook 1990/1991* (New York: United Nations, 1993).

might expect, education is also highly correlated with literacy. From an international marketer's standpoint, consumers must be able to read advertising messages and product labels as well as understand warranty and guarantee information. If large percentages of consumers are illiterate in certain markets, advertising programs and product packaging may need to be modified. Level of education is also of interest because it reflects the degree of consumer sophistication. Complex messages and products that require instructions may need to be adapted depending on educational trends in a particular country. Table 3.3 lists sample rates of illiteracy by country.

Economic Factors

In addition to demographic information, international marketers require economic data in order to assess market potential. This is because the attractiveness of a market goes beyond sheer numbers of people—a nation's current and future attractiveness is also based on the willingness and ability of those people to spend. A clear understanding of a host country's economic environment—including type of economy, per capita income, and level of urbanization—is also essential in developing an appropriate marketing and communications strategy.

Classification Systems

Classifications of economic systems vary depending on the originator of the classification system as well as its intended use. The following system is commonly employed in the marketing literature:

▶ *Subsistence economies*—includes countries in which the vast majority of citizens are engaged in agriculture. They tend to consume much of what they produce and to barter any excess production. Overall, market opportunities here are still rather limited.

▶ *Raw-material-exporting economies*—includes countries that are rich in one or more natural resources but considered poor in most other ways. Their revenues generally come from exporting these resources—for example, Saudi Arabia (oil) and Zaire (copper and coffee). Such countries tend to be good markets for heavy machinery and tools.

▶ *Industrializing economies*—includes countries in which manufacturing accounts for roughly 10–20 percent of the national economy—for example, Brazil, Egypt, and the Philippines. As manufacturing increases, these countries may require imports of raw materials and heavy machinery. Industrialization often creates a new rich class as well as a growing middle class, both of which demand a variety of consumer goods.

▶ *Industrial economies*—includes countries that are major exporters of manufactured goods as well as investment funds. Industrial economies trade goods among themselves as well as export them to industrializing and raw-material-exporting economies. Industrial economies generally have large middle classes, making them ideal for most categories of consumer goods.

Historically, industrial economies have represented the greatest marketing opportunities for corporations, because consumers in these countries typically have the capacity to purchase goods offered by international marketers. In addition, the communications, transportation, financial, and distribution networks necessary to conduct business are in place. However, such markets also tend to have stable or even shrinking population bases, and as a result, markets for many goods and services may already be saturated. Thus, marketers are increasingly turning to less developed nations, which tend to have expanding populations and therefore potentially greater growth opportunities. Gillette, for example, typically begins marketing efforts in subsistence and raw-material-exporting countries with its traditional double-edged disposable razors. If the razors are popular, a variety of other products are introduced, including pens, deodorants, shampoos, and toothpaste. When Gillette introduced its aerosol shaving cream to the Guadalajaran/

TABLE 3.4   1992 Economic Development and per Capita Income

LOW-INCOME ECONOMIES—$390		UPPER-MIDDLE-INCOME ECONOMIES—$4,020	
China	$470	Venezuela	$2,910
Kenya	310	Brazil	2,770
Pakistan	420	Portugal	7,450
Indonesia	670	Greece	7,290
LOWER-MIDDLE-INCOME ECONOMIES—$1,530		**HIGH-INCOME ECONOMIES—$22,160**	
Zimbabwe	$570	United Kingdom	$17,790
Guatemala	980	United States	23,240
Thailand	1,840	Japan	28,190
Costa Rica	1,960	Switzerland	36,080

SOURCE: World Bank, *World Development Report 1994* (New York: Oxford University Press, 1994), pp. 162–163.

Mexican market, however, it found the product to be too expensive for consumers. In response, Gillette created a customized product for the market—Prestobarba—a tub-packaged shaving cream. After initial success with this product, Gillette went on to promote the product in Colombia and Brazil.[6]

Income

A statistic commonly used to describe the economic condition of a country is *per capital income,* a widely accepted indicator of a country's economic development, as well as the potential purchasing power of its individuals. Per capita income is often examined in relation to a country's total national income, or *gross national product (GNP).* As Table 3.4 shows, there is a wide range in the per capita income figures among the nations of the world. For example, in 1992 dollars Switzerland had a per capita income of $36,080, while China had a per capita income of little more than $470.

Note that per capita figures are averages and give no indication of income distribution. Typically, the more developed the country, the more even the distribution of income. In many developing countries, however, there is a bimodal distribution of income—a very rich segment of the population and a very large, very poor segment with literally no middle class. The following serves as a useful classification system:

> ▶ *Very low family incomes*—subsistence economies characterized by rural populations in which consumption relies on personal output or barter. Some urban centers may provide markets.

▶ *Mostly low family incomes*—economies that are beginning to industrialize. Most goods are produced domestically.

▶ *Very low, very high family incomes*—economies that exhibit strongly bimodal income distributions. The majority of the population may live barely above the subsistence level, while a minority provides a strong market for imported or luxury items. The affluent are truly affluent and will consume accordingly.

▶ *Low, medium, and high family incomes*—economies in which industrialization has produced an emerging middle class with increasing disposable income. However, due to traditional social class barriers, the very low and very high income classes tend to remain.

▶ *Mostly medium family incomes*—advanced industrial economies with institutions and policies that reduce extremes in income distribution. The result is a large and comfortable middle class able to purchase a wide array of both domestic and imported products and services.[7]

Household income may be a more telling statistic than per capita income. In many developing countries, the extended family rather than the nuclear family is the norm. For example, in Latin American countries the typical household includes aunts, uncles, cousins, grandparents, and sometimes even great-grandparents. Several family members may be wage earners, directly impacting the buying power of the family unit. And while the nuclear family is still the norm in the United States, today that unit typically includes two wage earners. As a result, international marketers often pair household income with household size in analyzing a market's willingness and ability to spend.

Urbanization

One of the most telling economic indicators is the degree to which a country is urbanized. Table 3.5 shows the degree of urbanization for the world's four broad economic groupings. The averages for these groupings reveal a strong correlation between degree of urbanization and level of economic development. However, even within the broad economic groupings, there is significant variation. Typically, the more urbanized markets tend to be more appealing to international marketers. Developing countries are generally much less urbanized and, as a result, tend to be less attractive markets, particularly for consumer goods. Even less developed countries, however, may contain sizable pockets of high-income consumers. Products targeted to the urban markets in such countries may need only minimal changes from those marketed in developed countries. On the other hand, if the marketer is at-

TABLE 3.5 Economic Development and Urban Population (as percentage of total population)

LOW-INCOME ECONOMIES—27%		UPPER-MIDDLE-INCOME ECONOMIES—72%	
Ethiopia	13%	Portugal	35%
Bangladesh	18	Mexico	74
India	26	Brazil	77
China	27	Venezuela	91
LOWER-MIDDLE-INCOME ECONOMIES—53%		**HIGH-INCOME ECONOMIES—78%**	
Thailand	23%	Ireland	58%
Cameroon	42	United States	76
Philippines	44	United Kingdom	89
Romania	55	Hong Kong	94

SOURCE: World Bank, *World Development Report 1994* (New York: Oxford University Press, 1994), pp. 222–223.

tempting to reach both the rural and urban populations in developing countries, a greater degree of product specialization is likely to be required.[8] In any case, whether consumers live in predominantly urban or rural areas directly influences the media selected to disseminate advertising messages.

Geographic Characteristics

Geography, which refers to the earth's surface, climate, continents, countries, and available resources, is an uncontrollable environmental element that the international marketer cannot ignore. Topography and climate are of particular interest here. A market's physical characteristics may affect the international marketer's appraisal of a market and may well influence a number of the marketing mix factors.

Topography refers to the surface features of a country—its rivers, lakes, deserts, forests, and mountains. These characteristics are of interest to the international marketer in that they may impact product distribution. For example, large mountain ranges or bodies of water may complicate the physical distribution of products. In contrast, predominantly flat surface areas typically translate into easy transportation by road or rail, and navigable rivers likewise enable economical transportation. Further, the topography may serve to separate groups within the larger market. For example, consumers living in the highland regions of a country may display differing consumption behavior from those living in the valleys or flatlands.

Altitude, humidity, and temperature are all features of a country's climate. The climate and its degree of variation throughout the year can potentially impact what products a firm offers for sale, how they are distributed, and even how they are priced. Products consumers need vary depending on whether they live in tropical, temperate, desert, or arctic regions. For example, whether an automobile manufacturer equips vehicles with air conditioners or heaters depends on where those autos are being shipped.

The Political-Legal Environment

International marketers must have a good understanding of the political systems as well as the laws and regulations of the market in which they operate. Both the political system and local laws shape a given country's business environment and may directly impact various aspects of the marketing program, including whether a product can be sold in a particular country and how it will be distributed, priced, and, in particular, advertised. Legal and political constraints can be particularly challenging for the international marketer to overcome. A variety of factors influence the political-legal relationship between an international firm, its home country, and the host country in which it hopes to operate.

Political-Legal Environment of the Home Country

The political environment in most countries typically provides support for the international marketing efforts of firms located in that country. Governments may engage in efforts to reduce trade barriers or to increase trade opportunities. The United States, for example, has traditionally had a liberal attitude toward exports and imports. In other instances, however, foreign policy or national security concerns may result in constraints on free trade.

Trade Sanctions Governmental actions that restrict the free flow of goods and services between countries are known as *trade sanctions*. Sanctions often are used during times of war as a means of forcing countries to behave peacefully. In the 1992 Gulf War, for example, the United States imposed severe trade sanctions against Iraq and encouraged other countries to do the same. Trade sanctions may also be employed in the hopes of changing a nation's government or its policies. Reasons for the imposition of trade sanctions have varied, ranging from violations of human rights to terrorist activities and even nuclear armament. For instance, the United States currently prohibits firms from dealing with Cuba, North Korea, and Vietnam, although Vietnamese officials are requesting the lifting of this ban. In fact, several firms, including Coca-Cola, are set to move into this country once the trade ban is lifted. And, in anticipation of the lifting of the ban, at least six advertising agencies have moved to establish relationships in this market.[9]

With regards to South Africa, on which the United States imposed economic sanctions in 1988, Steven Burgess, a marketing professor at the Witwatersrand University School of Business Economics, noted: "If we have a nonracial government here tomorrow morning, South Africa becomes a boom town."[10] Burgess's prophecy has proven correct. Despite continued outbursts of violence, multinational firms have returned to South Africa in record numbers since the fall of apartheid and the subsequent lifting of the economic sanctions. For example, PepsiCo, which divested in protest against apartheid in the mid-1980s, is once again selling its products in this nation. Following the decision by Pepsi to re-enter South Africa, its worldwide lead agency, BBD&O, also announced its return. BBD&O was one of South Africa's biggest shops until it was liquidated when the ban was imposed.[11] Multinationals such as Eastman Kodak, General Motors, Honeywell, IBM, Procter & Gamble, and Sony see this nation of 35 million potential consumers as an appealing jumping-off point for the rest of southern Africa.

Clearly, if trade with certain countries or regions is cut off, the international firm may incur significant loss of business. Therefore, international firms must actively monitor the political climate in the countries in which they do business in order to anticipate potential sanctions and prepare for the consequences.

Export and Import Controls Two additional governmental activities that may directly impact the international marketer are export controls and import controls. *Export controls* are usually designed to prevent adversaries from acquiring strategically important goods, or at least to delay their acquisition. In the United States, exporters of defense-related equipment, for example, must obtain a license permitting shipment from the U.S. Department of Commerce. In fact, in order for any good, service, or idea to be exported from the United States, the exporter must obtain an export license from the Department of Commerce, which administers the Export Administration Act.[12] The Department of Commerce has available a list of commodities whose export is considered sensitive. Goods may be ranked high on this list due to concerns over national security, foreign policy, limitations in supply, or nuclear proliferation. An additional list ranks countries according to their political relationship with the United States.

If an industry—particularly a strategic industry—faces strong competition from imports, it may pressure government for protection against foreign goods. It is often argued that such protection is necessary to save jobs and that increased imports may further worsen the U.S. balance of payments. In response to such pressure, minimum prices may be set for imported goods. While import barriers often encourage foreign firms to invest in the domestic market, resulting in capital inflows, all too often consumers bear the brunt of protective measures—paying higher prices for goods and finding fewer choices available.

Political-Legal Environment of the Host Country

In evaluating a host country, the international marketer also must gauge its degree of political stability. Because entering a foreign market generally translates into a long-term commitment, firms seek assurance of relatively stable governmental policies regarding foreign business. In most countries the political environment is relatively stable. However, a glance at world headlines in recent years, and even recent months, reveals that political environments can change rapidly. In 1990 the Soviet Union was a socialist country; today, Russia and most of the republics are taking steps toward capitalism. Similarly, East Germany no longer exists, and the nations of Eastern Europe are evolving before our very eyes from Soviet satellites to viable political and economic entities.

Political Risk A number of political risk assessment techniques are available to assist the international marketer in determining which markets represent high levels of political risk.[13] Multinationals often purchase country trend data from political and economic consultants, some spending $50,000–$75,000 per year for such intelligence.[14]

Among the countries ranked as the worst political risks are El Salvador, Iran, Cuba, Bolivia, Libya, Pakistan, and Chile. The status of several other countries is changing. For example, major multinationals and advertising agencies are returning to Lebanon as the government there begins its ambitious reconstruction of a country ravaged by fifteen years of civil war. Following the end of the war in 1990 and the formation of a new government in late 1992, a degree of political stability has returned to the country, although hostilities still flare occasionally. Procter & Gamble has already introduced two products—Oil of Olay and its Vicks Cough and Cold line—and Saatchi &

Saatchi recently opened an office in Beirut.[15] The ascent of the Khmer Rouge in Cambodia in the 1970s brought more than a decade of civil war and social upheaval; an estimated 3 million Cambodians died during the Khmer's brutal regime. Most multinationals, including PepsiCo, fled the country in the mid-1970s. Since the United States lifted its trade embargo in early 1992, Pepsi has already invested in a joint venture to begin bottling Pepsi and 7-Up. Brand awareness for both products is already high, as faded outdoor billboards from the early 1970s still dot the Cambodian landscape.[16]

Should a firm choose to operate in a country where the political risk is high, it may face civil disturbances, terrorism, and possibly even warfare. Political unrest is often associated with an anti-industry element, making the company and its employees potential targets for violence. Even when such violence seems unlikely, the international marketer may still be faced with adverse governmental actions. A foreign company's property may be taken over, its currency holdings blocked, and its employees even taken hostage.

Expropriation refers to the takeover of a foreign investment by the host government. While it does not relieve the host government from providing some compensation to the former owners, compensation negotiations are often protracted and often result in settlements unsatisfactory to the owners. Moreover, if expropriation occurs, it can ward off other foreign firms. *Confiscation* is similar to expropriation in that ownership of the firm is transferred to the host country. However, when a firm is confiscated, no compensation is forthcoming. Certain industries are more prone than others to expropriation or confiscation—particularly those considered by the host nation to be critical to national defense or national wealth. Many countries, however, are turning from expropriation and confiscation to *domestication*. Here, the host government demands partial transfer of ownership and management responsibility and imposes regulations to ensure that a large share of the product is locally produced and a large share of the profit is retained in the country.

Restrictions affecting imports can be classified as tariff and nontariff barriers. A *tariff* is simply a tax imposed by a government on goods entering its borders. A tariff may be imposed either to generate revenues or to discourage the importation of goods in an attempt to protect domestic products from being outpriced by cheaper imports, and as such tariffs can serve as a very effective form of protectionism. Worldwide, tariffs range from nonexistent to quite hefty. For example, Canadian tariffs average 10 percent, but range from 0 to 27 percent. The European Union has tariffs ranging from 0 to 30 percent, and the Saudi tariff averages 12 percent. Generally, if a U.S. business finds no domestic production of a good within the targeted country, tariffs are likely to be low.

Nontariff barriers are equally serious impediments to trade. One form of nontariff barrier is the *quota*—a numerical or dollar limit applied to a specific category of goods. Quotas are not something only other countries do.

For example, in the early 1980s the U.S. government imposed quotas on Japanese auto imports in order to reduce the number of autos shipped to this country. Standards are another form of nontariff barrier. Whether imposed by design or accident, stringent requirements affecting the product, its packaging and labeling, and testing methods serve to restrict the entry of foreign goods. Bureaucratic red tape (such as customs guidelines or extensive documentation) also may effectively serve to discourage imports.

In addition to controlling the movement of goods across borders, host countries also influence the movement of capital into and out of their markets. *Exchange controls* may be employed by host governments that face a shortage of foreign currency; such controls can make it difficult for the international firm to remove its profits and investments from a country. When a country's balance of payments is unfavorable or unstable, it will not want precious capital to cross its borders. Thus, for instance, rather than selling cola to the former Soviet Union, PepsiCo engages in barter—trading cola for vodka.

Foreign countries may also exercise control over exchange rates. Currency needed to purchase foreign luxuries often carries high exchange rates while necessities receive more favorable rates. Such controls may be implemented in an effort to reduce the importation of goods that are considered unnecessary. Countries may also raise the tax rates applied to foreign investors in an effort to control the firms and their capital. Such tax increases may result in much-needed revenue for the host country, but they can severely damage the operations of the foreign investors.

In order to reduce the risk of adverse governmental actions, the international firm must demonstrate genuine concern for the welfare of the host country and not simply for its own profits. International firms can convey this message in a variety of ways. They can employ locals, particularly in management and decision-making positions, and offer fair pay and favorable working conditions. Local production of goods, production utilizing local materials, and the use of local suppliers all help to strengthen the image of the firm as a good corporate citizen.

While international marketers may still find it profitable to do business with an unstable country, the situation will certainly affect how business is conducted. International marketers must assess the political risk of each country the firm considers entering and, once operations have been set up, must continually monitor the risk level.

Nationalism The degree of nationalism a foreign market exhibits may make it more or less appealing to the international marketer. Some nations are quite receptive to foreign firms and may actively encourage investment from abroad, while others are quite hostile. Firms will clearly receive a better reception from a host country that has positive relations with its own country. A wide spectrum of factors can impact these relations. For example, if a host country is critical of some aspect of the foreign policy of the international firm's home country, the firm may be subject to fallout from this criticism. Another factor is the relationship of the home country with other nations. If a home country has particularly friendly or antagonistic relations with other nations, it may influence the relationship with the host country. If nationalism runs high, it will likely influence marketing communications. Advertisements, for example, may play down rather than emphasize the advertised product's country of origin.

International Law

A variety of international laws and agencies regulate business across national boundaries.

The International Monetary Fund Marketers typically exchange goods and services for money. Either gold or an internationally acceptable currency is necessary for this exchange. The International Monetary Fund (IMF), created at the end of World War II, promotes international monetary cooperation and facilitates the expansion of trade among member countries. The IMF works to diminish the degree of nationalistic actions taken by countries, thereby decreasing financial barriers to international trade. The IMF also lends money to member countries facing deficits in their international debt payments, allowing them to continue trading on the world market. At present the fund has 140 member countries, accounting for about 80 percent of total world production and 90 percent of world trade. The Commonwealth of Independent States is expected to become the IMF's newest member.

World Bank Membership in the World Bank is open to all members of the IMF, and the bank is owned and controlled by its 129 member governments. Each member country subscribes to shares for an amount reflecting its relative economic strength. The United States is the bank's largest shareholder, providing 25.3 percent of the subscription capital. The primary purpose of the bank is to provide both financial and technical assistance to developing countries. The World Bank currently lends about $8 billion a year to help raise the standard of living in poor countries. The bank provides loans for a variety of projects related to agriculture, rural development, education, population planning, electrical power, transportation, telecommunications, and water supply. The bank evaluates the prospects for repayment before granting loans. Loans are usually repayable over a twenty-year period.

General Agreement on Tariffs and Trade (GATT) The General Agreement on Tariffs and Trade (GATT) was organized in the aftermath of World War II to ensure that the discriminatory trade practices of the 1920s and 1930s would not again plague international business. The United States and twenty-two other countries signed this agreement. Today, the multinational, intergovernmental treaty, which operates within the framework of the United Nations, has approximately the same membership as the IMF. GATT's rules govern trade relations between member countries. The goal of member countries is the reduction of trade barriers and the further liberalization of world trade. The growth achieved during the past twenty years in the world economy is due in no small part to the efforts of GATT. Russia recently applied to join GATT, noting that membership would be a powerful boost to its struggling economy. Membership for Russia is an essential step toward integrating that country into the international trade system.

Summary

The international marketing environment contains a variety of elements: demographic characteristics (market size, population growth and distribution, education), geographic characteristics (topography and climate), economic factors (per capita income, GNP, distribution of income, household income, education), and the political-legal system (tariff and nontariff barriers, exchange controls, political risks, degree of nationalism). Acquiring and interpreting marketplace information relating to each of these areas are of fundamental importance to the development of marketing and advertising strategies. The one key area that we have not yet addressed is the cultural environment. Chapter 4 will be devoted to exploring this topic.

Additional Readings

Alexander, Ralph S., ed. (1965). *Marketing Definitions.* Chicago: American Marketing Association, p. 9.

Buzzell, Robert D. (November/December 1968). "Can You Standardize Multinational Marketing?" *Harvard Business Review,* pp. 102–113.

Committee on Definitions. (1985). *Marketing Definitions: A Glossary of Marketing Terms.* Chicago: American Marketing Association.

Douglas, Susan P., C. Samuel Craig, and Warren Keegan. (Fall 1982). "Approaches to Assessing International Marketing Opportunities for Small and Medium Sized Businesses." *Columbia Journal of World Business,* pp. 26–32.

"The Global Economy." *The Washington Post* (January 19, 1986), p. H1.

McCarthy, E. Jerome. (1960). *Basic Marketing: A Managerial Approach.* Homewood, IL: Irwin.

Terpstra, Vern. (1987). *International Marketing,* 4th ed. New York: Holt, Rinehart & Winston/Dryden Press, p. 427.

Notes

1. World Bank, *World Development Report 1994* (New York: Oxford University Press, 1994), pp. 210–211.

2. "Fortune's Global 500," *Fortune,* July 26, 1993, pp. 188–231.

3. U.S. Department of Commerce, Bureau of the Census, *1993 Statistical Abstracts of the United States* (113th ed.) (Washington, DC: GPO, 1993).

4. Ibid.

5. Engel, James F., and Roger D. Blackwell, *Consumer Behavior* (Chicago: Dryden Press, 1982), p. 20.

6. Hill, John, and William James, "Products and Promotion Transfers for Consumer Goods Multinationals," *International Marketing Review,* 8(2), 1991, p. 617.

7. Kotler, Philip, *Marketing Management* (Englewood Cliffs, NJ: Prentice-Hall, 1988), p. 383.

8. Hill, John, and Richard Still, "Effects of Urbanization on Multinational Product Planning: Markets in Lesser Developed Countries," *Columbia Journal of World Business,* 19, Summer 1984, pp. 62–67.

9. Butler, David, and Laurel Wentz, "Marketers Target Viet Nam," *Advertising Age,* February 15, 1993, p. I1.

10. Barnes, Kathleen. "Big Marketers Poised to Flood into South Africa," *Advertising Age,* May 17, 1993, p. I1.

11. Koenderman, Tony, "Pepsi, BBD&O Thirst for S. Africa," *ADWEEK,* July 4, 1994, p. 12.

12. Springer, Robert, Jr., "New Export Laws and Aid to International Marketers," *Marketing News,* January 3, 1986, pp. 10, 67.

13. Friedmann, Roberto, and Jonghoon Kim, "Political Risk and International Marketing," *Columbia Journal of World Business,* Winter 1988, pp. 63–74.

14. Bertrant, Kate, "Politics Pushes to the Marketing Foreground," *Business Marketing,* March 1990, pp. 51–55.

15. Holliday, Kalen, "Marketers Again Hear Call of Lebanon," *Advertising Age,* June 21, 1993, p. I1.

16. Geddes, Andres, "Soft Drink Giants Arrive in Cambodia," *Advertising Age,* October 26, 1992, p. I2.

CHAPTER 4

The Cultural Environment

The final aspect of the marketing and advertising environment that the international marketer must consider is the culture of a particular country. Marketers have traditionally examined a potential market's demographic and geographic characteristics, as well as economic and political factors, in order to determine if and how they might impact the marketing mix. However, only in recent years has greater attention been paid to the cultural environment. Each country exhibits cultural differences that influence the consumers' needs and wants, their methods of satisfying them, and the messages they are most likely to respond to. The international business literature reveals hundreds of blunders that have resulted from miscalculating—or simply ignoring—the cultural environment. This chapter explores the concept of culture and its various elements and discusses tools potentially useful to international marketers attempting to analyze foreign cultures and penetrate foreign markets.

The Concept of Culture

Over a century ago E. B. Taylor defined culture as "a complex whole which includes knowledge, beliefs, art, morals, law, custom, and any other capabilities and habits acquired by individuals as members of a society."[1] Adamson Hoebel referred to culture as the "integrated sum total of learned behavioral traits that are manifest and shared by members of society."[2] Culture has also been defined as a "learned, shared, compelling, interrelated set of symbols whose meaning provides a set of orientations for members of a society.[3]

Well over 160 different definitions of culture have been identified in the anthropological literature.[4] Clearly, no shortage of definitions of this concept exists. Yet, even the three definitions provided here reveal some commonalities. It is generally agreed that culture is not inherent or innate, but rather is learned. Learning typically takes place in institutions such as the family, church, and school. Most definitions also emphasize that culture is shared by members of a group. It is this shared aspect that enables communication between individuals within that culture. Cross-cultural communication is so difficult, in large part, because of the lack of shared symbols.

For the most part we live our lives relatively unaware of the tremendous impact our culture has on us. We automatically drive on the right-hand side of the road, try to arrive on time for appointments, and shake hands when we first meet someone. Without thought we react to our environment in a manner that is socially acceptable because that is how we have been socialized. Edward T. Hall points out: "No matter how hard man tries, it is impossible for him to divest himself of his own culture, for it has penetrated to the roots of his nervous system and determines how he perceives the world . . . people cannot act or interact in any meaningful way except through the medium of culture."[5] When we move into another culture, we carry our cultural map with us, responding to the foreign environment in ways that would be acceptable in our own culture but that may or may not be acceptable in different surroundings.

Self-Reference Criterion and Ethnocentrism

When we examine other cultures, we tend to view them through "culturally tinted glasses." For example, if our own culture places a high value on education or cleanliness, we may assume—correctly or incorrectly—that other cultures share these same values. James Lee terms this unconscious reference to one's own culture the *self-reference criterion*.[6] Because of this unconscious reference to one's own cultural values, marketers operating abroad may behave in a culturally myopic fashion.

Ethnocentrism poses another obstacle to understanding foreign cultures. Literally defined, *ethnocentrism* means "culturally centered"; it refers to people's tendency to place themselves at the center of the universe and not only evaluate others by the standards of their own culture but also believe that their own culture is superior to all others. A fundamental assumption of ethnocentric people is that their way of doing things is right, proper, and normal and that the ways of culturally different people are wrong and inferior.[7] Not surprisingly, this tendency toward an "us versus them" mentality is universal. People in all cultures, to some degree, display ethnocentric behaviors. Ethnocentrism limits our ability to accept cultural differences, which diminishes the chance of developing effective marketing programs. The best defense against ethnocentrism is an awareness of the tendency toward ethnocentrism.

Subcultures

While the focus of this text is international in scope, it is important to recognize that variations within cultures may be even greater than variations between cultures. In each culture there exist *subcultures*—groups of people with shared value systems based on common experiences. People belonging to various nationality groups (Italian-, Polish-, and Scandinavian-Americans), religious groups (Protestants, Jews, Catholics), racial groups (blacks, Asians, Hispanics), political groups (democrats, republicans, socialists), and geographic groups (westerners, easterners, southerners) may well exhibit characteristic patterns of behavior that serve to distinguish them from other subgroups within a country. The same can be said about people who belong to specific age or income groups. Clearly, an individual can belong to more than one subculture. To the extent that these patterns of behavior impact wants and needs, these subcultures can be targeted by marketers.

Hispanics and blacks represent two subcultures that have only recently received significant attention from American marketers. By the year 2000, Hispanics in the United States are expected to number 40 million. They are the second-largest as well as the fastest-growing minority, and as a group their annual purchasing power totals over $134 billion. Consumer research has revealed a particularly appealing characteristic of this subgroup from a marketer's standpoint—extreme brand loyalty. Just over 12 percent of the

U.S. population is black, which translates into 31 million consumers with an estimated $278 billion in spending power. A number of marketers have found success in tailoring products and messages to these groups. For example, J. C. Penney intends to become the first national department store chain to sell merchandise geared specifically toward Hispanic and black consumers. It plans to aim its new marketing program at areas with Hispanic and black populations of at least 25,000 and begin stocking stores with clothes and home furnishings that research has shown to have more appeal to these minority shoppers.[8]

An understanding of subcultures is essential because the failure to recognize distinctive subcultures can lead to an illusion of sameness within a market that simply does not exist. Additionally, understanding a subculture in one country may also help the marketer to understand a similar subculture in a foreign market. Knowing what motivates a New York businessman who earns $100,000 annually may well assist in the understanding of his counterpart abroad. A Paris businessman is likely to be much more similar to his colleague across the ocean than he is to a fellow Frenchman who works in the vineyards of Burgundy.

The study of culture is central to international marketing and advertising. Many cultural differences, and their impact on elements of the marketing mix, are rather obvious. Clearly, if one wishes to communicate with consumers in Kenya, language differences must be taken into account, and all promotional materials must be translated into the local tongue. Many cultural differences are, however, quite subtle. For example, one American shoe manufacturer promoted its product through advertisements with photos of bare feet. Although such a message would pose no problem in most countries, the campaign failed miserably in Southeast Asia, where exposure of the foot is considered an insult. The problem of communicating to people in diverse cultures has been called one of the greatest challenges in marketing communications.[9] International marketers, if they are to be successful in their efforts, must become culturally sensitive—that is, tuned into the nuances of culture. Indeed, they must become students of culture.

The Elements of Culture

Among the important elements of culture marketers must take into consideration are the verbal language (both spoken and written), various forms of nonverbal communication, needs and values, religion and the related moral and ethical standards, and customs and consumption patterns.

Verbal Language

In deciding which markets to enter and how to enter them, the international marketer must speak with governmental and business leaders in foreign countries as well as with potential employees and suppliers. Marketers likely will deal with the local language when collecting market data. And, in attempting to communicate with potential customers, marketers are faced with choosing a brand name, selecting copy or text to be included on product packaging, developing advertising slogans, creating advertising messages.

Because language plays such a central role in international marketing, it's crucial to understand the close relationship between culture and language. Culture and communication are inextricably linked. It has been said that it is impossible to truly understand a culture without understanding the language spoken by its people.[10] Conversely, a language cannot be fully understood outside its cultural context. As Gerhard Maletzke explains: "The art and manner in which one understands the world is determined to a large extent by language; but language, at the same time, is an expression of a specific group-experiencing of the world, and therefore may itself be shaped by the Weltanschauung as well as the wishes, expectations, and motivations of the group using it."[11] Put more simply, culture both influences and is influenced by language.

That culture influences the specific language spoken by a group can be demonstrated by examining the vocabulary it employs. Consider the classic example of the word *snow*. The Eskimo language has many words to describe snow. The complex classification system for different forms of snow developed because snow plays such a crucial role in the daily life of the average Eskimo. Similarly, the Arabic language has hundreds of different words for *camel* and all of its various parts. For most Americans the single words *snow* and *camel* generally suffice. On the other hand, the average speaker of the English language knows hundreds of words relating to technology and industry—such as *software, microwave,* and *fax*. The vocabularies of all languages are adapted to the elements considered important in that particular culture.

The Sapir-Whorf hypothesis suggests that language is not merely a mechanism for communicating ideas but is itself a shaper of ideas.[12] This view has also been referred to as "linguistic determinism," which simply means that people who speak different languages are likely to think and perceive reality differently. For example, Whorf's work with the Hopi Indians revealed that they do not conjugate verbs in terms of past, present, and future as English language speakers do. In Hopi the single word *wari* would be used to convey both that someone is now running and that the individual ran in the past. For the Hopi the statement of fact is what is considered important rather than whether it is a present or past event. Because of such linguistic differences, Whorf proposes that speakers of Hopi and English perceive time differently.

Languages also differ in their levels of formality. In the Japanese language the level of formality depends on the gender and status of the speaker and listener as well as the context of the conversation. This has a number of implications for marketing communications. For example, the language used by the seller is much more deferential than that of the buyer—the buyer is always placed in the position of superior status. Moreover, the female speaker is always required to use more polite, deferential language. As a result, saleswomen or female characters in broadcast advertisements tend to give a product a "feminine" image. While this association may be beneficial for certain kinds of products, such as household items, for others it may hurt sales.[13]

Linguists claim that well over three thousand different languages are spoken around the globe—some spoken by millions, others by no more than several hundred. Multilingual societies constitute the majority of the world's nations. For example, Zaire has over one hundred different tribal languages, and in India over two hundred languages and dialects are spoken. Any country in which a number of different languages are spoken undoubtedly will also have a number of different cultures. Consider Canada, where citizens speak predominantly English or French, or Belgium, where French and Flemish are spoken. In both Canada and Belgium, the differing linguistic groups have clashed on occasion. In Zaire and India, such confrontations have even ended in violence.

While language helps to define a cultural group, the same language can also be spoken in a number of different countries. English is spoken in the United States, England, much of Canada, Australia, and Ireland, while Spanish is spoken in Spain, Mexico, Argentina, and Peru. Often, however, different words are used for the same thing or the same words have different meanings. For example, a major paper towel producer learned the hard way that even British and American English are sufficiently dissimilar when it attempted to use its successful U.S. advertisement in England. The slogan was "There is no finer paper napkin for the dinner table." The problem? In England a napkin or "nappy" refers to a diaper.

According to Maletzke, "The extent to which individuals or groups understand one another, fail to understand, or misunderstand, is determined by the degree to which the World Views and frames of reference of the partners in communication overlap. The larger the common ground of Weltanschauung is, the more simple it is that there will be an adequate meeting-of-minds. The less common ground there is, the fewer frames of reference, then the more likely it is that there will be serious misunderstandings and non-comprehension."[14]

Errors in the translation of brand names, packaging copy, and advertising messages have cost businesses millions of dollars, not to mention damaging their credibility and reputation. It is not enough for translators merely to be familiar with the native tongue. In order to avoid translation blunders, translators must also be familiar with nuances, idioms, and slang. Consider the following:

▶ In Latin America the brand name *Chevy Nova* (a bright shining star in General Motor's dictionary) translated into "doesn't run" in the local dialect.

▶ One firm sold shampoo in Brazil under the name *Evitol.* Little did it realize that it was claiming to be selling a "dandruff contraceptive."

▶ In the 1960s Pepsi's slogan "Come alive, you're in the Pepsi Generation" was translated into German. The result? "Come alive out of the grave."

▶ The name *Esso* was a great handicap to that firm in Japan because it meant "stalled car" when pronounced phonetically. The original replacement name of *Enco* wasn't much of an improvement since it referred to a sewage disposal truck.

One useful technique in revealing translation errors is called back-translation.[15] One individual is responsible for the initial translation of the message. A second individual then translates the message back into the original language. If the message does not translate back, it's likely that there is a translation problem. While back-translation is a helpful tool, it's no guarantee against translation bloopers. Hiring only native speakers of the language into which the message is to be translated also helps to reduce problems, as does acknowledging that some words and phrases simply cannot be translated.

Nonverbal Language

We communicate not only through spoken language but also via nonverbal language. Indeed, it has been estimated that little more than 20 percent of communication between two individuals within the same culture is verbal in nature. The bulk of communications, then, takes place nonverbally—via a nod of the head, a wave of the hand, a smile, or even a step toward or away from another person.

A number of classification systems of nonverbal language exist, some containing up to twenty-four different categories of behaviors.[16,17] Most classification systems include facial expressions, eye contact and gaze, body movement (such as hand gestures and posture), touching, smell, space usage, time symbolism, appearance or dress, color symbolism, and even silence. It is important to note that nonverbal methods of communication are no more universal than verbal methods. Just as one word can mean different things in different countries (in the United States *closet* refers to a place to hang your clothes whereas in England it refers to the toilet), so, too, nonverbal cues vary in their meaning. The American "OK" gesture communicated by making a circle with one's thumb and index finger means zero or worthless in France and a willingness to give money in Japan. In Greece and Brazil, however, it carries a quite vulgar connotation. The "thumbs up" sign used in a recent AT&T campaign presented a problem when it had to be translated into other languages. For most Americans this gesture signifies positive affirmation. But to Russians and Poles, because the palm of the hand was visible, it gave the print advertisement, produced by N. W. Ayer, an entirely different— even offensive—meaning. YAR Communications, an agency specializing in translations, was engaged to reshoot the graphic element of the advertisement so that only the back of the hand was seen, thereby conveying the intended meaning.[18] Exhibit 4.1 shows the revised version of the ad.

Nonverbal communication regulates human interaction in several important ways: (1) it sends messages about our attitudes and feelings, (2) it elaborates on our verbal messages, and (3) it governs the timing and turn-taking between communicators.[19] A thorough discussion of all of the aspects of the silent language, as it's often called, is beyond the scope of this text. However, because of their importance to the international marketer, four areas will be addressed briefly: touch, space usage, time symbolism, and signs and colors.

Touch One of the earliest senses to mature is touch. Humans touch for a variety of reasons, and each culture has a well-defined system of meanings for different forms of touching, whether it be patting, slapping, pinching, punching, pushing, stroking, kissing, kicking, or even tickling. For example, according to Weston LaBarre:

> [The] Copper Eskimo welcome strangers with a buffet on the head or shoulders with the fist, while the northwest Amazonians slap one another on the back in greeting. Polynesian men greet one another by embracing and rubbing each other's back; Spanish-American males greet one another by a stereotyped embrace, head over the right shoulder of the partner, three pats on the back, head over reciprocal left shoulder, three more pats. . . . An Ainu, meeting his sister, grasped her hands in his for a few seconds, suddenly released his hold, grasped her by both ears and gave the peculiar Ainu greeting cry; then they stroked one another down the face and shoulders. . . . Andamanese greet one another by one sitting down in the lap of the other, arms around each other's necks and weeping for a while.[20]

Some generalizations can be made with regards to high-touch versus low-touch cultures. Americans, the English, Germans, and northern Europeans are said to belong to low-touch cultures, exhibiting very limited tactile

СамаЯ высокая степень сервиса, предоставляемого сегодня,
не предел для AT&T. Уже завтра, с помощью программы "Я План",
я смогу получить большее.
Как только я позвоню в AT&T по номеру 1 800 542-2025.

EXHIBIT 4.1 Revised AT&T Advertisement Targeted to Russian Audience

contact in public. In contrast, Hispanics, people of Eastern European descent, Italians, the French, Arabs, and Jews are all said to belong to high-touch cultures. Care must be taken, however, not to overgeneralize. Each culture, whether considered to be high- or low-touch, defines for its members whom they can touch, as well as when and where they can touch them. Thus, even in high-touch Arabian culture, inappropriate use of touch in advertising messages may cause problems. As shown in Exhibit 4.2, the European advertisement for Drakkar Noir men's perfume shows a man's hand holding the perfume bottle and a woman's hand clutching his bare wrist. This was seen as too direct and too sensual for the Saudi Arabian market. The photo had to be modified to show the man's arm clothed in a jacket sleeve and the woman's hand just slightly touching the man's arm with her fingertip.[21]

Space Usage How humans use space is referred to as *proxemics*. Edward T. Hall suggests that "each person has around him an invisible bubble of space

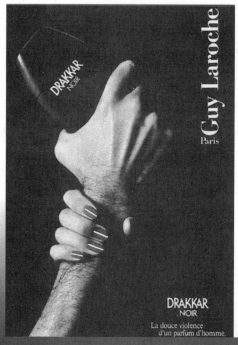

EXHIBIT 4.2 European and Saudi Arabian Ads for Drakkar Noir

which expands and contracts depending on his relationship to those around him, his emotional state, and the activity he is performing."[22] Based on his observations of North Americans, Hall developed four categories of distance in human interactions:

1. *Intimate distance:* ranging from body contact to 18 inches, this distance is used for personal contact, comforting, and protecting. Here, olfactory and thermal sensations are at their highest.

2. *Personal distance:* from 18 inches to 4 feet, depending on the closeness of the relationship, in this distancing mode people have an invisible "space bubble" separating themselves from others.

3. *Social distance:* from 4 to 12 feet, this distance is used by acquaintances and strangers in business meetings and classrooms.

4. *Public distance:* from 12 to 25 feet, at this distance recognition of others is not mandatory, and the subtle shades of meaning of voice, gesture, and facial expression are lost.[23]

However, the use of space is culture-bound—members of different cultures do not necessarily conform to Hall's four categories of distance. Americans are said to demonstrate a particularly high level of territoriality when compared with members of other cultures. In contrasting Europeans and Americans, Hall notes that "in Northern Europe the bubbles are quite large; moving south to France, Italy, Greece and Spain, the bubbles get smaller and smaller so that the distance that is perceived as intimate in the north overlaps personal distance in the south, which means that Mediterranean Europeans get too close to the Germans, Scandinavians, the English, and Americans of northern European ancestry."[24] Imagine the diversity when we compare how space is used in Africa or Asia. For example, most Americans feel quite uncomfortable when trapped on a crowded commuter train or in a full elevator. However, space is used differently by members of Japanese society. Japanese tend to stand and sit much closer together than Americans and appear to endure crowded conditions in public areas without much discomfort. As further evidence that Japanese and Americans use space differently, consider that in the United States top executives are typically separated from their employees—often inhabiting the top floor of the company building or, at the very least, sequestered in private offices. Because the Japanese are a group-oriented people, top executives rarely occupy private offices, preferring instead to work shoulder to shoulder with their employees. Clearly, each culture develops its own set of rules for space, and proper usage of space must be employed when developing visuals for advertising messages destined for foreign markets.

Time Symbolism Just as the use of space is culturally influenced, so, too, is our use of time. A culture's concept of time refers to the relative importance it places on time. Edward T. Hall notes that two time systems have evolved—monochronic and polychronic. "Monochronic time means paying attention to and doing only one thing at a time. Polychronic time means being involved with many things at once. Like oil and water, the two systems do not mix."[25] In a *monochronic* time (M-time) system, schedules often take priority over everything else and are treated as sacred and unalterable. Planes and trains must always run on time. Individuals raised in M-time systems constantly check their calendars and watches, worry about being prompt for appointments, and take it as an insult if kept waiting by others. Although this may seem natural and logical, it is merely a learned product of northern European culture. Hall explains that M-time systems grew out of the Industrial Revolution in England, wherein the factory labor force was required to be on hand and in place at the appointed hour. While examples of purely monochronic societies are rare, it can safely be said that Western cultures, in particular the United States, Switzerland, Germany, and Scandinavia, are dominated by M-time.

Polychronic time (P-time) systems are the antithesis of M-time systems. P-time is characterized by the simultaneous occurrence of many things and by a much greater involvement with people. In P-time systems, schedules and agendas mean very little, and appointments are often forgotten or re-arranged at the last minute. No eyebrows are raised if one arrives at a meeting 45 minutes late. Middle Eastern and Latin American cultures often exhibit P-time behaviors. Within the United States, Hopi Indians place little value on time—believing that each human and animal has its own time system.

What does all this mean for businesses operating in the international arena? Consider the agency–client relationship—and the confusion that might result if each participant in the relationship is operating on a different time system. A Western client might rush to ensure arriving on time for a meeting with a Middle Eastern agency executive—and feel quite irritated if left sitting for nearly an hour in an outer office. Consider the potential impact on advertising message content. A telephone company did not take time orientation into account when developing a television spot for its Latin American audience. In the ad the wife told her husband to "run downstairs and phone Mary. Tell her we'll be a little late." In fact, this commercial contained two major cultural errors. First, almost no Latin American would feel obligated to phone to warn of tardiness since it is expected. Second, Latin American wives seldom dare to order their husbands around.[26] It is impossible to estimate how much business has been lost because marketers failed to take into account differences between monochronic and polychronic peoples.

Colors and Other Signs and Symbols International marketers may encounter problems with the connotative meanings of colors and other signs and symbols as they vary from culture to culture. Laurence Jacobs and colleagues note: "Like language, marketers in a particular nation often take color for granted, having experienced certain color associations all their lives, and do not even question whether other associations may exist in different societies."[27] However, the significance of and meanings associated with specific colors vary from culture to culture. For example, while black signifies mourning in many Western cultures, white is the color most associated with death in Japan, Hong Kong, and India. White lilies are the appropriate flower for funerals in England, Canada, and Sweden, yet in Mexico white flowers are said to lift the spirits. Yellow flowers connote death in both Mexico and Taiwan, while purple is the color of death in Brazil and purple flowers are considered most appropriate for funerals. In the former Soviet Union yellow flowers are considered a sign of disrespect to a woman, and in Taiwan, wearing a green hat signifies an unfaithful wife. Red is considered a positive color in Denmark but associated with the occult in many African countries.

International marketers need to know what associations a culture has in terms of colors and how they might affect product design, packaging, and advertising messages. David Ricks points out that the "choice of package and product coloring is very tricky. Sometimes companies have failed to sell their products overseas and have never known why. Often the reason was a simple one; the product or its container was merely an inappropriate color."[28] For example, a number of years ago a leading U.S. golf ball manufacturer targeted Japan as an important new market for its product. However, sales of the company's golf balls were well below average. As it turned out, the firm had offered its product in white packaging—a color often associated with mourning. To make matters worse, it had packaged the balls in groups of four—the number signifying death in Japan.[29] While the number 4 sounds like "death" in both Japanese and Chinese, it also happens to sound like "loin" in other languages.

Numbers and shapes both mean different things to different peoples. The number 7 is considered bad luck in Kenya and good luck in the former Czechoslovakia, and it has magical connotations in Benin. In another example, recounts Michael Christie, " a U.S. company exporting its goods to the Middle East inadvertently stylized designs vaguely resembling crosses and stars on its packaging. In this market, where Islam is the dominant religion, this was highly offensive and the company was booted out of the market for using Judeo-Christian symbols on its packaging."[30]

Even the use of animals can prove problematic. A well-known marketer of eyeglasses initiated a campaign in Thailand with billboards showing cute pictures of the animals wearing eyeglasses. Sales, however, failed to materialize. The marketer only later discovered that the Thais regarded animals as a lower level of creation and found advertising using animal themes to be unappealing. In another example of an advertising faux pas, a print ad for a men's cologne pictured a man and his dog in a rural American setting. This ad worked well in America but failed in Northern Africa. The advertiser simply assumed that "man's best friend" was loved everywhere and failed to recognize that Muslims usually consider dogs to be either signs of bad luck or symbols of uncleanliness.

Needs

In attempting to understand foreign cultures, international marketers may look at the needs that motivate purchase behavior. A useful theory of human motivation was developed by Abraham Maslow, who hypothesized that people's needs can be arranged in a hierarchy reflecting their relative potency.[31] At the base of the hierarchy are physiological needs. As humans our need for food, water, and shelter from the elements dominates our behavior. As these fundamental or "lower" needs are met, higher needs emerge, such as the need for safety—for security and protection from dangers in the environment. Once this need has been provided for, social needs arise—for affection from family and friends and to belong to a group. Higher-order needs include the need for esteem (self-respect, prestige, success, and achievement) and, finally, the need for self-actualization (self-fulfillment). People are not, however, locked into a particular level; clearly, an individual attempting to fulfill esteem needs also must address basic physiological needs.

Maslow's model has relevance to the international marketer in that the needs that dominate a particular culture are closely tied to that country's level of development. Apparently, the more highly developed the market, the greater the proportion of goods and products devoted to filing social and esteem needs as opposed to physiological needs. An examination of American advertisements reveals this to be the case in this country. Consider the many products promoted as status-enhancing goods—from automobiles to clothing to bottled water. The advertising appeals employed in cultures at different stages of economic development are likely to be quite different. While Maslow's hierarchy of needs is a useful tool, caution should be exercised in employing it in a cross-cultural setting. The hierarchy is a theory based on Western behavior and has not been proven applicable to non-Western or developing countries.

Values

Defining and Analyzing Values Chances of success in a foreign market can be maximized if marketers also examine cultural values. Milton Rokeach provides a classic definition of a *value:* "an enduring belief that a specific mode of conduct or end state of existence is personally and socially preferable to an opposite or converse mode of conduct or end state of existence."[32] Put more simply, Edward C. Steward states that values "represent a learned organization of rules for making choices and for resolving conflicts."[33] Articles on values and consumer behavior that have appeared in scholarly journals suggest that values may indeed be one of the most powerful explanations of, and influences on, consumer behavior.[34] Because people from different cultures are generally perceived as holding a set of values different from our own, it is essential to explore their impact on the elements of the marketing mix.

While an examination of value systems can prove quite beneficial to the international marketer, it is often fraught with problems. A major stumbling block in analyzing value systems is that we cannot escape our own cultural orientation—and thus our perceptions are bound to be distorted to a certain degree. Another problem associated with making generalizations about the value systems of other cultures is that many nations are multicultural. The United States, often called a cultural melting pot, is an example of a particularly heterogeneous culture. If we state that a particular value is characteristic of the United States, that is not to say that each and every member of this society will possess that value. Rather, the concept of values should be used to assist in identifying primary differences between consumers in two different societies. Thus, it is possible to make broad statements with regards to the value systems that tend to dominate in the United States as compared to those of Japan, for example. While individualism has been shown to be a dominant American value, the Japanese tend to have a strong commitment to the group.[35] A well-known saying in Japan—"Deru kugi wa utareru" (the nail that sticks up is hit)—reminds Japanese people of the pain experienced when one fails to blend harmoniously into the group.[36] Because of this value orientation, advertisements stressing individuality and nonconformity have traditionally not been prevalent in Japan.[37]

Classifying and Assessing Values A number of different classification systems have been outlined for assessing the dominant values of a culture. For example, Rokeach has developed a means of quantifying personal value systems.[38] As shown in Table 4.1, the Rokeach value survey identifies eighteen terminal and eighteen instrumental values. *Terminal* values concern desired end states of existence that are socially and personally worth striving for. *Instrumental* values relate to desired modes of conduct and represent beliefs that are socially and personally preferable in all situations with respect to all objects. Value systems are established by having individuals complete a survey that asks them to arrange all thirty-six values in order of their importance as guiding principles in their lives.

This framework can be effectively employed to discriminate people of culturally diverse backgrounds.[39] For example, the instrumental value of ambitious means hardworking and aspiring. The degree to which consumers in different cultures perceive themselves as hardworking (or aspire to this value) may vary from one culture to the next, and this may have implications for promotional efforts. A recent survey of young people around the world found significant differences in the percentage who would describe themselves as "hardworking" versus "into having a good time." The "work hard/play hard" ethic appears to be most common in English-speaking countries. While 93 percent of American respondents, 84 percent of Australian respondents, and 61 percent of British respondents perceived themselves as hard workers, a mere 34 percent of German and 30 percent of Brazilian respondents gave themselves credit for working hard—indicating instead that they value having a good time. Surprisingly, Japanese youth are the least likely to describe themselves as either hardworking or fun-loving.[40]

TABLE 4.1   Rokeach's Eighteen Terminal and Eighteen Instrumental Values

TERMINAL VALUES	INSTRUMENTAL VALUES
A comfortable life (a prosperous life)	Ambitious (hardworking, aspiring)
An exciting life (a stimulating, active life)	Broadminded (open-minded)
A sense of accomplishment (lasting contribution)	Capable (competent, effective)
A world at peace (free of war and conflict)	Cheerful (lighthearted, joyful)
A world of beauty (beauty of nature and the arts)	Clean (neat, tidy)
Equality (brotherhood, equal opportunity for all)	Courageous (standing up for your beliefs)
Family security (taking care of loved ones)	Forgiving (willing to pardon others)
Freedom (independence, free choice)	Helpful (working for the welfare of others)
Happiness (contentedness)	Honest (sincere, truthful)
Inner harmony (freedom from inner conflict)	Imaginative (daring, creative)
Mature love (sexual and spiritual intimacy)	Independent (self-reliant, self-sufficient)
National security (protection from attack)	Intellectual (intelligent, reflective)
Pleasure (an enjoyable leisurely life)	Logical (consistent, rational)
Salvation (saved, eternal life)	Loving (affectionate, tender)
Self-respect (respect, admiration)	Obedient (dutiful, respectful)
Social recognition (respect, admiration)	Polite (courteous, well-mannered)
True friendship (close companionship)	Responsible (dependent, reliable)
Wisdom (a mature understanding of life)	Self-controlled (restrained, self-disciplined)

SOURCE: Milton Rokeach, *The Nature of Human Values* (New York: Free Press, 1973), p. 28.

Such insights clearly have implications for the design of advertising message content targeted to this segment in various markets.

The Values and Life Styles (VALS) segmentation method was developed at the Stanford Research Institute (SRI) in 1978.[41] The original model, based on Maslow's work as well as the concept of social character,[42] categorized the U.S. population according to their values and then identified consumer behaviors associated with those values. As shown in Exhibit 4.3, information regarding consumers' self-image, aspirations, and products used, as well as their orientation (outer- or inner-directed), was employed to divide Americans into nine different values and life style clusters (the VALS 1 segment). At the bottom of the model are the Survivors (struggling for survival, distrustful) and the Sustainers (hoping for improvement over time, concerned with safety). Two separate paths lead from the bottom of the model to the top. The outer-directed path contains Belongers (preservers of the status quo,

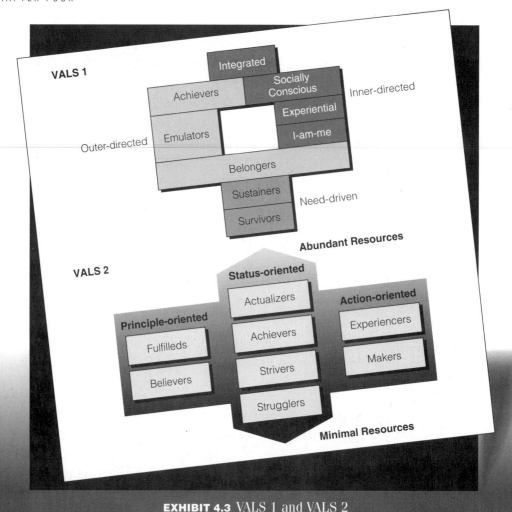

EXHIBIT 4.3 VALS 1 and VALS 2

SOURCE: Adapted from *American Demographics*, July 1989, p. 26. © 1989. Reprinted with permission.

seeking to be part of the group), Emulators (upwardly mobile, emulating the rich and successful), and Achievers (materialistic and comfort loving, oriented to fame and success). These groups take their cues from the world around them. The inner-directed path contains I-am-me's (very individualistic), Experimentals (seeking direct experience, valuing intense personal relationships), and Socially Conscious (simple, valuing natural living, socially responsible). These groups tend to make their own rules. At the top of the model are the Integrateds (psychologically mature, tolerant, having a world perspective).

This widely used scheme proved useful to international marketers in examining the percentage of consumers in foreign markets falling into each of these categories. For example, it was shown that according to VALS 1, about one-third of the U.S. population could be characterized as "belongers"; the corresponding figure in Japan was a full 80 percent, suggesting that consumers in that country were notably unwilling to stand out and strongly desired to belong to a peer group.[43] The "need-driven" grouping, which accounted for about 11 percent of the U.S. population, apparently had no direct counterpart among the Japanese, perhaps reflecting the greater cultural heterogeneity in America.[44]

In 1989 the system was updated to reflect the changes in American society that had taken place since the late 1970s, and SRI introduced VALS 2.[45] As with the original VALs typology, consumers are said to purchase specific types of goods and services because of their type of personality. VALS 2 holds that purchase behavior is influenced by individuals' available resources as well as their self-orientation. Resources can be both material (money, position, education) and psychological (intelligence, inventiveness, energy, and even health and self-confidence). Again as shown in Exhibit 4.3, VALS 2 divides consumers into three categories: principle-oriented, status-oriented, and action-oriented. Individuals with principle orientations generally look within themselves to make choices. In contrast, those with a status orientation generally make decisions based on the anticipated reactions of those within the group to which they belong, while those with an action orientation value feelings only when they result from action. There are eight subcategories: Fulfilleds, Believers, Actualizers, Achievers, Strivers, Strugglers, Experiencers, and Makers. Backer Spielvogel Bates Worldwide used VALS 2 to examine two groups the agency identifies as the largest in the developed world: Strivers (young people working hard for the material trappings of the good life) and Achievers (slightly older than Strivers, probably married, college-educated, sophisticated professionals). Although both groupings exist in Japan and the United States, some significant differences were found, reported *ADWEEK:* "Japanese Achievers are far more attached than their American counterparts to traditional male and female roles. As for the Strivers, the community support structure of Japanese society alleviates some of the pressures from which American Strivers suffer, including fear of unemployment."[46] Such insights into differences in values and life styles among consumers from different cultures can influence advertising strategy selection.

An examination of cultural values can do more than assist marketers in segmenting consumers. With regards to the relationship between values and advertising, values may be among the major influences on human be-havior, and advertisements that take this notion into account may be among the most effective. As noted in *Social Values and Social Change,* "Value-linked advertisements may animate affect, creating an affective response closer to the value-induced affect than to the product or advertisement with-out the value link. To the extent that affective advertisements are more in-fluential than bland ads, values may be a mechanism to explore when trying to understand the sources of affect."[47] In short, if marketers hope to formu-late more effective messages for foreign markets, they must become sensi-tive to the core values of a given country.

Religion, Morals, and Ethical Standards

Robert Bartels notes that "the foundation of a nation's culture and the most important determinant of social and business conduct are the religious and philosophic beliefs of a people. From them spring role perceptions, behavior patterns, codes of ethics and the institutionalized manner in which economic activities are performed."[48] As such, knowledge of the moral and religious traditions of a country are essential to the international marketer's under-standing of why consumers behave the way they do in a particular market.

Although numerous religious groups exist in the world today, Buddhism, Christianity, Hinduism, Islam, and Shinto are considered the major religions in terms of numbers of adherents. The influences of religion on interna-tional marketing are manifold. In some countries references to god or reli-gion are taken very seriously. In cultures practicing Islam, it is considered highly inappropriate to use Quranic quotations, the prophet's name, god's name, or pictures of Islamic shrines on products or in promotional materi-als.[49] In a marketing blunder tied to religion, a shipment of Chinese shoes whose soles featured a design that apparently meant "god" in Arabic was sent to Egypt. It took China's ambassador to Egypt to ease the tension that resulted.[50] When Hyatt Hotels enters a new market, it takes religious cus-toms very seriously. In Singapore ceiling arrows point in the direction of Mecca. The Grand Hyatt in Bangkok boasts both a house god and a house temple. In Bali, Hyatt asked religious leaders for help in approving the art-work before the hotel opened. Artifacts the hotel had purchased to be placed near the restaurant were repositioned elsewhere when company officials were informed that the artifacts were too holy to be close to an area where people eat.[51]

Religion directly impacts the way its adherents feel about work and the value they place on material goods. At the heart of Buddhism, for example, is the belief that suffering is caused by attachment to material possessions and selfish enjoyment of any kind. Islam also considers an emphasis on material wealth immoral. Such views stand in direct contrast to the Protestant ethic of hard work, wherein acquisition of wealth is a measure of achievement. The doctrine "for the good of all" is at the heart of the Shinto religion, practiced extensively in Japan. This doctrine is reflected in the Japanese work ethic: to live is to work and to work is to be conscientious and to make everyone proud. The Japanese dedication to hard work has resulted in twelve-hour work days, often six days per week.

Religious traditions may forbid altogether the sale, or at least the advertising, of various products. In Saudi Arabia, for example, alcoholic beverages are completely banned. While for most brewers such a ban would pose a distinct liability, Strohs has found success in selling nonalcoholic beer to consumers in this market. Gillette faced quite a challenge in promoting its razors to consumers in Iran because Islam discourages followers from shaving. As Laurel Wentz tells it, in attempting to obtain media space for Gillette's Blue II advertisements, a representative from an affiliate agency went from one paper to the next. Finally, he came across a newspaper advertising manager without a beard and noted that "shaving is not just for your face . . . if you have a car accident and someone has to shave your head, Gillette Blue II is the best." Using this argument, the newspaper advertising manager consulted his clergyman and returned with permission to run the ad.[52] Other products that are banned in this market because of the very conservative application of Islamic teachings include cigarettes, lighters, and even candy and chocolates. Islam also forbids the consumption of pork, while followers of the Hindu religion don't eat beef. An advertising blunder occurred some years ago when an appliance manufacturer ran an advertisement depicting an open refrigerator containing a centrally placed chunk of ham. Ads often feature a refrigerator stocked with delicious food, and because such photos are rather difficult to shoot, they generally are used for as many promotional purposes as possible. Unfortunately, the company used the stock photo in an ad headed for the Middle East. Locals considered the portrayal of pork to be insensitive and unappealing.

Religion may influence male/female roles, which may, in turn, impact various aspects of the marketing program. In attempting to gather market information on female consumers in the Middle East, one marketer planned to conduct a series of focus group interviews. Because of the very secluded role of women in this society, the marketer had to invite husbands and brothers to the focus group sessions instead. Similarly, hiring men to conduct face-to-face interviews with or even telephone surveys of women or addressing mailed questionnaires to women for the purpose of collecting market data would be considered highly inappropriate.[53] Historically, sales of cameras in Saudi Arabia were quite limited, because Islamic tradition requires that women be veiled. However, Polaroid instant photography allowed Arab men to photograph their wives and daughters in the privacy of their homes, without the need for strangers to handle the film in a processing lab.

What is considered moral behavior is also directly influenced by religion. Warner Lambert had its share of marketing problems in the late 1960s when it attempted to introduce Listerine to Thai consumers. In Thailand, Warner Lambert produced commercials fashioned after a well-known American TV spot showing a young man and woman kissing and otherwise expressing affection. Sales remained minimal, and company executives were puzzled by the turn of events. Finally, the problem was discovered—such public portrayals of male–female relationships was objectionable to the Thai people. The commercial was quickly reshot to show two young women instead. The ad caught on, and increased sales confirmed the effectiveness of the modifications.[54] In developing commercial messages for the Muslim world, human nudity is to be avoided at all costs as it is regarded as highly offensive. In other countries, such as France and, increasingly, the United States, nude models in advertisements hardly raise an eyebrow.

Many major holidays are also closely tied to religion. We are all familiar with the fervor with which American businesses gear up for the Christmas season. As early as September, many retailers begin to decorate their stores and shops with garlands and Christmas trees to stimulate holiday shopping. In December retailers generally extend their business hours in response to dramatic increases in consumer purchases. In many countries where Christianity plays a major role, Sundays are considered a type of holiday, and no or very few business establishments are open for business. In the Muslim world the entire month of Ramadan is a religious holiday, and Muslims are required to fast from dawn to dusk. Because of the rigors of such fasting, there is a marked drop-off in productivity during this period. At the same time, Ramadan is a significant holiday in terms of marketing and advertising because, at the end of the holiday, "Idul Fitri" is celebrated, and every man, woman, and child receives a gift of clothing. Obviously, local holidays must be taken into account in the development of all aspects of a marketing program.

Customs and Consumption Patterns

The customs of a society affect the kinds of products that are consumed as well as when and how they are consumed, by whom they are purchased and consumed, and how much is consumed.

What Consumers Buy and How Much They Consume Some products face nearly insurmountable challenges. Laundry product manufacturers have had little success in introducing dryer-activated fabric softeners in many European countries because of the custom of hanging out clothes to dry on a clothesline. And sometimes, consumers in foreign markets may expect products that are not available. For example, after successfully opening a park in Tokyo, Disney decided to expand to the European market, opening Euro-Disney just outside Paris. Just as with the parks in the United States and Tokyo, all alcoholic beverages were banned. However, Disney failed to consider the European penchant for drinking wine and beer with meals. In addition, the park did not offer sufficient restaurant seating for European customers, who expected to sit down at the accustomed dining time and enjoy a leisurely meal. Disney was criticized strongly for sticking too closely to its homogeneous "It's a small world after all" philosophy. Euro-Disney estimated that it would lose almost $350 million during its first year of operations. Disney has since introduced both beer and wine at all park restaurants.[55]

How a product is consumed can vary from market to market. In the United States beer drinkers prefer their brew cold, while in the United Kingdom and much of Europe, beer is served at room temperature. Many beer manufacturers in the United States portray their brands being served up icy cold in their advertisements; clearly, such positioning would be less than appropriate in England or Germany.

Who Makes Purchase Decisions The marketer must know who in the family is the primary decision maker, and for which products. In some cultures the female holds the purse strings while in others it is the male. In Japan, for example, note Edward T. and Mildred Hall, the "housewife makes most of the major purchases for the family and buys the family's food, household supplies and clothing. Usually, she receives her husband's paycheck, manages the household budget, and allocates funds for different categories of expenses, including savings for children's education, vacations, leisure activities, and retirement. She is the person advertisers must try to reach."[56] In the United States, for an increasing number of product categories, children and teens are the primary decision makers. It is estimated that 4- to 12-year-olds annually spend $6.2 billion of their own money purchasing items such as snacks, candy, and toys. Total spending for the 28 million consumers ages 12–19 rose to some $55 billion—an amount that approximates the gross national product of Turkey. However, claims Patricia Sellers, the impact of teenagers on the U.S. economy is much larger: "In addition to the $55 billion that came from kids' allowances and after-tax earnings and the $11.2 billion that they saved for future purchases, there's another $33.5 billion that busy moms and dads gave their offspring for family grocery shopping last year. Youngsters also influenced almost $150 billion in family purchases of such products as stereos, breakfast cereals and . . . frozen pizza."[57] Of course, not all young people around the world display such consumer clout. Many cultures place much greater value on the elders in the community and emphasize the wisdom that comes with age. This respect for the elderly stands in marked contrast to the extreme youth orientation in this country.

How Much Consumers Buy Even the amount or quantity of a product that consumers in different cultures purchase is not constant. In the United States shoppers typically purchase the economy size of products, as shopping is typically done on a weekly basis. In both Europe and Japan, where shopping is often done on a daily basis and where household storage space is more limited, consumers tend to purchase smaller-sized packages. Once Philips introduced a smaller version of its coffee-makers to fit into smaller-sized Japanese kitchens, sales took off. Two-liter bottles of Coca-Cola failed to move from retail shelves in Spain because few consumers had refrigerators with large enough compartments to store the beverage container. In contrast, in Mexico Campbell sells its soup in cans large enough to serve four or more, as families in this market are typically larger. Even deodorant consumption varies dramatically.[58] Americans consume almost twice as much deodorant as the French and nearly four times as much as Italians. Consumers in the United States are perceived by much of the rest of the world as quite fanatical with regards to personal hygiene.

Consumption patterns clearly have importance for advertisers in deciding how to introduce a brand. Where a group of products enjoys widespread acceptance, the message will likely be directed toward obtaining the largest share of the market. Where consumption is low or nonexistent, the marketing communications will have an educational character.

With regards to breakfast cereal, for example, U.S. citizens consume 9.3 pounds per person, while the British consume 12.9 pounds and the Irish a whopping 13.3 pounds. When Kellogg runs ads for Frosted Flakes and Corn Flakes in these markets, it is competing with other brands of cereals. In contrast, the German and Japanese cereal markets are comparatively undeveloped. Per capita cereal consumption is a mere 1.6 pounds in Germany and an almost negligible 0.1 pound in Japan. Traditionally, Germans eat bread with cheese or meat in the mornings or, occasionally, a type of whole grain cereal, while the Japanese eat primarily rice-based breakfasts. It is also important to note that many Japanese suffer from lactose intolerance, which further complicates the promotion of a breakfast consisting of cereal and milk. Kellogg initially faced quite a challenge in marketing its cereals in Germany and, in particular, in Japan, where they are only now making a serious breakthrough. Early messages for both Frosted Flakes and Corn Flakes tended to be predominantly educational in nature. Interestingly, even in the 1960s, Western-style soups had little trouble making it to the Japanese table . . . even the breakfast table. George Fields notes: "It was easier for soup to be served for the Japanese breakfast than cereal, because, traditionally, Japanese bean-paste soup (misoshiru) was always served for breakfast; thus, when breakfast started to turn Western, with toast and margarine, etc., Western-style soup had no conceptual problems being positioned. In a traditionally salt-oriented Japanese breakfast, cereals with milk and sugar had problems in this respect."[59]

Communicating Across Cultures

Many firms, especially smaller ones, or those entering foreign markets for the first time, do not have the resources, time, or personnel required to assess all the cultural elements that might potentially influence the marketing mix. Nevertheless, the international marketer can draw on various tools in analyzing a country's culture for the purpose of making promotional decisions.

Cultural Distance

The concept of cultural distance has its origins in early international trade theory as an explanation for why trade tended to be concentrated in foreign markets most similar to domestic markets. Migration patterns are at the core of this concept. When migrant groups settle in foreign countries, they carry with them their culture—their language, religion, values, and learned behaviors—all of which affect the goods and services they tend to purchase. Marketers in the host country thus acquire knowledge with regards to these consumption styles and habits, and this information influences their views on other foreign markets. Foreign markets are then seen as more or less similar to what the marketers know about their home market. In turn, this perceived similarity influences managerial preferences and choices of foreign markets, the international expansion strategies firms select, and the magnitude and direction of international trade.[60]

In communicating with consumers in foreign markets, regardless of perceived cultural distance, messages encoded in one culture must be decoded in another. However, when messages are communicated cross-nationally between similar cultures, the decoding effect of the receiver produces results more nearly like those intended in the original message encoding by the sender. Conversely, when messages are communicated cross-nationally between highly dissimilar—or distant—cultures, the decoding effect of the receiver may not produce the intended results. The model of cross-cultural communication outlined in Exhibit 4.4 incorporates economic, political-legal, and demographic differences in addition to cultural differences. This model is useful in that it refers to the degree of homogeneity or heterogeneity between markets in general.

Larry Samovar and Richard Porter propose that the degree of similarity or dissimilarity between senders and receivers may be viewed on a continuum of compared cultures, as shown in Exhibit 4.5. The authors explain the scale as follows:

> If we imagine differences varying along a minimum-maximum dimension, the degree of difference between two cultural groups depends on their relative social uniqueness. Although this scale is unrefined, it allows us to examine intercultural communication acts and gain insight into the effect cultural differences have on communication. To see how this dimensional scale helps us understand intercultural communication we can look at some examples of cultural differences positioned along the scale.
>
> The first example represents a case of maximum differences—those found between Asian and Western cultures. This may be typified as an interaction between two farmers, one who works on a communal farm on the outskirts of Beijing in China and the other who operates a large mechanized and automated wheat, corn and dairy farm in Michigan. In this situation we should expect to find the greatest number

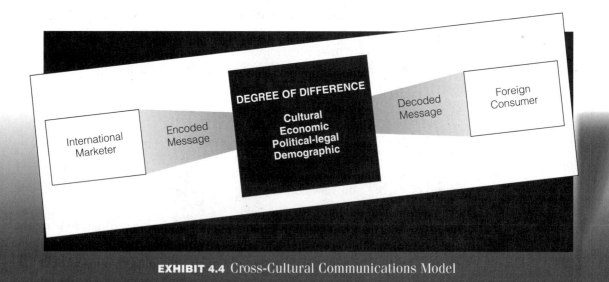

EXHIBIT 4.4 Cross-Cultural Communications Model

SOURCE: Adapted from Vern Terpstra, *International Dimensions of Marketing,* 3rd ed. (Chicago: Dryden, 1983), p. 413.

of diverse cultural factors. Physical appearance, religion, philosophy, economic systems, social attitudes, language, heritage, basic conceptualization of self and the universe, and the degree of technological development are cultural factors that differ sharply. We must recognize, however, that these two farmers also share the commonality of farming, with its rural life style and love of the land. In some respects, they may be more closely related than they are to members of their own

Maximum Sociocultural Differences

Western/Asian

Italian/Saudi Arabian

U.S. American/Greek

U.S. American/German

U.S. American/French-Canadian

White Anglo-American/Reservation Indian

White Anglo-American/African American, Asian American, Mexican American, or Urban Indian

U.S. American/British

U.S. American/English-Canadian

Urban American/Rural American

Catholic/Baptist

Male Dominance/Female Equality

Heterosexual/Homosexual

Environmentalist/Developer

Minimum Sociocultural Differences

EXHIBIT 4.5 Continuum of Compared Cultures, Subcultures, and Subgroups

SOURCE: Larry Samovar and Richard Porter, *Intercultural Communication: A Reader,* 7th ed. (Belmont, CA: Wadsworth, 1994), p. 22.

cultures who live in large urban settings. In other words, across some cultural dimensions, the Michigan farmer may have more in common with the Chinese farmer than with a Wall Street securities broker.

Another example nearer the center of the scale is the difference between American culture and German culture. Less variation is found: Physical characteristics are similar, and the English language is derived in part from German and its ancestor languages. The roots of both German and American philosophy are found in ancient Greece, and most Americans and Germans share some form of the Judeo-Christian tradition. Yet there are some significant differences. Germans have political and economic systems that are different from those found in the United States. German society tends toward formality while in the United States we tend toward informality. Germans have memories of local warfare and the destruction of their cities and economy, of having been a defeated nation on more than one occasion. The United States has never lost a war on its own territory.

Examples near the minimal ends of the dimension can be characterized in two ways. First are variations found between members of separate but similar cultures—for instance, between U.S. Americans and English-Canadians. These differences are less than those found between American and German cultures, between American and Greek cultures, between American and British cultures, or even between American and French-Canadian cultures, but greater than generally found within a single culture. Second, minimal differences also may be seen in the variation between co-cultures, within the same dominant culture. Socio-cultural differences may be found between members of the Catholic church and the Baptist church; environmentalists and advocates of further development of Alaskan oil resources; middle-class Americans and the urban poor; mainstream Americans and the gay and lesbian community; the able and the disabled; or male dominance advocates and female equality advocates.

In both these categorizations, members of each cultural group have more in common than in the examples found in the middle or at the maximum end of the scale. They probably speak the same language, share the same general religion, attend the same schools, and live in the same neighborhoods. Yet, these groups to some extent are culturally different; they do not fully share the experiences, nor do they share the same perception. They see their worlds differently.[61]

Map of Culture

Via his map of culture, Edward T. Hall provides a different way of understanding foreign cultures. His framework consists of ten cultural rules for ten human activities: interaction, association, subsistence, bisexuality, territoriality, temporality, learning, play, defense, and exploitation.[62] These ten "primary message systems" are outlined in Exhibit 4.6.

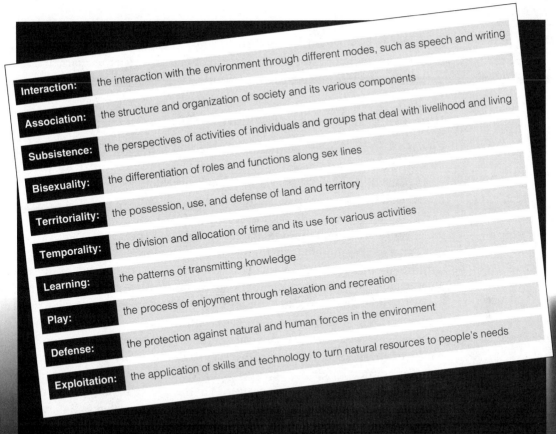

Interaction:	the interaction with the environment through different modes, such as speech and writing
Association:	the structure and organization of society and its various components
Subsistence:	the perspectives of activities of individuals and groups that deal with livelihood and living
Bisexuality:	the differentiation of roles and functions along sex lines
Territoriality:	the possession, use, and defense of land and territory
Temporality:	the division and allocation of time and its use for various activities
Learning:	the patterns of transmitting knowledge
Play:	the process of enjoyment through relaxation and recreation
Defense:	the protection against natural and human forces in the environment
Exploitation:	the application of skills and technology to turn natural resources to people's needs

EXHIBIT 4.6 The Primary Message Systems in Hall's Map of Culture

SOURCE: Edward T. Hall, *The Silent Language* (Garden City, NY: Doubleday, 1959), pp. 62–81.

For a broad-based understanding of the cultural environment of a foreign market, Hall suggests investigating each of the primary message systems. Such an analysis can assist marketers in divorcing themselves from the self-reference criterion and enables the exploration of the complexities of foreign markets. One of the greatest benefits of this system lies in its flexibility. An international marketer or advertiser short on time or funds may not need to engage in such an in-depth analysis. The model allows the marketer to analyze only those elements of culture that directly relate to the specific marketing decision. For this type of analysis, Hall suggests that marketers explore the intersection of message systems. For example, if marketers wish to understand how a particular culture shapes an individual's attitude toward work, they might explore how people interact in work situations or what roles are reserved for instructing others. Work messages are associated with each of the other message systems. Thus, by analyzing just one or two primary message systems, the international advertiser or marketer can obtain an overall perspective of the culture.

High-Context Versus Low-Context Cultures

Edward T. Hall also developed the concept of high and low context as a means of understanding different cultural orientations. Low-context cultures place high value on words, and communicators are encouraged to be direct, exact, and unambiguous. In contrast, high-context cultures consider verbal communications to be only a part of the overall message, and communicators rely much more heavily on contextual cues. Hall writes: "Context is the information that surrounds an event and is inextricably bound up with the meaning of that event. The elements that combine to produce a given meaning—events and context—are in different proportions depending on culture."[63] Thus, messages in high-context cultures tend to be a good deal more implicit and ambiguous, with communicators relying much more on nonverbal behavior, the physical setting, social circumstances, and the nature of interpersonal relationships. Hall further explains that "a high context communication or message is one in which most of the information is already in the person, while very little is in the coded, explicit, transmitted part of the message. A low context communication is vested in the explicit code."[64] Cultures typically are not perceived as either high- or low-context but, as Exhibit 4.7 shows, are arranged along a continuum. Note that this continuum should not give the impression of equal intervals.

The differences between communications styles in high- versus low-context cultures have direct implications for the international advertiser. Messages constructed by writers from high-context cultures might be difficult to understand in low-context cultures because they do not come to the point. Similarly, messages constructed by writers from low-context cultures may be difficult to understand in high-context cultures because they omit essential contextual material.[65] For example, Japan is considered to be a high-context culture while the United States is considered a low-context culture. Japanese marketers tend to be more intuitive, subjective, and oriented toward communications and human relations; American marketers tend to be more logical, scientific, and oriented toward data, systems, and procedures.[66] As might be expected, the advertising messages created in these two markets differ dramatically. A number of studies have documented that Japanese ads, both broadcast and print, contain fewer information cues than ads appearing in the United States and many other countries.[67,68] Japanese advertising is less likely to focus on the product's merits; the direct or hard-sell

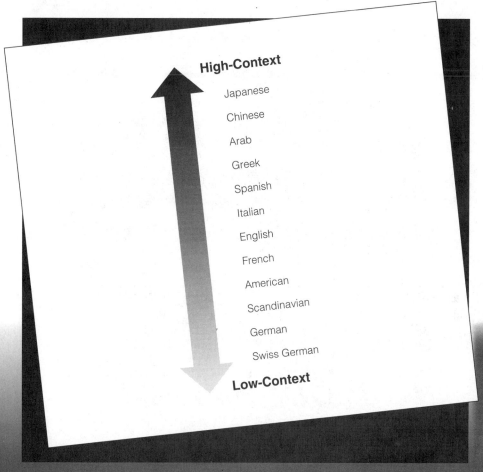

High-Context

Japanese

Chinese

Arab

Greek

Spanish

Italian

English

French

American

Scandinavian

German

Swiss German

Low-Context

EXHIBIT 4.7 High-Context Versus Low-Context Cultures

SOURCE: Gary P. Ferraro, *The Cultural Dimension of International Business* (Englewood Cliffs, NJ: Prentice-Hall, 1990), p. 56.

approach so common in American advertising seems to leave the Japanese consumer cold.[69] Comparative claims, a mainstay in American advertising, are almost unheard of in Japan. Instead, note Edward and Mildred Hall, "Japanese advertising evokes a mood and is designed to appeal to emotions, produce good feelings, and create a happy atmosphere. The approach is soft-sell."[70] Indeed, much of Japanese advertising is so soft-sell that it is often difficult to determine what the product is from viewing an advertisement. For example, a quick glimpse at the Japanese advertisement in Exhibit 4.8 would not reveal that this ad is promoting mayonnaise, nor would the headline,

カルシウムがミルクの2倍あることは、知られていない。

カルシウムを意識するとミルクを飲む。小魚を食べる。しかし、植物を連想する人は
いないようです。緑黄色野菜に目をむけてください。緑の濃い野菜は、土のミネラル
カルシウムをいっぱい吸収しています。パセリ100g中のカルシウムは190mg。これは
ミルクの約2倍。コマツナ、290mg。ダイコンの葉、210mg。シュンギクにも、ほぼ
ミルクと同量、90mgあります。乳製品だけでは不足するミネラルを、植物の食事で。
●新鮮な野菜にキューピーマヨネーズ。ビタミンA・D・B₁・B₂がいっぱいの卵の黄味、
ビネガー、サラダオイルが原料。着色料、乳化剤、防腐剤はいっさい使っていません。

キユーピーマヨネーズ
野菜をもっとたべましょう。

EXHIBIT 4.8 Soft-Sell Japanese Advertisement for Mayonnaise

which reads, "Parsley contains twice as much calcium as milk." The entire first paragraph discusses the calcium content of various vegetables. It is not until the final two sentences that the reader is encouraged to enjoy fresh vegetables with Kewpie brand mayonnaise.

Universals

Much has been said about differences between cultures, in part because cultural differences have a tendency to stand out more so than similarities. However, the similarities between cultures must not be overlooked. Cultural universals are defined as modes of behavior common to all cultures. As human beings, we share basic biological similarities. For example, all humans sense hunger, and the eating of food to ensure survival is a universal behavior. However, just how we respond to this biological drive—what we eat, as well as when, how, where, and with whom we eat—is shaped by culture. Beyond biological drives, all humans are confronted with universal needs. For instance, each society must ensure that its young learn the ways of the community, but just how this accumulated knowledge is passed on to the next generation differs from culture to culture. In some societies, the elders are responsible for sharing the wisdom of the tribe. In other cultures, such training is conducted in a formal manner—at primary and secondary schools as well as colleges and universities.

George Murdock has developed a list of cultural universals that includes athletic sports, bodily adornments, calendars, cooking, courtship, education, etiquette, family, folklore, funeral rites, gestures, gift giving, incest taboos, joking, kin groups, law, magic, marriage, mealtimes, mourning, mythology, property rights, religious rituals, tool making, and weather control.[71] To the extent that some aspects of the cultural environment may be perceived as universal as opposed to unique to each distinct society, it may be possible for the international marketer or advertiser to standardize various aspects of the marketing mix. Theodore Levitt, called a global marketing guru by some, proposes that the "world is becoming a common marketplace in which people—no matter where they live—desire the same products and life styles. Global companies must forget idiosyncratic differences between countries and cultures and instead concentrate on satisfying universal drives."[72]

Summary

To operate effectively in foreign markets, international marketers and advertisers must recognize the pervasive influence of culture. Failure to understand the cultural environment can lead and has led to misunderstandings, miscommunications, and marketing failures. In this chapter we examined only a few of the more prominent elements of culture—including verbal language, nonverbal communications, signs and symbols, needs and values, religion, and customs—as they impact consumer behavior. In addition, we outlined a number of tools for assessing foreign cultures. In the next chapter we turn to the standardization versus specialization controversy.

Additional Readings

Ferraro, Gary P. (1990). *The Cultural Dimension of International Business.* Englewood Cliffs, NJ: Prentice-Hall.

Fields, George. (1989). *Gucci on the Ginza: Japan's New Consumer Generation.* Tokyo: Kodansha International.

Hall, Edward T. (1977). *Beyond Culture.* Garden City, NY: Anchor Books.

Samovar, Larry, Richard Porter, and Nemi Jain. (1981). *Understanding Intercultural Communication.* Belmont, CA: Wadsworth.

Terpstra, Vern, and Kenneth David. (1991). *The Cultural Environment of International Business,* 2nd ed. Cincinnati, OH: Southwestern.

Notes

1. Taylor, Edward B., *Primitive Culture* (London: John Murray, 1871), p. 1.

2. Hoebel, Adamson, *Man, Culture and Society* (New York: Oxford University Press, 1960), p. 168.

3. Terpstra, Vern, and Kenneth David, *The Cultural Environment of International Business,* 2nd ed. (Cincinnati, OH: Southwestern, 1991).

4. Kroeber, A. L., and C. Kluckhohn. "Culture: A Critical Review of Concepts and Definitions," Papers of the Peabody Museum of American Archeology and Ethnology, 41(1), 1952.

5. Hall, Edward T., *The Hidden Dimension* (Garden City, NY: Anchor Press/ Doubleday, 1966), p. 177.

6. Lee, James A., "Cultural Analysis in Overseas Operations," *Harvard Business Review,* March/April 1966, p. 47.

7. Ferraro, Gary P., *The Cultural Dimension of International Business* (Englewood Cliffs, NJ: Prentice-Hall, 1990), p. 34.

8. Thompson, Karen, "Penney's Strategy Targets Black, Hispanic Buyers," *San Diego Union Tribune,* September 10, 1993, p. C1.

9. Ricks, David, "International Business Blunders: An Update," *Business and Economic Review,* 34, January/February/ March 1988, pp. 11–14.

10. Whorf, Benjamin Lee, *Language, Thought, and Reality* (Cambridge, MA: Technology Press of Massachusetts Institute of Technology, 1956).

11. Maletzke, Gerhard, "Intercultural and International Communication," in Heinz-Dietrich Fischer and John Calhounn Merrill, eds., *International and Intercultural Communication* (New York: Hastings House, 1976).

12. Sapir, Edward, *An Introduction to the Study of Speech* (New York: Harcourt, Brace and World, 1921); and Whorf, *Language, Thought, and Reality.*

13. Shane, Scott, "Language and Marketing in Japan," *International Journal of Advertising,* 7, 1988, pp. 155–161.

14. Maletzke, "Intercultural and International Communication," p. 412.

15. Miracle, Gordon, "An Empirical Study of the Usefulness of the Back-Translation Technique for International Advertising Messages in Print Media,"

in John D. Leckenby, ed., *Proceedings of the 1988 Conference of the American Academy of Advertising*, p. RC-51.

16. Hall, Edward T., *Beyond Culture* (New York: Anchor Books, 1976), p. 16.

17. Condon, John, and Merrill Rathi Yousef, *Introduction to Intercultural Communication* (Indianapolis, IN: Bobbs-Merrill, 1975), pp. 123–124.

18. Davis, Riccardo, "Many Languages— 1 Ad Message," *Advertising Age*, September 20, 1993, p. 50.

19. Ferraro, *The Cultural Dimension*, p. 69.

20. LaBarre, Weston, "Paralinguistics, Kinesics, and Cultural Anthropology," in Larry Samovar and Richard Porter, eds., *Intercultural Communication: A Reader*, 2nd ed. (Belmont, CA: Wadsworth, 1976), pp. 121–129.

21. Field, Michael, "Fragrance Marketers Sniff Out Rich Aroma," *Advertising Age*, January 30, 1986, p. 10.

22. Hall, Edward T., and Mildred Reed Hall, *Hidden Differences: Doing Business with the Japanese* (New York: Anchor Books, 1987), p. 12.

23. Hall, *The Hidden Dimension*.

24. Hall and Hall, *Hidden Differences*, p. 13.

25. Hall, *The Hidden Dimension*, p. 16.

26. Ricks, David, *Big Business Blunders: Mistakes in Multinational Marketing* (Homewood, IL: Dow Jones–Irwin, 1983).

27. Jacobs, Laurence, Charles Keown, and Kyung-Il Ghymn, "Cross-cultural Color Comparisons: Global Marketers Beware," *International Marketing Review*, 8(3), 1991, pp. 21–30.

28. Ricks, *Big Business Blunders*, pp. 32–33.

29. Glover, Katherine, "Do's and Taboos: Cultural Aspects of International Business," *Business America*, 8(15), pp. 2–6.

30. Christie, Michael, "Slips of the Tongue Result in Classic Marketing Errors," *Advertising Age*, June 20, 1994, p. I15.

31. Maslow, Abraham, "A Theory of Human Motivation," in Harold Leavitt and Louis Pondy, eds., *Readings in Managerial Psychology* (Chicago: University of Chicago Press, 1964), pp. 6–24.

32. Rokeach, Milton, *The Nature of Human Values* (New York: Free Press, 1973).

33. Steward, Edward C., *American Cultural Patterns: A Cross Cultural Perspective* (Pittsburgh: Intercultural Communications Network, 1972), p. 74.

34. Rokeach, Milton, *Beliefs, Attitudes and Values* (San Francisco: Jossey-Bass, 1968).

35. Nakane, Chie, *Japanese Society* (Berkeley: University of California Press, 1970).

36. Cathcard, Delores, and Robert Cathcard, "Japanese Social Experience and the Concept of Group," in Samovar and Porter, eds., *Intercultural Communication: A Reader*, p. 58.

37. Mueller, Barbara, "Reflections of Culture: An Analysis of Japanese and American Advertising Appeals," *Journal of Advertising Research*, June/July 1987, pp. 51–59.

38. Rokeach, *Beliefs, Attitudes and Values*.

39. Munson, J. Michael, and Shelby H. McIntyre, "Personal Values and Values Attributed to a Distant Cultural Stereotype," in H. Keith Hunt, ed., *Advances in Consumer Research*, Vol. V (Ann Arbor, MI: Association for Consumer Research, 1978), p. 103+.

40. Yankelovich Partners, "When It Comes to Pop Culture, We Are the World," *ADWEEK*, November 2, 1992, p. 62.

41. Mitchell, Arnold, *The Nine American Life Styles* (New York: Macmillan, 1983).

42. Riesman, David, Nathan Glazer, and Revel Denny, *The Lonely Crowd* (New Haven, CT: Yale University Press, 1950).

43. Mitchell, *The Nine American Life Styles*.

44. Johansson, Johny K., "Japanese Consumers: What Foreign Marketers Should Know," *International Marketing Review*, Summer 1986, pp. 37–43.

45. Graham, Judith, "New VALS 2 Takes Psychological Route," *Advertising Age*, February 13, 1989, p. 24.

46. "Comparing Consumer Segments in the U.S. and Japan," *ADWEEK*, June 22, 1992, p. 12.

47. Kahle, Lynn R., ed., *Social Values and Social Change: Adaptions to Life in America* (New York: Praeger, 1983).

48. Bartels, Robert, "National Culture—Business Relations: United States and Japan Contrasted," *Management International Review*, 2, 1982, p. 5.

49. Hashmi, Mahmud S., "Marketing in the Islamic Context," presented to the 6th annual Conference on Languages and Communication for World Business and the Professions, May 8, 1987, Ann Arbor, Michigan.

50. Ricks, David, "International Business Blunders: An Update," *B & E Review*, January/March 1988, pp. 11–14.

51. Greenberg, Peter, "Cultural Sensitivity Is Becoming New Aim for International Hotels," *San Diego Union Tribune*, October 3, 1993, p. F4.

52. Wentz, Laurel, "Smooth Talk Wins Gillette Ad Space in Iran," *Advertising Age*, April 27, 1992, p. I40.

53. Hashmi, "Marketing in the Islamic Context."

54. Diamond, R. S., "Managers Away from Home," *Fortune*, August 15, 1969, p. 50.

55. Wentz, Laurel, and Bruce Crumley, "Magic Doesn't Travel During Euro-Disney Visit," *Advertising Age*, September 20, 1993, pp. 1, 3.

56. Hall and Hall, *Hidden Differences*, p. 137.

57. Sellers, Patricia, "The ABC's of Marketing to Kids," *Fortune*, May 8, 1989, p. 115.

58. A. C. Nielsen Co. Orbit International Database, *Advertising Age*, April 27, 1992, p. I30.

59. Fields, George, *Gucci on the Ginza: Japan's New Consumer Generation* (Tokyo: Kodansha International, 1989), p. 115.

60. Reid, Stan, "Migration, Cultural Distance and International Market Expansion," in Peter W. Turnbull and Stanley Paliwoda, eds., *Research in International Marketing* (London: Croom Helm, 1986), pp. 22–33.

61. Samovar, Larry, and Richard E. Porter, *Intercultural Communication: A Reader*, 7th ed. (Belmont, CA: Wadsworth, 1994), pp. 21–22.

62. Hall, *The Silent Language.*

63. Hall and Hall, *Hidden Differences*, p. 7.

64. Hall, *Beyond Culture.*

65. Wells, William, "Global Advertisers Should Pay Heed to Contextual Variations," *Marketing News*, February 13, 1987, p. 18.

66. Lazer, William, Shoji Murata, and Hiroshi Kosaka, "Japanese Marketing—Toward a Better Understanding," *Journal of Marketing*, 49, 1985, pp. 69–81.

67. Lin, Carolyn, "Cultural Differences in Message Strategies: A Comparison Between American and Japanese Television Commercials," paper presented at the AEJMC Annual Conference, April 8–11, 1992, Montreal.

68. Ramaprasad, Preponderant, and Kazumi Hasegawa, "An Analysis of Japanese Television Commercials," *Journalism Quarterly*, 67, Winter 1990, pp. 1025–1033.

69. Mueller, Barbara, "Standardization vs. Specialization: An Examination of Westernization in Japanese Advertising," *Journal of Advertising Research*, 32(1), January/February 1992, pp. 15–24.

70. Hall and Hall, *Hidden Differences*, p. 139.

71. Murdock, George P., "The Common Denominator of Cultures," in Ralph Linton, ed., *The Science of Man in the World Crises* (New York: Columbia University Press, 1945), pp. 123–142.

72. Lynch, Mitchell, "Harvard's Levitt Called Global Marketing Guru," *Advertising Age*, June 25, 1984, p. 49.

CHAPTER 5

Coordinating and Controlling International Advertising

hapter 2 focused on the four P's of the marketing mix—product, price, place (distribution), and, briefly, promotion. In Chapter 3 we highlighted the importance of examining various characteristics of foreign markets—demographic and geographic characteristics, economic factors, and the political-legal environment—and in Chapter 4 we explored the cultural environment. Now we turn our attention to the coordination and control of international marketing communications. Once international marketers have developed a product that meets the needs of a specific group in a foreign market, have priced it properly, and have distributed it via the appropriate channels, they must still inform consumers abroad of the product's availability and benefits. Advertising's goal is to generate awareness, interest, desire, and, ultimately, action. In this chapter we will focus on centralized versus decentralized control of international advertising, advertising agency selection, and marketing and advertising strategy options.

Centralized Versus Decentralized Control of International Advertising

One of the first decisions a company must make when it decides to communicate with consumers in the various markets in which it intends to do business is how to organize international promotional functions—including advertising, personal selling, direct marketing, publicity, and sales promotions. In international advertising, marketers have three basic approaches: (1) Centralize all international advertising decisions at company headquarters, (2) decentralize all decisions for foreign markets, or (3) utilize some combination of centralized and decentralized control.

Centralization

Complete *centralization* of international advertising implies a high level of head office control—advertising agency selection, campaign planning, creative strategy and message development, media strategy and selection, budgeting, and sales promotion efforts all are conducted in the country in which the firm's headquarters is situated. One of the major advantages associated with centralization is that it affords the marketer complete control over all promotional efforts. This degree of control is essential if the marketer is planning on integrating marketing communications. In addition, it eases coordination efforts in multiple markets. The centralized approach is highly correlated with the use of standardized advertising—employing virtually the same campaign in both domestic and foreign markets. Conversely, a low level of head office control (decentralization) suggests that local development of advertising campaigns is more likely to be employed.[1] This issue of standardization as it relates to creative strategy will be dealt with in detail in the following chapter.

A centralized approach also is significantly more likely to be employed if the marketing environments of the message sender and receiver(s) are highly similar. In particular, centralization is commonly used if there is little variation in both the media available for advertising and the regulation of advertising from one market to the next. Depending on the foreign market, the international marketer may not feel that local managers possess sufficient marketing and advertising experience to engage in extensive decision making. In many instances foreign managers are quite relieved to turn over responsibility for advertising decisions to headquarters.

However, there are weaknesses associated with highly centralized control as well. For example, a firm employing such an organizational approach may find it lacks (1) the ability to sense changes in market needs occurring away from home, (2) the resources to analyze data and develop strategic responses to competitive challenges emerging in foreign markets, or (3) the managerial initiative, motivation, and capability in its overseas operations to respond imaginatively to diverse and fast-changing environments.[2]

Decentralization

Complete *decentralization* of international advertising means that all or nearly all advertising decisions are made by local managers in the foreign markets. The philosophy here, according to Christopher Bartlett and Sumantra Ghoshal, is that international subsidiaries shouldn't just be "pipelines to move products. Their own special strengths can help build competitive advantage."[3] A primary benefit of decentralization is that promotional programs are tailored to the specific needs of each market. Nationals may be perceived as knowing the local market best and thus are better equipped to make necessary modifications to advertising campaigns as a result of differences in the local media scene, political-legal environment, or culture. An international marketer may also opt for a decentralized approach if markets are small or the volume of international business and advertising is too limited to warrant close attention from headquarters. Local managers are likely to be more highly motivated when given responsibility for the promotional programs in their market. In some instances this approach is employed because foreign managers can be resentful if the home office centralizes control over advertising functions and then mandates the specific messages to be used in their markets. Certainly, a degree of control over promotional efforts is relinquished if a decentralized approach is adopted.

Combination Approach

With the *combination* approach, as the label implies, some promotional decisions are made by headquarters while others are left up to local managers. The combination approach can take many forms. For example, an international or network agency may be designated as the lead agency, responsible for developing what is termed *pattern advertising*. Pattern advertising refers to centralization of the "what" of an advertising campaign and localization of the "how."[4] Thus, the basic advertising strategy or approach is provided to each subsidiary; however, local managers are then free to modify copy, visuals, or other elements of the message to meet local needs.

In another variation of the combination approach, the lead agency may develop a series of advertising messages that utilize a similar theme, encouraging local managers to select those they believe will be most effective in their particular marketing environment. For example, Seagram & Sons, distributors for Chivas Regal, utilizes what is in effect a combination approach. In 1991 Seagram created a global brands division and restructured its brand management system along those lines. Later that year, DDB Needham Worldwide New York, Seagram's lead agency, created a $40-million global print and billboard campaign. Media buying, however, was handled locally. Seagram tested four campaigns in seven countries before choosing a series of twenty-four print ads using the theme line "There will always be a Chivas Regal." John Hartrey, Jr., senior vice president for marketing for Seagram's global brands division, notes: "The idea of a global campaign is not to say here's one ad and everybody will use it around the world; it's having the flexibility of global execution." The campaign runs in thirty-four countries and is translated into fifteen languages, but marketing executives in each region are allowed to choose specific ads in the series best suited to their market.[5] Regardless of the specific form it takes, the combination approach allows for local input and adaption while still permitting a degree of uniformity in a firm's international promotions.

Agency Selection

Firms marketing their goods and services abroad must decide who should plan, prepare, and execute their promotional campaigns. International marketers have a variety of options, including (1) employing their domestic agency (and then exporting advertising messages), (2) using their domestic in-house agency or a foreign subsidiary's in-house agency, (3) calling on the services of an international agency with domestic and overseas offices, or (4) hiring a foreign advertising agency.

Domestic and In-House Agencies

Smaller firms exporting their goods abroad may choose to rely on their domestic advertising agency to prepare advertising messages for their foreign markets. A firm's domestic agency may be affiliated with foreign shops capable of providing necessary translation services and assistance with media planning and buying. A domestic agency might also belong to an international network offering similar services. A very real danger of employing a domestic agency is that it may not be familiar with the many pitfalls associated with international advertising.

Some companies, in particular manufacturers of industrial goods, rely on their in-house advertising departments for foreign advertising assistance. On the plus side, the in-house agency is likely to be intimately familiar with the product or service to be promoted. However, domestic in-house agencies may lack the necessary experience in dealing with foreign markets. When international advertisers turn to a foreign subsidiary's in-house agency, while they gain familiarity with the local market, they lose a degree of control over promotional efforts. Further, there is no guarantee that the quality of the work produced will live up to the firm's expectations.

International Agencies and Global Networks

International firms leaning toward a centralized approach are three times more likely to employ an international agency or global network than they are to use a foreign agency.[6] Clearly, it's easier for international marketers to deal with a single international agency than with a separate agency in each market in which they operate. Although agency networks offer multi-country coverage, there is no guarantee that offices in each country will be equally strong. Clients may find agency work in one market of especially high quality, but less so in another market.

As noted in Chapter 1, many U.S. advertising agencies began aggressive expansion abroad in the 1960s in order to meet the needs of their multinational clients. Today, Backer Spielvogel Bates Worldwide, BBD&O Worldwide, Bozell, Leo Burnett, D'Arcy Masius Benton & Bowles, DDB Needham Worldwide, Grey Advertising, and McCann-Erickson Worldwide all have offices in more than thirty-four countries around the world. U.S. agencies are not alone in their expansion plans. Dentsu, Japan's agency giant, is continuing its expansion outside its home turf with moves into the Middle East and Europe in order to better meet its clients' increasing demands. In late 1992 the agency acquired a minority stake in Publi-Graphics, a $70-million Middle Eastern agency network, as well as Brussels-based BLD Europe. In addition, Dentsu has made a number of other European acquisitions in the past two years.[7] Exhibit 5.1 shows a recent Dentsu spot appealing to foreign advertisers; the ad appeared in U.S. publications read by American marketing managers.

In an attempt to become the first advertising agency capable of meeting the needs of increasingly global clients, London-based Saatchi & Saatchi introduced its global orientation in 1984 in an advertisement headlined, "The new opportunity for world brands." The advertisement reflected the philosophy of global marketing outlined by Harvard Business School professor Theodore Levitt, who stated: "The world's needs and desires have been irrevocably homogenized by technology. The global corporation accepts that technology drives consumers relentlessly towards the same common goals, i.e. the alleviation of life's burdens and the expansion of discretionary time and spending power. . . . Successful global companies sell the same things

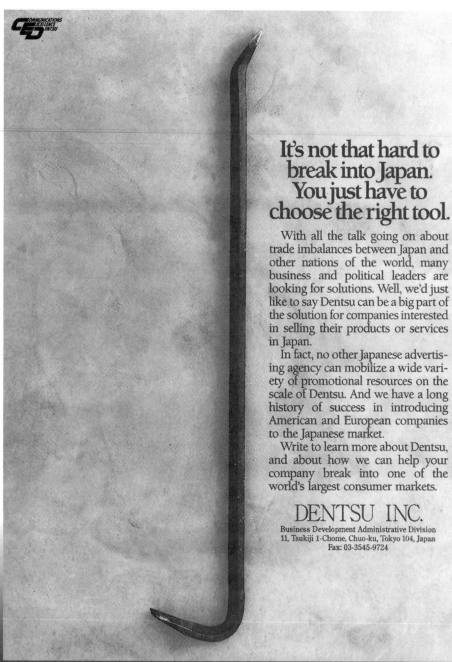

It's not that hard to break into Japan. You just have to choose the right tool.

With all the talk going on about trade imbalances between Japan and other nations of the world, many business and political leaders are looking for solutions. Well, we'd just like to say Dentsu can be a big part of the solution for companies interested in selling their products or services in Japan.

In fact, no other Japanese advertising agency can mobilize a wide variety of promotional resources on the scale of Dentsu. And we have a long history of success in introducing American and European companies to the Japanese market.

Write to learn more about Dentsu, and about how we can help your company break into one of the world's largest consumer markets.

DENTSU INC.
Business Development Administrative Division
11, Tsukiji 1-Chome, Chuo-ku, Tokyo 104, Japan
Fax: 03-3545-9724

EXHIBIT 5.1 Dentsu Spot Aimed at Foreign Advertisers

the same way everywhere and different cultural preferences, national tastes and standards are vestiges of the past."[8] Not surprisingly, Levitt is now a member of the Saatchi board. In late 1991 Saatchi & Saatchi further enhanced its global orientation by restructuring its North American and non–North American operations into a single unit. The agency even offers rewards to employees creating successful international campaigns, a practice reflecting its recognition that major clients, such as Procter & Gamble, are looking for advertising ideas that can run globally.[9] Saatchi's major international accounts also include British Airways, Sara Lee, Johnson & Johnson, and Toyota.

Apple Computers provides a classic example of a firm seeking to globalize. After years of allowing international divisions to coordinate their own advertising, Apple has centralized management of worldwide communications at its Cupertino, California, headquarters. In a parallel move Apple's longtime agency, BBD&O Worldwide, has centralized supervision of Apple's global advertising in its Los Angeles office, which formerly was responsible only for U.S. campaigns. Apple management has communicated to BBD&O that it wants to have the same campaigns running worldwide to the extent that it makes sense to do so. The change is designed mainly to build worldwide brand images for Apple as it diversifies beyond its best-known product line, the Macintosh personal computer. This move toward centralized control is rather ironic in that Apple has long built its corporate structure on the idea that power should be spread among individuals. In addition, Apple's former policy of delegating considerable control to international divisions so that advertising campaigns would reflect local values and culture seemed to work for the firm—international sales were growing faster than domestic sales and in 1992 accounted for 45 percent of Apple's record $7.1 billion in revenues.[10]

Although not all global marketers are turning to a single agency for worldwide promotions, an increasing number are lining up their brands with just a few international agencies—a strategic trend called *alignment fever*. Firms are paring down their rosters to just a few agencies, which are virtually guaranteed any new major business from clients that have committed to these designated agencies. B.A.T. provides a perfect example. The U.K.-based tobacco manufacturer's agency roster used to include practically every agency network in the world. Then, in 1992, the firm centralized marketing activities and aligned the entire B.A.T. portfolio with just two agencies, Grey Advertising and Backer Spielvogel Bates Worldwide.[11]

This alignment fever has spelled success for international agency networks. The top 10 agency networks' combined share of global advertising spending has more than doubled, from 22.9 percent to 48.3 percent, in the past decade—which has been dubbed the "decade of alignment." The large networks with their long international client lists appear to be in the best position for growth. But agencies do take risks when they take on large portions of their clients' worldwide business and often are forced to make concessions with regards to account conflicts. Clients understandably expect aligned agencies to be available for assignments around the world and in any category they choose to enter.

Table 5.1 lists the top agencies in Europe, Latin America, and Asia/Pacific for 1993. McCann-Erickson Worldwide was the dominant agency in Latin America as well as the leading Western agency in the Asia/Pacific region. Dentsu, with $1.3 billion in gross income, was the top-ranked agency in the Asia/Pacific region. Euro RSCG was the top agency in Europe with a gross income of $677 million.[12] Rankings are based on gross income in dollar amounts that an agency organization derives from the region.

Foreign (Local) Agencies

If the multinational firm adheres to decentralization, giving a good deal of autonomy to foreign managers, the advertiser is significantly more likely to select foreign (local) agencies to coordinate promotional activities for each market in which it operates. The selection of a local agency may even be left to overseas managers. Academics and practitioners who encourage the use of foreign (local) agencies argue that only such agencies can truly appreciate the local culture and, as a result, can develop messages best able to communicate with foreign consumers. A recent survey undertaken by Advertising Age International/Yankelovich Clancy Shulman revealed that while Europeans regularly purchase brands from other countries, when it comes to advertising messages they prefer the home-grown variety.[13] Foreign agencies thus can act as a cultural bridge between the international firm and the local market.[14] Because foreign agencies are often independent and typically smaller in size, they may demonstrate an innovativeness that agency networks cannot—and this may be just what a marketer is looking for. On the downside, utilizing a separate local agency for each foreign market makes coordinating worldwide campaigns quite challenging. International marketers must be aware, however, that the availability of advertising agencies in various markets varies greatly. Some countries, mostly in Africa, have just a single local agency. At the other end of the spectrum are countries such as the United States and the United Kingdom, each with well over five hundred advertising agencies.

A major reason that foreign (local) agencies continue to prosper is nationalism. Many countries resent the role played by foreign firms in their economy and particularly the effect of foreign-produced messages on their culture. Increasingly, countries are mandating local production of advertising messages. For example, Canada, Australia, and Venezuela all have laws banning commercials produced outside the native country, while Peru bans advertising messages containing foreign-inspired content or foreign models in an attempt to enhance its own national culture. Not only do such policies promote the local culture, but they also ensure the good health of the local advertising industry and provide employment for nationals.

Agency Selection Criteria

In addition to considering the organizational approach (centralized, decentralized, or combined), the international marketer should focus on a number of additional criteria in selecting the best agency or agencies to help the firm achieve its set goals:

▶ *Market coverage:* The firm must determine whether the agency or network under consideration provides coverage for all relevant markets.

▶ *Quality of coverage:* The firm must assess the agency's or network's reputation in each market.

▶ *Market research, public relations, and other marketing services:* If the firm needs market research, public relations, or other marketing services in addition to advertising, it must compare what the different agencies offer.

▶ *Relative roles of the firm's in-house advertising department and agency:* Some firms have a large in-house staff that takes on significant portions of advertising campaign development. These firms require fewer services from an advertising agency than do companies that rely on an agency for almost everything relating to advertising.

▶ *Size of the firm's international business:* The smaller the firm's international advertising expenditures, the less likely it will be to divide its expenditures up among numerous agencies. A firm's advertising volume may determine agency choice to assure some minimum level of service. An advertising budget multiplied by a number of markets may be of interest to an international agency even if it is of little interest to a single agency in any one market.

▶ *Image:* The firm must decide whether it wishes to project a national or international image. Desire for local identification and good local citizenship might indicate that the firm should select a number of national agencies rather than one international one.

▶ *Level of involvement:* In joint-venture arrangements the international firm typically shares decision making. The foreign partner may have already established a relationship with a local agency, which would be the decisive factor. In the case of licensing agreements, the licensee is typically responsible for the advertising

TABLE 5.1   Who's on Top in Europe, Latin America, and Asia/Pacific, 1993 (in U.S. million $)

EUROPE Rank/Agency	1993 European Gross Income by Equity	Change from 1992 (%)	1993 European Billings by Equity
1 Euro RSCG	$677.7	−8.1%	$4,752.7
2 Publicis Communication/Publicis-FCB	543.8	−10.8	3,620.5
3 McCann-Erickson Worldwide	372.4	−11.0	2,484.0
4 Ogilvy & Mather Worldwide	328.9	10.1	2,606.0
5 J. Walter Thompson	323.7	0.4	2,317.5
6 Young & Rubicam	323.3	−13.2	2,195.1
7 Lintas Worldwide	311.6	−4.0	2,078.3
8 Grey Advertising	311.5	0.2	2,130.6
9 BBD&O Worldwide	286.8	−8.7	2,068.8
10 DDB Needham Worldwide	284.9	−4.3	2,046.9
11 Saatchi & Saatchi Advertising	256.7	−4.2	2,062.9
12 D'Arcy Masius Benton & Bowles	241.4	−4.8	1,917.3
13 Backer Spielvogel Bates Worldwide	238.1	−10.4	1,905.0
14 BDDP Group	201.6	−5.8	1,171.5
15 Lowe Group	168.6	−5.5	1,122.9
16 Leo Burnett	155.1	−10.9	1,063.3
17 TBWA Advertising	99.6	−6.1	685.1
18 Amando Testa Group	61.0	−17.6	477.6
19 Conquest Europe	54.0	−2.6	455.9
20 Gold Greenlees Trott	36.6	−18.9	282.8
LATIN AMERICA Rank/Agency	1993 Latin America Gross Income by Equity	Change from 1992 (%)	1993 Latin America Billings by Equity
1 McCann-Erickson Worldwide	$150.0	63.6%	$1,000.5
2 J. Walter Thompson	69.3	12.0	419.1
3 Lintas Worldwide	60.8	22.8	405.7
4 Young & Rubicam	60.8	27.0	405.4
5 Leo Burnett	60.7	31.1	404.4
6 Ogilvy & Mather Worldwide	59.9	18.8	337.4
7 Duailibi, Petit, Zaragoza Propaganda	43.6	71.8	166.5
8 BBD&O Worldwide	40.3	6.1	183.1

(continued)

TABLE 5.1 *continued*

LATIN AMERICA (continued) Rank/Agency	1993 Latin America Gross Income by Equity	Change from 1992 (%)	1993 Latin America Billings by Equity
9 Grey Advertising	$34.3	18.4%	$201.6
10 Foote, Cone & Belding Communications	31.5	24.2	205.9
11 D'Arcy Masius Benton & Bowles	13.9	26.1	89.6
12 Saatchi & Saatchi Advertising	10.3	−4.4	82.1
13 Bozell Worldwide	4.2	1.0	33.5
14 DDB Needham Worldwide	3.9	32.7	26.2
15 Lowe Group	3.7	−16.7	24.6
ASIA/PACIFIC Rank/Agency	1993 Asia/ Pacific Gross Income by Equity	Change from 1992 (%)	1993 Asia/ Pacific Billings by Equity
1 Dentsu	$1,302.3	1.5%	$10,116.6
2 Hakuhodo	632.3	11.1	4,670.0
3 McCann-Erickson Worldwide	189.8	11.2	1,266.1
4 Daiko	182.0	3.5	1,395.5
5 Asatsu	171.3	3.3	1,308.8
6 J. Walter Thompson	127.1	15.5	855.8
7 I&S Corp.	105.0	−8.7	804.0
8 Dentsu, Young & Rubicam Partnerships	103.9	−2.0	691.8
9 Dai-Ichi Kikaku	103.7	−9.1	858.4
10 Cheil Communications	95.0	−5.5	414.0
11 Backer Spielvogel Bates Worldwide	90.8	9.2	736.0
12 Ogilvy & Mather Worldwide	81.7	12.0	534.8
13 Leo Burnett	80.7	2.3	537.9
14 DDB Needham Worldwide	65.9	8.3	439.5
15 Lintas Worldwide	58.6	3.7	391.1
16 Chuo Senko	51.9	3.0	370.7
17 Foote, Cone & Belding Communications	47.3	−17.6	312.5
18 Saatchi & Saatchi Advertising	46.1	14.9	369.0
19 D'Arcy Masius Benton & Bowles	45.2	11.9	269.9
20 Grey Advertising	33.5	8.5	228.7

SOURCE: Laurel Wentz et al., "Asian Gains Lift McCann as Saatchi Shops Suffer," *Advertising Age*, May 16, 1994, p. I1+. Reprinted by permission of the publisher.

131

function. Selling through distributors also reduces the degree of control the international firm has over promotional efforts. Generally, international marketers can choose agencies only for the advertising paid for by their firms. If a firm is engaging in a cooperative program with its distributors, its influence in agency selection may be somewhat greater.[15]

An international marketer may use different types of agencies for different purposes. For example, a recent study of Fortune 500 firms revealed that the choice of agency employed may vary depending on the stage of the advertising campaign. With regards to campaign development, the study showed that 17.8 percent of the firms used the company's in-house agency; 23.3 percent employed a foreign subsidiary's in-house agency; 24.5 percent turned to an international agency with overseas offices; and 34.4 percent selected the services of a foreign advertising agency. The numbers differed slightly with regards to campaign placement. Here, only 14.4 percent of the firms used the company's in-house agency; 27.8 percent sought out the services of a foreign subsidiary's in-house agency; 22.2 percent used an international agency with overseas branches for placement services; and 35.6 percent requested assistance from a foreign agency. Several of the Fortune 500 firms indicated that they used more than one type of organization, assigning campaign preparation and placement to different agencies.[16]

Marketing and Advertising Strategy Options

An in-depth investigation of successful worldwide marketers of consumer goods conducted at the request of the J. Walter Thompson agency by an independent research firm addresses the issue of control of the international advertising function and the question of standardization versus specialization of advertising and marketing efforts. On the question of centralism versus decentralism, reports Harold Clark, the "respondents come down squarely in the middle: the successful companies combine vision at the top, in-depth knowledge of each local market and the ability to merge these two perspectives in an organization culture that respects each perspective."[17] The individuals running these successful international companies noted that a global selling strategy is an absolute requirement for survival due to several factors. As Clark states: "First, the cost of new product technology forces manufacturers to look beyond their borders for a sufficient market to earn an efficient return on investment. The ability of competitors quickly and dev-

	STRONGLY AGREE (%)	STRONGLY DISAGREE (%)
To implement effective global marketing it is absolutely essential:		
To find the right balance between headquarters and local control	100%	0%
To stimulate the right degree of communication and exchange on an ongoing basis	100	0
To find people with the right talent, experience, and philosophy to carry out effective global marketing	96	4
To develop products that make sense as global brands	86	14
To get company people worldwide to believe in the global marketing approach and support it fully	82	18
To train and develop people to be effective global marketers	82	18
To establish the right organizational structure worldwide	82	18
To integrate the marketing research function on a global basis so that information obtained from national markets is comparable	68	32
To find an ad agency network that can be an effective partner in carrying out a global strategy	54	46
To establish packaging, pricing, and product specifications that make sense on a global basis	54	46
To develop advertising that can be effective on a global basis	46	54

TABLE 5.2 Ranking the Elements of Effective Global Marketing

SOURCE: Private study by Warren Keegan Associates Inc. for J. Walter Thompson. Study results published in Harold F. Clark, "Consumers and Corporate Values: Yet Another View on Global Marketing," *International Journal of Advertising*, 6, 1987, pp. 29–42.

astatingly to copy product advantages and features creates this pressure on innovators to deliver a fast return on their own innovations. They naturally look to as many markets as possible to provide that return."[18]

The study asked respondents to rank a number of elements of global marketing in order of importance. Their responses are shown in Table 5.2. Clark interprets the survey data in this way: "It is not the execution of a single idea that is vital in the minds of successful manufacturers. They do not even need a single global network—the assumption is the best agency in each local market-place is what is required."[19]

These same successful executives were asked the following questions: (1) "With an existing global product/brand, which parts of the marketing mix would your company be the most reluctant to change for a local country?" and (2) "What is the headquarters role and the local role in determining the final decision on each of these points?" Responses to these questions are outlined in Table 5.3.

TABLE 5.3 Executives' Ranking of Changes to Marketing Mix Elements and Influences on the Decision

	ATTITUDE		DOMINANT ROLE	
MARKETING MIX ELEMENT	Resist Change	Readily Change	Headquarters	Local
Brand name and logo	85%	7%	82%	0%
Product specifications	68	14	57	7
Product positioning and strategy	43	29	50	14
Packaging (surface design)	39	21	43	14
Advertising strategy	32	35	25	35
Packaging (functional)	25	39	21	46
Pricing	14	64	17	68
Advertising execution	14	54	11	61
Public relations program	11	57	7	61
Package size	7	64	10	64
Percentage of budget allocated to ad/sales promotion/publicity for a given brand	7	64	18	54
Types of distribution outlet used	3	82	4	86
Trade promotion programs	0	86	4	86
Types of specific media used	0	82	4	82
Media strategy	0	79	4	71
Consumer promotion program	0	78	4	79

SOURCE: Private study conducted by Warren Keegan Associates Inc. for J. Walter Thompson. Study results published in Harold F. Clark, Jr., "Consumer and Corporate Values: Yet Another View on Global Marketing," *International Journal of Advertising*, 6, 1987, pp. 29–42.

The one element these marketers indicated they would be most reluctant to change was the product's brand name or logo. Almost one-third indicated they would consider changing products to meet local needs, while a surprising 14 percent noted they would be "readily" willing to do so. It may well be that those manufacturers willing to consider product modification have a greater chance of success in global markets than those with a less flexible approach. Over 85 percent of the respondents revealed that they would not resist a change in advertising execution, and almost two-thirds noted that such decisions were generally made at the local level. Clearly, one-world messages are not nearly so important to these marketers as the literature would lead readers to believe.

The framework outlined in Exhibit 5.2 can assist international marketers in assessing marketing and advertising strategy options. It highlights that globalization of both marketing and advertising should be viewed on a continuum. As the exhibit shows, marketers must examine each step in a

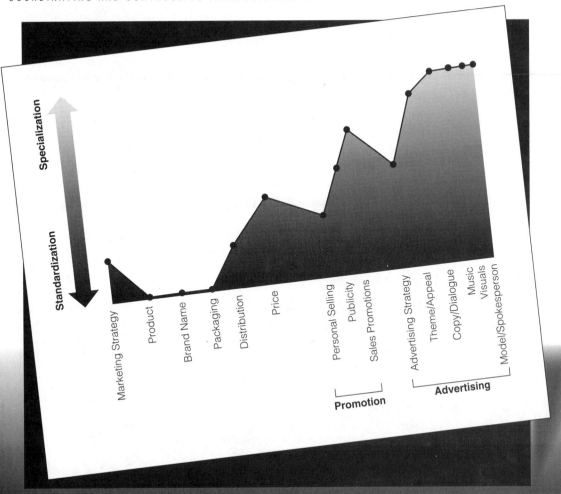

EXHIBIT 5.2 Strategic Options in the Marketing Mix: An Illustrative Mixed Strategy

SOURCE: Adapted from Susan P. Douglas and Yoram Wind, "The Myth of Globalization," *Columbia Journal of World Business*, 22(4), Winter 1987, pp. 19–29.

marketing program, taking into consideration the specific product to be marketed as well as the given marketing environment (characterized by its demographic, economic, political-legal, and cultural profile). Only then can the marketer evaluate the potential outcomes of steps taken toward the standardization or specialization end of the continuum. The framework can assist international marketers and advertisers in thinking globally with regards to marketing and advertising strategy yet acting locally as market circumstances warrant.

Summary

Clearly, global marketing and the role of international advertising in selling products in foreign markets is a complex issue. Marketers must decide whether to use a centralized, decentralized, or combination approach with regards to the coordination of promotional programs. A firm planning on selling products abroad may rely on its own in-house agency or on the in-house agency of a foreign subsidiary. Or a marketer may turn to the firm's domestic agency for assistance in preparing marketing communications for foreign markets. Use of a foreign (local) agency or an international agency/network are additional options. A framework outlining the strategic options in the marketing mix can assist the international marketer in making creative decisions for foreign markets—the focus of Chapter 6.

Additional Readings

Bartlett, Christopher A., and Sumantra Ghoshal. (November/December 1986). "Tap Your Subsidiaries for Global Reach." *Harvard Business Review,* 64, pp. 87–94.

Boddewyn, J. J., Robin Soehl, and Jacques Picard. (November/December 1986). "Standardization in International Marketing: Is Ted Levitt in Fact Right?" *Business Horizons,* pp. 69–75.

Kanso, Ali. (1991). "The Use of Advertising Agencies for Foreign Markets: Decentralized Decisions and Localized Approaches?" *International Journal of Advertising,* 10, pp. 129–136.

Kirpalani, V. H., Michel Laroche, and Rene Darmon. (1988). "Role of Headquarters Control by Multinationals in International Advertising Decisions." *International Journal of Advertising,* 7, pp. 323–333.

Levitt, Theodore. (May/June 1983). "The Globalization of Markets." *Harvard Business Review,* pp. 92–102.

Notes

1. Kirpalani, V. H., Michel Laroche, and Rene Darmon, "Role of Headquarters Control by Multinationals in International Advertising Decisions," *International Journal of Advertising,* 7, 1988, pp. 323–333.

2. Bartlett, Christopher A., and Sumantra Ghoshal, "Tap Your Subsidiaries for Global Reach," *Harvard Business Review,* 64, November/December 1986, pp. 87–94.

3. Ibid.

4. Roth, Robert F., *International Marketing Communications* (Chicago, IL: Crain Books, 1982), pp. 290–293.

5. Levin, Gary, "Ads Going Global: Marketers Cross Borders with New Efforts," *Advertising Age,* July 22, 1991, p. 4.

6. Kanso, Ali, "The Use of Advertising Agencies for Foreign Markets: Decentralized Decisions and Localized Approaches?" *International Journal of Advertising,* 10, 1991, pp. 129–136.

7. Kilburn, David, "Dentsu Expanding into Middle East, Europe," *Advertising Age,* September 7, 1992, p. 4.

8. Levitt, Theodore, "Globalization of Markets," *Harvard Business Review,* May/June 1983, pp. 92–102.

9. Wentz, Laurel, "Saatchi Thinks Global with International Bonuses," *Advertising Age,* June 3, 1991, p. 49.

10. Johnson, Bradley, "Apple Wants Unified Worldwide Image," *Advertising Age,* April 12, 1993, p. 2.

11. Wentz, Laurel, "Global Brands: Shops Flourish in 90's: Decade of Alignment," *Advertising Age,* September 20, 1993, p. I1+.

12. Wentz, Laurel, Elena Bowes, Andrew Geddes, and Todd Pruzan, "Asian Gains Lift McCann as Saatchi Shops Suffer," *Advertising Age,* May 16, 1994, p. I1+.

13. Giges, Nancy, "Europeans Buy Outside Goods, but Like Local Ads," *Advertising Age,* April 27, 1992, p. I1.

14. Terpstra, Vern, *International Dimensions of Marketing* (Boston: PWS-Kent, 1988).

15. Terpstra, Vern, *International Marketing,* 4th ed. (Chicago: Dryden Press, 1987), pp. 432–433.

16. Kanso, "The Use of Advertising Agencies," pp. 129–136.

17. Clark, Jr., Harold F., "Consumer and Corporate Values: Yet Another View on Global Marketing," *International Journal of Advertising,* 6, 1987, pp. 29–42.

18. Ibid.

19. Ibid., p. 39.

CHAPTER 6

Creative Strategy and Execution

C harles Frazer offers a generally accepted definition of *creative strategy:* "a policy or guiding principle which specifies the general nature and character of messages to be designed. Strategy states the means selected to achieve the desired audience effect over the term of the campaign."[1] One of the most important strategic considerations is whether to standardize advertising worldwide or to adapt it to the specific needs of each market. Scholars and practitioners alike are divided with regards to the benefits and disadvantages associated with each strategic approach. It should be reiterated, too, that this debate carries a variety of labels. Standardized campaigns have also been referred to as globalized and universal in the literature; specialized campaigns have been called localized, adapted, and even customized. In this chapter we will use the terms interchangeably in examining standardization versus specialization as it relates to creativity in advertising. We will also touch on the creative development and production of advertisements, examining the use of advertising appeals and both verbal and nonverbal aspects of commercial messages.

Strategic Decisions

Standardization of Advertising

An increasing number of advertising and marketing executives agree with Harvard's Theodore Levitt that the needs and desires of consumers around the world are growing ever more homogenized. These experts contend that the world is one large market and that regional, national, and even international differences are at best superficial. Therefore, the consumer may well be satisfied with similar products and services. There's no arguing with the fact that, today, Campbell soup, Crest toothpaste, and Camel cigarettes are at home in markets around the globe. Levitt went on to note that not only would consumers around the globe be satisfied with similar products, but advertisers could sell them with similar messages.[2] Narrowly defined, *standardized advertising* refers to messages that are used internationally with virtually no change in theme, illustration, or copy—except, perhaps, for translation where needed.

Standardization of international campaigns generally takes one of two routes. One option is to adopt a campaign deemed successful in the national or domestic market for a firm's foreign markets. Esso's "Put a tiger in your tank" campaign is a classic example of a promotional effort that proved effective in the United States and was subsequently exported to numerous other countries. Another option is a preplanned effort to develop a campaign for use in multiple markets. For example, an international task force—with talent from New York, Paris, and London—was assigned to work on developing the centrally conceived global campaign for Chivas Regal discussed in Chapter 5.

Advertisers and agencies alike perceive very real benefits associated with this approach. For one thing, coordination and control of marketing and promotional programs is greatly simplified, and as a result, foreign campaigns can be implemented much more quickly. This simplification may assist in faster product rollouts. Anthony Rutigliano notes: "As product life cycles shrink, companies will be hungry for quicker worldwide product roll outs, leaving less time to develop scores of local or national advertising campaigns."[3]

In addition, fewer marketing and advertising personnel are required at the local level to administer advertising campaigns developed at headquarters than are required to customize promotional efforts. Staff reductions lead to cost savings, and advertising production costs are reduced dramatically. It's certainly much less expensive to produce a single campaign for a number of markets than it is to produce a separate campaign for each specific market. Similarly, the cost associated with developing one television commercial for the European market and translating the dialogue or dubbing the spot into seven languages is significantly less than it is to develop seven separate television spots. McCann-Erickson claims to have saved Coca-Cola over $90 million in production costs over a twenty-year period by producing worldwide commercials.

Further, good ideas can be exploited. If a campaign has proven successful in one market, there may be no need to "reinvent the wheel" in others. Kenneth Robbins, deputy chairman at SSC&B Lintas Worldwide, notes that really good ideas are extremely hard to find. As an example, he shares his experiences with Snuggle, introduced in Germany in 1970 as a liquid fabric softener that made clothes incredibly soft. The big idea was the use of a teddy bear as a spokesperson. Research revealed that the depth of feeling for teddy bears was enormous—the stuffed animals personified security, comfort, love, and, most importantly, softness. Within one year of completing national distribution, the brand claimed a 26 percent market share. The brand was subsequently introduced into twelve additional countries, and the teddy bear was dearly loved throughout Europe and the United States.[4]

Finally, a consistent international brand or company image can be achieved. A uniform image serves to reduce message confusion in areas where there is media overlap or a good deal of cross-border travel—such as is the case in many European countries.

Numerous firms have adopted the standardized approach. For example, L'Oreal's subsidiary Helena Rubinstein is rolling out Golden Beauty, a line of seventeen sun-care products in eighty-three countries backed by a single campaign, even though, writes Elena Bowes: "Each country has different obsessions—Germans want to tan very quickly and darkly, Spaniards are obsessed with wrinkles, and Italians are concerned with the beauty of their skin."[5] The campaign was developed by a single agency—FCA International. Shiseido is launching its new perfume in twenty-five countries in Europe, Asia, and the Americas. Although the advertising campaign was developed by Shiseido's in-house agency, Shiseido is using local agencies for media placement.[6]

Products Suitable for Standardization

Standardization of advertising is viewed by many marketers as a challenging task. Clearly, however, some international marketers are successfully employing this approach. Progress has been made in understanding under what conditions standardized advertising works best and for which products global campaigns are particularly well suited.[7]

Products for Which Audiences Are Essentially Similar Young people in the United States, Europe, and Southeast Asia have similar levels of education and disposable income and are heavily influenced by international communications media. These similarities may be sufficient to make the youth market one for which standardized messages might be appropriate. A recent study found the life styles and spending habits of people age 14–34 around the world to be quite similar. Conducted in Australia, Brazil, Germany, Japan, the United Kingdom, and the United States, the study revealed that the average person surveyed spent about $60 per week on discretionary items, ranging from a low of $56 in the United Kingdom to a high of $89 in Brazil. Respondents' consumption of a variety of items over a three-month period was also measured. Rates of consumption of soft drinks, beer, and cigarettes were found to be quite similar among all respondents, while young adults in the United States and United Kingdom were more likely to have purchased athletic footwear than their counterparts in other countries.[8]

Exhibit 6.1 shows advertisements for Esprit (a garment manufacturer appealing to young people) appearing in the United States and in Germany. The same campaign was used for both markets; here, we see two different executions.

Products That Can Be Promoted Via Image Campaign "Many of the packaged goods products that account for much of the advertising dollars spent in the United States are difficult to differentiate on a functional . . . basis. Thus, creative strategy used to sell these products is based on the development of a strong, memorable identity or meaning for the brand through image advertising."[9] Image advertising has been used to promote a variety of products and services, including liquor, soft drinks, perfumes, clothing, airlines, and financial services. For an example of a successful international image campaign, see the Martell advertisement in Exhibit 6.2.

Luxury Products Targeting Upper-Class Markets Luxury goods have been identified as a product type particularly amenable to the standardized approach. Such highly priced items are often sold on the basis of their ability to enhance social status. Exhibit 6.3 shows an advertisement for Tag Heuer watches (made in Switzerland) that appeared in U.S., Australian, and Japanese publications and that targeted upper-class markets.

High-Tech Products Standardized messages may be appropriate for products coming to the world market for the first time, because such goods generally are not steeped in the cultural heritage of a particular country. Examples of products in this category include calculators, VCRs, camcorders, and computers. Recent research among personal computer and software companies shows a definite trend toward standardization in advertising strategy. Bob Nelson explains: "High tech products are purchased and used in the same manner everywhere, are most often standardized and utilitarian, share a what would you do?

there'd
be no
guns
no guns
at all

meredith snaider, new york

tell us what you'd do. write to esprit, p.o. box 77909, san francisco, ca 94107.
for more information about gun control write The Center to Prevent Handgun Violence,
1225 eye street, nw #1150, washington, d.c. 20005.

was würdest du tun?

nicht nur gegen
rassismus, sondern
für
die vielfalt der kulturen

nach dem erfolgreichen gemeinsamen musikleben in ökologischen jugend-camps von estland bis ungarn, von frankreich bis
bulgarien hatte billy boyd (27), schottland, den traum vom young musicians europe, der kreation eines multikulturellen
musikbaums, in dem junge umweltorientierte künstler aus ost und west gemeinsam musik machen, aber in ihren eigenen
sprachen singen. in diesem sommer wurde billy's traum wahr, ein internationaler friedenszirkus wird diesen traum
weitertragen: mit jongleuren, theater und feuerschluckern, sowie kreativen aktionen, über gewaltfreiheit und friedensarbeit.

friedenszirkus, postbox 780, 6130 at sittard, niederlande

was würdest du tun? esprit de corp., vogelsanger weg 49, 40436 düsseldorf

EXHIBIT 6.1 U.S. and German Esprit Advertisements

THE ART OF THE TRIBUTE.

EXHIBIT 6.2 Image Campaign for Martell Appearing Internationally

Reprinted with permission of Joseph E. Seagram & Sons, Inc.

EXHIBIT 6.3 Advertisement for Tag Heuer Watches Appearing
in U.S., Australian, and Japanese Magazines

Used by permission.

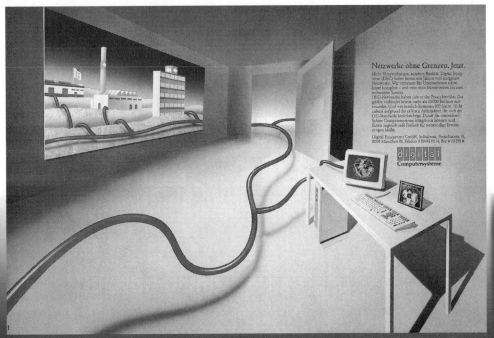

EXHIBIT 6.4 Digital Computer Systems Advertisement
Appearing in a German Magazine

Reprinted by permission of Digital Equipment Corp.

common technical language and use information appeals."[10] Exhibit 6.4
shows a Digital Computer Systems ad appearing in a German magazine.

Products with a Nationalistic Flavor If a country has a reputation for producing high-quality goods of a certain type or in a specific field, those goods may
well be sold via global advertising messages. Examples of this category include Beck's beer from Germany, Swatch watches from Switzerland, Bur-
gundy wine from France, and the Lexus automobile from Japan. Likewise,
products from the United States have been sold on the basis of their country
of origin—Levi's blue jeans, Coca-Cola, and McDonald's food all are promoted as fundamentally American. Exhibit 6.5 shows a Levi's advertisement
appearing in a German magazine.

Note that the benefits of employing a standardized approach, whatever
the product, accrue to the firm using that approach—not to its customers
around the world. For example, consumers of laundry detergent in Bavaria,
Germany, are not likely to be overly impressed that they are being exposed

EXHIBIT 6.5 Levi's Advertisement Appearing in a German Magazine

to the same television campaign as their counterparts in Beverton, Oregon; however, both groups do care about purchasing a detergent that will get their laundry clean.

Specialization of Advertising

While globalization has been hailed as the new wave in marketing and advertising by some, others contend that while people's basic needs and desires may well be the same all around the world, how they go about satisfying them may vary from country to country. The "global market" still consists of hundreds of nations, each with its own customs, life styles, economies, and buying habits, and marketers are urged to take these differences into account.[11,12] Advertising has been positioned as one of the most difficult of the marketing mix elements to standardize. Skeptics note that it is impossible to ascertain whether the success of brands such as Coke, Pepsi, Marlboro, and McDonald's was due to their internationalism or not. The fact is, claims Greg Harris, "One cannot prove in any scientific way . . . the specific contribution that advertising integration has made to the international sales performance of these brands."[13] In other words, these brands potentially might have been even more successful had the promotional messages been adapted for each market.

In the case of a fully adapted or "specialized" campaign, the advertiser localizes message content for several countries or even for each country in which the firm operates. Proponents of specialization argue that by concentrating on similarities in geographically divided marketplaces, firms may ignore or oversimplify many significant differences. The primary benefit of specialization is simply that it allows for differences in the international environment. In terms of demographics, for example, the proportion of individuals attending school or having completed various levels of education affects message development and the media employed to disseminate those messages. In many southern African nations, illiteracy rates are particularly high. In these markets an advertising medium was developed that would be considered quite foreign in the eyes of a Madison Avenue advertising executive: Boats travel up and down rivers to broadcast product messages to folks standing on shore.

With regards to the political-legal environment, a variety of political issues may present problems with regards to marketing communications. For example, attitudes toward advertising may differ from one market to the next. The Indonesian government commissioned a study of the impact of television and then proceeded to ban TV for a period of ten years. The government decided that television—and TV ads—could potentially promote consumerism and aggravate tensions between the rich and the poor.[14]

In addition, laws and regulations imposed on the advertising industry differ among nations. Legal and regulatory considerations will be addressed in detail in Chapter 9. For now, we'll focus on two areas to demonstrate that the legal environment has a direct impact on the development of international advertising campaigns. First, the content or type of creative approach that may be employed can vary widely. For example, France does not permit comparative advertising while Germany frowns on it and requires that a rigorous fairness test be passed before comparative claims are allowed. International advertisers face many more hurdles than just the use of comparative claims in developing messages for use in multiple markets. Lu Biscuits had to develop twenty different versions of a TV spot to satisfy all the legal requirements necessary to market their cookies in Europe. In Italy children are not allowed to look at the camera while speaking of the product. In Austria and Germany children must always appear in the company of adults. In the Netherlands a child may eat chocolate on the screen—provided a toothbrush is also shown.

Second, the media that advertisers are permitted to employ can also vary widely. The media scene abroad does not resemble that in the United States. For instance, Sweden and Norway still do not permit radio or television advertising. Denmark finally began phasing in this type of advertising on a limited basis as recently as 1987. And in Germany, even though TV advertising is allowed, it is severely restricted—limited to twenty minutes per day and typically aired only in the evenings (5:00–8:00 P.M.) in blocks of five–seven minutes that do not interrupt programming.

As noted in previous chapters, cultural differences also can pose formidable hurdles to standardization. Erno Laszlo, an American skin-care firm, tried from 1982 to 1985 to sell its products identically around the world. In contrast to the success L'Oreal experienced in utilizing a standardized approach, Laszlo found it impossible to sell the identical skin-care regimen to fair-skinned Australians, swarthy Italians, and delicate Asians. In Asia, in particular, skin-care customs varied widely from region to region.[15] Just as skin-care habits differ, so do eating customs. McDonald's sells beer along with its hamburgers in Germany, and wine in France. Australian outlets offer mutton pot pie, and in the Philippines, McDonald's serves up McSpaghetti to compete with the local noodle houses that are popular with the locals. McDonald's joint-venture partners, who run the firm's franchises abroad, have complete responsibility for local marketing.[16]

If a specific product's brand name differs from one market to the next, the international marketer may have no choice but to employ a specialized approach to advertising. For example, Unilever markets a cleaning liquid called "Vif" in Switzerland, "Viss" in Germany, "Jif" in Britain and Greece, and "Cif" in France.[17] Given that each of these brands is well established in its respective country, standardized messages would not prove particularly effective. The Japanese company Kao is entering its first nonoriental detergent market with the introduction in Australia of the laundry product that leads the Japanese market. The concentrated detergent is marketed as "Attack" in Japan, Singapore, Hong Kong, Taiwan, Malaysia, and Thailand, but it was renamed "Bio-z" for the Australian market. "Taking account of history, we felt the name Attack was not suitable for a Japanese product in Australia; we felt it might sound a little too aggressive. In any case, rights to that name are owned by another company in Australia," a Kao spokesman explained.[18]

Finally, if a specific foreign market is in a different stage of market development than the U.S. market, a given product may find itself in a different stage of the life cycle in that country. For instance, the Polaroid Swinger camera was said to have failed in France because the company pursued the same strategy there as in the United States when the two markets were in different stages of development. The U.S. market was in the mature stage whereas the French market was in the introductory stage.[19] In some markets an international firm will compete against other international marketers; in other markets the competition may be purely national. Sound advertising strategy in one market will not necessarily be appropriate in another market with a different competitive environment.

A number of firms that adopted the global approach have since soured on the concept. In the early 1980s Parker Pen was manufacturing about five hundred styles of pens in eighteen plants. Local offices in over a hundred and fifty countries were responsible for creating their own advertising and packaging. Putting Theodore Levitt's theory into practice, Parker consolidated to one hundred pen styles manufactured in only eight plants. It also hired a single advertising agency to create a global advertising campaign, which was then translated into myriad local languages. However, Parker did not anticipate the resistance of local managers, who resented that the U.S. firm was mandating what the advertising should be and which advertising agency they should employ. Profits plunged almost immediately—Parker had a $12-million loss for fiscal 1985, and the firm almost went broke. By 1986 a group of its British managers had bought the pen business. Today, the company is once again profitable, and local managers are allowed to select advertising for their own markets.[20]

Previously committed to a standardized approach, Colgate-Palmolive likewise shifted back to a country-by-country advertising strategy in 1990. As part of the move toward specialization, an approach intended to be a basic element of the firm's long-term growth plans, Colgate-Palmolive decided to decentralize the advertising function and turn responsibilities over to individual operating units. All future advertising will be tailored specifically to local markets and countries.[21]

Most recently, the House of Chanel has come to grips with the fact that global advertising doesn't always work. The fragrance company's current Chanel No. 5 campaign features French actress Carole Bouquet seductively whispering hate words to an unseen man. While very popular in Europe, the spot was nixed for U.S. release after four months of test marketing. Apparently, notes Penelope Rowlands, U.S. audiences associated the words of hate with unacceptable violence, "proving that global advertising may not be what it has been cracked up to be."[22]

The Standardization/Specialization Continuum

Examples of effective standardized campaigns clearly do exist, just as do examples of ineffective ones. Similarly, there are numerous examples of both more and less successful specialized campaigns. The pros and cons of both approaches to international advertising will continue to be debated. Many companies have moved away from viewing standardization as an all-or-nothing phenomenon and instead have chosen to employ a modified approach—standardizing some elements of their promotional plan while specializing others. The question is, in fact, one of degree, with standardization and specialization at opposite ends of a continuum, and with many "shades" of adaptation between the two extremes.

An excellent example of this modified approach is a campaign developed by Coca-Cola. Several years ago, the firm's advertising agency, McCann-Erickson Worldwide, created an award-winning commercial showing Pittsburgh Steeler football star "Mean" Joe Greene giving his jersey to a young boy who had offered him a bottle of Coke after a tough game. However, the advertisement could not be used outside the United States for two reasons. First, Joe Greene was unknown in foreign markets, and second, American football is not nearly so popular abroad as it is in the United States. Rather than abandon the concept, the agency adapted it to other countries by creating advertisements featuring stars of the more popular international sport of soccer. Advertisements in South America used the popular Argentinian player Diego Maradona, and those in Asia used Thai star Niwat as the heroes of the spots.

The Polaroid One-Step provides another example of a campaign that is neither completely standardized nor fully specialized. The One-Step was introduced in the United States in the early 1980s with the unique selling proposition that it was the "simplest camera in the world." The creative approach employed a well-known couple in the United States: James Garner and Mariette Hartley. Four months after introduction, the One-Step became a best-seller. Based on such positive results, Polaroid and its agency launched the camera internationally by adopting both the same positioning strategy and the same advertising campaign worldwide. Fortunately, the agency, Doyle, Dane & Bernbach, pretested the spot for recall, comprehension, and knowledge in several European markets. The research revealed that while the unique selling proposition was well accepted and credible, Garner and Hartley were virtually unknown. In response, the agency decided to keep the U.S. creative concept overall, but to search out local presenters with equal popularity abroad. The solution was to use actors H. J. Felmy and K. Eickelbaum for the German market, R. Briar and F. Kendall for the United Kingdom, and an individual—Sacha Distel—for France. The campaign subsequently received the highest advertising recall and brand awareness scores in Polaroid's history, and the One-Step became the best-selling camera in all three countries.

Execution Decisions

If strategy refers to "what is said" in a campaign, then execution refers to "how it is said." The advertising strategy adopted for a specific international campaign thus guides the execution—selection of advertising appeals as well as copy and illustrations.[23]

Advertising Appeals

According to George and Michael Belch, advertising appeals "refer to the basis or approach used in the advertisement to attract attention or interest consumers and/or to influence their feelings toward the product, service or cause."[24] The advertising appeals employed should be consistent with the values and tastes of the target audience. Indeed, a recent survey found that, on the whole, consumers seem to prefer domestically generated commercials. Foreign-produced advertisements did not appeal to more than half of European respondents in the three categories surveyed: taste, product differentiation, and likability. The English and French were rated as the most closed cultures toward foreign ads, while the Italians and Germans were rated as the most receptive.[25] This reinforces the view that advertising carries its culture with it. It is not surprising, then, that commercial messages created in various markets differ significantly. Note Abhijit Biswas and colleagues: "Cross cultural differences in advertising expression [are] a growing and important area of research, primarily because an understanding of these differences is needed in order to take on the creative challenge of communicating to people of diverse cultural backgrounds."[26]

Japan offers a prime example of a country that differs significantly from the United States in terms of culture and creative message content. Japanese print messages tend to employ indirect communications, rely on soft sell and status appeals, and demonstrate a greater respect for the elderly than do advertisements in the United States.[27] This contrasts sharply with the American emphasis on rational appeals with a focus on presenting features and benefits in order to showcase a product's superiority. In Japanese messages, write C. Anthony DiBenedetto and colleagues, "The goal is to transfer intended feelings to the consumer rather than detailing specific product attributes and quality. This is because the latter approach can be perceived as an insult to the consumers' intelligence concerning their ability to make a sound judgement about their company preference."[28] Recall the very soft sell approach employed in the Japanese mayonnaise advertisement shown in Exhibit 4.8.

This very preference for soft sell and indirect means of communication hinders the effectiveness of some creative techniques commonly used in the West. For example, Procter & Gamble's Cheer detergent was initially advertised in Japan using slice-of-life TV commercials similar to those used in the United States. Though quite innocuous to American viewers, the spots were found in a survey to be among the "most hated" in Japan. Cheer's initially poor sales were also attributed to this campaign, which was quickly replaced with a new series.[29] Table 6.1 lists typically American appeals that don't work well in Japan as well as recommendations for those that communicate effectively to Japanese consumers.

TABLE 6.1   Typical Advertising Appeals for the U.S. Versus the Japanese Markets

<table>
<tr><th colspan="2">UNITED STATES</th></tr>
<tr><th>Appeal</th><th>Explanation</th></tr>
<tr>
<td>"Be the first person in your neighborhood to own the Frammis washing machine . . ."</td>
<td>Japanese buyers would never want to be out of step with their neighbors, nor would they wish to appear to be superior. This is considered to be very bad taste.</td>
</tr>
<tr>
<td>"FREE . . . this $4.96 volume . . . no strings attached . . ."</td>
<td>The average Japanese buyer would simply not believe that something is given for nothing.</td>
</tr>
<tr>
<td>"Less work for mother . . ."</td>
<td>The Japanese housewife wants her family to know that she has personally prepared every bite of food. TV dinners are virtually unknown in Japan. Several years ago, food processors were introduced in Japan. They were a dismal failure. Why? Because Japanese housewives want to do all that chopping and blending by hand. Anything less would be considered an insult to the family.</td>
</tr>
<tr>
<td>"Act today—and save 10 percent off this price of this brand-new model hi-fi phonograph . . ."</td>
<td>Price is not considered a significant appeal to the Japanese buyer. They are more concerned with the dependability and reliability of the company.</td>
</tr>
<tr>
<td>"Here's a great way to express your individuality and set yourself apart from the crowd . . ."</td>
<td>The Japanese consider individuality to be a bad thing. There is a saying that Japanese children learn—almost from the first day of school: The nail that stands the highest is the nail that gets hit by the hammer.</td>
</tr>
<tr>
<td>"Now . . . for the very first time . . ."</td>
<td>In America, a phrase like this would be very appealing. In Japan, it is guaranteed to lose customers. The Japanese buyer simply does not want to be first to own something.</td>
</tr>
</table>

(continued)

As highlighted in the continuum of compared cultures shown in Exhibit 4.5, the United States and Japan fall at the "maximum sociocultural differences" end of the scale. Yet, significant differences in message content also are found when comparing the advertising of European countries with that of the United States. While France and the United States have a good deal in common, the advertisements produced in each country are quite distinct. One study found that French advertisements resorted more to emotional appeals and contained fewer information cues than did American advertisements. Sex appeals also were employed more frequently—a finding consistent with the perception that France is a more sexually liberated country than the United States. Overall, French advertisements employed humor appeals

TABLE 6.1 *continued*

JAPAN

Appeal	Explanation
"Our company has been in business for over 35 years . . ."	Stability is considered a great virtue in Japan—and this appeal is viewed as very important to the people of Japan.
"Our TV set is guaranteed to last longer than any other TV set on the market . . ."	Reliability is the major value that the Japanese look for when buying a product.
"Our company has the strength of the Rock of Gibraltar . . ."	Image is very important to the Japanese.
"This is an idea whose time has come . . ."	The Japanese are great believers in timing. Even if an idea seems incredibly "hot," they will wait—until the time is right. Once they are committed to a course of action, it would take wild horses to get them to change.
"Buy this product . . . it will help bring greater harmony to your life . . . at home and at the office . . ."	Beyond a doubt, this is the most appealing thing you could be saying to the Japanese. They are intensely concerned about their human relations. Any product that claims to improve human relations is guaranteed to sell in Japan.

SOURCE: Adapted from Milton Pierce, "Direct Response in Japan," *Direct Marketing,* November 1986, p. 160. Reprinted by permission.

to a greater extent than did their American counterparts. Based on the results of this study, the researchers suggest that multinational corporations advertising in France should be aware of these differences and adapt their messages accordingly.[30]

Likewise, despite the many cultural similarities between the United States and the United Kingdom, another investigation found substantial differences between American and British television advertising as well. British ads tend to make frequent use of features inherent in British culture, such as the persistence of class divisions and the affection for eccentricity, and often employ understated humor. In addition, they generally contain less information, employ a softer-sell approach, and attempt to entertain rather than educate the consumer.[31] Thus, Terence Nevett suggests, "American advertisers operating in that country should be wary of introducing different styles that may strike a discordant note. The current preoccupation with standardized global campaigns might lead to superficial consideration being given to subtle but important cultural differences."[32] Indeed, the findings of each of these studies should give pause to practitioners who advocate a complete standardization of commercial messages for international markets.

Verbal Communication: Copy and Dialogue

In Chapter 4 we addressed the cultural aspects of verbal communication. Here, we will focus on challenges in the translation of advertising copy and dialogue. As Barney Raffield points out: "Seemingly harmless brand names and advertising phrases can take on unintended or hidden meanings when translated into other languages, but such errors can make a marketer look somewhat like a buffoon to foreign consumers."[33] For example, Ford Motor goofed when it named its low-cost Third World truck *Fiera*, which means "ugly old woman" in Spanish. Market research showed that American Motor's *Matador* name meant virility and excitement, but when the car was introduced in Puerto Rico, it was discovered that the word meant "killer"—an unfortunate choice for Puerto Rico, which has an unusually high traffic fatality rate. An ad in a Middle Eastern country featured an automobile's new suspension system that, in translation, said the car was "suspended from the ceiling."[34] The list of blunders continues. Ford stumbled again when it introduced its Comet automobile to Mexican consumers as the *Caliente*—a Mexican slang term for "streetwalker." Sunbeam attempted to persuade German women to purchase its hair curling iron—with the innocuous-sounding name *Mist Stick*. Unfortunately, in German the word *mist* means "manure," and consumers understandably had little use or desire for a "manure wand."[35] While many of these bloopers were quickly corrected and resulted in little more than a temporary embarrassment to the company, in other instances the errors were not caught and emended so quickly and led to long-term losses of sales, market credibility, and international goodwill.

The disasters just cited should make advertisers aware that the most effective translation for advertising purposes is not likely to be the most literal one. The task of the advertising translator is to translate thoughts and ideas rather than words. Yuri Radzievsky, president of Euroamerica Translations, notes with amazement that advertisers spend thousands on what something says in one language, but only pennies to ensure that it says the same thing, the same way, when put into another language.[36]

The most effective approach in preparing copy for foreign markets is to begin from scratch and have all verbal communications entirely rewritten by a speaker of the foreign language who understands the complete marketing plan—including objectives, strategies, and tactics. With regards to translations from one language to another, says Robert Roth, "As far as can be determined, there has never been a 100 percent acceptable translation—certainly not of advertising or public relations material."[37] For copy to be translated, advertisers should be aware of some linguistic and managerial guidelines.[38, 39]

Linguistic Guidelines

1. Think multilingual. Remember from the start that copy will be translated. Copy should contain neither slang and idioms nor puns, rhymes, figures of speech, similes, or metaphors—all of which are extremely difficult and sometimes impossible to translate.

2. Remember that language is alive and changing. The dictionary should be avoided as a translation tool because the language of the dictionary is not necessarily the language of the people.

3. Recognize that translated words may have different shades of meaning. Some words simply cannot be translated, and others can only be translated in lengthy or awkward forms.

4. Use English at the fifth- or sixth-grade level to ensure ease of translation. Overly technical terms and industry jargon should be avoided.

5. Keep copy for translation relatively short, because many foreign languages invariably take more time/space to say the same thing the English-language copy says.

6. Remember that some languages distinguish between the familiar and the formal (*Du/Sie* for "you" in German and *tu/usted* for "you" in Spanish). Others employ honorific expressions depending on the relationship between speakers (inferior/superior in Japanese). Such differences can make translating from one language to another difficult.

Managerial Guidelines

1. Choose translators with care. Use only professional translators, preferably those with advertising copy translation experience. Translators may have specialties—medical, legal, or technical.

2. Use native speakers of the language into which the copy is being translated. Ideally, the translator should currently live in the country where the advertising will appear to ensure both familiarity and currency. Because language evolves, even a native tends to lose track of slang and idioms after being away from home for several years.

3. Examine the region in which translators were born, educated, and lived for significant periods of time. Such exposure may impact dialects. Within Germany, for example, each region speaks its own dialect. Similarly, the French spoken in France, Canada, Belgium, and Switzerland differs significantly.

4. Provide translators with full background on marketing and advertising objectives and strategies.

5. Give translators access to all necessary reference materials dealing with the appropriate subject and industry. Ensure that the translator has an adequate understanding of any required technical terms.

6. Settle on style issues before translation begins. American advertising copy is often considered brusque or staccato, which may not be appropriate for some markets.

7. Allow sufficient time for translations. Forcing translators to work under pressure benefits no one.

8. Don't be stingy—hire the best translators available.

9. Employ the back-translation technique. Here, one individual is responsible for the initial translation of the message, and a second individual then translates the message back into the original language. If the message does not translate back, there is likely a translation problem. Back-translation is a helpful tool, however, it's no guarantee against translation bloopers.

The same translation guidelines apply to both print and broadcast messages. In the production of advertisements for television, it may be preferable to design a spot that does not employ on-camera sound. While it is possible to dub spots for use in the international arena, the result is almost always rather unnatural sounding, and the technique is not inexpensive. With regards to both radio and television, music seems to travel across borders quite well—due, no doubt, to the immense popularity of many international music stars. For instance, Tina Turner, Michael Jackson, and Steve Miller all have been employed to sing and play to a global audience.

Nonverbal Communication: Visuals and Illustrations

According to several experts, including Martin Mayer, sight, sound, and motion are the future of international advertising: "Words will become very much less important, especially if the product is standardized, like Coca-Cola, Levi's or Marlboro."[40] The growing use of visual presentation (pictures and illustrations) minimizes the need for translations. Vern Terpstra and Ravi Sarathy write: "More and more European and Japanese ads are purely visual, showing something, evoking a mood and citing the company name. Emphasis on such simple illustrations also avoids part of the problem of illiteracy in poorer nations."[41] As an example, the many different languages spoken in Europe posed a formidable barrier to Levi's in selling its jeans on the continent. Therefore, the company and its advertising agency created broadcast and cinema advertisements that consisted solely of moving pictures and music. Unworried by problems of language or complicated dubbing procedures, Levi's advertising agency in London was able to utilize the Levi's 501 spots for use throughout Europe.[42] The development of international media is also influencing this trend. Ronald Beatson, director-general of the European Association of Advertising Agencies, had this to say:

> What satellite broadcasting is going to mean for us, apart from reach, is greater emphasis on non-verbal communication: the big visual idea, and the use of visual symbols. Where the message transcends national frontiers, it will often transcend national languages. Remember, we have 9 different, national languages within the EU. This is going to put a premium on the visual and musical content of commercials, with less emphasis on verbal communication; and, as brands develop expertise in non-verbal communication, I think we shall see this phenomenon appearing in print media too, with much more emphasis laid on graphics than on copy.[43]

Much as with singers and musicians, film stars and models are increasingly appearing in international advertising campaigns. In Japan alone at least twenty-seven international stars are appearing in current campaigns, including Harrison Ford for the Honda Legend, Jodie Foster for the Honda Civic, Michael J. Fox for the Honda Integra, Sean Connery for Suntory beer, and Don Johnson for Freixenet sparkling wine.[44] Each of these celebrities earns well over $7 million for appearing in a single commercial. Though some actors and actresses are quite selective about appearing in commercials in their home markets, they apparently welcome overseas opportunities. Top models are also known worldwide. In some instances specific models are selected for advertisements because they look "very American" or "very French." In other cases models appearing in advertisements must appeal to a wide audience. For example, in selling Badedas shower gel in Malaysia, SmithKline Beecham faced the challenge of selling the product to an ethnically diverse audience. To appeal to a wide variety of consumers, a model of mixed race was employed.[45]

Care should be taken in the selection of visual backgrounds and settings employed in both print and broadcast advertisements destined for foreign markets. These nonverbal communications should either reinforce the local culture in adapted campaigns or remain neutral enough to be accepted in all markets for those campaigns employing a standardized strategy. The creative team must attend to every visual detail in an advertisement. For example, according to Marieke De Mooij and Warren Keegan, "Landscapes, buildings, traffic signs, etc., must all be neutral. Dutch, Danish and Belgian houses may look similar to the Japanese or Americans, but they look different to the Dutch, the Danish and the Belgians! As soon as they cross each other's borders, they feel they are in a foreign country, not only because of the language, but because of the landscape, houses and churches."[46]

Creativity in the International Arena

At the prestigious 1994 International Cannes Advertising Film Festival, the United States won a film Grand Prix—the highest honor—with a Chrysler spot for Jeep Grand Cherokee. In the "Snow-Covered" spot, shown in the first panel of Exhibit 6.6, a molelike trail is burrowed through a snowy landscape. It halts at a nearly buried stop sign and turns left revealing a Jeep. A scale-model Jeep was pulled under snow to create the mounds. The images were composited by computer.[47] In addition, the United States also won seven of the twenty-two Gold Lions awarded, compared with three for the United Kingdom, its closest rival.

Winners of the Grand Prix and Gold Lions receive more than just the praise of their peers. Donald Gunn, director of creative resources worldwide for Leo Burnett, notes: "Research shows that commercials that win awards are at least twice as likely to be successful in the marketplace as commercials on average. My theory . . . is that there is some definite link between what pleases juries and what pleases viewers when they see advertising in their homes."[48] Cannes winners are significantly more likely to report dramatic increases in market shares, sales, volume growth, brand awareness, and favorable image ratings during and after the campaigns' flights.[49]

For decades New York was known as the center of American advertising creativity. Indeed, the rest of the advertising world took lessons from Madison Avenue. And, consumers around the globe read American-produced print advertisements and viewed American-produced broadcast messages. However, during the past ten to fifteen years, a gradual shift has been taking place. As a creative force the United States no longer stands alone. During the previous six years, as shown in Exhibit 6.6, agencies located in Tokyo, Barcelona, Paris, London, and Madrid garnered coveted awards at Cannes.

Increasingly, U.S. agencies must share the creative limelight with foreign shops. For example, recent winners of *Advertising Age*'s annual International Agency of the Year honor include Spain's Casadevall Pedreno & PRG (1993); South Africa's Hunt Lascaris TBWA (1992); Australia's Lintas (1991); Canada's Baker Lovick (1990); Spain's Contrapunto (1989); Britain's DDB Needham (1988); Japan's Dentsu (1987); Australia's Mojo MDA (1986); Britain's Lowe Howard-Spink (1985); and the Netherlands' Prins, Meijer, Stamenkovits & van Walbeek (1984).[50]

Theories abound as to why the United States no longer ranks No. 1 in advertising creativity. Alex Biel of the Ogilvy research operation offers one explanation of why European advertising, in particular, has become generally more imaginative than American advertising: "It's because [European] corporate structures are smaller. The head of the agency deals with the pres-

1994: "Snow-Covered" for Jeep
Grand Cherokee.
Agency: Bozell; New York

1993: "Moa Bird" for Nissin Cup
Noodles Soup.
Agency: Hukuhodo; Tokyo

1992: "Nuns" for Talens Rubber
Cement. Agency: Casadevall;
Pedreno, Barcelona

1991: "Le Lion & La Lionne" for
Source Perrier.
Agency: Ogilvy & Mather; Paris

1990: "Israelites/Masses of Lamb"
for Maxell Tapes. Agency: Howell
Henry Chaldecott Lury; London

1989: "Leaving Home" for TVE/TV
Espana state network.
Agency: Contrapunto; Madrid

1988: "Launch II" for Volkswagen
Passat.
Agency: DDB Needham; London

EXHIBIT 6.6 Cannes Grand Prix Winners, 1988–1994

ident of the company. It's the chain of nay-sayers in the United States that gives us such bland advertising." Another agency executive noted that the dominant compensation system in Europe (fees rather than commissions) encourages creativity.[51] Regardless of the reason, top creative ideas clearly are born in agencies operating in Europe, Asia, and many other world regions.

Summary

As a strategy advertising standardization may work well for some products, marketers, and audiences, and in some situations. In other instances specialization or adaption will prove to be more effective. And, sometimes, something in between will be most appropriate.[52] International marketers must carefully evaluate where along the standardization–specialization continuum a campaign destined for a specific foreign market should fall. Advertisers also must employ appeals suited to each culture and understand how cultural differences impact advertising content. Finally, advertisers must exercise caution in the use of both verbal and nonverbal messages. Translations must be conducted with care, and every aspect of the illustration or visual must be analyzed to ensure a proper cultural fit. And whatever the product, advertisers must select the best media—the subject of Chapter 7.

Additional Readings

Harris, Greg. (1984). "The Globalization of Advertising." *International Journal of Advertising*, 3, pp. 223–234.

James, William, and John Hill. (June/July 1991). "International Advertising Messages: To Adapt or Not to Adapt." *Journal of Advertising Research*, 31(3), pp. 65–71.

Onkvisit, Sak, and John Shaw. (Fall 1987). "Standardized International Advertising: A Review and Critical Evaluation of the Theoretical and Empirical Evidence." *Columbia Journal of World Business*, pp. 43–55.

Rijkens, Rein. (1992). *European Advertising Strategies.* London: Cassell.

Notes

1. Frazer, Charles, "Creative Strategy: A Management Perspective," *Journal of Advertising*, 12(1), 1983, pp. 36–41.

2. Levitt, Theodore, "Globalization of Markets," *Harvard Business Review*, May/June 1983, pp. 92–102.

3. Rutigliano, Anthony, "The Debate Goes On: Global vs. Local Advertising," *Management Review*, June 1986, pp. 27–31.

4. Robbins, Kenneth, "Does Standardization Work in International Marketing?" *European Management Journal*, 5(4), 1987, p. 253.

5. Bowes, Elena, "From Cookies to Appliances, Pan European Efforts Build," *Advertising Age*, June 22, 1992, pp. I1, I29.

6. Kilburn, David, and Bruce Crumley, "Shiseido Scents Global Market," *Advertising Age*, June 22, 1992, p. I1.

7. Fannin, Rebecca, "What Agencies Really Think of Global Theory," *Marketing and Media Decisions*, December 1984, pp. 74–82.

8. Giges, Nancy, "Global Spending Patterns Emerge," *Advertising Age*, November 11, 1991, p. 64.

9. Belch, George E., and Michael A. Belch, *Introduction to Advertising and Promotion: An Integrated Marketing Communications Perspective* (Erwin: Homewood, IL: 1993, p. 344).

10. Nelson, Bob, "High Tech Firms Lead the Way with Global Campaigns," *Advertising Age*, August 1, 1994, p. 22.

11. Hornik, Jacob, "Comparative Evaluation of International vs. National Advertising Strategies," *Columbia Journal of World Business*, Spring 1980, pp. 36–45.

12. Green, Robert, William Cunningham, and Isabella Cunningham, "The Effectiveness of Standardized Global Advertising," *Journal of Advertising,* 4(3), 1975, pp. 25–30.

13. Harris, Greg, "The Globalization of Advertising," *International Journal of Advertising,* 3, 1984, pp. 223–234.

14. Anderson, Michael H., *Madison Avenue in Asia* (Cranbury, NJ: Associated University Presses, 1984).

15. Bowes, "From Cookies to Appliances."

16. Lipman, Joanne, "Marketers Turn Sour on Global Sales Pitch Harvard Guru Makes," *Wall Street Journal,* May 12, 1988, p. 1.

17. Marcom, John, "Cable and Satellites Are Opening Europe to TV Commercials," *The Wall Street Journal,* December 22, 1987, p. 1.

18. Kilburn, David, "Kao Enters Australia, but Its Detergent Is No Attack," *Advertising Age,* June 22, 1992, p. I3.

19. Jain, Subhash, "Standardization of International Marketing Strategy: Some Research Hypotheses," *Journal of Marketing,* 53(1), January 1989, pp. 70–79.

20. Lipman, "Marketers Turn Sour."

21. Freemen, Laurie, "Colgate Axes Global Ads, Thinks Local," *Advertising Age,* November 26, 1990, pp. 1, 51.

22. Rowlands, Penelope, "Global Approach Doesn't Always Make Scents," *Advertising Age,* January 17, 1994, pp. 1+.

23. Kaynak, Erdener, *The Management of International Advertising: A Handbook and Guide for Professionals* (New York: Quorum Books, 1989).

24. Belch, George E., and Michael A. Belch, *Introduction to Advertising and Promotion: An Integrated Marketing Communications Perspective* (Homewood, IL: Irwin, 1993).

25. Giacomotti, Faboma, "In Europe, There's No Place Like Home," *ADWEEK,* June 7, 1993, p. 13.

26. Biswas, Abhijit, Janeen E. Olsen, and Valerie Carlet, "A Comparison of Print Advertisements from the United States and France," *Journal of Advertising,* 21(4), 1992, pp. 73–81.

27. Mueller, Barbara, "Reflections of Culture: An Analysis of Japanese and American Advertising Appeals," *Journal of Advertising Research,* 27(3), 1987, pp. 51–59.

28. DiBenedetto, C. Anthony, Mariko Tamate, and Rajan Chandran, "Developing Creative Advertising Strategy for the Japanese Marketplace," *Journal of Advertising Research,* 32(1), 1992, pp. 39–48.

29. Burton, Jack, and Dennis Chase, "Sun Still Not Shining on P & G in Japan," *Advertising Age,* December 20, 1982.

30. Biswas, Olsen, and Carlet, "A Comparison of Print Advertisements."

31. Nevett, Terence, "Differences Between American and British Television Advertising: Explanations and Implications," *Journal of Advertising,* 21(4), 1992, pp. 61–71.

32. Ibid., p. 68.

33. Raffield, Barney T., III, "Marketing Across Cultures: Learning from U.S. Corporate Blunders," in *Languages and Communication for World Business and the Professions,* Conference Proceedings, Ann Arbor, MI, May 1987.

34. Cateora, Philip, *International Marketing* (Homewood, IL: Irwin, 1990), p. 468.

35. Ricks, David, *Big Business Blunders: Mistakes in Multinational Marketing* (Homewood, IL: Dow Jones–Irwin, 1983).

36. Radzievsky, Yuri, "The Invisible Idiot and Other Monsters of Translation," in *Viewpoint,* a publication "By, For and About Ogilvy & Mather," Fall 1983/84.

37. Roth, Robert F., *International Marketing Communications* (Chicago, IL: Crain Books, 1982), p. 135.

38. Ibid.

39. Miracle, Gordon E., "An Empirical Study of the Usefulness of the Back-Translation Technique for International Advertising Messages in Print Media," in the Proceedings of the 1988 Conference of the American Academy of Advertising, John D. Leckenby ed., p. RC51–61.

40. Mayer, Martin, *Whatever Happened to Madison Avenue: Advertising in the*

90s (Boston, MA: Little, Brown, 1991), p. 213.

41. Terpstra, Vern, and Ravi Sarathy, *International Marketing* (Hinsdale, IL: Dryden Press, 1991).

42. Rijkens, Rein, *European Advertising Strategies* (London: Cassell, 1992).

43. Beatson, Ronald, "Europe 1993," presentation to the Point-of-Purchase Advertising Institute Marketplace 1989, New York, October 31–November 2, 1989, as quoted in Rijkens, *European Advertising Strategies*, p. 15.

44. Skur Hill, Julie, "International Stars Warm Up to Ad Climate Outside of U.S.," *Advertising Age,* June 22, 1992, p. I10.

45. *Advertising Age,* Global Gallery, June 22, 1992, p. I15.

46. De Mooij, Marieke K., and Warren Keegan, *Advertising Worldwide* (New York: Prentice-Hall, 1991).

47. Wentz, Laurel, "U.S. Lions Roar at Cannes," *Advertising Age,* June 27, 1994, p. 1.

48. Jaffe, Andrew, "Burnett's Donald Gunn on What Wins at Cannes," *AD-WEEK,* June 6, 1994, p. 46.

49. Tilles, Daniel, "Commercials Do Win Awards and Sales," *ADWEEK,* July 11, 1994, p. 16.

50. Klosky, Deborah, "International Honors to Casadevall Pedreno," *Advertising Age,* April 13, 1994, p. 4.

51. Mayer, *Whatever Happened to Madison Avenue.*

52. Quelch, John A., and Edward J. Hoff, "Customizing Global Marketing," *Harvard Business Review,* 64(3), May/June 1986, pp. 59–68.

CHAPTER 7

Advertising Media in the International Arena

An area that proves to be particularly challenging and often quite frustrating for most international marketers is that of the media function. The basic principles of media planning and purchasing are generally the same whether the planner is operating in New York or New Delhi—the selection of those media and vehicles that most efficiently and effectively reach the target audience. However, the application of these principles will vary from one market to the next.

The intention of this chapter is not to provide an overview of the media situation in each of the numerous markets around the world. First, a complete survey is beyond the scope of this text, and second, such information would soon be outdated. Rather, the goal here is to outline the media options available to international media planners and to highlight the diversity in the various media environments.

International Versus National/Local Media

Media planners zeroing in on foreign markets have the option of using local/national media or employing media that cross national borders—better known as international media. Using a combination of the two is clearly an alternative as well. The decision of whether to employ local/national or international media is impacted by a number of factors, including but not limited to (1) how much centralized control the firm has, (2) what target audience the advertiser is attempting to reach, (3) whether the firm has chosen to employ a localized or globalized campaign, and (4) whether the firm works with national or multinational advertising agencies.

The tendency toward decentralized decision making, the use of campaigns tailored to the local market, and the preference for domestic agencies generally result in more extensive employment of local media than international media. Even where a standardized campaign is employed, media planning and buying usually is conducted on a local basis. Decentralizing this aspect allows for greater input from local advertising experts, which greatly simplifies the execution of media plans. This trend is documented in a study of agency media buyers which revealed that international media buying still represents a very small fraction of agency business.[1] While the amount of advertising in national media is still vastly greater than that appearing in international media, this may well change significantly in the years to come.

National/Local Media

National or local media offer advertisers a greater variety of vehicles—television, radio, newspapers, magazines, outdoor, direct mail, and transit, as well as many rather unique forms. They also permit use of the local language, which is generally more effective in reaching the local market. However, there are drawbacks to using local media. The practice of media planning and buying at the local level is quite complex because the media environments rarely resemble one another. These differences can take the form of media availability, viability, coverage, cost, quality, and the role of advertising in the media.

Media Availability

Advertisers in the United States are accustomed to the availability of a wide variety of media and vehicles. Yet, media that commonly are employed in domestic campaigns may quite simply be unavailable in foreign markets. Until quite recently, for example, Denmark and Sweden did not allow broadcast advertising. Television stations in Saudi Arabia still accept no commercial messages. As a result, a firm marketing its products in a number of nations may well find it impossible to employ the same media mix in all markets. Even when the same media are available, commercial time may be severely restricted. In Germany, commercial time is limited to twenty minutes a day and is banned on Sundays as well as holidays on each of the government-owned stations. In addition, advertisements are shown in three or four blocks approximately five minutes in length, and as a result, viewership tends to be rather low. However, Germany's privately owned stations are considerably more liberal—allowing up to 20 percent of airtime to be devoted to television commercials.

Table 7.1 highlights the differences existing among countries with regards to how extensively specific media are used, and thereby reveals the relative importance of various media from one market to the next. For example, print's share of advertising dollars ranges from a low of 14.3 percent in Mexico to a high of 90.4 percent in Norway. Similarly, TV's share ranges from a low of 1.4 percent in Sweden to a high of 75 percent in Mexico. While cinema advertising does not even register for the United States, it ranks comparatively high in Argentina. Such variation necessitates adaptation to the local media environment.

Media Viability

Beyond media availability Dean Peebles and John Ryans note the importance of media viability. They suggest that the international advertiser look beyond simple media availability and also explore whether the medium is "available in the quality and quantity and at a cost that will permit the international advertiser to successfully employ it."[2] As an example Peebles and Ryans note that while commercial television is available in Australia to the international advertiser, governmental restrictions require local production of commercials. The added cost of producing a commercial in Australia may well preclude the use of the medium of television if the international advertiser sees a limited market for the product in this country or had planned to use a commercial produced in the domestic market. There may also be severe restrictions on the number of TV messages an advertiser can run during

TABLE 7.1   Percent Distribution of Measured Media, 1991–1992

COUNTRY	TV	PRINT	RADIO	CINEMA	OUTDOOR/TRANSIT
Argentina	36.2%	37.9%	10.5%	4.0%	11.4%
Australia	34.3	49.3	8.9	1.8	5.7
Austria	26.0	54.3	12.2	0.6	7.0
Belgium	29.3	53.1	3.3	1.3	13.0
Brazil	57.7	35.5	4.8	—	2.0
Canada	26.7	50.2	11.8	—	11.3
Chile	43.2	43.0	10.9	0.2	2.6
China	18.6	33.8	4.0	3.8	39.7
Colombia	59.5	21.7	18.8	—	—
Denmark	5.3	92.1	0.9	0.5	1.2
Ecuador	66.2	22.7	9.4	0.2	1.5
Finland	15.1	77.5	4.3	—	2.6
France	27.2	53.7	6.5	0.6	12.0
Germany	15.8	75.9	4.0	1.0	3.3
Greece	52.2	37.7	5.0	0.4	4.7
Hong Kong	49.9	41.0	4.7	1.2	3.2
India	17.2	70.4	2.3	0.6	9.6
Indonesia	25.2	53.6	12.0	1.1	8.1
Ireland	28.4	54.2	10.0	1.0	6.5
Israel	4.0	81.8	6.0	1.2	7.0
Italy	48.1	42.1	3.6	0.2	6.1

(continued)

a given period of time. Finally, while a given medium may be available, the cost may be so high in certain markets that the international advertiser's budget prohibits the use of the medium.

Media Coverage

Media coverage also varies from one market to the next. Table 7.2 presents data on numbers of newspapers, television sets, and radio receivers in countries around the world. In the case of broadcast media, both the range of exposure and the ownership of radio and television receivers affect coverage. In the United States there are 815 television sets for every 1,000 Americans, and 620 sets for every 1,000 Japanese. This stands in sharp contrast to the 5 receivers per 1,000 inhabitants in Bangladesh or the 2 receivers per 1,000

TABLE 7.1 *(continued)*

COUNTRY	TV	PRINT	RADIO	CINEMA	OUTDOOR/TRANSIT
Japan	38.9%	40.3%	5.6%	—	15.2%
Malaysia	41.3	52.4	2.1	0.5%	3.7
Mexico	75.0	14.3	10.7	—	—
Netherlands	16.1	73.5	2.5	0.3	7.6
New Zealand	33.7	45.0	13.4	1.3	6.6
Norway	4.9	90.4	1.4	1.3	2.1
Pakistan	44.6	48.5	3.1	0.2	3.6
Philippines	60.8	22.6	15.6	—	1.0
Portugal	37.5	32.9	6.6	13.1	9.7
Singapore	29.8	62.3	2.5	0.8	4.6
South Africa	28.4	58.3	10.2	1.0	2.1
South Korea	27.7	49.1	5.2	—	2.1
Spain	60.1	33.7	3.3	0.4	2.6
Sweden	1.4	94.1	—	0.7	3.8
Switzerland	6.8	77.3	1.9	0.9	13.1
Taiwan	32.8	45.4	4.8	—	17.0
Thailand	46.1	40.1	9.8	0.1	3.9
United Kingdom	30.9	63.1	2.0	0.6	3.5
United States	35.3	52.5	10.9	—	1.9
Venezuela	65.1	31.1	1.9	—	1.0

SOURCES: European Marketing Data and Statistics, 1994, and International Marketing Data and Statistics, 1994 (published by Euromonitor, 87–88 Turnmill St., London, ECl M5QU).

Ethiopians. The pattern is similar for radio receivers. Ownership is again highest in the United States, with 2,123 receivers for every 1,000 inhabitants. In the United Kingdom there are 1,146 receivers for every 1,000 residents. At the other extreme there are fewer than 80 receivers for every 1,000 Indians and only 65 receivers per 1,000 Guatemalans. These figures clearly suggest that the issue of receiver ownership is particularly relevant in developing countries, where a large percentage of the population simply cannot afford individual ownership of radios or television sets.

Coverage of print media is impacted by both national literacy levels and subscription levels to publications, because illiterate consumers generally do not subscribe to magazines and newspapers. Levels of illiteracy vary significantly from country to country. At the high end 81 percent of Afghanis, over 50 percent of Indians, and 27 percent of Chinese are functionally

TABLE 7.2 Newspapers, Televisions, and Radios per 1,000 Inhabitants

COUNTRY	NEWSPAPERS[a]	TELEVISION RECEIVERS[b]	RADIO RECEIVERS[c]
United States	250	815	2,123
Algeria	51	74	233
Argentina	124	222	681
Australia	249	486	1,280
Austria	357	481	624
Bangladesh	6	5	42
Belgium	305	452	778
Bolivia	55	163	599
Brazil	54	213	379
Bulgaria	451	250	438
Burma	5	2	82
Cambodia	NA	9	113
Canada	228[d]	641	1,026
Chile	455	205	342
China, Mainland	37[f]	31	184
Colombia	61	115	170
Costa Rica	102[g]	149	259
Cuba	124	207	345
Cyprus	111	150	292
Czechoslovakia	507	412	587
Denmark	352	535	1,030
Dominican Republic	32	84	170
East Germany	338[e]	514	952
Ecuador	87	83	315
Egypt	57	109	324
El Salvador	87	90	404
Ethiopia	1	2	191
Finland	559	497	998
France	210	406	896
Ghana	13	15	266
Greece	140[e]	196	423
Guatemala	21	52	65
Honduras	39	72	385
Hong Kong	632	274	649
Hungary	233	410	595

(continued)

TABLE 7.2 *(continued)*

COUNTRY	NEWSPAPERS[a]	TELEVISION RECEIVERS[b]	RADIO RECEIVERS[c]
Iceland	467[f]	320	787
India	26[f]	32	79
Indonesia	28	60	147
Iran	27	70	247
Iraq	34	69	205
Ireland	159	276	583
Israel	261	266	471
Italy	107[d]	424	797
Jamaica	63	130	411
Japan	587	620	907
Kenya	15	9	125
Kuwait	221	285	343
Lebanon	118	330	840
Luxembourg	389	255	630
Madagascar	4	20	200
Malaysia	140	148	429
Mexico	127	139	243
Morocco	13	74	209
Netherlands	311[e]	906	1,106
New Zealand	324	442	929
Nicaragua	65	62	249
Nigeria	16	32	172
Norway	614	425	798
Pakistan	15	17	87
Panama	70	165	223
Paraguay	39	59	171
Peru	79	97	253
Philippines	54	48	138
Poland	127	293	429
Portugal	38	177	218
Puerto Rico	131	267	721
Romania	158[f]	194	198
Saudi Arabia	42	283	318
Singapore	280	376	643
South Africa	38	105	326

(continued)

TABLE 7.2   *(continued)*

COUNTRY	NEWSPAPERS[a]	TELEVISION RECEIVERS[b]	RADIO RECEIVERS[c]
South Korea	280	210	1,006
Soviet Union	482[d]	329	686
Spain	82[e]	396	306
Sri Lanka	32	35	197
Sudan	24	71	250
Sweden	533	474	888
Switzerland	463	407	855
Syria	22	59	251
Thailand	72	112	185
Trinidad and Tobago	NA	302	468
Tunisia	37	80	196
Turkey	72	175	161
United Kingdom	395[e]	435	1,146
Uruguay	233	233	603
Venezuela	142	167	436
West Germany	338[d]	514	952
Yugoslavia	96	198	246
Zimbabwe	21	31	85

NA = Not available.   [a]Publications containing general news and appearing at least four times a week; may include copies sold outside the country.   [b]Estimated number of sets in use.   [c]Data cover estimated number of receivers in use and apply to all types of receivers for radio broadcasts to the public, including receivers connected to a radio "redistribution system" but excluding television sets.   [d]For 1989. [e]For 1988.   [f]For 1985.   [g]For 1991.

SOURCE: U.S. Bureau of the Census; *Statistical Abstract of the United States, 1993*, 113th ed. (Washington, DC: U.S. Department of Commerce, 1993).

illiterate. At the low end, less than 4 percent of Italians, about 2 percent of citizens of the former Soviet Union, and less than 1 percent of Americans are illiterate.[3] Differences also exist in the illiteracy levels between males and females. In every instance illiteracy levels are higher among females, and in some instances the illiteracy rate is over 25 percent higher among women. This suggests that in many countries it is still the male who receives formal education and that, as a result, print may be a more appropriate medium for targeting males in many markets. Another factor that comes into play in terms of media coverage is income. In countries with a low per capita income, consumers likely cannot afford to subscribe to print publications. In certain markets a wide variety of media and numerous media vehicles may be required in order to reach the majority of the market. The international advertiser faced with such a situation may no longer find it profitable to attempt to reach the mass market, particularly in many less developed countries.

Media Cost

In markets where a limited number of media are available or where shortages of advertising time/space are common, considerably higher advertising rates can be expected by the media planner. For example, multinational advertisers and agencies are seething over the doubling of advertising rates on Hungary's most watched television channel—Magyar Television 1. The channel recently increased rates by 100 percent after having bumped them up by 40 percent—a situation that would likely not be tolerated in a more competitive television market. Currently, a sixty-second prime-time spot costs $8,750—up over 98 percent from previous rates. Because it has the largest viewership, the station receives more than twice the number of requests for prime-time spots than are available. And despite these hefty increases in advertising rates, the station's service is poor—often spots are placed back-to-back with those of competitors, and the station rarely confirms bookings.[4]

In many markets variable pricing for time and space is the norm, with rate cards simply providing a basis for negotiations. In China, for example, both local companies and joint ventures pay in local currency to advertise, but rates are higher for joint ventures. And foreign companies pay the highest rates—in U.S. dollars. Print rates also don't take into account quantitative or qualitative factors such as circulation levels or readership profiles. Indeed, a provincial publication in the remote city of Urümqi charges the same for ad space as the prestigious *People's Daily.* Finally, many large-circulation dailies demand payment as soon as the booking order is signed but then raise rates—requiring additional payment. Rate protection is an unknown concept in this market.[5] Local media buyers are more likely to be aware that media rates may fluctuate due to unstable currencies and economic/political conditions. In addition, the local buyer may well be in a better position to negotiate more successfully than a foreign media buyer; such local representation may ensure that the international advertiser is indeed obtaining the best deal.

Media Quality

Even if a particular medium is available, the quality may vary from that in the home market. For example, newsprint quality is so poor in many countries—India, for one—that it is nearly impossible to obtain adequate halftone reproduction. Many markets still do not have color television, which may play a central role in a visually oriented campaign.

Role of Advertising in the Mass Media

As in the United States, advertising is the principle source of revenue for mass media throughout much of the world. However, the international advertiser should be aware that in numerous markets one or more of the media may be government-owned or -controlled. For example, in many European countries television is subsidized or owned by the government. In Germany, Italy, and Sweden, as well as a number of other countries, television owners pay annual fees to the government for television viewing, and these fees subsidize programming. With regard to the print media, in many countries readers pay a significantly greater percentage of the cost via subscription rates than do consumers in the United States. As a result, these media are much less dependent on advertising revenues in these countries. In some instances they may choose not to accept commercial messages or to severely restrict the time allotted to advertising.

Throughout the world, however, the overall trend is toward commercialization of both the broadcast and print media. For instance, two state-owned television channels currently exist in Poland. Although those stations do accept advertising messages, they frustrate advertisers by lumping together up to twenty spots at a time with competing brands airing in the same blocks. Competition exists in the form of fifteen illegal stations, which have begun broadcasting in cities across the country. The stations, which applied for licenses as long as three years ago, started up without official sanction because the Polish government took so long to make decisions. Although the government has fined several pirate stations, it has few resources for enforcement. The government plans to complete its review of license applications for commercial networks and then to award one or two licenses for national commercial networks as well as an undetermined number of licenses for local channels.[6]

Israel provides another example of the trend toward commercialization of media. For the past two years Israel has been testing transmissions for its first semiprivately owned commercial TV channel. The government-owned Channel 1 accepts program sponsorships but no advertising, and the government prohibits local companies from advertising on the country's plethora of cable channels, putting local firms at a disadvantage with global competitors. For example, Gali, a local shoe marketer, cannot advertise; however, Nike and Reebok International's commercials reach Israeli consumers via cable channels.[7] Critics of the current system note that per capita advertising spending lags compared to that in Europe mainly because of the lack of TV advertising. The situations in Poland and Israel are not unique—government-owned media around the world are facing increased competition from a growing number of private stations and publications.

Media Spillover

There are two kinds of media spillover—incidental and deliberate. *Incidental spillover* refers to those cases in which a local television channel, for example, may be viewed by individuals in other countries as well. Along the northern and southern borders of the United States, both radio and television broadcasts spill over into Canada and Mexico. The Netherlands receives broadcasts from Germany, Belgium, and other countries, too. Such spillover does not play a significant role in media planning because in most cases only small groups of consumers are reached and little audience measurement of such spillover is available.

Deliberate spillover refers to media created with the specific objective of broadcasting across national borders. An example of deliberate spillover is Rupert Murdoch's British Sky Broadcasting, a primarily British satellite service making forays into Europe. BSB, for instance, is expected to take its Sky News channel pan-European in 1994 and possibly even globally. A country's broadcasts may spill over into another nation via cable, terrestrial stations, or satellite dishes. However, spillover is not limited to the broadcast media. For example, some German publishers promote significant circulation of their magazines and newspapers in Austria and Switzerland.

Certain problems are associated with media spillover as well. For instance, India's state-run Doordarshan Television bans the advertising of a number of product categories, including liquor, baby food, and foreign banks. However, Hong Kong–based Star TV, the pan-Asian network, reaches 4 million households in India and accepts ads for the products banned on Doordarshan TV. Until recently, liquor companies in India have skirted the ban by running ads for fake mineral water and soda products carrying the same names as the liquor. However, all major Indian liquor producers are expected to begin advertising on Star TV. Indian officials are busy looking for ways to ward off the potential challenge.[8]

Local Broadcast Media

Television The medium most commonly employed in attempting to reach broad national markets in most developed countries is television. In these markets coverage is generally not a problem. Table 7.3 lists data on household penetration rates for television sets, videocassette recorders, teletext, remote control, and cable for a number of European, Asian, and Pacific Rim markets as contrasted with U.S. penetration rates. In most categories the U.S. market leads; however, teletext penetration is significantly higher in Austria, France, Germany, Italy, Sweden, and the United Kingdom.

TABLE 7.3 Percentage Household Penetration of Broadcast Media

COUNTRY	TV	COLOR TV	VCR	TELETEXT	REMOTE CONTROL	CABLE
United States	98%	97%	70%	1%	72%	60%
Australia	99	98	57	1	56	—
Austria	98	90	39	15	69	19
China	63	27	—	—	—	—
France	97	90	31	19	60	3
Germany	93	90	46	26	79	32
Hong Kong	97	97	40	—	—	—
Hungary	100	52	17	—	—	—
India	66	16	3	—	—	—
Italy	99	85	18	19	80	—
Japan	100	99	64	1	—	14
Malaysia	86	—	30	—	—	—
New Zealand	98	95	45	8	35	—
Norway	100	85	50	—	—	37
Philippines	51	16	8	—	—	—
Singapore	100	98	76	8	30	—
Spain	99	91	38	—	38	—
Sweden	96	95	56	48	72	40
Thailand	88	62	19	—	13	—
Turkey	96	49	33	—	—	—
United Kingdom	97	90	54	27	54	1

SOURCE: McCann-Erickson, 1991 Asia/Pacific Media Facts and 1991 European Media Facts.

However, television is also one of the most highly regulated communications media. Even in developed markets, the availability of television advertising time may be quite limited or even nonexistent. This is often true in cases where television is government-owned and -controlled. What can be advertised, and how, is also restricted in most every country. Much as in the United States, many countries prohibit the advertising of cigarettes and alcohol other than beer, while other countries also forbid advertising by financial institutions and baby food producers. Regulation of this medium will be discussed in greater detail in Chapter 9.

A recent study revealed that TV advertising is more highly regarded today by consumers worldwide than in the late 1980s. The study, which measured attitudes toward TV advertising in general and in thirteen specific product categories, was based on phone and in-person interviews with more than five thousand consumers in thirty-two countries. Exhibit 7.1 summarizes

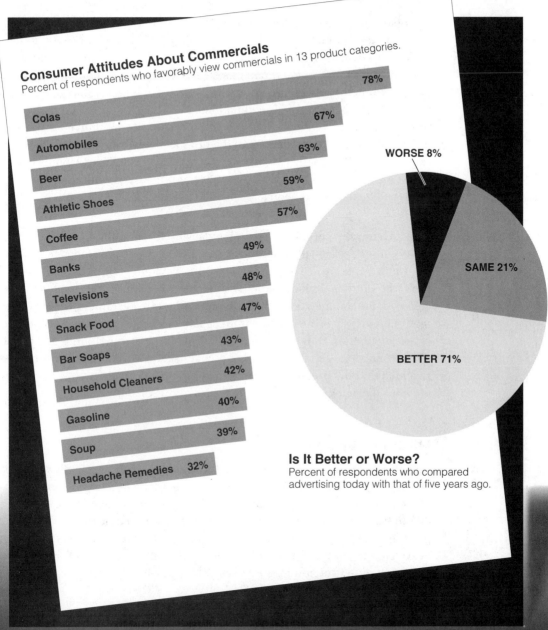

Consumer Attitudes About Commercials
Percent of respondents who favorably view commercials in 13 product categories.

- 78%
- Colas — 67%
- Automobiles — 63%
- Beer — 59%
- Athletic Shoes — 57%
- Coffee — 49%
- Banks — 48%
- Televisions — 47%
- Snack Food — 43%
- Bar Soaps — 42%
- Household Cleaners — 40%
- Gasoline — 39%
- Soup
- Headache Remedies — 32%

WORSE 8%

SAME 21%

BETTER 71%

Is It Better or Worse?
Percent of respondents who compared advertising today with that of five years ago.

EXHIBIT 7.1 Global Consumer Attitudes Toward TV Advertising

SOURCE: Pat Sloan, "TV Ads Gaining Favor Worldwide," *Advertising Age,* November 25, 1991, p. 28. Reprinted by permission of the publisher.

key results of the survey. Over 70 percent of respondents perceived advertising as better than it was five years ago, while only 8 percent found it to be worse. TV advertising also received high marks for entertainment and information value. And, as Pat Sloan observes: "The study did find the greatest net attitudinal improvement among consumers in less developed countries and the least in more developed nations. In Malaysia, for example, net improvement in the way advertising is perceived was more than 85% while in the U.S. it was just 15 percent."[9] Of the product categories studied, cola messages appeared to be the clear winner, with 78 percent of participants worldwide responding favorably. Automobiles and beer ads ranked second and third, and headache remedies received the fewest positive responses.

Radio Generally perceived as a secondary medium in the United States, in many countries radio plays a much more dominant role. As revealed in Table 7.1, radio as an advertising medium enjoys relative popularity in countries such as Colombia, Indonesia, Kenya, and New Zealand. A major plus associated with the medium is its ability to reach illiterate customers; moreover, in many countries it is the only medium capable of delivering to large segments of the population. However, the medium's popularity is not limited to developing countries. A study examining media usage in five European countries revealed that the greatest percentage of Europeans listened to radio on the previous day and also spent most minutes per day listening to radio.

Local Print Media

The role that print media will play in the media advertising plan is generally directly correlated with the literacy level of the target audience in each country. The more highly developed the nation, the more heavily newspapers and magazines will be used by consumers in those countries. Overall, the print media tend to receive the lion's share of advertising dollars in almost every country in the world. However, the extent of market saturation that can be obtained via newspapers or magazines will vary from one country to the next.

Newspapers In some countries, such as Britain, Japan, and the United States, one or more newspapers can be said to have a truly national circulation. It wasn't until 1983 that the first general-readership national newspaper began being circulated in this country. Despite its current paid circulation of over 1.3 million, however, *USA Today* has been unprofitable for every year of its existence. In contrast, *The Wall Street Journal* and *The New York Times* are two examples of successful nationally distributed newspapers in the United States, although both are read by a predominantly business-oriented audience. For instance, an advertisement promoting *The New York Times* to media planners notes that the publication reaches "66% of those in the Executive Branch of the Federal government, and 71% of those in the Congressional Branch. And, the Times is read by 66% of opinion leaders in the communications and media industries."

International advertisers must be aware of national newspapers that may be available as an advertising medium in each market. For example, Japan has five national newspapers, the largest of which reaches over 7 million readers. Exhibit 7.2 shows a message promoting *Asahi Shimbun*—Japan's leading newspaper—to international advertisers. The copy lists previous advertisers, including BMW, MasterCard, Swatch, Du Pont, and Estée Lauder, to demonstrate the paper's popularity with advertisers.

In many countries, newspapers tend to be predominantly local or regional rather than national and, as such, serve as the primary medium for local advertisers. Attempting to use a series of local papers to reach a national market is considerably more complex and costly. Unlike in the United States, in many nations there is heavy competition among local newspapers, which tends to benefit advertisers by holding advertising costs down. Advertisers must examine several issues when considering the use of local papers. For instance, some publications are sponsored by a particular political party, and the international advertiser must exercise caution in placing advertisements in particularly controversial papers. Also, the quality of newspapers may not be consistent from one country to the next. Therefore, for each market, the international advertiser must investigate whether the publication offers high-quality, four-color production or low-quality black-and-white.

In the United States most newspapers clearly distinguish between editorial and advertising content. Such is not the case in many other countries, where editorial space is regularly sold for advertising purposes, occasionally making it difficult for readers to distinguish between the two. Advertisements even crop up on the front page of many newspapers around the world. For example, J. Walter Thompson, which rewards creativity in media planning, presented its 1993 global White Pea award (named after the rare white pea standing out from the green ones in a pod) to its Bombay office for an ad created for Nestlé chocolates. In India, the market leader, Cadbury, was almost a generic word for chocolate, so JWT needed to make a big impression on potential consumers. To do so, the Bombay office negotiated several unprecedented deals with newspapers—including buying the entire front page of a leading Bombay daily and replacing all the day's news with a huge headline reading "No News," followed by the announcement that Nestlé had

AIR NEW ZEALAND   ALITALIA   AMERICAN AIRLINES   AMERICAN DRUG   AMERICAN EXPRESS   AMERICAN HOME ASSURANCE

AMERICAN LIFE INSURANCE   APPLE   ARAMIS   AT&T   AUDI   BENETTON   BERLITZ   BMW   BRISTOL-MYERS   BRITISH AIRWAYS

CARTIER   CATHAY PACIFIC   CHANEL   CHRISTIAN DIOR   CHRYSLER

CIBA-GEIGY   CIGNA INSURANCE   CITIBANK   CITROËN   CLINIQUE

DELTA AIR LINES   DINERS CLUB   DU PONT   ESTÉE LAUDER   FORD

GARUDA INDONESIA   GENERAL MOTORS   GLAXO   GIVENCHY   GUERLAIN   HERMÈS

IBERIA   IBM   JAGUAR   JOHNSON & JOHNSON

KLM   KOREAN AIR   LANCÔME   LOEWE

LOUIS VITTON   LUFTHANSA

MASTER CARD   MERCEDES-BENZ   MOTOROLA   NESTLÉ   NORTHWEST AIRLINES   OLIVETTI

OPEL   PEUGEOT   PFIZER   POLAROID   PORSCHE   QUANTAS AIRWAYS   RALPH LAUREN   REEBOK

ROCHE   ROVER   ROYAL INSURANCE

SAAB   SANDOZ   SAS

SINGAPORE AIRLINES   SWATCH   SWISSAIR

UNISYS   UNITED AIRLINES   UNITED DISTILLERS   VIRGIN ATLANTIC AIRWAYS   VOLKSWAGEN   VOLVO   WATERFORD WEDGWOOD

YVES SAINT LAURENT   **These International Advertisers Have Chosen Asahi Shimbun.**   ZURICH INSURANCE COMPANY

A Key
to Your Success
in the
Japanese Market.

There is a reason that Asahi Shimbun is the premier choice of the world's leading advertisers:
It is Japan's foremost national newspaper, preferred by those who move and shape Japanese public opinion.
Its readership includes opinion leaders in the nation's industrial, educational, judicial,
governmental and commercial fields—people who have tremendous
influence over consumer's purchasing behavior.
In fact, Asahi Shimbun has the largest readership among the households
with an annual income exceeding ¥8 million (US$76,000).
Supported by such an elite readership, the circulation of the morning edition has
grown to reach eight million, a number almost equivalent to one-fifth of Japan's 42 million households.
In terms of both quality and quantity,
Asahi Shimbun is the newspaper that optimizes your chance of breaking
into the Japanese market and expanding your business in Japan.

Asahi Shimbun
JAPAN'S LEADING NEWSPAPER
5-3-2 Tsukiji Chuo-ku, Tokyo 104-11 Tel:+81-3-5540-7755 Fax:+81-3-5540-7741

EXHIBIT 7.2 Message Promoting Japan's Asahi Shimbun as an
International Advertising Medium

arrived. In another buy the agency superimposed the words "Nestlé Premium Chocolates now in Delhi" like a dark watermark over the entire sports page of a Sunday paper. The award-winning campaigns garnered more than sixty articles in the Indian press and an estimated $50,000 worth of publicity for the $2,000 spent on media space.[10] Knowing local media regulations can be of great benefit in developing a media plan for a local market.

Magazines In general, magazines have nowhere near the broad readership of newspapers, although readership levels are considerably higher in many foreign markets than in the United States. Rarely, however, can a single magazine reach a majority of a market. In most countries magazines serve to reach specific segments of the population dependent on their subject matter or area of emphasis. It is this selectivity—or ability to reach narrowly targeted audiences—that is one of the main benefits of this medium in many advertisers' eyes. For example, for fashion and beauty tips, young women in Germany read *Freudin,* in France they read *Marie Claire,* and in the United States they read *Glamour.*

Other Local Media

Billboards Billboards are an important medium in many markets—both developed and developing. In crowded metropolitan areas, literally millions of consumers may be exposed to a single billboard message, and in countries with high levels of automobile ownership, billboards located along highways also prove an effective medium. Outdoor billboards in the Netherlands are even using interactive techniques to attract attention in a crowded media environment. As Derek Suchard reports, an increasing number of outdoor billboards in this country are "taking on elements not usually associated with the medium, including live models sitting in board-mounted displays and the use of boards to offer free samples. In one recent example, Westimex, a Belgian potato chip marketer, attached bags of Croky chips on 100 boards along streets across the country, inviting sampling with the headline 'Bet these are the best-tasting chips in Holland.' Passers-by accepted the offer, pulling down individual sized bags that were within reach."[11] Apparently, both consumers and the trade responded positively to the approach. In developing markets, where high levels of illiteracy are common, billboards, with their heavy emphasis on visuals and limited use of advertising copy, are a dominant medium. The primary disadvantage related to the use of the billboard medium encountered by international advertisers lies in the different standard sizes offered in different markets.

Transit Transit advertising is playing an increasingly significant role in many markets. For example, transit advertising is the most effective advertising medium in Romania, according to a survey conducted by the Economic University in Bucharest. Of all consumers surveyed, 91 percent said they remembered the content of transit ads, compared with 82 percent who remembered the content of TV ads and only 44 percent who remembered the content of print ads. Transit ad space there is available on two hundred buses, and recent advertisers have included R.J. Reynolds, Colgate-Palmolive, PepsiCo, Rank Xerox, and Philip Morris. Transit advertising may well rank higher than television because there is only one television station in Romania. In addition, magazines and newspapers are not nearly as sophisticated as Western publications and therefore are less attractive to advertisers.[12]

The use of transit media is expanding rapidly in China as well. A small firm in Singapore recently acquired the worldwide rights to sell on space on buses, trains, ferries, and airports throughout the vast territory of China. Until now, little transit advertising has been sold in this market. However, observes Ian Stewart, the potential for the development of this medium is enormous: "More than half a million people are carried up and down Changan Avenue in central Beijing every day and in Shanghai more than 160 ferries operate daily."[13] Moscow provides an example of an innovative use of transit media. Recently, Mandara—a Swedish firm—signed an agreement with the Moscow Post Office for exclusive twenty-year rights to broker advertising on the sides of Moscow's 800 postal vehicles and on the walls of the city's 660 post offices. Under the agreement the Swedish firm also may use postal vehicles for client deliveries and outfit 10,000 Moscow postal carriers in uniforms highlighting a client's logo. The first marketer signed by the company is a Stockholm-based brewery, which bought rights to advertise on 100 postal trucks and at least one post office wall for three months. Mandara is also targeting companies such as Japanese electronics manufacturers and European food companies.[14]

Cinema Cinema advertising is commonly overlooked by U.S. marketers because the medium is in its infancy in this country. In many countries, however, where it is common to subsidize the cost of showing movies by running advertising messages both prior to and after the feature film, cinema advertising has become an important medium. For example, India has the highest film audience and the highest level of per capita movie attendance of any country in the world, and as a result, cinema ads play a much greater role in this country than in the United States. Indeed, this medium offers access to market segments that would be impossible to reach via any other medium.

Direct Mail In a large number of markets, direct mail campaigns are hampered by a lack of reliable mailing lists. In addition, various national regulations impact the viability of this medium for many international marketers. In Saudi Arabia, for example, sending consumers a direct mail piece is considered an invasion of privacy. And in Chile letter carriers collect additional postage from recipients for every item delivered because senders pay only part of the postage. Clearly, the use of the direct mail medium is quite limited in this country—customers generally do not take kindly to paying for unsolicited advertisements.

Media Unique to Developing Countries In developing countries, which tend to lack the media resources of advanced nations, marketers often adopt unusual promotional strategies. For example, Group Africa, a firm based in Johannesburg, developed Roots Television (RTV), an innovative means for reaching South Africa's rural population. Through a network of 550 TV sets and VCRs in country stores, ladies clubs, and traveling shows mixing advertising and entertainment, RTV claims it reaches 3.2 million rural Africans each month—consumers who could not be easily reached via more traditional media. Every four to six weeks, RTV representatives visit rural stores and deliver videotapes featuring six hours of entertainment along with eighteen minutes of commercials per hour. The entertainment is tailored to the local village—RTV representatives tape weddings, initiations, coming-of-age ceremonies, gospel music, and sporting events. The raw footage is edited and commercials are inserted in RTV's Durban studios. On the next trip through the village, a premiere of the local tape is held, which remains with the store owners. The ladies clubs are included to help draw customers to participate in a day of fun and games, songs and contests, and free samples once every three months. Up to several thousand villagers come from far and wide for an opportunity to see themselves on screen. Group Africa's clients include Lipton, Colgate-Palmolive's Stay Soft fabric softener, Nestlé's Nespray baby milk formula and Gold Cross condensed milk, and Unilever's Van Den Bergh Foods' Rama margarine. Shop owners pay RTV $42 a month for TV and VCR rentals.[15]

Media Unique to Advanced Markets While the international marketer will face unexpected media forms in developing countries, the same is true in many more developed markets as well. Japanese advertisers are finding dramatic spaces and new techniques for ads, including giant outdoor video screens and train tunnels. Units of major Japanese agency giants such as Dentsu are at the forefront in developing these new media forms. David Kilburn and Julie Skur-Hill report: "Dentsu PROX, for instance, has developed a commercial purpose for the sky. With Search Vision, images can be freely suspended by using projectors and aircraft or balloons as screens."[16] Recently, a Japanese department store used the method to announce its new store in front of Sapporo Station. Dentsu PROX also developed TunnelVision, using train tunnels as an ad medium. A series of images behind boards placed at ten-meter intervals are lit when the train passes, creating images like those made by flip cards.[17]

Interactive television and interactive kiosks are examples of two new media forms that are being tested in Europe. Interactive Systems, an Oregon-based firm, has been operating TelePick in Spain since early 1993. The service, which allows viewers to play along with game shows, print out coupons, and vote in electronic polls, connects to the viewer's TV and telephone and includes a remote control, a printer, and a small monitor. The company has already sold over 16,000 units to Spanish consumers for about $170 each. Participating advertisers include Gillette, Pizza World, and Chesebrough-Ponds, which runs a weekly infomercial that quizzes viewers through the set-top box and rewards them with beauty-tip booklets and other prizes. If an advertiser is offering a coupon, the consumer will be alerted by a beep and a message on the screen and can then hit a button to print out the coupon from a small printer attached to the set-top box. A similar program was initiated in the Netherlands, where companies such as Coca-Cola, McDonald's, and Procter & Gamble tested various interactive commercials. Currently, Interactive Systems is beginning a two-month test of its system in Portland, Oregon, and will then introduce the system to other U.S. markets.[18]

Similar technology has been incorporated in the development of the world's first interactive kiosk. In late 1992, *Paris Vogue* and French department store Le Printemps sponsored a multimedia interactive kiosk called "Sensaura" that helps customers select perfumes. Sixteen fragrances from such companies as Chanel and Estée Lauder participated in the promotion, which ran for two weeks in Le Printemps. Debra Aho describes the process: "The kiosk used a touch screen to guide customers through a series of questions about what they liked to do or wear. After answering the questions, customers got a short analysis of their personality and the names of two perfumes that might suit them. The customer could then go to the fragrance counter and request a sample of one of the perfumes."[19] Consumers responded favorably to the promotion, waiting in line up to thirty minutes to use Sensaura. In addition, the promotion was a traffic builder for Le Printemps and netted extra ad pages for *Vogue*. Both the publication and the department store are planning to use Sensaura again in the future. The technology uses multimedia computer software that also runs on online services and CD-ROM and that will eventually run on interactive TV. The system currently is being marketed to cosmetics, apparel, and computer companies.

International Media

While television, via satellites and cable, can send the Olympic games, royal weddings, and space shots into the homes of consumers in literally hundreds of countries, no single network controls this global transmission. However, international media that provide nearly global market coverage offer a means for international advertisers to reach consumers across many markets. The number of international media and the expenditures on them are rising rapidly.

International Print Media

International Magazines Print remains the dominant international medium, and magazines are considered the first of the internationalists. A number of U.S.-based magazines have international editions, including *Time, Newsweek, Reader's Digest, National Geographic,* and even *Playboy.* Time Warner's *People* magazine has just made its debut in a Chinese edition for Taiwan and Hong Kong. The publication's first issue carried twenty-five pages of ads for companies such as Lancome's Clinique, Estée Lauder, Polo Ralph Lauren, and Benetton.[20] *Cosmopolitan* has thirty-four international editions; Exhibit 7.3 shows an advertisement for *Cosmopolitan* appearing in a South American publication.

It is not only U.S. magazines that make their way across foreign borders. *Marie Claire,* a French monthly magazine with twenty-two editions published worldwide through joint ventures and licensing deals, recently debuted in the United States, becoming the newest member of the Hearst Magazine family. In many markets *Marie Claire* already competes with the international editions of *Vogue* and *Elle.*[21]

While many of these publications are translated into many different languages and are available in many different markets, their foreign readers are a quite different group in terms of demographics from those who read these publications in their country of origin. In foreign markets these publications appeal predominantly to international travelers and upscale, high-income consumers. However, the publications are generally less effective in reaching mass consumer markets and thus are of less value in promoting mass consumption items.

Business-oriented publications that reach businesspeople on a worldwide basis include *Forbes, Business Week, Fortune,* and *Harvard Business Review.* A major plus associated with such publications is that they provide verified circulation and audience data. In addition, they tend to lend the magazine's

EXHIBIT 7.3 Advertisement in a South American Publication Promoting *Cosmopolitan* as an Advertising Vehicle

prestige to advertised products. One of the drawbacks of such publications, however, is that they generally offer only English, French, and Spanish editions. *Forbes,* which already has foreign-language editions in Japan, Germany, and Hong Kong, plans to enter the Chinese and Latin American markets by 1995. The China edition is awaiting a license to begin publishing; to date, the Chinese government has never approved any foreign publication. The mainland China edition, which will be published monthly with a target circulation of 50,000, will have ad rates starting at $6,000–$7,000 for a color-page ad.[22] In an advertisement promoting *Business Week* to international advertisers, the copy notes: "Every issue delivers an elite international audience: 92% of our subscribers are citizens of their country of residence, 93% are in business, industry or the professions. Of these, 75% are in senior management and 57% are a member of the board of directors of their company."

International Newspapers Most of the international newspapers are directed toward the business community. In the past decade the *International Herald Tribune* has extended its distribution worldwide, opening nine new printing sites and boosting circulation by more than 60 percent to more than 200,000 copies in 164 countries. The newspaper is looking toward Latin America, Australia, Africa, Eastern Europe, and the former Soviet Union for additional growth opportunities.[23] Exhibit 7.4 shows an advertisement promoting the *International Herald Tribune;* the message boasts that this newspaper is read by more continental Europeans listed in the *International Who's Who* than any other international publication.

A Russian-language edition of *The New York Times* was introduced in Moscow in 1993, with plans for distribution in sixty cities in the former Soviet Union. This is the first foreign-language edition of the 141-year-old paper, and initial circulation is estimated at 100,000. Many publishers realize that similar life styles and interests in many different markets can be catered to using the same or similar publishing formulas. The fact that launching multilocal editions of newspapers spreads costs across several markets is not lost on international publishers.

International Broadcast Media

International Television International commercial television is increasingly appealing to a number of companies, including Sony, Coca-Cola, McDonald's, and Gillette. The growth and development of satellite technology is making multinational television networks a reality.

Cable has served to bring satellite TV into the homes of consumers and will likely remain the major means of receiving satellite transmissions. Those satellites with stronger transmitters allow households to receive signals

EXHIBIT 7.4 Advertisement Promoting the *International Herald Tribune* as an International Advertising Vehicle

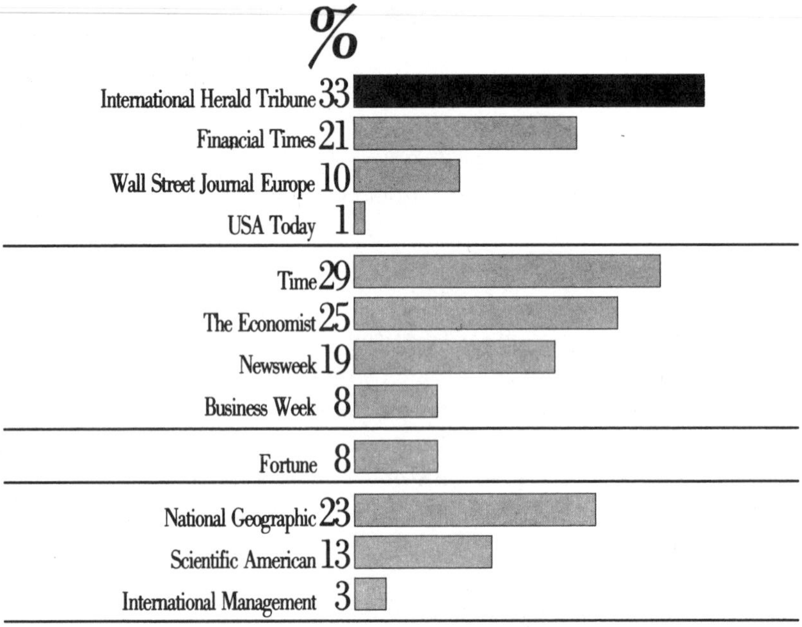

Reprinted by permission of the publisher.

directly via their own small dish antenna; however, penetration of such satellite dishes in most markets is still rather limited. Future developments in high-powered direct broadcast satellites (DBS) will make reception even easier. This will prove to have significant impact for those regions lagging in cable infrastructure.

Satellite television plays a particularly dominant role in Europe. Currently, four main satellites serve Europe: Intelsat, Kopernickus, Astra, and Eutelsat. Over 50 percent of total viewing by individuals in Germany, the Netherlands, Sweden, and the Flemish-speaking part of Belgium is done via commercial channels transmitted by satellite and cable, compared with 40.8 percent watching state-run TV, according to a survey conducted by Pan European Television Audience Research.[24] Note that numbers add to more than 100 because some respondents said they watch both. Only in Denmark is state TV considerably more popular than satellite/cable. Less than ten years ago, the traditional state-owned and public service sector enjoyed a secure collective audience share of about 90 percent in the countries surveyed.

Currently, the United States has the largest number of cable stations to choose from—but they are all American cable stations. In some developing markets (Indonesia, for example), middle-class consumers can watch TV programs from all over the world—Australia, Malaysia, the Philippines, and the United States. Interestingly, consumers in less developed markets are thus receiving the widest selection of viewpoints.

The following ten pan-European television channels provide service on the continent: Superchannel, MTV: Music Television, Eurosport/TESN, Euronews, Cable News Network, Children's Channel, Discovery, NBC's Super Channel, Cartoon Network, and The Movie Channel. The list is likely to grow longer in the near future. Cable News Network (CNN) began providing twenty-four-hour news coverage in the United States in 1980, and within a decade it was offering programming in over eighty countries worldwide. AT&T, MCI Communications, Delta Air Lines, and General Electric are primary advertisers on CNN. In an advertisement appealing to media planners, CNN invites the reader to "join the leading companies of the world who have included CNN International in their strategic global planning."

In addition to MTV Europe, there is also MTV Australia, MTV Brazil, and a program called MTV Internacional in Latin America; MTV Japan is on the drawing board. As shown in Exhibit 7.5, MTV reminds advertisers that its programming is viewed in eighty-seven countries on five continents—reaching 235 million homes internationally.

Severely limited program choices and limited advertising opportunities on government-controlled stations in much of Europe have proved to be a growth incentive to these satellite networks and channels. Yet, many nations are attempting to restrict both advertising and programming beamed into their country over foreign satellite channels because of a concern with

IN 87 COUNTRIES, IT'S THE
UNIVERSAL PASSION.
(OKAY. SO IT'S THE OTHER
UNIVERSAL PASSION.)

EXHIBIT 7.5 Advertisement Promoting MTV as an International Advertising Medium

preserving national identity. This is of greater concern to some nations than others. For example, the United Kingdom offers a relatively friendly regulatory environment as authorities have largely ignored a European Union directive, in effect since 1991, called "Television Without Frontiers." As Laurel Wentz reports:

Strict adherence to the guidelines in other European countries may present some obstacles to satellite TV. For example, the French are strictly interpreting the directive's requirement that at least 60% of the programming be European-made where practical. After scrutinizing TNT and Cartoon Network's proposed first two weeks of programming, France's Conseil Superieur de l'Audiovisuel has simply banned the channels from France's one million cable homes. The channels can be seen now only by 100,000 homes with their own dishes. The council has warned French cable operators [that] anyone telecasting the channels would be subject to penalty because the two channels showed no intention of complying with the directive.[25]

Other channels in other countries may well face similar restrictions.

International Radio International commercial radio plays its most significant role worldwide in Europe, where a number of stations reach several nations. These stations have transmitting power up to five times that allowed in the United States, enabling them to cover much of Europe. The leading station is Radio Luxembourg, broadcasting in five languages with over 40 million listeners from the British Isles to Germany, Austria, and Switzerland.

Table 7.4 details worldwide and regional distribution of international media. The profiles include information about numbers of editions, languages published, and costs of advertising. Criteria for inclusion of broadcast media in the table are (1) reception on at least three continents, (2) advertising support, and (3) programming that runs on at least three continents as a network. Print media criteria for inclusion in the table are (1) substantial mass circulation on at least three continents, (2) worldwide circulation of at least 50,000 of international editions equal to at least 10 percent of the domestic circulation, and (3) advertising support.

International Media Data

Audience profiles and circulation data are closely monitored in most highly developed nations. Advertisers in these markets have come to expect and rely on data supplied by large, independent, syndicated research services in making virtually all media decisions. One such service is A.C. Nielsen, the primary TV audience measurement service in the United States, which is also contracted to collect data in Canada, Australia, and Japan. Its entry into Europe has been somewhat slower, however. Although Nielsen provides service in Sweden, Norway, and Finland, it recently failed to win the audience measurement business in Germany, the United Kingdom, and France.[26]

TABLE 7.4 Global Media Lineup by Circulation and Household Reach

MEDIA	TOTAL DISTRIBUTION 1994	1993	% CHANGE
Dailies			
Financial Times, London	297,463	288,967	+2.9%
International Herald Tribune, Neuilly, France	190,705	195,315	−2.4
USA Today, Arlington, VA	2,108,830	2,064,808	+2.1
The Wall Street Journal, New York	2,937,059	1,994,863	+47.2
Weeklies			
Business Week, New York	1,006,762	1,013,602	−0.7
The Economist, London	568,683	534,122	+6.5
The Guardian Weekly, Manchester, England	102,221	106,177	−3.7
Newsweek, New York	4,108,000	4,075,000	+0.8
Paris Match, Paris	194,434	203,699	−4.5
Time, New York	5,616,000	5,491,000	+2.3
Monthlies			
Cosmopolitan, New York	5,755,795	5,812,085	−1.0
Esquire, New York	1,207,478	1,174,558	+2.8
Good Housekeeping, New York	5,715,865	5,657,739	+1.0
Harper's Bazaar, New York	1,056,711	1,028,198	+2.8
National Geographic, Washington	9,367,954	9,555,722	−2.0
Reader's Digest, Pleasantville, NY	27,584,000	27,925,000	−1.2
Redbook, New York	3,826,869	3,941,694	−2.9
Runner's World, Emmaus, PA	519,000	510,000	+1.8
Scientific American, New York	633,653	626,157	+1.2
The WorldPaper, Boston	1,698,100	1,300,000	+30.6
Other Print			
Fortune, New York	870,000	870,000	0
TV			
BBC Worldwide TV, London	23,800,000	—	—
CMT: Country Music Television, New York	34,900,000	33,800,000	+3.3
CNN, Atlanta	143,000,000	141,000,000	+1.4
Cartoon Network, Atlanta	34,400,000	24,000,000	+43.3
The Discovery Channel, Bethesda, MD	85,000,000	64,000,000	+32.8
ESPN, New York	130,700,000	110,000,000	+18.8
MTV: Music Television, New York	250,800,000	252,000,000	−0.5
Middle East Broadcasting Centre, London	7,029,000	—	—
NBC, New York	181,100,000	—	—
TNT, Atlanta	84,500,000	76,400,000	+10.6

SOURCE: *Advertising Age*, January 6, 1995, p. 119. Reprinted by permission of the publisher.

			REGION		
North America	Central/South America	Europe	Middle East/ Africa	Asia	Australia/New Zealand
29,748	1,299	255,246	3,000	7,689	301
10,867	1,436	129,577	5,204	42,984	362
2,038,830	—	48,317	—	19,349	—
1,854,901	977,000	59,201	—	45,957	—
886,326	19,710	62,981	—	37,745	—
258,698	10,927	224,225	16,108	45,925	12,800
26,994	3,043	22,253	32,178	8,303	15,000
3,100,000	73,000	290,000	50,000	225,000	110,000
32,395	1,399	121,894	16,833	649	—
4,443,000	96,000	530,000	91,000	306,000	150,000
2,528,280	636,343	1,781,489	110,272	398,000	301,411
739,828	—	112,650	—	355,000	—
5,056,700	203,129	456,036	—	—	—
738,647	77,652	158,035	—	82,377	—
7,942,463	101,654	911,605	—	158,933	229,958
16,706,000	1,111,000	7,176,000	390,000	1,071,000	630,000
3,253,746	—	423,123	—	—	150,000
430,000	—	77,000	12,000	—	—
518,167	9,370	76,191	4,023	9,952	15,950
3,000	204,500	510,000	30,000	950,600	—
740,000	—	65,000	—	55,000	—
7,000,000+	—	2,000,000+	—	7,200,000+	—
26,800,000	—	8,000,000	—	3,236	400
62,000,000+	1,600,000	50,000,000+	—	4,400,000	—
12,000,000	1,500,000	20,400,000	—	500,000	—
67,100,000	5,000,000	10,000,000	—	2,800,000	—
63,000,000	4,300,000	56,000,000	200,000	7,200,000	—
59,400,000	13,400,000	57,800,000	—	13,838,000	—
—	—	414,000	6,615,000	—	—
95,000,000	1,100,000	65,000,000	—	20,000,000	—
61,000,000	2,600,000	20,400,000	—	500,000	—

Overall, research on international media is quite limited, in large part because of the high costs involved. However, a number of services conduct research for specific media and in specific regions, including the Pan-European Television Audience Survey (PETAR), the European Business Readership Survey (EBRS), International Financial Management in Europe Survey (IFME), the Pan European Survey (PES), the Asian Businessman Readership Survey (ABRS), and Asian Profiles 5.[27]

For data in most other countries, comparable services tend simply not to be available, particularly in developing countries. What data are made available may well be supplied by the media themselves, and such unaudited statistics are often viewed by international marketers as rather suspect. Verification of such figures clearly is a difficult task. When data are available, local differences in auditing procedures may make country-by-country comparisons nearly impossible. Data provided are also often outdated and quite simplistic. For example, figures with regard to pass-along circulation are typically not provided, yet such secondary circulation can be quite substantial in many markets. This lack of accurate media information presents one of the primary headaches for media planners operating in foreign markets.

International Media Buying Services

There are a number of ways that the media planning and/or buying function can be handled in the international setting. The traditional model has all planning and buying conducted by the client's domestic or lead agency. Another option is to conduct media planning centrally but to handle media buying on a local basis in each country in which the international advertiser operates. A third option is to turn the function (either all or part) over to an independent international media buying service; such services have been cropping up over the past few years. These firms work either directly for international clients or for their advertising agencies. They are generally responsible for finding the local media best suited to the client's needs and the target audience to be reached, providing accurate media data, conducting the negotiations and obtaining the best rates, making the purchase, and monitoring placement.

Increasingly, media conglomerates are launching global media buying systems. Such systems package magazines, newspapers, and broadcast and other media properties in order to maximize international cross-media possibilities and to integrate agency and client media needs. CNN, a pioneer in global media buys, today reaches 70 million households in about 125 countries. In a deal with CNN in 1992, Coca-Cola purchased a schedule that represented the first time an advertisement appeared simultaneously around the world. General Electric has also used CNN to promote its corporate image spots worldwide.[28] In a deal between Hachette, a global media concern, and Ford Motor, the auto manufacturer purchased space in eighty-four Hachette magazines, including the company's sixteen U.S. titles, as well as magazines in Europe, South America, and Asia. While the initial buy involved only print, Ford is considering adding other Hachette media properties including TV, radio, newspaper, outdoor, and book publishing operations.[29] And many agency executives predict that there will soon be a wave of such media packages.

Summary

In this chapter, by no means were all forms of local and international media available to the international advertiser addressed. A media planner may also turn to taxi cab advertising and to sponsored events and trade shows, among a multitude of other media that in many cases may be specific to a particular market. An advertiser planning on entering a specific market must undertake an in-depth analysis of the media situation particular to that country. Basic questions that must be asked relate to the availability and viability of both traditional and "unique" media; the coverage, costs, and quality of various media; the role of advertising in the media of a specific country; the selection of local or international media, or a combination of the two; the availability of reliable media data; and the decision whether the client, agency, or independent media service should be responsible for media planning and buying. It should also be understood that media change in the international arena is rapid and that many of the facts and statistics presented here may well be out of date in just a few short years. Therefore, in Chapter 8 we discuss research in the international arena as a means of ensuring the best data possible.

Notes

1. Stewart, David, and Kevin J. McAuliffe, "Determinants of International Media Purchasing: A Survey of Media Buyers," *Journal of Advertising,* 17(3), 1988, pp. 22–26.

2. Peebles, Dean M., and John K. Ryans, *Management of International Advertis-* *ing: A Marketing Approach* (Boston: Allyn & Bacon, 1984), p. 173.

3. World Bank, *World Development Report 1994: Infrastructure for Development* (New York: Oxford University Press, 1994), pp. 162–163.

4. Kasriel, Ken, "Rates Double for Air-time in Hungary," *Advertising Age,* September 28, 1992, p. I22.

5. Geddes, Andrew, "Chinese Media Resist Call for Change," *Advertising Age,* November 8, 1993, p. I14.

6. Marsh, Ann, "Private TV Nears OK in Poland," *Advertising Age,* July 19, 1993, p. I10.

7. Parnes, Sharone, "Open Israel Cable to Ads, Marketers Say," *Advertising Age,* October 26, 1992, p. I20.

8. Lingam, T.S.K., "Star TV Skirts India Ad Limits," *Advertising Age,* September 28, 1992, p. I20.

9. Sloan, Pat, "TV Ads Gaining Favor Worldwide," *Advertising Age,* November 25, 1991, p. 28.

10. Wentz, Laurel, "Media Buying Adds Creativity," *Advertising Age,* July 19, 1993, p. I15.

11. Suchard, Derek, "Netherlands Boards Get Added Dimensions," *Advertising Age,* May 17, 1993, p. I19.

12. Kelly, Janice, "Bus Ads Ride High in Romania," *Advertising Age,* April 27, 1992, p. I36.

13. Stewart, Ian, "Chinese Ad Space Open to New World," *Advertising Age,* November 8, 1993, p. I14.

14. Bartal, David, "Ads Leave Stamp on Moscow Mail," *Advertising Age,* July 5, 1993, p. 8.

15. Barnes, Kathleen, "Reaching Rural S. Africa," *Advertising Age,* April 19, p. I3.

16. Kilburn, David, and Julie Skur-Hill, "Creativity Cracking Through Ad Clutter," *Advertising Age,* December 10, 1990, p. 41.

17. Ibid.

18. Donaton, Scott, "Interactive System Tries U.S. Market After Test in Spain," *Advertising Age,* November 8, 1993, p. 24.

19. Aho, Debra, "France Says Oui to Interactive Kiosk," *Advertising Age,* November 8, 1993, p. 25.

20. Geddes, Andrew, "Chinese *People* Arrives in Taiwan, Hong Kong," *Advertising Age,* February 14, 1993, p. I2.

21. Donaton, Scott, "Hearst in '94 to Unveil Marie Claire, Lauren," *Advertising Age,* December 13, 1993, p. 4.

22. Kilburn, David, and Andrew Geddes, "Forbes Edition to Enter China by Mid-1994," *Advertising Age,* April 19, 1993, p. I17.

23. Crumley, Bruce, "Bruce Huebner—How He Grew *International Herald Tribune* into Global Paper," *Advertising Age,* October 26, 1992, p. I15.

24. Downer, Stephen, "Satellite, Cable TV Take Lead in Europe," *Advertising Age,* April 19, 1993, p. I4.

25. Wentz, Laurel, "Satellite TV Risk Pays for Murdoch," *Advertising Age,* September 20, 1993, p. I2.

26. Bowes, Elena, and Dagmar Mussey, "Nielsen Finds Tough Going As It Seeks TV Business for Europe," *Advertising Age,* July 19, 1993, p. I3.

27. De Mooij, Marieke, and Warren Keegan, *Advertising Worldwide* (New York: Prentice-Hall, 1991), p. 227.

28. Fahey, Alison, "New GE, Coke Deals Boost CNN," *Advertising Age,* January 27, 1992, p. 4.

29. Donaton, Scott, "Hachette Signs Ford in Global Media Deal," *Advertising Age,* February 10, 1992, p. 3.

CHAPTER 8

Research in the International Arena

The role of research is equally important in domestic and international marketing and advertising. Its basic purpose is to assist advertising and marketing managers in making more informed, and therefore better, decisions. When planning to sell goods to foreign consumers, each element of the marketing mix must be investigated. As noted in Chapter 2, the product must be appropriate for a given market. In some cases the same product can be marketed around the globe; in others modifications may be required. The marketer must determine the most appropriate price, which may be influenced by the firm's short- and long-term objectives, the competitive environment, and a variety of other factors. The marketer must establish the availability of various channels and select the most efficient means of distribution. Marketing research can address each of these areas. Finally, the international marketer must consider promotion of the product: personal selling, sales promotion, direct response, public relations efforts, and, of course, advertising. Advertising research may involve life style studies, concept testing, message pre- and post-testing to determine reactions to different types of advertising appeals and executions, and, finally, determination of appropriate media vehicles. Each of the marketing mix decisions will be influenced by the international marketing environment, outlined in Chapter 3. The marketer must familiarize him- or herself with demographic factors such as market size and population growth, economic factors including degree of urbanization and income distribution, geographic characteristics such as topography and climate, and the political-legal climate in terms of potential political risk and regulatory restrictions. In addition, the marketer must understand the cultural environment—verbal and nonverbal language, values and attitudes, and religion and ethical standards, as well as customs and consumption patterns, as explored in Chapter 4. Jean-Pierre Jeannet and Hubert Hennessey note that "the complexity of the international marketplace, the extreme differences from country to country, and the frequent lack of familiarity with foreign markets accentuate the importance of international market research."[1] Research can help to prevent a multitude of marketing blunders.

Despite the importance of undertaking such research, it is not as frequently employed internationally as it is domestically. Indeed, for many reasons, a significant number of both consumer and industrial goods firms conduct little or no research in most of the foreign markets in which their products are sold. The dominant reason is the high cost associated with conducting research, particularly if primary research is deemed essential. Many companies for which foreign markets represent a relatively low profit potential find it difficult to justify such an investment. In addition, conducting international research is no easy task. Coordinating research and data collection across a number of countries can prove quite challenging, and there is the associated difficulty of establishing comparability and equivalence.[2] Finally, all too many marketers have a rather limited appreciation for the significantly different character of foreign marketing environments. As a result, management relies on little more than casual observations or generalizations drawn from other markets, rather than basing their marketing and advertising decisions on solid research. In this chapter we outline the basic steps in international marketing and advertising research.

Steps in Research Design

The procedures and methods related to conducting marketing and advertising research in the international arena are conceptually and methodologically similar to conducting such research in domestic markets. Most research studies involve a common series of tasks: (1) define the research problem, (2) identify information sources, (3) design the research, (4) collect data, and (5) analyze and report the research data.

Problem Definition

Subhash Jain defines *marketing research* as the process of "gathering, analyzing and presenting information related to a well-defined problem. The focus of the research is a specific problem or project with a beginning and an end. Marketing research differs from marketing intelligence, which is information gathered and analyzed on a continual basis."[3] Defining the problem is the most important task in international research because at this stage the researcher determines precisely what information is required. Problems may even vary from one market to another. This may reflect differences in socioeconomic conditions, levels of economic development, cultural forces, or the competitive market structure.[4]

Determination of Information Sources

Next, the researcher must determine where necessary information can be found. In some instances research may be limited to the collection of secondary data. *Secondary data* refers to information that has previously been collected and is available from another source—for example, governmental bodies, trade associations, or syndicated research suppliers. The collection of secondary data is generally considered the appropriate starting point for all international investigations, as it is most easily accessible and least expensive to obtain. Secondary data can assist in identifying areas of interest not adequately addressed and therefore deserving of additional attention. Marketers may then collect primary data. Presumably, *primary data* provides more relevant information because it has been collected for the sole purpose of addressing the researcher's stated problem. Both qualitative and quantitative methods can be employed in the collection of primary data. The advantages and disadvantages of both secondary and primary data will be discussed in detail later in the chapter.

Research Design

As Brian Toyne and Peter Walters explain: "A research design is simply a framework or plan adopted to study a particular research problem. It is the blueprint followed when collecting and analyzing data. Its dual purpose is to ensure that the study is relevant to the problem and that it employs economic, effective procedures."[5] The research design typically entails determination of research techniques and instruments to be employed as well as the sampling plan. Each of these areas will be discussed in greater detail later in this chapter. The researcher may choose among several research techniques: observation, focus group interviews, experimental techniques, and surveys. The most commonly employed instrument for gathering primary data is the survey questionnaire. Issues critical to the design of survey questionnaires include functional equivalence, instrumental equivalence, measurement, scaling, and wording. For surveys the investigator must know how to draw a sample from the population to be studied that is both representative and comparable.

Data Collection

Tracking down secondary data sources can be both time consuming and labor intensive. Further, the marketer must realize from the outset that secondary data is unlikely to be available for all variables or in all markets. With regards to secondary data, the issues of accuracy, comparability, and timeliness will be of concern. In the case of primary data collection, the sample must be drawn and the survey instrument must be administered, generally via telephone, mail, or in-person interviews. Here, the researcher must watch for and guard against nonresponse bias, topic bias, and social bias as well as researcher and respondent bias. Again, each of these issues will be discussed in greater detail in a later section.

Data Analysis and Reporting

Because secondary data was originally collected to serve other purposes, analyzing it requires combining and cross-tabulating various data sets in order for the information to be of use to the researcher. In the case of primary data, the information collected must first be edited and coded. Care must be taken in applying those analytical tools appropriate to the quality of the data collected. Only then can interpretation take place. Finally, the researcher compiles a report that highlights how the research results relate to the originally stated research problem. This report is generally presented to headquarters management as well as local subsidiaries.

Secondary Data

Secondary data, or preexisting statistics or information gathered for a purpose other than that of the immediate study, offers some real advantages to the international marketer.[6] Collection and analysis of secondary data is typically the first step in market research for most firms, because a tremendous amount of information can be obtained in this fashion. In addition, secondary data generally can be collected fairly quickly and easily, and, most importantly, relatively inexpensively—most secondary sources provide the information free or for only a minimal fee. The primary cost, then, for accessing this information can be viewed in terms of the time and energy spent by the research staff. Secondary data is particularly valuable for firms planning on entering smaller markets, because their more limited profit potential may permit only modest research expenditures.

Problems with Secondary Data

A major problem international marketers face with regards to secondary research is data availability. While the United States is unmatched in terms of the abundance of demographic and economic information available to marketers, this is certainly not the case in every country. In developing markets in particular, secondary data is relatively scarce. Indeed, a direct relationship seems to exist between the availability of secondary data in a country and its level of economic development. Further, while much demographic or economic information may be accessible, more specific types of data, such as information regarding consumer needs or life styles, are nearly impossible to obtain from secondary sources. Available data must be evaluated in terms of accuracy, comparability, and timeliness.

Secondary data often is less accurate than the international marketer would prefer. The data available in developing markets in particular tends to be a good deal less accurate than information from developed nations. Industrially advanced countries typically tend to be quite skilled in market research and to possess well-developed data collection mechanisms. In less sophisticated markets, data collection is generally rather rudimentary and experienced research personnel are not abundant. This directly impacts the quality of the data. For example, if a sample has not been randomly drawn, the results cannot be assumed to be representative of the total population. Data collection methods should always be examined to determine whether proper research methods were employed. More often than not, statistics available in Third World nations represent little more than estimates or even, in some cases, wishful thinking. International marketers should be wary of who collected the data and for what reason. In many countries the primary data-gathering organization is the government, which may have reason to under- or overrepresent certain statistics. For instance, a specific country may wish to downplay statistics that might be associated with a negative image, such as high levels of illiteracy or disease; or politicians may overemphasize favorable items, such as industrial production levels, in an attempt to attract foreign investment. Such manipulation of the data is often associated with a country's attempt to obtain assistance from various donor organizations, nations, or agencies.

Even when secondary data is available and accurate, it may not be comparable. If the international marketer is to evaluate foreign countries, the data collected must be comparable. Items of interest to the international marketer may be defined differently from one country to the next. For instance, explain Susan P. Douglas and C. Samuel Craig, how the term *urban* is defined varies from market to market:

> In Japan, for example, urban population is defined as a *shi* (city) with 50,000 inhabitants or more, or *shis* (population usually 30,000 inhabitants) with urban facilities. In India it includes all places with 5,000 inhabitants or more. In Nigeria, it includes the forty largest towns; and in Kenya and Zaire, agglomerations with at least 2,000 inhabitants. Similarly, in France and West Germany, it includes communities with 2,000 or more inhabitants, while in Norway and Sweden it goes down to localities or built-up areas with as few as 200 inhabitants.[7]

Likewise, one researcher attempted to collect international data on the number of women in the work force in different countries. As Table 8.1 shows, she obtained wildly conflicting estimates depending on the source. Explanations for the diversity in figures are myriad. For instance, some figures are based on different age parameters. Some are gathered by survey rather than census, and censuses and surveys do not always collect the same information. Some figures represent estimates, while others represent hard data. Finally, different definitions of what constitutes the "work force" impacts the ultimate number.[8]

There is also the question of the *timeliness* of the data. In some countries data may be collected annually, while in others literally decades pass before a survey is again undertaken. There is often a very good reason for this lag in data collection activity. Information gathering is an expensive endeavor, so that in a country with limited resources, data collection may simply not be a priority. Few countries—developed or not—can match the frequency of U.S. data collection efforts.

Data from secondary sources from any country (including the United States) must be checked and interpreted carefully. As a practical matter, the following questions should be asked in order to judge the reliability of the data sources:

▶ Who collected the data? Would there be any reason for purposely misrepresenting the facts?

▶ For what purposes were the data collected?

▶ How were they collected (methodology)?

▶ Are the data internally consistent and logical in light of known data sources or market factors?[9]

TABLE 8.1   Variations in Statistics Related to Percentages of Women in the Labor Force

COUNTRY	Census	PERCENTAGES BY DATA SOURCE				
		Organization for Cooperation and Economic Development	International Demographics	Statistical Abstract of Latin America	Statistics Canada	Annual Abstract of Statistics UK
United States	55 (1985)	63	54	—	—	—
Canada	52 (1981)	62	61	—	46	—
Japan	49 (1985)	57	57	—	—	—
Great Britain/ United Kingdom	47 46 (1981)	59 (UK)	57 (UK)	—	—	49
Australia	46 (1981)	53	52	—	—	—
Federal Republic of Germany	39 (1980)	49	49	—	—	—
Italy	33 (1981)	41	41	—	—	—
Venezuela	31 (1984)	—	24	21	—	—
Mexico	28 (1980)	—	—	17	—	—
Brazil	27 (1980)	—	39	20	—	—

SOURCE: Rena Bartos, "International Demographic Data? Incomparable!" *Marketing and Research Today,* 17(4), November 1989, pp. 205–212. Reprinted by permission of Elsevier Science.

International marketers may turn to both domestic and foreign sources of secondary data.

Domestic Sources of Secondary Data

The U.S. Government More information is collected by the U.S. government than any other source in the world. The data, which are characterized by their timeliness and accuracy, are generally available to the public either at no cost or for a minimal fee. The Department of Commerce is heavily involved in promoting the expansion of U.S. business in the international arena through its International Trade Administration Division. The International

Trade Administration regularly publishes a variety of materials of interest to the international marketer, and this data can be accessed at field offices in every major city in the country. One such publication, *Overseas Business Reports*, offers basic marketing background information for almost every market throughout the world. In addition to marketing and economic data, the reports include information on taxation and trade regulations, copyright and trademark law, and channels of distribution. *Business America,* a weekly newsletter, is an excellent source of trade leads and lists of foreign governments interested in doing business with U.S. firms. Another series of documents focusing on foreign market opportunities, *Global Market Surveys,* provides in-depth reports on products and industries with export growth opportunities in foreign markets. *Foreign Economic Trend Reports* reviews current business conditions country by country, including statistics on GNP, wage and price indices, foreign trade levels, unemployment rates, and construction starts. Also, the Department of Commerce keeps firms abreast of developments in Washington that might impact international business undertakings. Many other governmental agencies and departments—including the State Department, the Federal Trade Commission, the Department of Labor, the Bureau of Census, the Department of the Treasury, and the Department of Agriculture—also publish information pertaining to international trade.

Foreign Embassies and Consulates As Subhash Jain notes, virtually all foreign nations have embassies in Washington, DC, as well as United Nations mission offices in New York City. In addition, foreign governments may have one or more consulate offices in the United States. Jain writes: "For example, the government of Brazil maintains consulate offices in New York, Chicago, Dallas, San Francisco, and Los Angeles in addition to their embassy in Washington, DC. Usually an embassy has a commercial attache who may be a good source of secondary information on a country. The consulate and U.N. mission usually have basic information on their country to offer the researcher."[10]

Foreign Trade Offices A number of foreign governments also maintain foreign trade offices (FTOs) in the United States—mostly in Washington, DC, and New York. The function of these FTOs is to assist U.S. exporters and importers, the end goal being the stimulation of trade. These offices can provide the international marketer with brochures, booklets, and newsletters outlining various aspects of doing business in their countries. One example of such an FTO is the Japan External Trade Organization, which has available over one hundred complimentary publications and films on doing business in Japan.[11]

Industry and Trade Associations Industry associations are generally formed to represent entire industry segments. For example, the industry associations for the automotive and pharmaceutical industries gather both national and international data from their members and publish them in aggregate form. A variety of business groups, such as chamber of commerces, the Conference Board, and the National Foreign Trade Council, also can provide marketers with counsel and information on local markets.

Banks and Other Service Institutions Major U.S. banks that operate multinationally (such as BankAmerica Corp. and CitiCorp), foreign banks with branches in the United States (such as Sanwa), and national banks located abroad (such as the Bank of England) provide assistance to their client companies engaging in marketing efforts around the globe. Marketers may find these banks' annual reports or yearbooks to be useful sources of information. In addition, many of these banks maintain libraries accessible to both current and potential customers. These banks may also provide a variety of services, including suggesting overseas markets for goods and services, locating potential foreign investors, contacting distributors, and obtaining information on foreign exchange regulations. In addition to banks, the international marketer can turn to accounting firms and transportation companies (such as major airlines and freight services) for information on business practices in foreign markets as well as basic trade data.

Universities Universities in general, and schools of business administration in particular, both in the United States and abroad, are excellent sources of information. For example, Harvard has an abundance of case studies on almost every country worldwide. The University of Texas has published close to one hundred case studies on foreign markets. Similarly, libraries at the University of Washington, Pennsylvania State University, and the University of Southern California all house relevant bodies of information.

Research Firms Table 8.2 lists the world's top 25 research companies by non-U.S. revenue. Nielsen/IMS International, formerly reporting separately as A. C. Nielsen and IMS International, led the list at $1.158 billion. Parent company Dun and Bradstreet has merged the two operations, largely for expansion reasons. While Nielsen/IMS's foreign operations recorded a 2.2 percent decline from the previous year, the firm still earned more than eight times the revenues generated by second-place Video Research. U.S. firms are well represented among the top 10 research companies. Not unlike American advertising agencies, U.S. research firms have followed in the footsteps of their clients and turned to foreign soil for growth.[12] These organizations are devoted to the gathering and selling of marketplace information,

TABLE 8.2 The Top 25 Research Companies by Non-U.S. Revenue (in U.S. million $)

RANK			NON-U.S. RESEARCH REVENUE			NON-U.S. REVENUE AS % OF TOTAL	
1993	1992	COMPANY	1993	1992	% Change	1993	1992
1	1	Nielsen/IMS International	$1,158.0	$1,184.0	−2.2%	62.0%	62.5%
2	2	Video Research	132.5	133.9	−1.1	100.0	100.0
3	3	Research International Group	124.3	122.6	1.4	84.6	84.3
4	4	MRB Group	69.0	64.7	6.6	66.3	64.2
5	7	Walsh International/PMSI	54.0	39.0	38.5	42.9	38.2
6	5	Global Market Research	51.1	50.4	1.5	96.9	97.4
7	8	Information Resources	50.2	35.2	42.6	15.0	12.7
8	6	Millward Brown	46.7	44.5	4.9	61.4	62.7
9	9	Gallup Organization	27.0	21.0	28.6	26.2	24.7
10	11	Louis Harris & Associates	18.0	14.4	25.0	62.1	60.0
11	10	Macro International	17.0	15.0	13.3	56.7	55.6
12	12	NPD Group	15.7	13.1	19.8	23.8	22.9
13	13	Goldfarb Consultants	8.5	8.9	−4.3	30.3	33.5
14	14	Opinion Research	8.4	8.2	2.4	24.3	24.0
15	16	National Research Group	7.0	2.9	141.4	20.3	10.7
16	15	Pretesting	6.9	7.2	−4.2	79.7	88.9
17	17	BAI	2.2	1.7	29.4	25.1	24.0
18	18	Intersearch	2.0	1.6	25.0	6.2	5.3
19	21	BASES Group	1.8	1.3	39.5	5.8	4.4
20	19	Roper Starch Worldwide	1.8	1.5	16.7	7.0	6.6
21	22	M.O.R.-PACE	1.3	1.2	4.2	7.5	8.0
22	24	Griggs-Anderson Research	1.2	0.8	60.0	19.4	12.5
23	23	M/A/R/C	1.0	1.1	−6.3	2.3	2.0
24	96	Wirthlin Group	1.0	1.1	9.0	6.6	8.8
25	26	Lieberman Research West	1.0	0.5	89.2	6.3	3.8

SOURCE: Kenneth Wylie, "Special Report Research: U.S. Industry Spreads Toward $3 Billion," *Advertising Age*, November 28, 1994, pp. 27–30. Reprinted by permission of the publisher.

specializing in data related to consumer behavior so difficult to obtain from other sources.

Consulting Firms, International Advertising Agencies, and Other Sources A number of consulting firms gather, organize, and make available information of value to international marketers. For example, Business International (BI), headquartered in New York City, is an excellent source of information on GNP, population, foreign trade, and production for over one hundred and thirty countries. Weekly newsletters also highlight the experiences and challenges firms face in various international markets. In addition, BI conducts regular and ad hoc studies dealing with international marketing issues. Another service that can prove useful in evaluating international market environments is the Economist Intelligence Unit (EIU), which is based in London and associated with *The Economist* magazine. EIU reports on economic and political trends for over one hundred and fifty countries around the globe, publishes a large number of special reports, and also conducts customized market studies for international firms.

Major international advertising agencies, through their overseas offices, can provide clients with guidance in marketing goods in foreign countries. International advertising agencies may be affiliated with local research firms or may offer clients the services of their in-house research departments. Backer Spielvogel Bates Worldwide has invested more than $2 million in Global Scan, a program that sponsors annual surveys of consumers in seventeen different countries. Via a scale that measures 250 attitudes, including 130 that are specific to an individual country and 120 that cross cultural boundaries, Global Scan has identified five global psychographic types: Strivers, Achievers, Pressureds, Adapters, and Traditionals. Such research can often reveal cultural differences that can either make or break an advertising campaign. For example, reports Rebecca Purto:

> [Global Scan] found an important difference in how Strivers relate to their cars in the U.S. and Japan. In the U.S., Strivers are under both time and money pressure. Japanese Strivers are under time pressure, but they have enough money. What they don't have is space. The average young person in Japan gets married with $25,000 in the bank, while in the U.S., the average young person is at least $5,000 in debt. U.S. Strivers want cars that are fun, stylish, fast and a good value. Japanese Strivers consider their car an extra room, and they will spend extra to put in lace curtains or expensive stereo systems. So the price-oriented appeal that works on a U.S. Striver would be lost on a Japanese Striver who likes extra features.[13]

Finally, the international marketer should also investigate a number of trade journals and other periodicals as potential sources of secondary information. For example, *Business Week, Business International, The Economist,*

The New York Times, and *Advertising Age* often publish special reports on specific countries or regions as well as data reflecting global marketing trends.

International Sources of Secondary Data

Simply because secondary data is not available domestically does not mean it may not be available abroad. Various international organizations as well as regional bodies (such as the European Union) and even the governments of individual countries can be tapped for international marketing data.

International Organizations International organizations such as the United Nations, the World Bank, the International Monetary Fund (IMF), the General Agreement on Tariffs and Trade (GATT), the Organization for Economic Cooperation and Development (OECD) all provide extensive data of value to the international marketer.

The UN—and its affiliated organizations—is the official source of many international statistics. UN data is carefully compiled and generally acknowledged to be quite accurate. It should be noted, though, that UN statistics are not always completely reliable because the UN must occasionally depend on unsubstantiated statistics provided by member countries. The UN publishes the *Statistical Yearbook of the United Nations* (which provides demographic and economic development data plus political, geographic, and cultural information on over two hundred and fifty countries). A monthly statistical supplement to the *Yearbook* is available as well. The UN also publishes a variety of regional reviews including the *Economic Survey of Europe* and the *Economic Survey of Asia and the Far East* (which cover developments on topics such as trade and balance of payments). *The World Trade Annual* provides data from the principle trading nations by commodity and country. The UN Industrial Development Organization's (UNIDO) primary objectives are the advancement of developing nations and the fostering of industrial cooperation between regions and countries of the world. As part of these efforts, UNIDO publishes a variety of documents useful to the international marketer. UNIDO's annual report, *Industry and Development: Global Report,* presents forecasts of industry output for most countries and regions of the world.

The World Bank's *World Tables* summarizes for international marketers valuable data on living patterns for 124 countries, including such indicators as radio, television, telephone, and auto ownership per thousand households. *The World Bank Atlas,* published annually, presents information on population size, growth trends, GNP, life expectancy, infant mortality, and education levels for various countries. The World Bank is also an excellent source for information on production, industrialization, trade, energy usage, and social and military spending.

The IMF publishes *International Financial Statistics* on a monthly basis to provide information on the financial status of over one hundred countries. In addition, the IMF makes available data on a variety of national economic indicators, such as GNP, industrial production, inflation rate, and money supply, among other statistics.

GATT provides international marketers with a number of valuable resources, including the *Guide to Sources of Information of Foreign Trade Regulation* and the *World Directory of Industry and Trade Associations.*

The OECD conducts studies on the economic performance of its member countries, publishing both quarterly and annual data. Two publications in particular will be of interest to those conducting business internationally: *The OECD Economic Outlook,* which provides statistics from a semi-annual survey of trends in member nations, and *The OECD Economic Surveys,* which contains information on the economic standing of each member country.

International Marketing and Market Research Organizations A number of international organizations, including the International Advertising Association (IAA), the World Federation of Advertisers (WFA), the American Marketing Association (AMA), the American Academy of Advertising (AAA), and the European Society for Opinion and Marketing Research (ESOMAR), publish a wealth of marketing- and advertising-related information. Some also regularly undertake surveys—for example, the International Advertising Association conducts an annual survey of all international advertising agencies. Such organizations also organize conferences where delegates from around the globe present papers and exchange experiences.[14] Conference proceedings also serve as valuable resources.

Regional Organizations The European Union is an excellent resource for statistics specific to European countries. Eurostat, the statistical office of the EU, publishes *Demographic Statistics,* which provides, as the name implies, basic demographic information on member countries. Euromonitor, headquartered in London, publishes two volumes on European markets as well as an additional volume on all other markets. An incredible amount of detailed information is available in these publications, from population, employment, production, trade, and economic data to statistics on consumption, housing, health, education, communications, and standard of living. With regards to standard-of-living data, Euromonitor provides information on comparative wages and earnings, consumer prices, comparative costs, consumer durables, household expenditures, and ownership of radios, TVs, and autos.

Foreign Governments The governments of the countries that the international marketer is planning to enter can be an important source of secondary information, although both the quantity and the quality of the data is likely to vary from one market to the next. Even if the requested information is not available on hand, governmental employees are generally able to direct the international marketer to the appropriate source. Unfortunately, much of the data available in foreign markets may be published only in the native language.

The preceding provides just a brief overview of major sources of secondary data. Clearly, it is impractical to include a complete listing of all secondary sources available for all international markets. However, for an expanded discussion of the topic, see Edward Cundiff and Marye Tharp Hilger's "Compendium of Secondary Sources of Information on International Marketing"[15] and Susan P. Douglas and C. Samuel Craig's list of "Selected Secondary Sources."[16]

Primary Data

While secondary data is likely to reveal most basic demographic and economic information needed by international marketers in order to conduct business in a specific country, many marketing and advertising decisions require more specific kinds of information. As Philip Cateora and Susan Keaverney point out, "Consumer buying behavior, attitudes about products or promotional messages, relevance of product attributes, product positioning and other manifestations of cultural and societal norms are usually product- or industry-specific and must be gathered by primary research. This information may be critical to sound tactical decisions and usually warrants the time, energy, creativity and expense required to collect it."[17] This statement highlights the major advantage of conducting primary research—the fact that the data collected is specific to the firm's needs.

The greatest disadvantage associated with primary data collection is that it can be quite expensive. The international researcher's golden rule should be to exhaust all secondary sources before doing primary research, and then to obtain only the data that is absolutely necessary.[18] Research conducted abroad is generally a good deal more costly than comparable research conducted in the domestic market. For example, the cost of conducting a usage-and-attitude study with similar specifications was compared for a number of European countries. If the index average base equals 100, then Italy, for instance, would have a cost index of 136, France an index of 149, and Switzerland an index of 155.[19] Even in developing markets, research tends to be expensive. This increased cost stems from a number of factors, including limited availability of marketing research firms abroad and differences in the level of sophistication of such firms. For this reason the use of primary research in the international arena is a good deal less widespread than it should be, particularly in less industrialized markets. Yet, it is precisely in these countries that management is likely to be less familiar with market conditions and more prone to making marketing errors. Dean Peebles and John Ryans provide the following advice: "We recommend one particular criterion when considering the value of a research project: will the benefits obtained from the information be greater than the cost of conducting the research. In answering the question, the advertising manager must recognize both the short-term and long-term value of the information and its potential use across markets."[20] As might be expected, larger companies are more likely to conduct primary research in foreign markets than smaller or even medium-sized firms.

Primary Research Methods

The manner in which primary data is collected is strongly influenced by culture. U.S. managers tend to prefer methods allowing them to collect large quantities of data that can then be manipulated statistically. Quantitative methods are generally the tool of choice. In fact, suggests Joseph T. Plummer, "American marketers are number crazy and need numbers or scores to make decisions."[21] This is not to say qualitative techniques do not have a place in Western research. Focus group and in-depth interviews are commonly employed in advertising investigations. The preoccupation with numbers is not nearly so prevalent in other countries. For example, Japanese-style market research depends to a greater extent on nonquantitative approaches, including both soft data—obtained from visits to dealers and other distribution channels members—and hard data—dealing with shipments, inventory levels, and retail sales. Indeed, many Japanese managers express disdain for large-scale consumer surveys and other scientific research tools so commonly employed in the West. Johny K. Johansson and Ikujiro Nonaka write: "As the head of Matsushita's videocassette recorder division once said: Why do Americans do so much marketing research? You can find out what you need by traveling around and visiting the retailers who carry your product."[22]

Qualitative and quantitative research methods include observation, focus group and in-depth interviews, experimental techniques, and surveys. Because each method has certain strengths and weaknesses when used in foreign markets, international marketers and advertisers are increasingly relying on triangulation studies. Here, two or more entirely different methods are employed to study the same research question. If similar results are obtained by the various techniques, the researcher can feel relatively confident that the findings are both valid and reliable.

Observation

Here, the researcher plays the role of a nonparticipating observer, noting the activities or behaviors of members of another culture relevant to the stated research question. Subjects may be either aware or unaware of the fact that they are being observed. Many international marketers and advertisers believe that this data-gathering process, traditionally used by anthropologists, is too cumbersome and snail-like in its pace to be of any value to their more immediate needs. However, many international business situations warrant such an approach. For example, the researcher may wish to obtain a sense of purchasing behaviors in a real-world setting such as a retail outlet. As a methodology observation is also particularly valuable to marketers completely unfamiliar with a given market or market situation. Upjohn, for instance, hired a professionally trained anthropologist as part of its plans to begin marketing products in Indonesia. Using participant observation techniques, the anthropologist was able to transform relevant cultural data into a form usable by the company.[23]

Focus Group Interviews and In-Depth Interviews

In focus group interviews, some seven to ten members of the target audience are invited to discuss a specific topic related to the marketer's or advertiser's research question, typically in a home or laboratory setting. A focus group moderator guides the discussion, which can last from two to four hours. Participants may be more willing to discuss certain issues in such a group setting than they would be in a one-on-one interview. While focus group interviews do not provide statistically significant data due to the small sample size, they help provide insights into underlying consumer motives and attitudes. Focus group interviews are particularly effective in studying product positioning, packaging, and advertising themes and diagnosing the possible need for changes in advertising strategy.[24] In-depth interviews are basically unstructured means of collecting information from either individuals or small groups. Both techniques tend to be time consuming and costly. Also, there are significant cultural differences in the willingness of respondents to discuss their feelings openly. Because of this, a highly skilled interviewer or moderator capable of stimulating discussion is essential. Note, too, that neither focus group sessions nor in-depth interviews are amenable to statistical analysis.

Experimental Techniques

On the topic of experimental techniques, Susan P. Douglas and C. Samuel Craig state: "Experimental techniques are, at least in theory, potentially applicable to all cultural and socioeconomic backgrounds. In practice, however, it is often difficult to design an experiment that is comparable or equivalent in all respects in every country or socio-cultural context. Experiments, particularly field experiments, typically incorporate certain elements of the specific socio-cultural context in which they are conducted."[25]

Surveys

Surveys are employed where quantitative data are desired. Collection of primary data in foreign markets via survey methods presents a variety of challenges generally not encountered when conducting research in the domestic market. These include, but are not limited to, problems relating to data comparability, instrument design, sampling, data collection, and infrastructure limitations. Note Brian Toyne and Peter Walters: "At best, failure to recognize these problems results in findings that are of no value to the decision maker. At worst, it results in decisions that may prove extremely costly for the firm."[26]

Challenges Relating to Data Comparability The issue of comparability was discussed previously with regards to secondary data. However, it also plays a significant role in the collection of primary data. A researcher may examine a particular phenomenon in just a single market or undertake an investigation in a number of countries. For example, the research objective may be to explore the potential effectiveness of a specific advertising theme in Germany or to determine the feasibility of employing the same theme across the European Union. If cross-cultural research is being conducted, every effort must be made to ensure that the findings from different test markets can indeed be compared. The challenge of comparability increases with the number of markets under investigation. Even when the research program initially focuses only on a single country, similar research may be required for markets that the firm subsequently enters—again reinforcing the importance of comparability.

In order to achieve comparability, researchers engaging in cross-cultural investigations must deal with the external environmental factors of functional equivalence and conceptual equivalence. In addition, researchers must concern themselves with the internal measurement issue of instrument equivalence (which will be addressed in the next section). The researcher must be sensitive to *functional equivalence,* which refers to whether a concept, behavior, or product serves the same or a different function in the markets under consideration. For example, while refrigerators are used to store frozen foods in some countries and to chill water and soft drinks in others, in certain markets they serve as status symbols and are prominently displayed in the home—often in the living room rather than the kitchen. If similar products have different functions in different societies, their parameters cannot be used for comparative purposes.[27]

A second consideration in cross-cultural research is *conceptual equivalence.* Explains Yusuf A. Choudhrey: "Sometimes concepts have totally different meanings in different cultures and are thus inappropriate for use on an international scale. This means that proper care has to be exercised to ensure that the words used to elicit response carry similar meanings to individuals in different cultures."[28] For example, the word *family* has very different connotations in different parts of the world. In the United States it generally refers to the nuclear family consisting of mother, father, and children, whereas in other countries it could also include grandparents, aunts, uncles, cousins, and so on.

Instrument Design Challenges For purposes of comparative evaluation, the international researcher also must strive for *instrument equivalence,* which Choudhrey defines as "the necessity of an instrument that measures a phenomenon uniformly in different cultures. . . . Unfortunately, the most popular instrument for collecting consumer data, the survey questionnaire, is susceptible to considerable bias in cross cultural applications."[29] Fortunately, however, instrument design is one element over which the researcher does have some control.

The issues of measurement, scaling, and wording are central to the design of the research instrument.[30] Asking the right question—in the right way—is always a challenge in marketing research, whether conducted in domestic or foreign markets. In designing the survey instrument, the researcher must ensure that the questions are measuring the same thing in each market. Susan P. Douglas and C. Samuel Craig note that the "most significant problems in drawing up questions in multicountry research are likely to occur in relation to attitudinal, psychographic, and lifestyle data. Constructs such as aggressiveness, respect for authority or honor may not be relevant in all countries and cultures."[31] W. Fred Van Raaij provides an excellent example of a totally inappropriate questionnaire statement designed to measure social responsibility in a foreign market: " 'A good citizen is responsible for shoveling the sidewalk in front of his home.' This statement assumes private ownership of houses, one-family housing, and a climate with snow in winter, and is clearly not applicable in an African country."[32] Here, social responsibility would need to be measured with a completely different statement or perhaps even a series of statements.

The appropriateness as well as the effectiveness of various scales and response categories is dependent on the market in which the research is to be conducted. The semantic differential is one type of scale that is widely believed to be pan-cultural. However, even here the international researcher must exercise caution. While the 5- or 7-point semantic differential scale is commonly employed in the United States to rate objects and other items, in some countries consumers are much more familiar with 10- or even 20-point scales, while in still others respondents are most comfortable with a 3-point scale. When confronted with a verbal 7-point scale ranging from "excellent" to "terrible," Westerners tend to start from the extreme positions and then work inward, whereas Japanese tend to take a neutral position and move outward, seldom reaching the extremes.[33] Thus, the range of Japanese scores is generally much more limited than that of Westerners, making the use of such scales problematic. This seems to be a cultural phenomena—Japanese tend to arrive slowly at a fixed position, carefully weighing all known facts and consequences before responding.

Response categories may need to be expanded or collapsed depending on the specific market. For instance, in a study that required the determination of marital classification in Gabon, the standard categories of "married," "single," "divorced," and "widowed" were used. The category of "concubine" was not included even though about 20 percent of the female respondents fell into this category. This is a typical case of applying Western classifications and assuming that they will be inclusive in other cultures.[34] On the other hand, some categories may need to be dropped. When asking Third World customers where they purchase an item, it may be advisable to delete "supermarkets" as a possible response if a particular area is not blessed with this institution.

With regard to wording, the translation of a survey instrument into a foreign language can pose significant problems for the international researcher. While some questions are relatively easy to translate (such as those dealing with demographic information—age, sex, education), if the goal is to collect data regarding motivations and attitudes, the researcher must ensure that questions are understood by foreign respondents. Some questions simply cannot be translated into another language because the words do not exist to express precisely the same thought.[35] The problem of survey instrument translation is compounded in multilingual societies—for example, fourteen different languages are spoken in India. Here, the researcher may be tempted to use the official language (say, English or French), only to find that just a fraction of the population speaks that language.[36]

In order to minimize translation errors, many experts suggest that researchers employ the back-translation technique.[37] Back-translation, as noted in Chapter 6, involves independent translators translating the questionnaire into the foreign language and then back into the original language and finally comparing the two versions for equivalence. Even when using the same language, care must be taken in transporting the survey from one country to the next. Translation difficulties were experienced in a questionnaire designed for the United Kingdom. A question aimed at business executives was to have read, "Should advertising practitioners be certified?" but instead was understood as, "Should advertising practitioners be confined to an insane asylum?" The British word "certificated" should have been employed as it is the equivalent of the American "certified."[38] It is generally advisable to pilot test all survey instruments prior to undertaking the investigation, ideally with a subset of the population under investigation.

Problems with equivalence can be encountered in other areas of international research as well, including sampling, data collection procedures, and the analysis and interpretation of results.

Sampling Challenges After designing the survey instrument and translating it into the foreign language(s), the researcher must determine the appropriate respondents and the procedures best suited to selecting a sample from the population. Respondents selected for a survey may, in fact, vary significantly from one market to the next. For example, in examining purchase behavior of major household durables, researchers in the United States are likely to focus on women in their survey. In some foreign markets, however, men may be the primary decision makers. And in still others, several family members might be involved in the decision; thus, the focus would most appropriately be on the group rather than on an individual.

Sampling refers to the selection of a subset or group from a population that is representative of the entire population.[39] Most commonly employed sampling methods were developed for use in economically advanced markets, such as the United States, and as a result, these methods are not always transferable to other nations.[40] For example, in most Western countries researchers prefer to employ a probability sample because it allows an accurate prediction of the margin of error. Since the size of the population in a probability sample is known, data collected from the sample (if it is of adequate size) can be projected to the entire population. In a *random probability sample* each unit selected has an equal chance of being included in the sample. In a *nonrandom probability sample* each unit has a known probability of being selected.

In any probability sampling the researcher must have access to reliable information that can be used as sampling frames—such as census data, census maps, electoral lists, telephone listings, mailing lists, and so on. While such data are readily available in industrialized countries, they may simply not exist in many poorer markets—or if available, they may be sorely out of date. For example, as Philip Cateora and Susan Keaverney point out, "Neither Cairo nor Tehran have telephone books. Saudi Arabia has neither street names nor house numbers. Street maps are frequently unavailable in parts of South America."[41] A lack of infrastructure may further complicate sampling procedures. In many Third World countries only a small percentage of the population may own telephones, and it may be nearly impossible to access rural areas if adequate transportation is not available. In short, it is often extremely difficult to obtain a proper random sample in less developed markets. The researcher's only viable alternative may be to employ nonprobability sampling procedures, such as convenience sampling or judgment sampling. A convenience sample involves selecting any respondent who happens to be readily available. A judgment sample involves selecting respondents based on the assumption that certain individuals are likely to be better informed than others or possess expert knowledge in a given area. For example, the researcher may focus on village elders or local authority figures.[42] Such nonprobability samples generally do not lend themselves to inferential statistical analysis, and as a result, the data collected cannot be assumed to be representative of the entire population.

The researcher must also consider whether the same sampling procedures should be employed across markets. Sampling procedures may vary in their reliability from one country to the next; thus, employing identical procedures is no guarantee of comparability. It may be preferable to utilize different methods that have equivalent levels of accuracy or reliability instead.

Data Collection Challenges A variety of data collection methods can be employed, including mail, telephone, and in-person surveys. Each has its advantages and disadvantages, and the method ultimately employed depends largely on individual market conditions. The international marketing researcher must also consider the various forms of respondent bias, which may be related to the specific survey method selected, the country under investigation, the topic being explored—or a combination of these variables. One form is *nonresponse bias,* which refers to the fact that in some cultures individuals are more reluctant to answer questions posed by a stranger. While Americans are quite familiar with market surveys and generally willing to answer even the most personal questions, this is not the case in every country. In some markets respondents may be unwilling to share information because they suspect that the interviewers might, in fact, be government agents or perhaps tax auditors. The international researcher must also recognize that it may be extremely difficult to obtain responses from some segments of the population. For example, in Muslim countries women aren't allowed to speak with male interviewers, and the number of female interviewers is still quite limited because this is not considered to be an appropriate career choice for women.

Willingness to respond to questions dealing with certain topics is likely to vary from country to country as well. Some topics in certain cultures are simply perceived as more sensitive than others. For example, the subject of sex is considered taboo in India. Even in the United States many individuals are wary of responding to questions about their income. Therefore, potential areas of *topic bias* must be identified during the design of the research instrument. The international researcher is also likely to face some form of *social bias*. For instance, social acquiescence bias refers to the increased tendency for respondents in some markets—particularly in Asian countries where courtesy is highly valued—to provide the response they believe will most please the interviewer, rather than stating their true beliefs. In societies with a collective orientation, respondents are not used to making individual decisions; therefore, questions demanding individual answers may be problematic. Likewise, respondents may attempt to give an answer they think reflects popular opinion so as not to appear to deviate from the norm. This social desirability bias is a particular danger in group interviews, where a participant might look to others for the "appropriate" response.

When researchers from one country conduct an investigation in another country, they also must deal with what is termed *researcher bias*—the tendency to observe phenomena or behavior in the host country and define it in home-country terms.[43] One way to counter researcher bias is to incorporate the perspectives of researchers from a variety of different cultural backgrounds.

Finally, there is the danger of *researcher–respondent bias,* which refers to the interaction that may take place between the interviewer and respondent, thus tainting the survey results. If the interviewer is perceived to be a foreigner, there may be an increased level of mistrust, further contaminating the data collected.

Mail surveys are quite popular in industrialized markets for a number of reasons. First, the cost of administering mail surveys tends to be relatively low on a per-questionnaire basis. Respondents may also be more willing to respond to sensitive questions via a mail survey, and there is no potential for researcher–respondent bias. On the downside, nonresponse may be higher than with other survey methods, which can bias the results of the investigation. Also, all control over responses to the survey instrument is lost in mail surveys. For instance, the respondent may fail to answer some questions and respond incorrectly to others. The use of a mail survey may be inappropriate in many developing markets due to poor mail service or a lack of available mailing lists. In addition, many developing countries are characterized by high levels of illiteracy (up to 50 percent in some Asian and African markets); clearly, where illiteracy prevails, written questionnaires are of little use.

Much like mail surveys, costs per respondent are relatively low for telephone surveys—at least in developed markets. Telephone surveys are an extremely fast means of obtaining necessary data, and nonresponse rates tend to be low. A major disadvantage associated with telephone surveys is that the interview itself cannot take too long, and questions cannot be overly complicated. In addition, respondents may be rather reluctant to answer certain types of questions over the telephone. Researcher–respondent bias can also come into play with telephone surveys. Even in economically advanced markets, the researcher must exercise caution when attempting to employ telephone surveys. For instance, Germany's laws are such that, if followed to the letter, telephone interviews would not be permitted unless the interviewee had previously agreed to be interviewed. This would, in effect, require two interview attempts—one to gain permission and one to conduct the interview. In addition, telephone numbers are not a fixed length, making random-digit dialing almost impossible. Developing countries pose a number of additional challenges. If levels of telephone ownership are low, as they are in many less developed markets, other survey methods may be more appropriate, unless the researcher is limiting data collection to urban areas. Telephone numbers may be difficult to access given that telephone books are nonexistent in some Third World markets. Further, telephone costs tend to be higher in many developing countries, making this a rather expensive means of obtaining data.

With in-person interviews, nonresponse rates are particularly low. Given data and infrastructure limitations, this approach may be the most viable means of data collection in poorer markets. Yet, even this method is not without its disadvantages. With a largely rural population in many developing countries, reaching potential respondents becomes a major challenge. Roads are likely to be poor, and reliable public transportation may simply not be available. In addition, in-person interviews are the most expensive method of administering a questionnaire to a sample population in any market. Finally, interviewer bias is a very real problem.

In much the same way that sampling procedures vary from one country to the next in terms of comparability, so, too, do data collection procedures. For example, in one country telephone surveys may be known to offer a certain level of reliability, while in another market mail surveys offer the equivalent level of reliability. In collecting data international researchers must be sensitive to such cross-cultural variations because they directly impact the comparability of the research results.

Infrastructure Limitations Skilled marketing and advertising researchers can be found in primary overseas markets as well as a number of developing markets.[44] However, the researcher should be aware that obtaining facilities, field staff, and other resources will likely be a significantly greater challenge in Third World countries. Not only must these individuals be well trained in the area of marketing research, they should be familiar with the local culture and conversant in the local language(s). In addition, they should recognize that infrastructure limitations pose a major stumbling block in many international investigations. As noted above, mail surveys are not feasible without reliable postal service. Similarly, telephone surveys are not possible if ownership of telephones is limited. Finally, undertaking research abroad becomes a good deal more difficult without adequate roads and transportation systems.

Research Relating to Message Design and Placement

Message research can help marketers to avoid promotional blunders in the international arena. For example, research allows the marketer to determine whether creative strategies should vary by country or whether a single strategy can be adopted for all markets in which the firm plans to operate (the issue of standardization versus specialization was addressed in detail in Chapters 5 and 6). Message research must be conducted in each market, as findings do not necessarily cross borders. Just because a particular advertisement tests well in Austria does not ensure that it will be equally successful in Germany or Switzerland.

Some of the same tools employed in domestic markets are also used in international advertising research. Life style data is of particular value to marketers, yet it can be exceptionally difficult to access, especially in developing markets. The researcher should begin by exploring secondary data—the anthropological literature is ripe with detailed studies of life style patterns and cultural values in a large number of countries. In order to select concepts and position brands, international marketers may find it necessary to conduct life style research to determine which patterns are similar across markets.

If advertisers wish to know whether foreign consumers understand the basic selling idea or product benefit highlighted and whether the message elicits the desired response, they may employ concept testing. The use of concept testing in international advertising research is growing rapidly, because, although it employs qualitative methods such as focus group discussions or in-depth interviews, it can provide considerable insights quickly and relatively cheaply.[45] For example, an American manufacturer of dishwashers introduced its product to the Swiss market using the same product benefit employed in the United States—convenience. The firm did not research the effectiveness of the convenience appeal and assumed (incorrectly) that the

Swiss consumer would respond much as American consumers had. What the firm did not realize was that Swiss homemakers are much more involved in their role than their American counterparts. Swiss homemakers rejected the idea of being replaced with a machine, and consequently, sales were dismal. Later, in-depth interviews revealed the source of the problem, and the product was successfully repositioned in terms of hygiene. The Swiss apparently place great value on cleanliness and responded favorably to a "kills bacteria and germs" appeal.[46] Ideally, concept testing should take place in the early stages of creative development. The logic behind this approach, explains Joseph Plummer, is that "if the basic selling idea has little relevance or appeal in a significant number of the markets, there is no value . . . to proceeding further by testing executions."[47]

Once there is agreement on the strategy, the international marketer must determine whether the message execution will be appropriate. Pretest research focuses on the potential effectiveness of an advertising execution prior to its full-scale use in a market or markets. For example, a number of years ago, Colgate-Palmolive wanted to relaunch Alert shampoo throughout Latin America. The anti-dandruff shampoo had been reformulated to deliver a better fragrance with a creamier, thicker lather. Initial research revealed a dichotomy in the target audience's attitudes toward dandruff. While the prospects—younger men and women—were quite interested in impressing the opposite sex, they perceived dandruff as little more than a minor annoyance that could be easily treated. Therefore, the agency team developed a strategy that emphasized how "new Alert helps you look and feel your best because your hair is healthy, shiny *and* dandruff free." The execution of this strategy was problematic: how to deliver the message without making the dandruff problem too serious and how to handle the sex appeal angle so as not to offend specific cultural mores. The pretest research design used a test-and-control methodology—the test cell being the newly designed spot for Alert ("Rapunzel") and the control cell being the former commercial. The test employed both open-ended and closed questions, along with a series of questions that asked respondents for their impression of what type of person might use Alert. These questions were included to help determine whether the spot was portraying users as more fashionable, younger, and stylish. Reports Joseph Plummer: "The research study was conducted in both Mexico and Venezuela and results from the two countries were remarkably similar. Rapunzel performed well in each test, delivering the key strategic message in a relevant, meaningful and refreshing way."[48] In broader terms, notes Plummer, "A trend has begun to emphasize the need to pretest copy and creative approaches even if standardized advertising is used."[49] The advertising issue becomes: Will the execution work *equally well* across markets?

Focus groups and in-depth interviews are commonly employed techniques in pretest research. Post-test research, on the other hand, is employed to determine whether the advertisement or campaign has achieved its objective—whether that be to build awareness, convey knowledge, generate liking, or create preference for the brand in each market. Not only is such research necessary in determining the success or failure of a campaign, but insights garnered through posttesting can suggest how the message might be modified or adapted in the future. While focus group interviews may be employed here as well, telephone and mail surveys are more commonly conducted to measure recognition and recall as well as changes in attitude ascribed to the advertising.

International advertisers are increasingly employing ad-tracking studies— the continual monitoring of brand awareness, image, trials, and usage trends. However, different conditions in different markets make comparison of tracking study results difficult. These conditions include (1) the size of advertising expenditures, (2) the nature of the brands, (3) the differences in advertising styles and cultures, (4) media differences in advertising practice, and (5) differences in legal restrictions.[50]

With regards to message placement, marketers will require information relating to the availability of media for commercial purposes as well as data relating to advertising readership, listenership, and viewership and audience characteristics. The individual media in established markets are capable of providing such information to the marketer. This is increasingly true of the media in developing markets as well. In addition, media-generated research—such as audience profiles, product perception surveys, and brand preference or awareness studies—may be available without cost from various foreign print and broadcast media. A number of general resources are likely to be of value to the international marketer, including the *World Radio and Television Handbook,* the *Media Guide International for Business and Professional Publications and Newspapers,* and Euromonitor's *European and International Marketing Data.* The number of quality international media placement services is also on the increase.

Control of International Research

There are three major approaches to organizing international marketing and advertising research: (1) centralized control, (2) decentralized control, and (3) coordinated control. Each has its advantages as well as disadvantages. The approach ultimately adopted is largely influenced by the overall manner in which the marketer's organization is structured, as well as by the size of the firm's international operations in general and specific markets.

Where a centralized mode of control is employed, headquarters is responsible for all aspects of the investigation to be conducted in each market. This includes determining data sources, outlining the research design and sampling procedures, and specifying the data analysis to be performed. Fieldwork may be undertaken by either headquarters staff or an outside organization. One of the major benefits of the centralized approach is that it ensures maximum comparability of studies conducted across a number of markets. It is also a good deal less expensive to coordinate research design and data processing and analysis in the home office, particularly if the firm is doing research on a regular basis. In addition, it is an excellent way for a firm to gain familiarity with a particular market. The primary drawback of this approach is that local conditions may not be taken into consideration. Too often, headquarters will prefer a uniform research design that may not be sensitive to host country differences. Also, headquarters staff may be too limited in size or lack the necessary skills in the areas of marketing and advertising research to conduct multicountry investigations.

Where research efforts are decentralized, headquarters establishes the research objectives but assigns supervision of the research program to local personnel. Local units may then opt to hire domestic research firms to assist in the design and implementation of the investigation. Data collection and analysis are handled in the host market, and upon completion of the study, a representative from the research firm or local management presents a report to corporate headquarters. This is often the mode of choice when a firm is completely unfamiliar with a particular country or is undertaking a specialized or one-time-only investigation. It may also be employed in cases where the volume of business in a particular market is limited and does not warrant headquarters' full attention. The major advantage of this approach is that researchers can adapt to differences in the local culture and infrastructure. In addition, local management may be more likely to implement changes based on research in which they were involved. The use of an outside research firm may also provide an added degree of objectivity, which is often of great importance to management. The potential danger associated with a decentralized approach is that the research design and data collection techniques may not be comparable with efforts undertaken in other markets, thus limiting the usefulness of the findings.

With a coordinated approach headquarters maintains its involvement in defining the research objectives but turns over the coordination of the research efforts in different countries to either an international research agency or the corporation's regional headquarters. The research agency or regional headquarters generally involves, to varying degrees, both headquarters and staff in the local operating units in the research endeavor. As a result, local operating units may be less likely to object to plans based on such research. The coordinated approach increases, but does not guarantee, the comparability of research results between markets, particularly if modifications are incorporated based on local input.

Summary

As companies increase their involvement in foreign markets, they recognize the importance of conducting international marketing and advertising research. This process involves defining the research problem, identifying information sources, collecting data, and analyzing and reporting the data. The two means of obtaining marketing information are collecting secondary data and conducting primary research. Secondary data is quick and inexpensive to obtain, so almost all international research begins with the collection of previously compiled data. However, as the extent of a firm's international involvement increases, so does its recognition of the importance of primary research. While secondary data can provide the marketer with a wealth of information, only primary data can truly address the marketer's more specific questions. Data collection methods include observation, focus group interviews, in-depth interviews, and surveys—telephone, mail, and in-person. Firms must also recognize that conducting research in the international setting differs from doing so in domestic settings, as well as decide on a centralized, decentralized, or coordinated approach to research efforts. A sincere commitment by management to conduct both secondary and primary research in each of the foreign markets in which their firm operates is sure to reduce the potential for marketing blunders. We now turn our attention to international media decisions.

Additional Readings

Caller, Linda. (June 1990). "Effective Management of International Research and Planning in Brand and Advertising Development." *Marketing and Research Today,* 18(2), pp. 109–114.

Choudhrey, Yusuf A. (Winter 1977). "Pitfalls in International Marketing Research: Are You Speaking French Like a Spanish Cow?" *Akron Business and Economic Review,* 17(4), pp. 18–28.

Douglas, Susan P., and C. Samuel Craig. (1983). *International Marketing Research.* Englewood Cliffs, NJ: Prentice-Hall.

Van Hamersveld, Mario. (August 1989). "Marketing Research—Local, Multidomestic or International." *Marketing and Research Today,* 17(3), pp. 132–138.

Van Raaij, W. Fred. (1977). "Cross-Cultural Research Methodology: A Case of Construct Validity." *Advances in Consumer Research,* 5, pp. 693–710.

Notes

1. Jeannet, Jean-Pierre, and Hubert D. Hennessey, *International Marketing Management: Strategies and Cases* (Boston: Houghton Mifflin, 1988), p. 203.

2. Douglas, Susan P., and C. Samuel Craig, *International Marketing Research* (Englewood Cliffs, NJ: Prentice-Hall, 1983).

3. Jain, Subhash, *International Marketing Management* (Boston: PWS-Kent, 1984), p.

4. Douglas and Craig, *International Marketing Research.*

5. Toyne, Brian, and Peter G. P. Walters, *Global Marketing Management: A Strategic Perspective* (Boston: Allyn & Bacon, 1989), p. 200.

6. Ibid.

7. Douglas and Craig, *International Marketing Research.*

8. Bartos, Rena, "International Demographic Data? Incomparable!" *Marketing and Research Today,* 17(4), November 1989, pp. 205–212.

9. Cateora, Philip R., and John M. Hess, *International Marketing* (Homewood, IL: Irwin, 1979), p. 262.

10. Jain, *International Marketing Management,* p. 562.

11. Ferraro, Gary P., *The Cultural Dimension of International Business* (Englewood Cliffs, NJ: Prentice-Hall, 1990).

12. Endicott, R. Craig, "European Dream Captivates Researchers," *Advertising Age,* October 18, 1993.

13. Purto, Rebecca, "Global Psychographics," *American Demographics,* 12(12), December 1990, p. 8.

14. De Mooig, Marieke, and Warren Keegan, *Advertising Worldwide* (New York: Prentice-Hall, 1991).

15. Cundiff, Edward, and Marye Tharp Hilger, *Marketing in the International Environment* (Englewood Cliffs, NJ: Prentice-Hall, 1988), pp. 553–572.

16. Douglas and Craig, *International Marketing Research,* pp. 306–317.

17. Cateora, Philip, and Susan M. Keaverney, *Marketing: An International Perspective* (Homewood, IL: Irwin, 1987), p. 47.

18. Peebles, Dean M., and John K. Ryans, *Management of International Advertising: A Marketing Approach* (Newton, MA: Allyn & Bacon, 1984).

19. Honomichl, Jack J., "Marketing/ Advertising Research: Ranking Top Players in Growing Global Arena," *Advertising Age,* November 24, 1986, p. S1.

20. Peebles and Ryans, *Management of International Advertising,* p. 145.

21. Plummer, Joseph T., "The Role of Copy Research in Multinational Advertising," *Journal of Advertising Research,* October/November 1986, pp. 11–15.

22. Johansson, Johny K., and Ikujiro Nonaka, "Market Research the Japanese Way," *Harvard Business Review,* 65, May/June 1987, pp. 16–22.

23. Ferraro, *The Cultural Dimension.*

24. Douglas and Craig, *International Marketing Research.*

25. Ibid., p. 40.

26. Toyne and Walters, *Global Marketing Management,* p. 197.

27. Choudhrey, Yusuf A., "Pitfalls in International Marketing Research: Are You Speaking French Like a Spanish Cow?" *Akron Business and Economic Review,* 17(4), Winter 1977, pp. 18–28.

28. Ibid., p. 20.

29. Ibid., pp. 21–22.

30. Cundiff and Hilger, *Marketing in the International Environment,* p. 244.

31. Douglas and Craig, *International Marketing Research,* p. 180.

32. Van Raaij, W. Fred, "Cross-Cultural Research Methodology: A Case of Construct Validity," *Advances in Consumer Research,* 5, 1977, pp. 693–710.

33. Fields, George, "Advertising Strategy in Japan," *Dentsu's Japan Marketing/ Advertising,* Fall/Winter 1980, pp. 52–56.

34. Mueller, Barbara, "Cultural Pitfalls in International Advertising Research," *Proceedings of the 1990 Conference of the American Academy of Advertising,* Patricia Stout ed., pp. RST 194–196.

35. Cundiff and Hilger, *Marketing in the International Environment.*

36. Terpstra, Vern, *International Dimensions of Marketing* (Boston: PWS-Kent, 1988), p. 73.

37. Brislin, R., "Back-Translation for Cross-Cultural Research," *Journal of Cross Cultural Psychology,* 1, 1970, pp. 185–216.

38. Mueller, "Cultural Pitfalls."

39. Keegan, Warren J., *Multinational Marketing Management* (Englewood Cliffs, NJ: Prentice-Hall, 1984).

40. Cundiff and Hilger, *Marketing in the International Environment.*

41. Cateora and Keaverney, *Marketing,* p. 50.

42. Douglas and Craig, *International Marketing Research.*

43. Cateora and Keaverney, *Marketing.*

44. Peebles and Ryans, *Management of International Advertising.*

45. Ibid.

46. Douglas and Craig, *International Marketing Research,* p. 13.

47. Plummer, "The Role of Copy Research," p. 15.

48. Ibid., pp. 11–12.

49. Harvey, Michael G., "Point of View: A Model to Determine Standardization of the Advertising Process in International Markets," *Journal of Advertising Research,* 33(4), July/August 1993, pp. 57–64.

50. De Mooig and Keegan, *Advertising Worldwide.*

CHAPTER 9

Advertising Regulatory Considerations in the International Arena

Much as the media scene of a particular country changes rapidly, so, too, does the regulatory situation. In fact, the two are often related. As new media forms evolve, such as satellite broadcasting, new regulations regarding advertising messages that may appear in those media also develop. Currently, advertising regulations differ significantly among nations. A message considered perfectly acceptable in one market might well be deemed inappropriate in another. Product categories that can be advertised freely in one country may be banned altogether elsewhere. In this chapter we will highlight the various types of advertising regulations and regulatory agencies the international advertiser may encounter when promoting goods and services in foreign countries. We will also discuss the role of self-regulation in both national and international markets and the implications of advertising regulation for the international marketer. Each of these points is relevant, regardless of whether the international marketer plans to undertake a standardized campaign or anticipates localizing promotional efforts for each country. Because it is beyond the scope of this text to provide a complete overview of the regulatory environment of each and every market, instead examples will be provided to reinforce the variety of advertising regulations worldwide.

National Regulation

Influences on National Regulations

Much in the same way international marketers must familiarize themselves with the foreign marketing environment, as discussed in Chapter 3, so, too, must they investigate the regulatory environment. Indeed, demographic, economic, geographic, political-legal, and cultural factors may all directly influence the regulatory situation. In particular, the degree to which advertising is regulated, as well as the forms that regulations take, is inextricably intertwined with the political system and the dominant religion of a country. The political environment in a nation shapes the prevalent attitudes toward business. Edward Cundiff and Marye Tharp Hilger explain: "Differences in attitudes may be due to different political structures or to party philosophies, history and tradition, the roles of interest groups or the political elite, an unstable political environment and forces of nationalism."[1] In Albania until as recently as three years ago, for instance, foreign investment was forbidden by law and foreign investors were considered agents of treason. The Stalinist totalitarian regime that had ruled Albania since 1944 fell apart with the collapse of communism in Eastern Europe. In 1994 Coca-Cola, the first major foreign investor, opened a $10-million bottling plant just outside the capital.[2]

Legal restrictions often are based on religious foundations, and particular religions may frown on certain business practices. For example, writes Katherine Toland Frith:

> Islam is the national religion in Malaysia and there have been cases where commercials have been withdrawn from the media because of complaints from religious authorities. The Seiko watch company has been running a worldwide campaign using the theme: "Man Invented Time, Seiko Perfected It." A series of commercials with this theme ran on RTM networks . . . until RTM received a complaint from the Head of Islamic Studies at University Malaya charging that this commercial should be withdrawn because God, not man, invented time. RTM complied. The agency was told that if they wanted to advertise in Malaysia they must change their slogan. After lengthy consultations with the client, a new slogan was developed: "Man Invented Timekeeping, Seiko

Perfected It." The agency had to change all TV commercials, as well as outdoor and press ads. They are now able to advertise once more.[3]

In some countries regulation may be quite limited, and the laws that reinforce such regulation quite lax, particularly in the developing markets. In others advertising regulation may be perceived as quite extensive and often be stringently enforced. As Barbara Sundberg Baudot points out, "International law accords the host country sovereignty over all peoples, resources and activities within their territorial limits. The capacity, willingness and effectiveness of the host countries to perform such roles vary considerably."[4] In a study conducted by the International Advertising Association, international executives identified fourteen countries as being highly restrictive: Germany, the United Kingdom, the United States, France, Canada, Australia, Sweden, Austria, Belgium, Argentina, Mexico, Italy, Finland, and Denmark.[5]

At the national level deceptive advertising practices are considered a crime in every country. The U.S. criteria for defining deception include determining whether the claim is false, whether the information presented is partially true and partially false, whether the message lacks sufficient information, whether the claim is true but the proof is false, and whether the message creates a false implication. Similar standards hold in other countries and have been adopted by international regulatory bodies as well. Clearly, such deceptive practices should be avoided because they are harmful not only to the consumer but also to honest advertisers and the public image of advertising in general.

China, prompted by the growing influence of Western agencies, is preparing to bring its advertising and marketing laws in line with the rest of the world. Currently, the industry is governed by laws dating back to 1979, when China first opened its free-trade economic zones. These laws banned ads that jeopardized the dignity of Chinese ethnic groups in ads, were counterrevolutionary in nature, or were obscene, disgusting, or superstitious. However, there were no restrictions on claims by advertisers for any type of product.[6] As the government attempts to crack down on rampant false advertising, new laws are being developed that will impact a number of product categories. For example, new regulations, jointly issued by the State Administration for Industry and Commerce and the State Pharmaceutical Administration, will influence advertisements for medicines and medical devices purported to diagnose, cure, or prevent illness or regulate bodily functions. Annually, as many as three hundred new medicines and medical devices (many of them variations on traditional Chinese herbs and methods of treatment) hit the Chinese market, prompted by the profit incentive of economic reform. While some of the ads are harmless, others are quite outrageous, such as a TV spot for an anti-aging tea that shows older people becoming young and virile. Other messages are potentially dangerous. Love Solution, a "sterilizing spray," claims it can protect the user from contracting

AIDS; print ads claimed the product was approved by the Virus Institute of the Chinese Academy of Preventative Medicine. According to new guidelines, all Chinese advertisements must be true, accurate, and scientific. Violators are subject to having their product's ad certification revoked and being fined up to the equivalent of $925, among "other punishments."[7]

Although international advertisers normally are wary of increased advertising regulation, in the case of Hungary, they are avidly supporting it. As Christopher Condon reports, "The rules, dealing with misleading advertising and product misrepresentation, will clarify legal guidelines and, advertisers hope, add some luster to a fairly tarnished image of advertising [in Hungary]."[8] Drafted by the Ministry of Justice, the proposals set strict penalties for offenders. First, those found guilty of false product presentation—using a name or logo similar to a competitor's—will face up to three years in prison and a fine of approximately $38,000. While existing laws ban outright forgery of competing product names, use of slightly altered names and widely recognized symbols is widespread. For example, athletic bags can be purchased from street vendors that carry the Adidas symbol under the brand name "Adios." Second, those found guilty of making exaggerated product claims or offering false purchase incentives, such as phantom sweepstakes and contest prizes, will face up to two years in prison and a fine of approximately $38,000.

Advertising regulation also focuses on the type of products that may be advertised, the content or creative approach that may be employed in advertising, the media that all advertisers (or different classes of product/service advertisers) are permitted to employ, the amount of advertising that a single advertiser may employ in total or in a specific medium, the use of advertising materials prepared outside the country, the use of local versus international advertising agencies, and specific taxes that may be levied against advertising.[9] Each of these areas will be addressed in turn.

Types of Products That May Be Advertised

Numerous countries have bans or restrictions on advertising of various products, including but not limited to alcohol, cigarettes, and pharmaceutical products. France, the nation whose name is synonymous with wine, is also the nation with what may well be one of the world's most restrictive laws controlling the advertising of alcoholic beverages. Initial provisions of the law, which was enacted in 1991, banned all subtle and not-so-subtle references to social or financial success. Advertisements were limited to showing the product and naming the place where it was made, how it was made, and how it should be consumed. Also mandated was a warning that read: "The abuse of alcohol is dangerous to your health. Consume in moderation."[10]

The European Council of Ministers is currently meeting to review the pan-European ban on tobacco advertising. Economists have noted that a ban on such ads could cut smoking up to 5 percent. However, the proadvertising faction questions whether governmental banning of products is truly an effective means of changing consumer behavior, suggesting that advertising does not increase the number of smokers but simply maintains brand differentiation. Further, they argue that a ban would be an infringement on individual freedom and set a precedent for widespread censorship.[11] The United Kingdom, Germany, the Netherlands, Denmark, and Greece strongly oppose the ban, and together these countries form a blocking minority. If the tobacco ban is not approved, European Union health ministers may consider giving self-regulation a try for a period of several years.

In 1992 the Czech Republic banned all tobacco advertising in all media, including TV, print, radio, cinema, outdoors, and tram. However, legal loopholes as well as a lack of enforcement allow international cigarette marketers to get around the ban. In some countries the rules on cigarette and liquor messages change so rapidly that advertisers aren't really sure what can and what cannot be done. For example, in attempting to enter the Eastern European market, Saatchi & Saatchi debated as to whether to picture its client's cigarette package in the ad. The consternation came about because of the frequent shifts in what's legal with regards to tobacco advertising in Hungary and to what extent the laws are enforced. The ad produced by Saatchi & Saatchi ended up showing the package along with several cigarettes indicating each pack contains twenty-five cigarettes—five more than rival brands— even though other cigarette marketers had been fined for showing cigarettes in their messages. According to Dagmar Mussey, "The rule of thumb that most of the powerful multinational companies follow is: Lobby hard, then run as many ads as you can get away with. Even government officials admit there is vagueness in some rules," and repercussions are mild. The maximum fine in Hungary is $115 per court case.[12] China has an interesting way of regulating cigarette and liquor advertising—both product categories are totally banned except in hotels and establishments that foreigners frequent.

While most international marketers are accustomed to some form of restrictions on the products noted here, there are numerous unanticipated restrictions as well. For example, margarine cannot be advertised in France. In addition, the French government severely restricts the advertising of tourism because it encourages the French to spend their francs outside the country.[13]

The Content or Creative Approach That May Be Employed

Many countries have restrictions on the types of claims advertisers can make, the manner in which products can be presented, and the appeals that may be employed in advertisements. For example, France has just begun to permit comparative claims, while Germany discourages them by requiring messages to pass rigorous fairness tests before comparative claims are allowed. In Japan, until quite recently, comparative ads have been a rarity, not because of specific regulations, but rather because in Japanese culture direct confrontation and actions that cause another to lose face are considered taboo. Nonetheless, a recent General Motors ad asked Japanese consumers to "Compare our Seville's fuel efficiency with Infiniti's" in seven major newspapers.[14] In Canada rulings with regards to comparative claims are quite stringent. In essence, puffery, an acceptable practice in the United States, could be interpreted in Canada as false and misleading advertising. In the United States puffery is defined as "an advertiser's opinion of a product that is considered a legitimate expression of biased opinion."[15] However, in Canada puffery that goes beyond claims for the product and implies superiority over other brands may carry the potential for legal consequences. A statement such as the "strongest drive shaft in Canada" would be judged misleading unless the advertiser had absolute proof that the drive shaft was indeed stronger than any other drive shaft for sale in Canada.[16] South Africa's Advertising Standards Authority, the industry's self-regulatory body, is considering loosening its strict policy against comparative ads. Marketers currently are prohibited from naming competitors, showing rival brands, and making any comparisons that would identify a specific brand. Advertisers in the country favor relaxation of the policy and have made their opinions known to the Authority.[17]

In the past the lack of advertising regulation in Taiwan encouraged many marketers to use blatant puffery and even outright lies in product ads. Under new federal Taiwanese consumer protection guidelines expected to be enacted soon, advertising claims for the first time are considered a contract rather than a simple solicitation. Legal experts explain that whatever marketers now claim in ads becomes part of a contract if a consumer accepts the offer in the ad by purchasing the product. Advertisers, legally obligated to make sure that promises are carried out, would face a fine of up to three times the consumer's claimed damages.[18]

Not only are product claims regulated, but visuals are also carefully scrutinized. R. J. Reynolds, the manufacturer of Camel cigarettes, was prohibited from showing humans smoking cigarettes in messages targeted to French consumers. In order to overcome the restriction, the firm used a smiling camel smoking its brand of cigarette. "Joe Camel" has since become a most successful trade character for the brand.

The Media That Advertisers Are Permitted to Employ

Media availability is severely limited in many markets. For example, only in the last three years has advertising on television and radio been permitted in Saudi Arabia, while direct mail is considered an invasion of privacy and is not used. Denmark began phasing in broadcast advertising in 1987; however, Sweden did not allow commercials to be broadcast until 1992. While Italian advertisers know that billboard ads are banned on highways, they must now comply with a recent code that also bans the outdoor messages from panoramic roads, inside parks, and within fifty meters of bus shelters. The code also imposes strong limits on the colors that billboards can employ— only 20 percent of a poster's surface can be red (the only exception is for registered trademarks). These new restrictions are expected to result in an 80-percent reduction in outdoor revenues and a loss of some 25,000 jobs.[19]

Media bans may also be related to specific product categories. The newest provisions of the French alcoholic beverages law deal with the media to be used in the promotion of wine and spirits. In a country where cinema commercials play a dominant role, wine and liquor ads are no longer allowed in movie houses. Advertising on radio is limited to hours when children are not likely to be listening; billboards advertising wine or spirits are limited in size and banned in cities. Soon, ads will be banned in all airports and railroad stations. Drinks cannot be advertised on outdoor tables at street cafes or on the terraces of restaurants, but curiously, umbrellas advertising them are allowed. Posters are banned except in the region of production. And, finally, wherever they are displayed in France, no wine or spirits advertisements can be within a hundred meters of a school.[20] In Singapore cigarette ads have been banned in local media under a law providing for fines of up to $12,500 or six months in jail. However, the country has stepped up its antismoking campaign by also banning cigarette ads in foreign publications, including *Asian Business, Newsweek, Time, World Executive Digest,* and the Chinese-language edition of *Asiaweek.*[21]

The Use of Advertising Materials Prepared Outside the Country

A study conducted by the International Advertising Association in 1985 revealed that of the forty-six countries surveyed, 22 percent restricted foreign-produced ads and foreign talent and another 38 percent had partial restrictions.[22] The Malaysian Ministry of Information, for example, requires that all footage for and music in television commercials be produced locally and use local talent. Reports Katherine Toland Frith: "This means that all people involved in the production must be Malaysian—including actors and actresses, technical people, voice, etc. The government requires a 'made in Malaysia' (MIM) form to be submitted with the final checkprint (the finished, edited footage)."[23] No imported commercials may be used in Australia or the United Kingdom unless a local crew performs or attends the shooting, and in commercials intended for American audiences, a union agreement is required to film outside the United States if American personnel are not used.[24] Peru bans foreign-inspired models and materials in advertisements appearing in that country in an effort to protect and enhance its national identity. Beyond nationalistic and cultural objectives, restrictions on foreign-prepared materials often are motivated by economic considerations—such as the desire to provide jobs for the local print production and film industry.[25] There is also the fear that multinational ad agencies will hamper the development of the local advertising businesses.

Many countries are quite sensitive about the use of foreign words in advertising messages as well. The International Advertising Association survey mentioned previously also found that of the countries surveyed, while 90 percent permitted the use of foreign languages in print ads and direct mail, only 72 percent allowed foreign-language commercials on TV, on radio, or in the cinema. Over 25 percent of the countries restricted foreign-language ads to media targeted to foreigners in their country. France and Mexico are two examples of countries that resist the foreignization or anglicization of the local language in advertising messages. French law specifically forbids the use of foreign words and expressions when French equivalents can be found in the official dictionary. In a recent decision all foreign billboards and shop signs in Moscow must be accompanied by Russian translations. This also applies to advertising messages on kiosks. The rationale here is quite simple: Muscovites have been confused by the dizzying array of outdoor advertising and signs that have mushroomed since economic reforms were introduced in 1992. The move is designed to help consumers better understand the products being advertised.[26]

The Use of Local Versus International Advertising Agencies

An increasing number of advertising agencies are positioning themselves as "global," or capable of providing services to clients worldwide. J. J. Boddewyn notes that "such a reach requires that they be allowed to establish themselves, or to merge with and acquire others, rather freely around the world."[27] The previously mentioned IAA survey reveals that such maneuvers are generally allowed to enable advertisers to coordinate their international campaigns through a single or limited number of agencies. Of the forty-six countries surveyed, thirty-four (74 percent) allow full ownership of an ad agency, particularly in the developed countries. Even partial or total exclusion of foreigners does not prevent foreign agencies from entering into joint ventures as well as technical and managerial agreements with local agencies, and some locally owned agencies simply serve as shells for multinational ones in developing countries. Consequently, it often is possible to use a "global" agency to reach many markets.

The Specific Taxes That May Be Levied Against Advertising

U.S. advertisers have long battled the threat of an advertising tax. Firms in other countries have not been so successful in evading taxation. To prevent increasing government encroachment, the Australian advertising industry has decided to bolster its watchdog group, the Advertising Standards Council (ASC). To support this effort, beginning in 1992, advertisers were charged a 0.01 percent levy on gross media billings to raise funds for the ASC. While the levy has been endorsed by major advertisers such as Coca-Cola, Toyota, Kellogg, Colgate-Palmolive, McDonald's, Kraft Foods, and the Distilled Spirits Industry Council, some agency heads are uncomfortable with having to collect the funds from their clients and to educate and inform clients about the levy.[28] This is but one example of a tax levied against advertising. In this case support for the move may be strong. In other instances, however, governmental bodies may impose a tax on advertising for reasons that are less palatable, and most national advertising organizations typically attempt to block such moves. In some markets the ad tax is levied only on specific media. In England, for example, all media except newspapers and magazines are taxed.

With regard to advertising regulation at the national level, despite the efforts of organizations such as the International Advertising Association, the International Chamber of Commerce, and the International Advertising Association to minimize variations in regulations from country to country, the preceding discussion should make clear that much advertising still will likely need to be adapted to meet local legal conditions and requirements.

International and Regional Regulation

International and regional regulations consist of those rules and guidelines that states and nations consider to be binding upon themselves. The major bodies or organizations that have developed or are developing international or regional advertising regulations are the various United Nations agencies, the European Union, and the Gulf Cooperation Council.

The United Nations

The United Nations and its various agencies influence advertising regulation in member countries. The most important of these agencies are the World Health Organization (WHO); the Commission on Transnational

Corporations; the United Nations Educational, Scientific and Cultural Organization (UNESCO); and the UN Conference on Trade and Development.[29] Barbara Sundberg Baudot explains their functions:

> These organizations lack the attribute of sovereignty, or the legislative authority of a world government to legislate enforceable regulation. Thus their roles are restricted to the development of voluntary codes and guidelines whose effectiveness depends on moral suasion and public acceptance. However, these codes may be translated through national legislation into laws. By consensus, members also may decide to adopt regulations by treaty, which becomes enforceable law in ratifying countries. Alternately, countries may decide to adopt conventions or resolutions binding members in accordance with voting rules in organizational charters.[30]

Several issues appear to have top priority at the various UN agencies. First, the UN is beginning to perceive market data as a type of national resource. In a report on transborder data flow that highlighted the significant expansion in this area as well as the great value of such data to international marketers, the UN expressed concern over whether such data flow helps or hinders developing countries. The report implies that developing countries should limit the flow of information from their country to the headquarters of international firms and that they should use their data to negotiate advantageous contracts and agreements. Second, the various UN agencies have all targeted pharmaceutical advertising for special attention. The UN is particularly concerned with international firms that may be dumping substandard or hazardous pharmaceutical products on unsuspecting developing markets as well as with the costly, high-pressure marketing and promotional methods employed by many international pharmaceutical firms. Third, the UN agencies acknowledge that media depend on advertising for much of their financial support and are concerned that media dollars may not always support those media of greatest importance to developing countries. Unfortunately, the developing nation's most critical media forms may not provide the proper target audience coverage for the international marketer. Finally, several of the UN agencies likely will develop rules and regulations that cover advertising in the international arena.

The European Union

Twelve European nations—Belgium, France, Germany, Italy, Luxembourg, the Netherlands, Denmark, Ireland, the United Kingdom, Greece, Spain, and Portugal—banded together to form the European Union (EU) in December 1992. Their goal is the creation of a single European market. By lifting most physical, fiscal, and technical barriers to free trade among nations, the EU hopes that people, products, and services will be able to move among the member nations with much the same ease as they now cross U.S. state borders. In January 1995, Sweden, Austria, and Norway joined the EU, and the Eastern European countries as well as the republics of the former Soviet Union will soon join as well.

The EU has been years in the planning, and it will be many more before all the planned legislative changes are put into effect. Much the same can be said about the role that advertising regulation will play in the new economic community. In 1984 the EU adopted legislation, which went into effect in 1986, that set forth guidelines and standards for the protection of both consumers and businesses from misleading advertising. Article 2 of the directive defined "misleading" advertising as "any advertising which in any way, including its presentation, deceives or is likely to deceive the persons to whom it is addressed or whom it reaches and which, by reason of its deceptive nature, is likely to affect their economic behavior or which, for those reasons, injures or is likely to injure a competitor."[31]

Article 3 of the directive went on to explain the operational meaning of the term *misleading*. It stated that in the determination of whether advertising is misleading,

> account shall be taken of all its features, and in particular of any information it contains concerning: (1) the characteristics of goods or services, such as their availability, nature, execution, composition, method and date of manufacture or provision, fitness for purpose, uses, quantity, specification, geographical or commercial origin, or the results to be expected from their use, or the results and material features of tests or checks carried out on the goods or services; (2) the price or the manner in which the price is calculated, and the conditions under which the goods are supplied or the services provided; and (3) the advertiser's nature, attributes, and rights, such as identity and assets, qualifications and ownership of industrial, commercial or intellectual property rights, or awards and distinctions.[32]

Article 7, however, nearly undermined the entire legislative effort by stating that individual nations were not precluded from keeping or adopting provisions that furnish more extensive protection for consumers, businesses, and the general public.[33] This served to put advertising regulation right back into the hands of member states. While there is currently a drive toward overall harmonization of advertising regulation, member states still regularly make independent regulatory decisions.

As noted previously, the evolution of advertising regulation in the EU continues. At present the European Commission is preparing a document that may lead regulators to take a more liberal approach to advertising. The document admits that the Commission has tended toward overregulating advertising and has not viewed it as commercial freedom of speech. Over a period of several months, the director general of the Commission will communicate with ad agencies, marketers, and direct marketing, sales promotion, and public relations companies. This long consultation period is welcome news to the ad industry, which has often complained that the Commission has drafted unsuitable legislation without industry input.[34]

The Gulf Cooperation Council

Currently, Saudi Arabia, Qatar, Kuwait, Oman, the United Arab Emirates, and Bahrain are forging a common consumer and trade policy to ensure economic integration. Once this integration is complete, the Gulf Cooperation Council (GCC) will present significant marketing opportunities for multinational firms. An understanding of the advertising regulatory environment of these member states is essential for marketers interested in this region. Because Saudi Arabia is the largest and economically strongest member of the GCC, it plays a dominant role in shaping the regulations that will govern all commercial activity (including advertising) among member states.

With regard to the marketing environment, religion takes precedence over all other cultural considerations in Saudi Arabia. Mushtaq Luqmani and colleagues explain:

> The Saudi legal system is unique in that it identifies law with the personal command of the "one and only one God, the Almighty." The Islamic laws known as Sharia are the master framework to which all legislation is referred and with which it must be compatible. The Sharia is a comprehensive code governing the duties, morals and behavior of all Muslims in all areas of life, including commerce. Sharia is derived from two basic sources, the Quran or Holy Book and the Hadith, based on the life, sayings and practices of the Prophet Muhammad. The implications of religion on advertising regulation in this country are far-reaching.[35]

Several sets of Quranic messages have special significance for advertisers and advertising regulation. The most important have to do with strict taboos dealing with alcohol, gambling, and immodest exposure. For example, at no time may alcoholic beverages be consumed, and games of chance are illegal. Religious norms require women to be covered, both in public and in advertising messages. Therefore, international print messages may need to be modified by superimposing long dresses on models or by shading their legs with black. Also, advertisers may not picture sensuous-looking females. Instead, a pleasant-looking woman in a robe and headdress, with only her face showing, is reflective of the typical model. Cartoon characters are often employed to present women in messages because they are less likely to violate Islamic codes on exposure. Advertising messages may also be considered deceptive by religious standards. For example, according to

Islam, fraud may occur if the seller fails to deliver everything promised, and advertisers may need to use factual appeals based on real rather than perceived product benefits.

No specific governmental agency is responsible for controlling advertising behavior in Saudi Arabia. There is no self-regulatory industry group and no evidence of any plans to develop one. Companies are, however, involved in self-compliance, which may eventually lead to self-regulation. As Luqmani and colleagues state, "Possible violations are monitored in two ways. The government is involved through the Ministry of Commerce which ensures that ads remain within legal bounds, and the Ministry of Information which approves television commercials. Less formal oversight is provided by a voluntary religious group, the Organization for the Prevention of Sins and Order of Good Deeds. Members observe public and commercial behavior (including promotions) for any violations of Islamic law."[36] Obviously, advertisers must take great care to ensure that advertising content is compatible with the Islamic religion and its laws.

International and regional codes and guidelines contribute to the harmonization of national laws and, in doing so, pave the way for global advertising campaigns. International marketers planning on promoting their products or services in a particular region may be faced with a multitude of advertising regulations—many of which may conflict with one another—and therefore have little choice but to employ a localized campaign for each country. However, with standardized advertising regulation in the European Union or the Persian Gulf region, marketers have the option of employing the same or similar message strategy.

Self-Regulation

The Trend Toward Self-Regulation

During the past several decades, both consumer groups and governments have increasingly turned their attention toward the control of advertising. As a result, advertising, trade, and industry associations, as well as the media in many countries, have realized the importance of voluntary self-regulation. In addition to avoiding government-mandated regulation, self-regulation in advertising generally has three objectives:

1. To protect consumers against false or misleading advertising and against advertising that intrudes on their privacy through its unwanted presence or offensive content

2. To protect legitimate advertisers against false or misleading advertising by competitors

3. To promote the public acceptance of advertising so that it can continue as an effective institution in the marketplace.[37]

For example, to prevent more government regulation of advertising, the Spanish advertising industry is forming a group to police itself. The body will draw up and enforce a code of ethics and later hear complaints to keep them from reaching the legal system. This effort is a step toward attempting to establish regulations more in line with those of other European countries. Among the sanctions being considered is a requirement that challenged ads be withdrawn or corrected if deemed necessary and that official legal proceedings be initiated if offenders choose not to comply.[38]

Also hoping to combat government restrictions and censorship, industry groups from thirteen Latin American countries have formed the Inter-American Society for the Freedom of Commercial Speech. Members have signed the Caracas Pact, an agreement to create a self-regulatory code. Included in the group are agencies, media, and advertiser associations from Brazil, Colombia, Costa Rica, Chile, El Salvador, Guatemala, Honduras, Mexico, Nicaragua, Panama, Paraguay, Puerto Rico, and Venezuela; Argentina has also signaled its support but has not yet signed the pact. The new group will gather information about each country's current industry and government regulations before developing a pan–Latin American code. After the code is in place, the group proposes to foster a wider understanding of advertising's objectives and to sponsor campaigns in favor of freedom of commercial speech.[39]

The Russian Advertising Council, a coalition of advertising, news, and social organizations, was formed in mid-1993. The ultimate purpose of the council will be to draft legislation for Russia's emerging ad industry and to create a code of ethics to protect Russian consumers.[40]

The Canadian Direct Marketing Association, hoping to preempt government regulations, established self-regulatory guidelines that took effect in 1993. As in many countries, Canada's direct marketers have been under increasing pressure from consumers as well as government agencies to give consumers more control over when and how their names and personal information about them are used. The guidelines include the following:

1. To provide consumers with the opportunity to have their names removed from lists at least once every three years

2. To tell consumers how marketers obtain names and how lists will be used

3. To require association members, which make up 80 percent of direct marketers in Canada, to delete upon request names of customers

from the association's main database and to take appropriate measures to ensure that lists are protected against unauthorized use

4. To ensure that the privacy of medical, financial, and credit data is the responsibility of the industries that collect them, not direct marketers.[41]

National media are also involved in the monitoring of advertising content. Both media associations (such as the National Association of Broadcasters in the United States) and individual media are concerned about advertising messages that may be deceptive, offensive, or even contrary to public standards. For example, despite fears of public outrage, the South African Broadcasting Corporation (SABC TV) has received very few complaints about its new policy of accepting condom advertising. The ultraconservative, government-owned network aired its first condom ad in late 1992 in response to the AIDS epidemic in South Africa and the urgent need for population control. The three 20-second ads are quite discreet. One shows a couple strolling through a field of flowers with soft music playing in the background. As the lovers embrace and fall gently to the ground, a package of the condoms is flashed on the screen. The word *condom* is never used in any of the spots.[42]

In addition to advertising association, industry, and media codes, individual firms, including Procter & Gamble, General Foods, and Revlon, have begun to develop their own guidelines.[43] Developments in this area, however, have not been particularly well studied and deserve further attention.

The International Chamber of Commerce Code of Advertising Practice

The International Chamber of Commerce (ICC) was established in 1919 to promote the interests of international business. The ICC, which today is represented in over one hundred countries, is the most important international body influencing self-regulation of advertising. With the support of advertisers, agencies, and the media, the ICC developed the first formal internal self-regulatory code for advertising. The ICC Code of Advertising Practice states that all advertisers have an overall duty to be "decent, honest, legal and truthful" (see the Appendix for the complete ICC code). The code goes on to state that advertisements "should be prepared with a due sense of social responsibility . . . and not be such as to impair public confidence in advertising." With these words the ICC code moved away from addressing only "hard" matters that center on the deceptive character of

TABLE 9.1 Countries Rating Advertising Taste/Decency Issues as "Major" (out of 47)

TASTELESS/INDECENT (11)	SEXY (9)	SEXIST (7)	OBJECTIFICATION OF WOMEN (9)	VIOLENCE AGAINST WOMEN (6)
Bahrain*	Austria	India*	Argentina*	Chile*
Canada	Bahrain*	Ireland	Austria	Lebanon*
Chile*	Indonesia*	Lebanon*	Brazil*	New Zealand
Indonesia*	Ireland	Peru*	Lebanon*	Spain
Kenya*	Italy	Sweden	Portugal	Trinidad & Tobago*
Lebanon*	Kenya*	Switzerland	Singapore*	United States
Malaysia*	Lebanon*	United States	Spain	
Philippines*	Norway		Sweden	
Taiwan*	Philippines*		Switzerland	
Trinidad & Tobago*				
United States				

NOTE: The asterisk (*) denotes countries that are usually classified as "developing" or "less developed."
SOURCE: J. J. Boddewyn, *Sexism and Decency in Advertising: Government Regulation and Industry Self-Regulation in 47 Countries* (New York: International Advertising Association, 1989).

advertisements and on proper substantiation of advertising claims. It also encompassed "soft" issues, which include matters of sex and decency in advertising. Jean J. Boddewyn notes that, "reflecting these ICC principles, various clauses on decency, taste, public opinion and social responsibility are usually found in advertising self-regulatory codes and guidelines around the world."[44] Sex and decency can be broken into five major subcategories:

1. Tasteless/indecent ads, which do not conform to recognized standards of propriety, good taste, and modesty
2. Sexy ads, which use sexual imagery or suggestiveness
3. Sexist ads, which diminish or demean one sex in comparison with the other—particularly through the use of sex-role stereotypes
4. Objectification-of-women ads, which use women primarily as decorative or attention-getting objects with little or no relevance to the product advertised
5. Violence-against-women ads

An IAA survey conducted in 1988 inquired about the salience of these five advertising issues. Table 9.1 reveals that a larger number of developing countries (fifteen) than of developed ones (eleven) rated one or more of these issues as "major." Lebanon and the United States appeared to be most concerned with these issues, and these countries are the only ones represented in at least three columns. The subcategory of tasteless/indecent ads generated the most mentions, particularly in developing countries.

Some self-regulatory bodies refuse to handle soft issues, limiting themselves to the hard issues of truth and accuracy. This is true of the U.S.'s NAD/NARB system. The NARB (National Advertising Review Board) is the advertising industry's primary self-regulatory body and is responsible for policing misleading advertising. The NAD (National Advertising Division) is the policy-making arm of the NARB. Other bodies, including those in Germany and Canada, readily deal with "taste and opinion" complaints. Most bodies, however, stand in between, occasionally agreeing to handle soft cases on the basis of the general principles they apply—particularly when gross breaches of social standards occur, as in matters of obscenity, racism, and denigration.[45]

In developing self-regulatory guidelines, many countries have turned to the ICC code. Because latecomers often borrow from the ICC codes as well as from codes outlined by U.S., U.K., and Canadian associations, voluntary codes often appear to resemble one another. In addition to a code of advertising practices, the ICC also outlines codes of practice in marketing, market research practice, and sales promotion practice.

Industry, trade, and advertising associations have developed codes of ethics and guidelines in more than fifty nations, and the number is increasing each year. This is particularly true of developed markets and countries where advertising expenditures are relatively large. Increasingly, we will also see movement toward self-regulation in developing markets.

Implications for International Advertisers

Although it is nearly impossible for international advertisers to be familiar with the regulation of advertising worldwide, they are still responsible for making every effort to inform themselves of the regulatory environment of markets they plan to enter. Because of the changing regulatory environment, advertisers must develop a system for keeping abreast of new developments. Beyond the impact of the regulatory environment on a single campaign, the global regulatory climate will influence how successfully international advertisers can conduct their business in the years to come. In the meantime international advertisers should do the following:

1. Have their in-house and external legal counsels check and double-check the true nature of advertising restrictions in relevant foreign markets.

2. Monitor and oppose the spread of regulations, taxes, and other obstacles that hamper international advertising. In particular, advertisers

should support U.S. and other governments' efforts to liberalize trade and investment in services through GATT and other bilateral agreements. Defending the freedom of commercial expression and communication at home and abroad is part of this agenda.

3. Support and assist the development of advertising self-regulation around the world. Advertising self-regulation exists in only fifty-five countries and is well developed in only twenty. It is largely nonexistent or ineffective in most of the developing countries where the spread of regulation is imminent.[46]

With regard to the first suggestion, a variety of resources exist to update regulatory profiles. Several texts are mandatory reading for advertisers planning foreign market entry. *International Advertising Handbook: A User's Guide to Rules and Regulations* by Barbara Sundberg Baudot provides an excellent overview of the topic.[47] For marketers planning on operating in Europe, the European Association of Advertising Agencies has published a book on the regulatory environment in Europe entitled *Red Book on Laws and Regulations on Advertising in Europe.* On the same topic Rein Rijkens and Gorden Miracle authored an informative text entitled *European Regulation of Advertising.*[48]

Local and national resources should be tapped for current information on legislative or self-regulatory efforts. National advertising associations can provide invaluable assistance. In the United States the American Advertising Association (AAA), the American Association of Advertising Agencies (AAAA), and the American Advertising Federation (AAF) are all excellent resources. Most developed countries have similar associations. For example, in Europe the international advertiser may contact the European Association of Advertising Agencies (EAAA) or the Institute of Practitioners in Advertising (IPA). Likewise, the Asian Federation of Advertising Agencies (AFAA) provides current data to advertisers entering Asian markets.

Finally, the International Advertising Association (IAA), with members in over seventy countries, conducts numerous surveys that deal with governmental regulations as well as specific industry guidelines. In addition, the IAA publishes a report on government regulation and industry self-regulation in fifty-three countries entitled "Barriers to Trade and Investment in Advertising."

Summary

Some experts propose that the extent and severity of advertising regulation worldwide is likely to increase; others predict it will decline. On the one hand, many governments currently are developing tougher regulations with regard to advertising in general as well as stricter restrictions relating to specific product categories such as cigarettes, alcohol, and pharmaceuticals. On the other hand, many governments—particularly those in developed markets—are moving toward deregulation. Especially in markets facing slow- or no-growth economies, politicians are questioning the wisdom of further increasing the costs associated with doing business.

Regardless of the regulatory environment in which international marketers find themselves, every effort should be made to comply with both national and international rules and guidelines. In addition, international marketers should strive to operate abroad in a socially responsible fashion. Such efforts can assist in avoiding legal entanglements and stemming any erosion of consumer confidence in advertising worldwide. The issue of social responsibility and ethical standards in the international arena will be addressed in the next chapter.

Additional Readings

Baudot, Barbara Sundberg. (1989). *International Advertising Handbook: A User's Guide to Rules and Regulations.* Lexington, MA: Lexington Books.

Rijkens, Rein, and Gordon E. Miracle. (1986). *European Regulation of Advertising.* New York: Elsevier, 1986.

Notes

1. Cundiff, Edward, and Marye Tharp Hilger, *Marketing in the International Environment* (Englewood Cliffs, NJ: Prentice-Hall, 1988), p. 196.

2. Tagliabue, John, "Albania, Europe's Poorest State, Gets Big Coca Cola Bottling Plant," *San Diego Union Tribune,* May 20, 1994, p. A24.

3. Frith, Katherine Toland, "The Social and Legal Constraints on Advertising in Malaysia," *Media Asia,* 14(2), 1987, p. 103.

4. Baudot, Barbara Sundberg, *International Advertising Handbook: A User's Guide to Rules and Regulations* (Lexington, MA: Lexington Books, 1989), p. 31.

5. Ryans, John K., Jr., James R. Wills, Jr., and Henry Bell, "International Advertising Regulation: A Transnational View," *Midwest Marketing Association Conference Proceedings* (Carbondale: Southern Illinois University, 1979), p. 37.

6. Geddes, Andres, "China Plans New Advertising Rules," *Advertising Age,* June 21, 1993, p. I6.

7. Huus, Kari, "Look Out, Chinese Love Solution," *Advertising Age,* September 28, 1992, p. I6.

8. Condon, Christopher, "Hungary Regulations Could Polish Industry Image," *Advertising Age,* October 11, 1993, p. I6.

9. Peebles, Dean M., and John K. Ryans, *Management of International Advertising* (Boston: Allyn & Bacon, 1984), p. 196.

10. Prial, Frank J., "French Law Restricts Alcohol Ads," *San Diego Union Tribune,* June 2–3, 1993, p. Food 9.

11. Richmond, Susannah, "Cigarette Advertisers Under Fire in Britain," *ADWEEK,* December 13, 1993, p. 14.

12. Mussey, Dagmar, "Reemtsma Takes West Cigarette East," *Advertising Age,* April 19, 1993, p. I2.

13. Wentz, Laurel, "Local Laws Keep International Marketers Hopping," *Advertising Age,* July 11, 1985, p. 20.

14. Barrager, Dave, "Japan Tiptoes Toward Comparative Ads," *ADWEEK,* February 22, 1993, p. 10.

15. Russell, J. Thomas, and W. Ronald Lane, *Kleppner's Advertising Procedure* (Englewood Cliffs, NJ: Prentice-Hall, 1993), p. 666.

16. Cateora, Philip, *International Marketing* (Homewood, IL: Irwin, 1990), p. 198.

17. "Advertising Age Legal Briefs: Comparative Advertising Mulled," *Advertising Age,* March 15, 1993, p. I6.

18. Yi-Chun, Chen, "Taiwanese Consumer Law May Rein in Wild Ad Claims," *Advertising Age,* June 20, 1994, p. I6.

19. Giacomotti, Fabiana, "Italian Billboard Laws Prompt Fight," *ADWEEK,* April 26, 1993, p. 13.

20. Prial, "French Law Restricts Alcohol Ads."

21. "Advertising Age Legal Briefs," p. I6.

22. Boddewyn, Jean J., and Iris Mohr, "International Advertisers Face Government Hurdles," *Marketing News,* May 8, 1987.

23. Frith, "The Social and Legal Constraints," p. 101.

24. Boddewyn, J. J., "The One and Many Worlds of Advertising: Regulatory Obstacles and Opportunities," *International Journal of Advertising,* 7(1), 1988, p. 13.

25. Boddewyn and Mohr, "International Advertisers Face Government Hurdles."

26. "Advertising Age Legal Briefs: Russian Required Here," *Advertising Age,* March 15, 1993, p. I6.

27. Boddewyn, "The One and Many Worlds of Advertising," p. 14.

28. Warneford, Penny, "Aussie Agencies Boost Self Regulation," *ADWEEK,* November 16, 1992, p. 32A.

29. Dunn, S. Watson, "United Nations as a Regulator of International Advertising," *Proceedings of the 1982 Conference of the American Academy of Advertising* (Lincoln, NE: American Academy of Advertising, 1982). pp. 29–32.

30. Baudot, *International Advertising Handbook,* p. 36.

31. Greer, Thomas, and Paul Thompson, "Development of Standardized and Harmonized Advertising Regulation in the European Economic Community," *Journal of Advertising,* 14(2), 1985, p. 31.

32. Ibid., p. 31.

33. Ibid., p. 32.

34. Wentz, Laurel, "EC Readies More Liberal Advertising Stance," *Advertising Age,* June 21, 1993, p. I6.

35. Luqmani, Mushtaq, Ugur Yavas, and Zahir Quraeshi, "Advertising in Saudi Arabia: Content and Regulation," *International Marketing Review,* 6(1), 1989, pp. 59–72.

36. Ibid.

37. Rijkens, Rein, and Gordon E. Miracle, *European Regulation of Advertising* (New York: Elsevier, 1986).

38. "Advertising Age Legal Brief: Spain to Self-Regulate Ads," *Advertising Age,* October 11, 1993, p. I6.

39. Kirby, Catherine, "L. American Group to Push Self-Regulation," *Advertising Age,* September 26, 1992, p. I6.

40. Babakan, Genine, "Russian Ad Council Gets Ready for Biz," *ADWEEK,* July 12, 1993, p. 15.

41. Brown, Barry, "Canadian Mailers Come Up with Rules," *Advertising Age,* June 22, 1992, p. I6.

42. Barnes, Kathleen, "S. Africa OKs Condom Ads," *Advertising Age,* February 15, 1993, p. I6.

43. Boddewyn, J. J., "Advertising Regulation, Self-Regulation and Self-Discipline Around the World: Some Facts, Trends and Observations," *International Marketing,* 1(1), 1981, p. 52.

44. Boddewyn, Jean J., "Controlling Sex and Decency in Advertising Around the World," *Journal of Advertising,* 20(4), 1991, pp. 25–35.

45. Ibid., p. 29.

46. Ibid.

47. Baudot, *International Advertising Handbook.*

48. Rijkens and Miracle, *European Regulation of Advertising.*

CHAPTER 10

Social Responsibility and Ethics in the Global Marketplace

A dvertisers and agencies should take note of a number of trends that may well impact how business is conducted in the global marketplace of the future. First, there appears to be a growing concern with regard to the social responsibility and ethical standards of international advertisers, probably in large part because of a number of well-publicized incidents including the infant-formula controversy, a variety of cases related to the marketing of drugs in Third World countries, and the Bhopal disaster.[1] Second, the consumer movement is expanding in both developed and developing markets. As Dean M. Peebles and John K. Ryans point out, "Consumer protection groups . . . are focusing sharply on advertising that misleads, misrepresents, takes advantage of consumer's lack of knowledge, degrades local competition, or that is in poor taste according to local standards—and they are looking even more closely at multinationals that invade their markets."[2] Finally, in the past several years many nations have sharply increased their regulation of promotional activities.[3] In a growing number of countries, the advertising agency shares liability with the advertiser for any violation of advertising practices, so that both parties are fined or otherwise penalized equally.[4] Further, to encourage agencies to take greater responsibility for the content of the messages they produce, France now removes the blanket of anonymity by requiring that the agency name appear on its client's advertising. Other countries are considering similar measures.[5] If international marketers and advertisers are to avoid the wrath of increasingly powerful consumer associations as well as the limitations imposed by the associated increase in regulation, they must engage in socially responsible behavior when operating in both developed and developing countries. The adoption of codes of ethics may well serve as a means to this end. These issues will be discussed in this chapter.

The Growth of the Consumer Movement

Consumerism has been defined in a variety of ways. Stephen A. Greyser and Steven L. Diamond define it as "the organized movement to increase the rights and powers of buyers in relation to sellers in an imperfect market."[6] William T. Kelley defines it as an "effort to put the buyer on equal footing with the seller. Consumers want to know what they're buying. What they're eating. How long a product will last. What it will and will not do. Whether it will be safe for them and/or the environment."[7] Organized consumer groups are especially influential in the United States, the United Kingdom, Sweden, and Australia, and their success in these countries has spurred the development of similar groups in other nations. For example, the consumer movement in Malaysia has become quite strong, and the Consumer Association of Penang (CAP) is one of the harshest critics of advertising in that nation.[8] The consumer movement in general has made demands in three main areas:

1. *Consumer information:* data about products and services offered for sale and information to assist specific buying decisions, especially comparative data

2. *Consumer education:* the development of the knowledge base necessary to be an intelligent consumer, to know how the economy operates, how buyers and sellers interact, and how to deal with the people and institutions one encounters

3. *Consumer protection:* the call for governments and regulatory bodies to safeguard consumer rights, protect against deceptive practices, and set health and safety standards.[9]

In general, consumer organizations have not been overly impressed with industry attempts to produce an effective self-disciplinary system. They claim that the advertising industry in particular lacks the authority to be a viable alternative to state or national regulatory systems. Consumerists argue that regulation by governmental agencies is necessary to ensure that advertisers take responsibility for informing, educating, and protecting consumers. Given such views, the conflict between consumer organizations and advertisers is likely to continue, particularly in Third World countries.

Social Responsibility in the Global Marketplace

Because of growing concern on the part of consumers, consumer organizations, and governments with the practices of international advertisers and marketers, the highest standards of marketing behavior must be applied to each of the marketing mix elements—product, price, distribution, and promotion. With regard to product responsibility, firms should strive to produce high-quality goods that are safe for both consumers and the environment, as well as being culturally sensitive. Advertising agencies must question whether they will represent clients whose products do not live up to such standards. For instance, a number of chemical and pharmaceutical products that had been banned in developed markets because they were deemed unsafe were subsequently exported to less developed countries where such controls were lacking. In another example some German companies have been accused of using Poland as a dumping ground for packaged goods (such as condiments) with expiration dates that had already passed.[10] Such practices have led Poles to embrace domestically manufactured goods and eye foreign marketers with great suspicion. Environmental issues also are expected to receive increasing global attention in the future. Consumers around the world are concerned with issues such as toxic waste, pollution, depletion of the ozone layer, nuclear waste, and energy conservation—and with the degree to which international marketers contribute to such problems. Advertisers will increasingly be expected to produce environmentally sound products and limit wasteful packaging—and advertising agencies will be responsible for communicating such benefits to consumers. Agencies and advertisers together must take an active role in protecting the environment. Exhibit 10.1 shows an example of a foreign advertisement appealing to environmental concerns; the headline reads, "Recommended by Environmentalists."

Von Umweltschützern empfohlen.

Was tun Sie, wenn Ihr Kind das nächste Mal vor dem Kühlschrank steht und nicht nach Pudding oder Limo fragt, sondern danach, ob Ihr Kühlschrank vielleicht noch FCKW enthält, welches unsere Umwelt belastet? Wäre es nicht schön, wenn Sie dann antworten könnten, daß Sie einen Bosch-Kühlschrank* besitzen, mit dem selbst Umweltschutzverbände zufrieden sind, weil er weder FCKW noch FKW enthält? Daß er Klima und Ozonschicht nicht ge-

FCKW & FKW FREI

fährdet und trotzdem für kühlen Pudding und frische Limo sorgt. Wenn Sie den kritischen Fragen Ihres Kindes zuvorkommen wollen, schauen Sie doch mal bei Ihrem Fachhändler vorbei.

* KTR 1570 oder KDR 3700

 BOSCH

Gute Ideen in Bosch-Qualität.

Robert Bosch Hausgeräte GmbH, Hochstraße 17, D-81669 München · Robert Bosch AG, Hüttenbrennerstrasse 5, A-1030 Wien · Robert Bosch AG, Hohlstrasse 188, CH-8021 Zürich.

EXHIBIT 10.1 Environmentally Aware German Advertisement for Bosch Refrigerators

Pricing responsibility refers to charging only what the market will bear. Earlier in this text, we discussed the example of an international manufacturer of dog food selling its product in the new Commonwealth of Independent States; one must question whether it is socially responsible to sell a forty-pound bag of dog food at a price equivalent to a month's salary in the CIS. The international marketer also must evaluate whether the price charged offers grounds for foreign governments or competitors to claim that goods are being dumped. With regard to place responsibility, marketers must assess whether bribes or payoffs will be required in order to enter foreign markets and to distribute products. Goods must be distributed in a socially responsible fashion, and international marketers must ensure that products are made available to consumers where they require them. Promotion responsibility refers not just to advertising message content but to all promotional activities. Advertising's high visibility, however, makes it particularly vulnerable to criticism. Key questions facing advertising practitioners on a day-to-day basis include the following:

- ▶ Who should and who should not be advertised to?
- ▶ What should and should not be advertised?
- ▶ What should and should not be the content of the advertising message?
- ▶ What should and should not be the symbolic tone or actual character of the advertising message?
- ▶ What should and should not be the relationship among clients, agencies, and the mass media?
- ▶ What should and should not be advertising's business obligations versus its societal obligations?[11]

Engaging in socially responsible marketing and advertising means doing what's best for consumers in general or for specific groups of consumers. The manner in which marketers and advertisers have operated in Third World countries has generated a particularly high level of controversy.

Advertising in Developing Markets

Clearly, international marketers will continue to look to developed markets to sell their goods and services. A well of opportunities has been created by the formation of the European Union. Yet, despite the fact that this market is over 300 million consumers strong, it is not growing. The same is true of both the U.S. market (with its 253 million consumers) and the Japanese market (half the size of the U.S. market). Reports Bill

Saporito: "As a well-known packaged goods CEO tells his new product staff about the developed world: Just remember, nobody needs anything anymore."[12] However, this is definitely not the case for the vast majority of consumers worldwide. According to World Bank estimates, some 77 percent of the world's population live in developing areas. And while many advanced markets are mired in recession or, at the very least, face slow or no growth, the economy in the developing world is expanding at some 5–6 percent annually. Only in the past few decades have manufacturers and distributors begun to aggressively target consumers in developing markets. As a result, while a good deal is known about the role of marketing and advertising in markets with economic systems based on plenty, relatively little is known about how advertising operates in a situation of comparative scarcity and poverty.

Economic and Social Conditions in Developing Countries

Terms such as *developing markets, low-income countries, Third World economies*, and even *less developed countries* often are used interchangeably to refer to specific markets that share some common characteristics. The main criterion used to classify economies and broadly distinguish stages of development is GNP per capita. The world's economies are classified into three groupings: low-income ($610 or less in 1990), middle-income ($611–$7,619), and high-income ($7,620 or more).[13] Even with substantial efforts over the past quarter century, more than one-fifth of humankind still lives in acute poverty. On the positive side, estimates are that by the year 2000 the number of poor in Asia will have declined and the adverse poverty trends in Latin America and Eastern Europe will be reversed because of the economic recovery predicted in those regions. On the negative side, the situation is expected to deteriorate in sub-Saharan Africa; with increases in the proportion of the population in poverty, the number of poor is expected to rise by about 9 million a year on average.[14]

Despite their relative lack of resources, even the lowest-income groups become appealing to international marketers in terms of their aggregate disposable income. Consumer appetite for low-priced packaged goods is strong in Third World markets. For example, in developing Asia, a person earning just $250 annually can afford Gillette razors. Yet even high-end, durable goods find a market in developing countries—the poorest slums of Calcutta are home to some 70,000 VCRs, and in Mexico homes with television sets outnumber those with running water.[15]

Developing markets tend to have rapidly growing populations as well. Since the 1950s mortality has declined and life expectancy has increased dramatically. This trend can be attributed to progress in overall living standards, sanitary conditions, and public health practices. According to the *World Development Report 1992*, "Under the World Bank's projections, world population growth would decline slowly, from 1.7 percent a year in 1990 to about 1 percent a year by 2030. World population would more than double from current levels and would stabilize at about 12.5 billion around the middle of the twenty-second century. Two-thirds of the increase would occur by 2050, and 95 percent of population growth would take place in developing countries."[16]

Developing countries share other characteristics as well. They are generally agrarian or raw-materials-producing economies. Levels of labor productivity and literacy tend to be low. Further, they tend to have poor infrastructures—characterized by inadequate transportation and communication systems and storage facilities—and an overall shortage of consumer goods and services.

In less developed countries, for the most part, production is confined to meeting the limited needs of consumers. Generally, whatever is produced will find a buyer. Local manufacturers typically refrain from promotional efforts because of (1) financial restraints, (2) unfamiliarity with the concept of promotional strategy, and (3) an inability to perceive its effectiveness. The prevailing conditions of such "sellers' markets" typically do not stimulate the need for advertising.[17] Under such conditions marketers often are tempted to let their products sell themselves—to rely on word of mouth and perhaps personal selling rather than advertising. Of course, the larger the firm in such developing markets, the greater the likelihood that advertising will be employed. These trends are reflected in the relatively low levels of advertising expenditures in developing countries. Whereas in developed markets advertising expenditures usually account for approximately 3 percent of the GNP, in less developed countries they generally account for about 1 percent or even less. Similarly, per capita advertising expenditures are lower in less developed markets than in more economically advanced countries. For example, advertising expenditures per person in the United States are as much as forty to fifty times greater than in most less developed countries.[18]

The debate regarding advertising's effects on developing nations is a heated one. On the positive side, advertising serves to educate consumers by informing them of what goods are available and where they may be obtained; advertising enables consumers to compare goods, which often results in lower prices and improved product quality; advertising stimulates the local economy by encouraging consumption; and it has the potential to improve living standards. Agencies often offer employment to locals, as well as providing career training. In addition, many of the messages aired in developing countries serve to promote desirable social aims—such as increased savings, reduced illiteracy, lower birth rates, and improved nutrition and hygiene. Advertising has even been successfully employed in the fight against AIDS. Modern marketing techniques have substantially increased condom usage in Turkey, Ecuador, the Caribbean, and south-central Africa. Notes Dr. Jeff Harris, director of the AIDS program for the United States Agency for International Development, "Successful programs have borrowed sales techniques from consumer products. We market condoms like we would Coca Cola."[19] Indeed, many of the television spots employed have featured songs by well-known entertainers.

A good deal more attention has been paid to the negatives associated with the efforts of international advertisers in developing countries. Charles Frazer points out that "the idea that marketing, and particularly advertising, activities come to have disruptive, perverse and subversive effects in other cultures, especially the Third World, travels under a variety of labels, including cultural dependence, social mobilization . . . and cultural imperialism."[20] The dependency approach, claims Michael H. Anderson, suggests that "imported western institutions and values intentionally or unintentionally generate dependency and function as a hindrance to the development of genuinely independent nations."[21] According to social mobilization theory, writes John McGinnis, "It is not economic development or modernization that leads to political instability, but the rate of rising expectations and the failure to satisfy those expectations."[22] With regard to cultural imperialism, Herbert I. Schiller notes:

> No part of the globe . . . avoids the penetration of the internationally active American advertising agency. These transnational advertising agencies have made deep inroads into most of the already industrialized states, and many of the third world nations are experiencing the same loss of national control of the image-making apparatus and internal communications systems. Advertising, and the mass media that it eventually transduces are, therefore, the leading agents in the business of culture, and the culture of business.[23]

Regardless of the label, at the heart of the matter is the charge that international marketers attempt to re-create Western-style consumer cultures in countries outside the United States and Western Europe. Critics claim that consumers in these countries are particularly vulnerable to the efforts of international advertisers because they likely are poor and illiterate, lack experience with consumer goods, and have not been exposed to decades of media messages common in more developed markets. In addition, developing countries tend to lack legal systems for consumer protection. While there is much speculation on the possible impact of both multinational corporations and advertising agencies on developing countries, there exists little empirical evidence of these effects.[24] Specific charges as well as counterclaims will be discussed in greater detail in the next section.

Charges Against and Arguments for Advertising in Developing Markets

Advertising's Influence on Competition Critics claim that firms which advertise heavily make it impossible for competitors in developing countries to enter the marketplace because of the enormous sums spent on advertising. Supporters claim that by encouraging competition among producers, advertising actually stimulates the economy. Because there is little consensus as to the impact of advertising on competition in developed markets, not surprisingly, there is also a good deal of debate over its role in evolving economies. Although no significant studies document advertising's effect on competition, some interesting statistics suggest there may be some validity to this criticism. For example, multinational corporations outspend local firms by six to one in advertising. With so much exposure, international brands generally have substantially higher recall levels among consumers than do local brands. In some places, the international brand even serves as the generic name. Kellogg's, for example, has come to mean "breakfast cereal" in many developing markets. In addition, significant status is associated with foreign brands of consumer goods.

Advertising's Influence on the Domestic Media Scene A major criticism of international advertising is that it promotes commercialism of the media, as well as introducing Western media content. Wherever international corporations operate, the local mass media have been summoned to promote sales of consumer goods. As a result, the structure of national communications systems, as well as the programming offered, has been transformed according to the specifications of international marketers. In terms of media structure, many developing countries shifted away from public- or state-financing models to the U.S. model whereby the media are supported by advertising. The broadcast media appear to be particularly susceptible to the lure of advertising dollars. Today, the overwhelming number of radio and television stations in developing markets, both government-owned and private, are financed through advertising revenue. This model typically favors amassing profits over serving public needs. In Latin America, for example, 30–50 percent of newspaper content, over 33 percent of magazine content, and as much as 18 percent of television content is advertising. Not surprisingly, advertising clutter in many developing markets is even worse than in the United States.

With regard to media vehicles multinational corporations generally prefer Western programming in which to air their messages. Because such reliance on imported foreign programming reduces opportunities for locals, governments increasingly are taking steps to ensure that a certain percentage of programming remains domestically produced. However, foreign styles and production standards are often copied while traditional styles are abandoned. Lebanon, for example, produced its own version of *Playboy,* and Mexico developed a "60 Minutes"–like program. When the multinationals do utilize local programs, they prefer entertainment-oriented programming over more culturally oriented offerings. Further, they tend to prefer broadcast media over print, so that advertising revenues flow to the broadcast media rather than to print. The end result may well be ever-increasing costs for print media and ever-decreasing levels of readership, which does not bode particularly well for literacy levels. Finally, multinational corporations have been accused of attempting to influence media content by threatening withdrawal—thus exerting powerful pressure on local media.

Some researchers have emphasized the beneficial effects of advertising on the local media scene. Supporters claim that, given the limited governmental funding available in many developing countries, advertising support is indeed essential to the health of local media. For instance, international advertising revenues may help to make the media autonomous from politics.[25]

International Advertising Agencies' Influence on Local Advertising Institutions Critics claim that international advertising agencies have the ability to dominate advertising in ways that small, local advertising agencies in weak, poor nations cannot.[26] They suggest that powerful global agencies have a direct impact on a nation's efforts to build autonomous advertising institutions. It should be noted that this claim was a good deal more valid a decade ago than it is today. In the 1960s many agencies opened shop in the Third World—generally by setting up subsidiaries or purchasing local advertising firms. These agencies typically were staffed with Westerners who brought along not only their marketing skills but also their personal and professional values. Separating skills from values is difficult if not impossible, and tensions developed when host countries wanted some of the skills but not the full package of foreign professional values and styles.[27] Because of their high level of creative sophistication and innovation, multinational agencies more or less set the criteria by which all advertising was measured. Local agencies were forced to provide similar services (such as audience research) and were also expected to reproduce the quality and style of multinational advertising in order to remain competitive. Fred Fejes notes that "another very important way in which multinational agencies affect national advertising practices is through their dominance of national and regional advertising associations. Often multinational agencies are the driving force behind the creation of such associations and set the criteria for agency accreditation."[28]

Many developing nations, which at one time welcomed foreign agencies with open arms, have increasingly passed regulations limiting ownership and investment in domestic agencies. The advertising agency is seen in many developing nations as a national communications system that should not be handed over to foreigners. For example, in Latin America foreign investment is limited to 19 percent and in India it is limited to 40 percent. In addition to ensuring that the majority of an agency's ownership rests in the hands of locals, many nations are taking steps to ensure that agency personnel are also nationals and, as a result, are more likely to be familiar with the indigenous culture of the country. Despite such efforts, all too often, expatriates are hired in decision-making roles while locals are employed for the more routine tasks. For example, in the case of Ogilvy & Mather in Hong Kong, four key positions—president, managing director, head of creative, and head of media—are held by expatriates, all of whom came from Great Britain.[29]

Advertising's Influence on Consumerism Critics claim that international marketers promote consumerism in developing markets. For example, Malaysia's Consumer Association of Penang describes the situation as follows: "A worrying trend is the growing influence of negative aspects of Western fashion and culture on the people of the Third World countries, including Malaysia. The advertising industry has created the consumer culture which has in fact become our national culture. Within this cultural system people measure their worth by the size of their house, the make of their car and the possession of the latest household equipment, clothes and gadgets."[30]

International advertising messages are said to stimulate artificial wants and needs and to encourage consumers to demand goods inappropriate for their level of development. Such charges are difficult to answer empirically. Distinguishing between what is a real and an artificial want or need is no easy task. Even in markets where there are no active selling and promotional efforts, demand for Western-style products appears to be widespread. For example, despite the nineteen-year trade embargo imposed on Vietnam (which was finally lifted in 1994), Coca-Cola is extremely popular in this, one of the poorest countries in the world today. Apparently, brand-conscious and America-loving Vietnamese consumers have been purchasing Coca-Cola on the black market for years.[31] Conceivably, a variety of underlying social and environmental factors (such as church and school) play a more significant role in stimulating wants and needs than does advertising.

While consumerism is generally attacked as a negative consequence of advertising, it may also benefit a host society. Advertisements may, for example, convey messages about higher standards of living to a society and, as such, be viewed as a force contributing to the betterment and advancement of people's lives.[32] For example, every society has a need for clean laundry. In many developing nations clothing typically was laundered in a stream of running water or on a rock. To meet the needs of such consumers, a small, plastic, hand-powered washing machine was developed, marketed, and widely accepted.[33] Brazilians (like most Latin Americans) do not typically eat a morning meal. Kellogg's and its advertising agency, J. Walter Thompson, introduced the nutrition concept, highlighting the importance of eating breakfast, within telenovelas, Brazil's most popular form of television programming. The increased demand for this product category attests to their success in this "altruistic endeavor."[34]

Advertising and the Allocation of Precious Resources The criticism here is that scarce national resources are squandered for the production, promotion, and consumption of products that simply are not needed by consumers in developing markets. International businesses are accused of engaging in advertising to shift consumer behavior from rational consumption of locally produced goods to conspicuous consumption of foreign-made goods.[35] To compete with foreign advertisers, local firms increasingly must also employ promotional techniques. These monies, it is argued, could be better spent assisting the local population via health and welfare programs. For example, in Kenya, one study has documented that expenditures for soap advertising are higher than government expenditures for rural health care. Not only do businesses spend unnecessarily, but so do consumers in these countries, because the cost of many international products is significantly higher than that of local goods. U.S. products, in particular, carry a premium price. For instance, in India, Camay soap costs 27 cents while local soaps are priced at 19 cents; Head & Shoulders shampoo sells for $4.77 while local shampoos are priced at $2.00.[36] Clearly, the poor can ill afford such items, because the majority of their income is spent on sustenance. The counterargument here is that while multinational corporations and their advertising agencies may change the patterns of consumption, they do not impact levels of consumption.[37] Regardless of perspective, the question remains, who is to decide which expenditures are wasteful and which are not? From the viewpoint of many international marketers, this is a decision best left to consumers themselves. Critics argue, however, that local governments in developing countries must consciously decide where valuable resources are to be spent.

Advertising's Influence on Rising Frustrations In a related criticism, it's claimed that advertising creates demand for goods consumers cannot possibly afford. The concern here is that the associated dissatisfaction and frustration might possibly lead to social unrest or even political destabilization. In selling goods in developing countries, advertisers may communicate with three major markets: (1) the urban-center dwellers, consisting of foreign expatriates as well as sizable pockets of both high- and middle-income locals who often are as sophisticated in their tastes as their counterparts in developed markets; (2) suburbanites living in outlying areas some ten to fifteen miles from the urban centers; and (3) the rural population, whose life styles remain quite provincial and whose incomes are quite meager.[38] Note that nearly 80 percent of the population in most less developed countries lives outside the cities and that the cultural and economic gap between the urban centers on the one hand and the villages or rural areas on the other is quite substantial.[39] The problem lies in targeting promotional messages only to the most appropriate market segment. For example, international marketers may decide to offer a product to those consumers who are relatively well off with sufficient disposable income—primarily those in urban centers. This creates a taste for Western life styles and values that often trickles down to the lower classes. Inevitably, consumers in rural areas will seek ways to expend their limited resources to obtain these very same items. Ultimately, the lower sectors are perceived not simply as passive bystanders but as potential consumers of these very same products.[40] Philippine author Renato Constantino voiced his concern: "In the Philippines for example, where recent estimates place fully 70 percent of families below the poverty line, money sorely needed for food, shelter and basic health is often squandered on tobacco, cosmetics, soft drinks and the latest fashion jeans. Although the targets of transnational corporation sales are the elite and middle classes, their advertising is "democratically" heard via transistor radios, seen on billboards and to a lesser extent on television."[41]

Further, in many Third World countries upward mobility is virtually nonexistent. Generally, less than 10 percent of the population owns 60 percent or more of a nation's wealth. Many consumers in these countries do develop a desire—whether through advertising or other stimuli—for goods they can ill afford. In Mexico, for example, U.S. soft drinks control over 75 percent of the market, and schoolchildren will save money to purchase Pepsi, which costs three to five times what a local soft drink would cost. However, little evidence indicates that consumer frustrations have resulted in demands for radical change. Nonetheless, governmental bodies in some developing markets have undertaken steps to avoid the potential social or political unrest. For example, in 1981, the Indonesian government exerted a ban on commercial television in order to reduce the negative impact of advertising in remote villages where purchasing power is quite limited.[42]

Advertising's Influence on Indigenous Culture Advertising was heavily criticized in UNESCO's 1980 report, "Many Voices, One World: Communication & Society Today and Tomorrow," in which the McBride Commission took advertising to task for its uninvited cultural intervention in Third World countries. Paulo Freire, a philosopher from Chile, argues: "The invaders penetrate the cultural context of another group, in disrespect of the latter's potentialities; they impose their own view of the world upon those they invade and inhibit the creativity of the invaded by curbing their expression."[43] Note Katherine and Michael Frith: "While multinational marketers and advertisers might consider a western-style global marketing campaign to be an efficient way to reach new audiences in the developing countries, critics like Freire would characterize this as an act of violence against the persons of the invaded culture."[44] Much of the criticism of foreign messages asserts that the advertisements project nonindigenous values and beliefs. For example, although 85 percent of South Africa's population is black, points out Tony Koenderman,

> advertising continues to focus on the white minority and advertising is largely fashioned by whites, for whites. Creative concepts tend to be Western with little relevance for local lifestyles and values, according to the head of the country's only black-owned advertising agency. They use white models even when the main market for a product is black. Until recently, advertisers could justify this Euro-centric approach on the grounds that whites accounted for most of the buying power in the South African market, which spends $1.2 billion annually on advertising. But official statistics show that the white share of total household expenditures fell from 57 percent in 1978 to 49.5 percent in 1988. Today it is closer to 40 percent.[45]

Western advertising clearly presents Western values, particularly when standardized campaigns are employed. What it means to be successful or attractive, what roles men, women, and children should play, are all outlined for consumers in developing markets in thirty-second messages, radio jingles, and outdoor billboards. Sales messages are overlaid on cultural messages glamorizing Western lifestyles. To counter this, many countries have taken protective steps. The governments of some developing countries demand messages that are created exclusively for their local consumers— messages designed to preserve and strengthen their own culture rather than reflect imported values. In Peru, for example, 100 percent of advertising must be locally produced in order to ensure that local values are projected. In Malaysia, write Katherine and Michael Frith, "All television and radio commercials must be screened by the government's censor board before they are allowed to air. The ministry's advertising code provides guidelines that agencies must follow which are aimed at protecting the Malaysian national language, religion, culture and tradition. The code states: Adaption or projection of foreign culture, either in the form of clothing, activity or behavior is not allowed."[46] Real or imagined, fears of cultural imperialism have spurred numerous governments to take preventive action.

Advertising's Potential to Exaggerate Claims and Deceive Consumers That advertising often exaggerates claims and deceives consumers is widely accepted as a valid concern by both consumers and the advertising industry. This problem has always been associated with advertising, but in developed countries regulatory bodies developed alongside the advertising industry, offering consumers some degree of protection. In contrast, more than half of developing nations have no regulatory agencies to speak of. This leaves consumers in developing nations open to misleading advertising. In addition, there is little self-regulation of advertising in Third World markets, resulting in numerous instances of less than scrupulous advertising. The classic example of deceptive advertising—the infant formula scandal—will be addressed in detail later in this chapter. In another example, flame-retardant sleepwear that had been shown to cause cancer and therefore banned in the United States was sold freely in Third World countries. Only a few years ago in Kenya, advertising materials considered misleading were withdrawn only by a gentleman's agreement—there was no legislation to control deceptive messages.

Problems in Assessing Advertising's Effects in Developing Markets

The most striking factor in the preceding discussion is the lack of empirical evidence regarding the effects of marketing and advertising in developing countries. The claims made are complex—and not easily substantiated or refuted. More often than not, arguments are based on anecdotal or scanty evidence, and conclusions clash depending on whose perspective is embraced.[47]

Several problems are associated with assessing the influence of promotional efforts. First, in the debate regarding advertising's effects, the type of advertising often is not clearly defined. Criticisms are levied against advertising in general, yet advertising for specific product categories tends to generate more objections than others. For example, retail advertising, which brings together buyers and sellers and provides consumers with information about the local market, is generally not the target of criticism. Similarly, industrial advertising, directed not at the consumer population but rather at businesses, has received little criticism. This type of advertising also tends to be high in information content. On the other hand, advertising for brand-name products, such as soft drinks, sweets, alcoholic beverages, and, in particular, cigarettes, has received the greatest amount of criticism. Cigarette manufacturers, for example, have been targeted for aggressively marketing cigarettes in developing countries in order to replace lagging sales in the West.

Second, in assessing advertising's effects, oversimplified models of buying behavior often are employed. Critics of advertising in developing countries ascribe great power to advertising, assuming advertising directly causes purchase behavior. Clearly, many additional factors come into play in stimulating buyer behavior.

Finally, advertising is a process in which a great many intervening variables—some of which are not all that clearly defined—play a role. For example, research regarding the impact of international advertising on indigenous culture is complicated by the methodological problems associated with identifying exactly what indigenous culture is. A multitude of factors may impact the culture of a society, and each must be taken into consideration when analyzing both positive and negative claims against advertising. Charles Frazer notes that, unfortunately, advertising effects are not separable from those of other social forces: "How advertising effects might be disentangled from marketing, mass media, social, political, cultural and individual impetus is indeed a staggeringly complex undertaking."[48]

Promotional Strategies in Developing Markets

The promotional strategies destined for developing countries often require significant changes from those used in more advanced or industrialized countries, for several reasons:

▶ The illiteracy rate in many developing countries is often very high, so written communication is of limited value.

▶ The media infrastructure is often underdeveloped, so that the media frequently used elsewhere, such as television, may have limited uses for advertising purposes.

▶ Some countries may be multilingual, making translation quite costly.

▶ The company's products, brands, and so on may be unknown.

▶ The markets may be narrow because of wide variations in income and extremes in income distribution.

▶ The markets may be geographically diverse and dispersed and therefore difficult and expensive to reach.[49]

Yet, despite such differences, campaign adaptation is more common for developed markets than for developing markets.[50] Table 10.1 compares both sales platform decisions and creative context decisions for products sold in relatively poor markets (per capita GNP less than $6,000) versus relatively affluent markets (per capita GNP greater than $6,000). "Sales platform" refers to the product feature emphasized while "creative" context is defined as the way the message is expressed.

Changes in sales platforms and creative contexts were more likely to occur in more affluent markets than in less affluent markets. This may well be a primary reason that international advertising messages targeted to consumers in developing markets are so heavily criticized. International mar-

TABLE 10.1 Market Affluence and Strategic Campaign Decisions

	SALES PLATFORM DECISIONS	
MARKET AFFLUENCE	**Platform Changed**	**Platform Unchanged**
Per capita GNP less than $6,000	51%	49%
Per capita GNP greater than $6,000	74	26
	CREATIVE CONTEXT DECISIONS	
MARKET AFFLUENCE	**Context Changed**	**Context Maintained**
Per capita GNP less than $6,000	58%	42%
Per capita GNP greater than $6,000	72	28

SOURCE: John S. Hill and William L. James, "Effects of Selected Environmental and Structural Factors on International Advertising Strategy: An Exploratory Study," *Current Issues and Research in Advertising,* 12(1,2), 1990, pp. 135–153.

keters wishing to avoid further regulation and vicious social criticism should create advertisements that do the following:

1. Express local social values and needs (an admittedly difficult task because local values are complex and often in conflict with one another).

2. Encourage the economic austerity and personal savings needed to create domestic investment capital.

3. Foster greater awareness of the effect of personal consumption on the local environment.[51]

As Vern Terpstra notes, "Transferring promotional messages between markets is not difficult. Ensuring that they are at least appropriate for their market audiences is not so easy, especially in developing country circumstances where there is greater cultural diversity."[52]

The Future of Advertising in Developing Markets

As previously discussed, advertising in the Third World can have both positive and negative effects. It is, in many ways, a sword that cuts both ways. On the one hand, host nations obviously realize that international marketers and their agencies do make contributions to host societies, which is why they allow them to operate within their borders in the first place. Indeed, in numerous instances corporations and agencies are invited to enter these markets and are even offered concessions, incentives for foreign investment, and tax exemptions.[53] A good many products have proven to be both of value to Third World consumers and profitable for international marketers. And, as noted, advertising has been employed in combating social ills in many Third World markets. Promotional efforts have also assisted in improving both health and hygiene in numerous less developed countries.

On the other hand, there are real dangers associated with the use of marketing and advertising in developing countries. Overcommercialization of the media may well result in the decline of local programming unless protective steps are taken. Deceptive campaigns and the promotion of undesirable or dangerous products pose potential health and other risks for Third World consumers. Additional regulatory bodies are needed to fulfill a watchdog function. It is indeed possible to limit the negative effects with planning and regulation. Scholars and researchers must continue to attempt to understand the effects of advertising in developing markets. Michael H. Anderson summarizes:

> Generalizations about the precise costs and benefits that the transnational advertising agencies bring to their host nations are difficult to make. This is because nations and their development policies and patterns, problems and pressures are in a constant state of flux and are products of various interwoven factors operating within and between nations. What can be said with some certainty, however, is that the presence of the transnational advertising agencies in any Third World society *does* generate some tensions and conflict.[54]

Ethics in the International Arena

Corporations and their advertising agencies are required to make many difficult decisions when operating both in domestic markets and abroad. Granted, numerous laws govern what can and cannot be done. However, not every issue is covered by a written rule, and even where laws exist, there is a good deal of room for interpretation. With regard to business behavior, most marketers would agree that it is important to maintain high ethical standards, whether operating in domestic or international markets. Determining what is meant by "high ethical standards" is a good deal more complex. While interest in the ethical issues pertaining to international business has grown enormously in the past two decades, research on the ethical dimensions of international business and marketing has been relatively limited and nonempirical.[55]

Determining What's Ethical

Ethical standards are often perceived as difficult to define. However, cheating, stealing, lying, and taking or offering bribes are generally considered unacceptable behaviors. Bribery refers to voluntary payments by parties seeking unlawful advantage. For example, a U.S. pharmaceutical company and two U.S. advertising agencies (Young & Rubicam and Foote, Cone & Belding) recently were accused of ethical violations in relation to alleged involvement in an ever-widening kickback scandal in Italy. Prosecutors claim advertising managers bribed ministry officials in order to obtain portions of an AIDS awareness campaign.[56]

Indeed, the issue of bribery often is more than merely an ethical question, because the offering or taking of bribes is illegal in some countries. The U.S. Congress passed the Foreign Corrupt Practices Act (FCPA) in 1977, making it illegal for U.S. firms to bribe foreign officials, candidates, or political parties. The act provides for fines of up to $1 million for offending firms, and company executives, directors, and employees may be fined up to $10,000 and face five years in prison.[57] Other countries, however, may not have laws against bribery. In the international arena confusion often reigns because what is considered a bribe in one country may be perceived as just a "gift" in another. For example, report Gene Laczniak and Patrick Murphy, "Gift giving is part of the Korean business ethic although lavish gift giving is reserved for special occasions such as weddings and funerals. Gift giving has become the norm and those who choose not to follow the custom are socially ostracized." In contrast, the former Soviet Union "stipulated a penalty of death for bribery. Even dinners and small souvenirs are scrupulously accounted for."[58] Even within the category of bribery, a distinction is often made between "lubrication" and "subornation." Philip R. Cateora and Susan M. Keaverney explain:

> When a relatively small payment or gift is made to a low level official to facilitate or expiate otherwise legal transactions, this is referred to as lubrication. It is fairly common throughout the world and is not strictly considered a bribe and often not considered illegal. Subornation involves a fairly substantial payment, frequently not properly accounted for, designed to entice officials to turn their heads or to perform an illegal act. Subornation is a bribe and is usually considered illegal.[59]

A survey of over 1,000 top business executives of corporations whose annual sales exceed $500 million revealed that 95 percent of the respondents perceived that differences exist in business ethical standards even between developed countries.[60] In another study researchers surveyed American international business managers to determine the aspects of international marketing that pose the most difficult ethical or moral problems. The most frequent ethical problem faced was, in fact, bribery; the next most salient ethical problems faced related to governmental interference, customs clearance, transfer of funds, and cultural differences.[61]

In a related investigation, American managers were asked to respond to a series of ethical statements. Their views are presented in Table 10.2. Clearly, while the concept of ethics may be difficult to define, the issue plays a significant role in the lives of international marketers and advertisers. More than one-half of respondents agreed that the opportunities to engage in unethical behavior are many. Fortunately, the majority indicated that success in international undertakings was not dependent on compromising one's ethics. The response to the last statement in the table suggests that a particular level of ethical sensitivity is indeed necessary when engaging in business dealings with less developed markets.

There appears to be little agreement as to what principles should be used to guide business behavior in the international arena. For example, should the international marketer or advertiser adhere to the ethical mores of the home country, the host country, or the international marketplace? Advertisers likely will operate in markets that reflect a wide spectrum of ethical standards—standards that may well be in conflict. For example, an American marketer may adhere to the U.S.'s Foreign Corrupt Practices Act and refrain from engaging in bribery in markets where such behavior is considered perfectly acceptable. However, many businesspeople believe such strict adherence to home country laws places U.S. companies at a distinct disadvantage in foreign markets.

Another perspective is that the legal and political system of the host country should set the parameters for ethical behavior—that is, "When in Rome, do as the Romans do." The fundamental idea here is that as long as the international marketer and advertiser operate within the confines of these parameters, they need not be concerned with ethical issues. Yet, just because a specific foreign country deems a particular business behavior acceptable does not necessarily make it ethical. Indeed, a number of American firms have been criticized for engaging in business practices abroad that are quite legal in the host country but that are frowned on or even illegal in the United States. Moreover, this philosophy does not address the fact that in many developing countries the legal system may not sufficiently protect consumers.

There are numerous examples of multinational marketers who behaved highly irresponsibly in foreign markets but broke no laws. Swiss-based Nestlé, the world's largest food company, provides a classic example. The firm has been selling infant milk formula to developing countries for over fifty years. In the late 1970s the firm was heavily criticized for its aggressive marketing tactics. In selling the formula to consumers in third world markets, Nestlé failed to address a number of environmental factors that resulted in an international scandal. First, illiteracy rates in many developing markets were

TABLE 10.2   American Managers' Views on Ethical Statements

STATEMENT	AGREE (%)	NEUTRAL (%)	DISAGREE (%)
Managers in international business often engage in behaviors I consider unethical.	25%	25%	50%
There are many opportunities for U.S. managers in international business to engage in unethical behaviors.	56	16	28
In order to succeed in international business it is often necessary to compromise one's ethics.	15	10	75
U.S. managers encounter more ethical problems when dealing with less developed countries than when dealing with developed countries.	65	13	22

SOURCE: Robert Armstrong et al., "International Marketing Ethics: Problems Encountered by Australian Firms," *European Journal of Marketing,* 24(10), 1990.

quite high, and a large percentage of consumers in the target audience were unable to understand the instructions on product packaging. As a result, many consumers diluted the formula improperly, and many Third World children suffered from malnutrition. Many consumers also did not know to sterilize the bottles, often mixed the formula with impure water, and thus fed their babies contaminated milk. Studies revealed that the overall death rate of formula-fed babies was three times higher than among breast-fed babies. Another problem was related to price. To purchase just a one-week supply of the formula, the typical Nigerian family spent up to 67 percent of its household income. In the late 1970s consumer outrage around the globe led to a boycott of Nestlé products. During the same period a Swiss court ruled that Nestlé had to undertake fundamental reconsideration of its promotional efforts if it wished to avoid charges of immoral and unethical behavior. The boycott ended after seven years when Nestlé finally complied with the infant formula marketing codes established by the World Health Organization (WHO). The code banned all promotional efforts, including advertising, sampling, and any direct contact with consumers. Nestlé was required to limit its activities simply to taking orders for the product from distributors.[62] It is important to note, however, that the WHO code, which applies to all marketers of infant milk formula, contains only recommended guidelines; the code is mandatory only if adopted by individual governments. The United States, for example, has not adopted the WHO code, although most U.S. manufacturers abide by the guidelines.

The third perspective holds that the responsibility for ethical behavior rests squarely in the hands of international advertising managers and practitioners. Companies and agencies should apply high standards of ethical behavior regardless of what a particular system might allow. Universal standards should be outlined in codes of behavior to be followed in each and every market. The primary criticism of this philosophy is that cultures differ so greatly that the creation of a viable set of worldwide ethical standards becomes nearly impossible. Despite cultural differences a number of firms operating in the international arena have developed worldwide codes of ethics and expect the rules outlined therein to be followed in all areas of operation and in all markets. For example, Citicorp's code states:

> We must never lose sight of the fact that we are guests in foreign countries. We must conduct ourselves accordingly. We recognize the right of governments to pass local legislation and our obligation to conform. Under these circumstances, we also recognize that we can survive only if we are successful in demonstrating to the local authorities that our presence is beneficial. We believe that every country must find its own way politically and economically. Sometimes we believe that local policies are wise; sometimes we do not. However, irrespective of our views, we try to function as best we can under prevailing conditions. We have also felt free to discuss with local governments matters directly affecting our interests, but we recognize that they have final regulatory authority.[63]

Constructing Codes of Ethics

Increasingly, progressive firms such as IBM, Caterpillar, S. C. Johnson, and Citicorp have developed codes that outline their objectives, duties, and obligations in the international markets in which they operate. Many advertising agencies and professional organizations also have adopted codes of ethics. The goal of a code of ethics is to give expression to the actual core values of an organization and then to use these to guide management and marketing decisions.[64] Core values are beliefs that are so fundamental to the organizational structure that they will not be compromised. Codes may also embody peripheral values, which may be adjusted according to the local customs of various markets.[65]

The most effective codes of ethics recognize the importance of all individuals, agencies, and institutions relevant to the operation of the firm or agency, including customers, employees, the host community, relevant governmental agencies, the population at large, and so forth. A company must consider the impact of each of its decisions on these various publics. Such guides to ethical behavior may well assist international marketers and advertisers in avoiding some of the costly ethical mistakes of the past. Even the most detailed code, however, cannot cover each and every morally difficult situation. While most marketers and advertisers typically have little difficulty in making the "correct" decision with regard to health and safety issues, many other situations have no easy solutions and must be handled on a case-by-case basis. In some instances, when the gap between the values of the multinational corporation or advertising agency and the host country is too wide, voluntary suspension of all marketing and promotion activities must be considered.

Summary

International marketers need to behave in a socially responsible manner in terms of product development, pricing, distribution, and promotion. With the growth of consumerism worldwide, especially in developing countries, the need for ethical and socially responsible practices by international marketers and advertisers has become a crucial issue. Unfortunately, it is difficult to assess advertising's effects in a given market. Moreover, what is considered ethical business behavior in one country is not necessarily acceptable in another. A key consideration is whether the international marketer or advertiser should adhere to the ethical mores of the home country, the host country, or the international marketplace. To address these issues, international marketers as well as individual countries have stepped up the debate over what's ethical and have begun constructing codes of ethics for the international arena. In the final chapter we focus on this international arena by examining new marketing and advertising frontiers.

Additional Readings

Frazer, Charles. (1990). "Issues and Evidence in International Advertising." *Current Issues and Research in Advertising*, 12(1, 2), pp. 75–90.

Frith, Katherine Toland, and Michael Frith. (1990). "Western Advertising and Eastern Culture: The Confrontation in Southeast Asia." *Current Issues and Research in Advertising*, 12(1, 2), pp. 63–73.

Hill, John S., and Unal O. Boya. (1987). "Consumer Goods Promotions in Developing Countries." *International Journal of Advertising*, 6, pp. 249–264.

Hill, John S., and Richard R. Hill. (Summer 1984). "Effects of Urbanization on Multinational Product Planning: Markets in Lesser-Developed Countries." *Columbia Journal of World Business*, 19, pp. 62–67.

Hunt, Shelby, and Lawrence Chonko. (1987). "Ethical Problems of Advertising Agency Executives." *Journal of Advertising*, 16(4), pp. 16–24.

Laczniak, Gene, and Patrick Murphy. (Fall/Winter 1990). "International Marketing Ethics." *Bridges: An Interdisciplinary Journal of Theology, Philosophy, History and Science*, 2(3, 4), pp. 155–177.

Mayo, Michael, Lawrence J. Marks, and John K. Ryans. (1991). "Perceptions of Ethical Problems in International Marketing." *International Marketing Review,* 8(3), pp. 61–75.

Peebles, Dean, and John K. Ryans. (1984). "The International Advertiser's Responsibility to a Host Country—the Corporate Future." In *Management of International Advertising: A Marketing Approach.* Boston: Allyn & Bacon, pp. 269–289.

Notes

1. Armstrong, Robert, Bruce Stening, John Ryans, Lary Marks, and Michael Mayo, "International Marketing Ethics: Problems Encountered by Australian Firms," *European Journal of Marketing,* 24(10), 1990, pp. 5–18.

2. Peebles, Dean M., and John K. Ryans, *Management of International Advertising: A Marketing Approach* (Boston: Allyn & Bacon, 1984), p. 273.

3. Toyne, Brian, and Peter G. P. Walters, *Global Marketing Management: A Strategic Perspective* (Boston: Allyn & Bacon, 1989), p. 549.

4. Peebles and Ryans, *Management of International Advertising,* p. 273.

5. Ibid., p. 274.

6. Greyser, Stephen A., and Steven L. Diamond, "Business Is Adapting to Consumerism," *Harvard Business Review,* September/October 1974, p. 38.

7. Kelley, William T., ed., *New Consumerism: Selected Readings* (Columbus, OH: Grid, 1973), p. vi.

8. Frith, Katherine Toland, "The Social and Legal Constraints on Advertising in Malaysia," *Media Asia,* 14(2), 1987, p. 103.

9. De Mooij, Marieke, with Warren Keegan, *Advertising Worldwide* (New York: Prentice-Hall International, 1991), p. 399.

10. Marsh, Ann, "Polish-made Goods Come into Their Own," *Advertising Age,* July 19, 1993, p. I10.

11. Rotzoll, Kim B., James E. Haefner, and Charles H. Sandage, *Advertising in Contemporary Society* (Cincinnati: South-Western, 1986), p. 147.

12. Saporito, Bill, "Where the Global Action Is," *Fortune,* Autumn/Winter 1993, pp. 63–65.

13. World Bank, *World Development Report 1992,* "Development and the Environment" (Oxford: Oxford University Press, 1993).

14. Ibid.

15. Saporito, "Where the Global Action Is."

16. World Bank, *World Development Report 1992,* p. 26.

17. Kaynak, Erdener, *The Management of International Advertising: A Handbook and Guide for Professionals* (New York: Quorum Books, 1989), p. 26.

18. McGinnis, John, "Advertising and Social Mobilization," paper presented to the Association for Education in Journalism and Mass Communication, Portland, Oregon, 1988, p. 14.

19. *New York Times,* "A Lesson on AIDS Fight from Developing Nations," November 28, 1991, p. B15.

20. Frazer, Charles, "Issues and Evidence in International Advertising," *Current Issues and Research in Advertising,* 12(1, 2), 1990, pp. 75–90.

21. Anderson, Michael H., *Madison Avenue in Asia* (Cranbury, NJ: Associated University Press, 1984), p. 42.

22. McGinnis, "Advertising and Social Mobilization."

23. Schiller, Herbert I., *The Mind Managers* (Boston: Beacon Press, 1973), pp. 129–133.

24. Del Toro, Wanda, "Cultural Penetration in Latin America Through Multinational Advertising Agencies," paper presented at the annual meeting of the International Communication Association, Chicago, May 22–26, 1986.

25. Pollay, Richard W., "The Distorted Mirror: Reflections on the Unintended

Consequences of Advertising," *Journal of Marketing,* 50, April 1986, pp. 18–36.

26. Anderson, *Madison Avenue in Asia,* p. 61.

27. Ibid., p. 66.

28. Fejes, Fred, "Multinational Advertising Agencies in Latin America," paper presented at the annual meeting of the Association for Education in Journalism and Mass Communication, Boston, August 9–13, 1990.

29. Kim, Kwangmi Ko, and Katherine T. Frith, "An Analysis of the Growth of Transnational Advertising in Five Asian Countries: 1970–1990," *Media Asia,* 20(1), 1993, p. 51.

30. Consumer Association of Penang, *Selling Dreams: How Advertising Misleads Us* (Penang, Malaysia: CAP, 1986), as quoted in Katherine Toland Frith and Michael Frith, "The Stranger at the Gate: Western Advertising and Eastern Cultural Communications Values," paper presented at the International Communication Association Conference, San Francisco, 1989, p. 4.

31. Saporito, "Where the Global Action Is."

32. Kaynak, *The Management of International Advertising.*

33. Keegan, Warren J., *Multinational Marketing Management* (Englewood Cliffs, NJ: Prentice-Hall, 1984), p. 169.

34. Del Toro, "Cultural Penetration."

35. Tansey, Richard, and Michael R. Hyman, "Dependency Theory and the Effects of Advertising by Foreign-based Multinational Corporations in Latin America," *Journal of Advertising,* 23(1), March 1994, pp. 27–42.

36. Alam Khan, Mir Maqbool, "Another Day in Bombay," *Advertising Age,* April 18, 1994, p. I11.

37. Tansey and Hyman, "Dependency Theory."

38. Hill, John S., "Targeting Promotions in Lesser-Developed Countries: A Study of Multinational Corporation Strategies," *Journal of Advertising,* 13(4), 1984, pp. 39–48.

39. Hill, John S., and Richard R. Hill, "Effects of Urbanization on Multinational Product Planning: Markets in Lesser-Developed Countries," *Columbia Journal of World Business,* 19, Summer 1984, pp. 62–67.

40. Del Toro, "Cultural Penetration."

41. Constantino, Renato, "Mass Culture: Communication and Development," *Philippine Journal of Communication,* 1986, pp. 13–26, as quoted in Frith and Frith, "The Stranger at the Gate."

42. Napis, M., and R. F. Roth, "Advertising in Indonesia," *International Advertiser,* 3(3), 1982, p. 12.

43. Freire, Paulo, *Pedagogy of the Oppressed* (New York: Continuum, 1970).

44. Frith, Katherine Toland, and Michael Frith, "Advertising as Cultural Invasion," *Media Asia,* 1989, pp. 179–184.

45. Koenderman, Tony, "S. African Marketers Take New Direction," *ADWEEK,* January 3, 1994, p. 16.

46. Frith and Frith, "The Stranger at the Gate."

47. Del Toro, "Cultural Penetration."

48. Frazer, "Issues and Evidence."

49. Toyne and Walters, *Global Marketing Management,* p. 564.

50. Hill, John S., and William L. James, "Effects of Selected Environmental and Structural Factors on International Advertising Strategy: An Exploratory Study," *Current Issues and Research in Advertising,* 12(1, 2), 1990, pp. 135–153.

51. Tansey and Hyman, "Dependency Theory."

52. Terpstra, Vern, *The Cultural Environment of International Business* (Cincinnati: South-Western, 1978).

53. Del Toro, "Cultural Penetration."

54. Anderson, *Madison Avenue in Asia,* p. 61.

55. Taylor, R. E., D. Edwards, and J. R. Darling, "The Ethical Dimensions of Trade Barriers: An Exploratory Study," *Columbia Journal of World Business,* 1989.

56. Klein, Maureen, "Three U.S. Companies Dragged into Italian

Investigation," *Wall Street Journal,* June 25, 1993, p. A7.

57. "The FCPA Revisited: What Companies Should Know to Soften Its Impact," *Business International,* June 1, 1984, pp. 173–174.

58. Laczniak, Gene, and Patrick Murphy, "International Marketing Ethics," *Bridges: An Interdisciplinary Journal of Theology, Philosophy, History and Science,* 2(3, 4), Fall/Winter 1990, pp. 155–177.

59. Cateora, Philip R., and Susan M. Keaverney, *Marketing: An International Perspective* (Homewood, IL: Irwin, 1987), p. 144.

60. Touche-Ross, "Ethics in American Business," *American Business,* January 1989, p. 6.

61. Mayo, Michael, Lawrence Marks, and John K. Ryans, "Perceptions of Ethical Problems in International Marketing," *International Marketing Review,* 8(3), 1991, pp. 61–75.

62. Post, James E., "Assessing the Nestlé Boycott," *California Management Review,* 27, Winter 1985, pp. 113–131.

63. Naor, Jacob, "A New Approach to Multinational Social Responsibility," *Journal of Business Ethics,* 1, 1982, pp. 219–225.

64. Laczniak and Murphy, "International Marketing Ethics."

65. Ibid.

New Marketing and Advertising Frontiers

While the intent of this text is not to provide a country-by-country analysis of marketing opportunities and advertising challenges, its goal is to reinforce how environmental changes—political, legal, cultural, and otherwise—impact international marketing and advertising efforts. Among a number of regions undergoing tremendous environmental change, three will be discussed in detail: the European Union, the new Commonwealth of Independent States, and China. The EU, with its 360 million consumers, rivals the United States and Japan in world trade power. The former Soviet Union has evolved into a hot marketplace for many international firms. And China, according to many sources, has become the world's second largest economy, smaller than the United States but larger than Japan. Developments in the Pacific Rim region and Latin America will also be noted briefly. Each of these regions presents new marketing frontiers for international advertisers and their agencies.

Developments Influencing the Marketing and Advertising Environment

Despite its association with the year 1992, the development of the European Union (EU) actually can be traced back to the post–World War II period. As early as 1946, Winston Churchill encouraged Europe to unite. In 1951 the European Coal and Steel Community was formed; this early agreement established free movement of these commodities among the six core member countries (Belgium, France, Italy, Luxembourg, the Netherlands, and West Germany).[1] The arrangement proved quite successful and became the basis for the foundation of the EU as we know it today. The Treaty of Rome was signed in 1957. The vision of this treaty was the establishment of a customs union and the dismantling of tariff, quota, and nontariff barriers as well as the application of a common external tariff. In addition, the treaty contained provisions for the free movement of people, goods, services, and capital among member states. In 1973 Britain, Ireland, and Denmark joined the EU, followed by Greece in 1981, and finally, Spain and Portugal in 1986, to make up the original Community of Twelve. In early 1995, Austria, Norway, and Sweden joined the EU, increasing the number of member countries to fifteen.

Despite the ideals set forth in the Treaty of Rome, a variety of barriers to trade remained. These included customs barriers and border controls, barriers resulting from varying technical standards and product specifications, and financial barriers relating to differing rates of value-added tax (VAT) levied by various member countries. As an illustration of the costs associated with customs delays, customs formalities at each border post took an average of eighty minutes per truck, which raised by 5–10 percent the cost of the goods transported across borders.[2] The thirty-five different customs forms required for international transport were largely responsible for these delays. In the automobile sector, recounts Peter Danton de Rourrignac, "Different technical requirements between member states prevented the mass manufacture of over 90 components surveyed, so adding considerably to their cost." Likewise, differences in "packaging and labelling requirements affected up to a third of food items. Almost the same number were restricted by laws governing content or specific ingredients."[3] For example, Germany's Reinheits Gebot—a national law that set exceptionally high standards for the purity of beer—effectively prevented foreign brands that did not adhere to the strict ingredient requirements from entering the German market. Also, as a result of national differences in VATs, consumer product prices fluctuated widely from one market to the next. The purchase tax on autos, for instance, varied from a low of 12 percent in Luxembourg to up to 200 percent in Greece and Denmark.

Nearly three decades after the signing of the Treaty of Rome, member countries finally renewed their efforts to integrate economically. In 1986 twelve countries signed the Single European Act, which committed each nation to the goal of completing the process of transforming Europe into a community with no internal frontiers by December 31, 1992. The impetus for the single market was, in fact, born out of the recognition by Europeans that drastic changes were needed if they were to compete effectively in world trade. Rapid developments in both Japan and the United States in the areas of computers, telecommunications, energy, aerospace, and biotechnology had left Western Europe behind.[4] A single, common market would mean a bigger and more vital Europe—one better able to compete both at home and abroad.

Implementation of this agreement required the enactment of nearly three hundred legislative proposals designed to dismantle the last remaining barriers to free trade throughout Europe. Specifically, the act sought compliance with three general goals: (1) the elimination of physical barriers between countries, including each country's customs posts; (2) the suspension of all value-added or excise taxes on goods and services traded among member countries; and (3) the removal of regulations on goods and services (including technology), on bids for goods and services, and on capital requirements for investing across borders. In addition, health, safety, and other technical requirements were to be standardized.

Benefits of a Common Market The benefits associated with the development of a European Common Market are seen as substantial. An immediate goal of the European Commission (the legislative body of the EU) is the mutual recognition of national standards so that products judged acceptable in one country would also be allowed into other countries without further testing and approval. Thus, for example, the German Reinheits Gebot has already been ruled illegal, and as a result, beer manufacturers from around the globe have taken steps to introduce their brands to this market. The Commission's long-term goal is the development of a harmonized European standard, under the auspices of the European Standardization Committee (CEN) and the European Committee for Electrical Products (CENELEC), that will supplement the individual national standards.[5]

Despite the current economic slump, many experts predict that the unification will result in a significant increase in gross domestic product for Europe (potentially as much as 4–7 percent). While 18 million Europeans currently are unemployed, the European Commission estimates that new jobs will be created for 2–4 million people. Services industries are expected to be the fastest-growing sector. European consumers are likely to be confronted with an even wider choice of brands as more products from more countries become increasingly available. In addition, analysts estimate a reduction in consumer prices of up to 6 percent. Further, a common market is expected to lead to the creation of industries that are better able to compete internationally—almost half of American business leaders anticipated that a unified European market would generate economies of scale that would make European products more competitive in the American market and weaken the U.S. world trade position.[6] Finally, a common market will make it easier for foreign firms to do business on the Continent because they will need only a single base in the area rather than fifteen.

Key Issues to Be Resolved While numerous pluses are associated with the EU, several problems still must be resolved. One thorny issue has been the development of the European Currency Unit (Ecu), perceived as central to economic unification. Fearing the loss of some of its sovereignty, Great Britain has continued to refuse to promise to give up its pound sterling. Nonetheless, EU financial ministers have decided that a single currency will be created by 1999 at the latest. However, even countries that strongly support a common currency will be allowed to participate only if they meet certain criteria in terms of levels of inflation, interest rates, and debt.

Another problem area involves tax rates. VAT rates currently vary from 0 to 38 percent across Europe. With the removal of border controls within Europe, consumers likely will do their shopping—particularly for liquor, cigarettes, and high-end products—in those countries that levy the lowest taxes. Although the EU has recommended two common rates varying by no more than 5 percent, many European governments have refused to comply as this would necessitate revising their entire tax structures.

Continuing disharmony in the laws of member states also poses problems. The Single European Act requires that member states "approximate" their national laws in line with EU directives, with community law to take precedence over national law. Yet, individual countries are allowed to pass temporary local laws to help in an economic crisis. In addition, governments are permitted to protect local standards of public morality or consumer and environmental safety.[7] Clearly, such clauses muddy both legal and marketing waters. Danish law provides an excellent example. To protect the environment, in Denmark soft drinks may not be sold in cans; only glass bottles with refundable deposits are permitted. Suppliers of drinks normally sold in cans must either convert all European production back to glass, run a separate line for Denmark, or exclude Denmark from their market. Environmentalists would naturally prefer the first option, but most businesses, given the fact that Danes comprise only 1.5 percent of the total EU market, will simply opt to exclude this nation.[8]

Profile of the Euro-Consumer Market

Together, EU countries now contain over 360 million consumers—making it 44 percent larger than the United States and approximately three times the size of Japan. Collectively, the EU countries are one of the world's largest markets for goods and services. Moreover, there is little doubt that the EU will expand significantly in the near future; Turkey has already applied for membership. A number of Eastern European countries are also expected to join; indeed, Poland has already indicated an interest. At some point in the perhaps not-so-near future, many of the republics of the new Commonwealth of Independent States will also participate in the EU. Depending on who counts and which figures are included, the 360-million figure previously cited may well blossom to over 800 million consumers. This would result in a market a good deal larger than even the one established by the United States, Canada, and Mexico through the North American Free Trade Agreement (NAFTA).

A quick glance back at Table 3.1 reveals wide variations in the populations of European countries, with Germany, Italy, France, and the United Kingdom representing the largest markets, and Luxembourg, Ireland, and Denmark the smallest. Population growth will be slower than in either the United States or Japan. Half a million Euro-consumers will be added to the market annually until the year 2000—an increase of only 1.6 percent over the decade. In contrast, the U.S. market will grow at 5.5 percent per year, and the Japanese market at 4 percent.[9] However, age groups are more evenly distributed in Europe than in Japan or the United States, which makes the EU a particularly stable market. As Sandra Vandermerwe and Marc-Andre L'Huillier point out, "Companies will be faced with the same opportunities and challenges an older population brings. The EU is no exception to the industrialized world's aging market phenomenon."[10] Overall, population densities are significantly higher than in the United States. The Netherlands, Belgium, and the United Kingdom have the highest population densities, with well over 600 persons per square mile; Ireland and Spain have considerably lower densities, with under 200 persons per square mile.[11]

One of the most appealing aspects of marketing in the EU is that the market is not only large but also rich. The EU accounts for some 20 percent of world trade and exports goods and services at a rate three times that of the United States and four times that of Japan. While there is a good deal of variation between nations, EU countries overall are strong economically, and consumers have sufficient disposable income to make them of interest to international marketers. Table 11.1 presents GNP and GNP per capita figures for each of the EU countries as well as for the United States. The figures reveal that several European countries—Denmark, Germany, and Luxembourg—have a higher per capita GNP than the United States. The bottom line is, the EU represents a potential market of nearly $5 trillion.

TABLE 11.1   GNP and GNP per Capita

COUNTRY	GNP (1990 BILLION $)	GNP PER CAPITA (1990 $)
United States	$5,465.1	$21,863
Austria	158.0	20,493
Belgium	192.4	19,953
Denmark	123.5	24,027
France	1,187.7	21,044
Germany	1,507.1	23,885
Greece	67.3	6,697
Ireland	37.4	10,685
Italy	1,078.0	18,696
Luxembourg	9.0	24,270
Netherlands	276.1	18,481
Norway	105.0	24,764
Portugal	58.0	5,505
Spain	486.9	12,497
Sweden	224.7	26,250
United Kingdom	975.0	17,004
EU Total	5,889.4	EU Average: 16,895

SOURCE: U.S. Department of Commerce, Bureau of the Census, *Statistical Abstracts of the United States, 1993,* 113th ed. (Washington, DC: GPO, 1993).

Opportunities for Advertisers and Agencies

Both foreign and domestic marketers and advertisers are restructuring their organizations and fine-tuning strategies in order to operate more effectively in what is perceived to be a completely new environment. Marketers are hopeful that the changes that have been implemented to date, as well as those to take effect in the coming months and years, will make it easier to market and advertise goods and services throughout Europe. Many firms are making plans to approach Europe as a single market rather than as a group of distinct nations by realigning product lines and assigning budgets for brands on a pan-European basis. For example, 35 percent of Unilever's detergents are currently fully European brands, and another 50 percent are potentially European.

Some marketers are choosing to consolidate their advertising with one agency—or at most a few large agencies—rather than utilize a multitude of agencies in different countries. For example, United Pictures International, the export marketing organization for the American studios Paramount,

Universal, and MGM/UA, fired an assortment of ad agencies in national markets and appointed a single agency—Young & Rubicam—to manage $30 million worth of film promotion in Europe. In turn, many agencies are merging their foreign offices to strengthen their ability to serve clients targeting the entire EU. The alliance of Foote, Cone & Belding with Publicis in the late 1980s was an attempt by FCB to position itself with a strong European partner. As an outgrowth of this trend, agencies are increasingly hiring individuals with international experience, people who have worked in different countries and understand the major markets of Europe. Many agencies are restructuring to create more international staff positions.[12]

The Evolving European Media Landscape

Currently, a variety of pan-European, national, and local media alternatives serve those seeking both to address the Euro-consumer and to target a more narrowly defined audience. As the EU develops, the availability of advertising vehicles likely will continue to improve as well. Table 7.2 presents information on the number of newspapers, televisions, and radio receivers per 1,000 population for each of the EU countries as well as for the United States; overall, Europe clearly is a relatively sophisticated market in terms of media distribution.

Print Throughout the EU there are over 1,900 daily papers with a total circulation of over 74 million copies each day. Germany alone has some 1,300 daily papers. Other countries have significantly fewer; Belgium, Denmark, and the Netherlands each publish under 50 daily papers. Great Britain has a very strong national press, while the regional press dominates in other countries, such as Germany. In addition to nearly 2,000 daily papers, there are also weekly publications as well as weekly and monthly magazines—both general-interest and special-interest.

Pan-European publications are based on the shared interests of specific groups of consumers, such as media targeting businesspeople or segments with similar life styles and hobbies. In Chapter 7 we discussed the impact of international editions of U.S. publications, such as *Time, Reader's Digest, Cosmopolitan,* and *Playboy.* Several European publications are also popular in a number of Euro-markets. The list of titles with multicountry appeal includes *Marie Claire* (France, Greece, Italy, Portugal, Spain, Turkey, the United Kingdom, and the Netherlands), *Elle* (France, Germany, Greece, Italy, the United Kingdom, Spain, the Netherlands, Portugal, Sweden, and Turkey), *Expression* (Belgium, France, Germany, Italy, the United Kingdom, the Netherlands, Spain, and Switzerland), and *Auto Bild/Express* (France, Germany, Hungary, Italy, the Netherlands, Norway, and the United Kingdom).[13]

Broadcast During the past decade the television landscape has changed significantly in Europe. Previously, television had been tightly regulated throughout Europe, and many countries had only state-run channels. In recent years, however, the number of private channels has increased dramatically. For example, in 1980 Italy had 27 commercial and about 350 private local channels; by 1990 it had 53 commercial channels and almost 940 private local channels. Many nations, including Belgium and Denmark, launched commercial channels for the first time during the 1980s. Deregulation of television has driven up TV stations' revenues as well as the number of minutes of commercials shown each day. Satellite transmissions are playing an increasingly important role in Europe. In 1980 there were no satellite channels in operation; less than a decade later the number had jumped to over forty-five. Satellite channels present a real opportunity to communicate with European consumers utilizing a single medium. While there are no technological restrictions on pan-European television, language barriers and continuing national regulations challenge the usefulness of the medium.

Cable has been the primary means of bringing satellite TV into European homes. The current level and anticipated growth of cable and satellite penetration in Europe is shown in Table 11.2. Note that cable plays a more significant role in densely populated countries such as Belgium and the Netherlands. In less densely populated areas cable service tends to be relatively costly, and as a result, fewer houses are connected. National viewership levels for satellite channels also vary considerably from country to country, depending on the number of terrestrial channels available, the popularity of programming offered, the number of satellite channels available in the mother tongue, and the understanding of foreign languages. As satellite television continues to expand, advertisers will increasingly take advantage of this medium.

Overall, as the variety of broadcast programming increases, Euro-consumers increasingly turn to television as their medium of choice. Currently, the United Kingdom and the Netherlands tend to engage in the most TV viewing behavior, and Germany and Belgium the least.[14]

Other Media In markets where broadcast advertising has traditionally been heavily regulated, direct marketing is becoming increasingly popular. Indeed, the European Commission estimates that investment in direct marketing in Europe will exceed traditional advertising expenditures by the year 2000. Direct marketing presents some real pluses in comparison to other media forms. "Given the linguistic, cultural and regional diversity of Europe, the celebrated idea of a Euro-consumer is Euro-baloney," notes Tony Coad, managing director of the United Kingdom's NDL International, a London-based direct marketing and database firm. "Direct marketing's strength lies

TABLE 11.2   Current and Projected European Cable and Satellite TV Penetration

YEAR	CABLE PENETRATION	SATELLITE PENETRATION	COMBINED PENETRATION
1988	12.3%	0.1%	12.4%
1989	16.7	0.6	17.3
1990	19.3	1.2	20.5
1991	21.8	2.7	24.5
1992	24.8	4.2	28.9
1993	27.2	5.5	32.7
1994	30.0	6.8	36.8
1995	32.7	8.0	40.8
1996	35.2	9.0	44.2
1997	37.1	10.1	47.2
1998	39.2	11.3	50.4
1999	40.8	12.3	53.1
2000	42.2	13.4	55.5

SOURCE: "Television in Europe to the Year 2000," Saatchi & Saatchi Communications, February 1990.

in addressing these differences and adapting to each consumer."[15] At the same time, a shortage of information, caused by data protection and privacy laws as well as other regulations, makes obtaining good direct response lists quite an obstacle. By most estimates there are only about two hundred truly pan-European lists, due to the difficulty in harmonizing and incorporating data from a number of national statistical systems whose quality is not uniform and that use different definitions and methods.[16] The situation with national lists is only slightly better. There is great concern among citizens that data from various files will be combined and used for surveillance or repression. As a result, information regarding consumer tastes and buying habits, so common in the United States, is often difficult to come by. As Linda Kesler points out, "The technological forces driving direct marketing in the U.S.—such as computer data bases, credit card systems and toll free phone numbers—are not as prevalent in European countries. Most corporations still confine their European direct marketing strategy to one country at a time—tailoring the campaign to local language and culture."[17]

European countries offer the advertiser a wide variety of outdoor media, ranging from permanent and semipermanent billboards; neon as well as sports arena and stadia displays; bus, trolley, train, and underground metro cards; to the popular kiosks and airport advertisements. Outdoor media can be a particularly effective means to reach Euro-consumers because the messages typically are visually rather than verbally oriented. The primary drawback for the international advertiser lies in the differences in standard sizes and posting periods in the various countries. Standardization of both sizes and regulation is likely to evolve as outdoor media increasingly develop into an international advertising vehicle.

Guidelines for Creating Advertising

While many marketers and advertisers have become rather disillusioned with the concept of global marketing, some corporations and agencies operating in the EU agree that marketing to Europe as a whole—rather than on a piecemeal, country-by-country basis—may well be the wave of the future. DDB Needham Worldwide, for example, has coined the term *Euro-marketing* for its particular version of pan-European advertising. Notes Lloyd Highbloom, executive vice president for the agency, "Global marketing has mostly been reviewed and discussed at some theoretical level—I have found it always sounded very good, but it was an impossible task. Euro-marketing was developed as a method of moving from global theory to specific application."[18]

A number of factors are indeed driving pan-European advertising and marketing. First, consumers from one European country are increasingly visiting their neighbors in another; thus, it becomes important for a product to look the same on a shelf in Berlin as it does in Brussels. Second, some experts claim that life styles in Western Europe are becoming increasingly similar—especially among upper-class consumers and the young. Younger Euro-consumers tend to have considerable spending power, to have adopted American culture (MTV, Michael Jackson, and McDonald's), to be generally better educated, and to travel farther and more frequently than their parents. Third, a convergence in demographics across Europe (an increasing number of white-collar workers and the decreasing family size, for example) also supports similar marketing approaches. Finally, technical considerations come into play, such as the spillover of television programming and print media from one country to the next, which is significant in Europe. As a result of such spillover, combined with the popularity of pan-European media, there is an increase in cross-cultural influences that has the potential of creating even greater similarities among consumers.

Marketers moving toward a pan-European approach include Procter & Gamble, Black & Decker, and Gillette. Some marketers have even created new products intended specifically for a mass Euro-market. Swiss-invented Toilet Duck, so called because of its duck-shaped bottle neck, is distributed Euro-wide by Johnson & Johnson. To promote the cleaner, the company produced a single TV spot in English, based on the simple concept that the bottle's shape makes it easier to use. The voice-over for the spot was then translated into various languages. Johnson & Johnson believes that the success of the product (which is a market leader in a number of European countries) defies the old marketing notion that consumers have different buying patterns based on nationality. As Madlyn Resener writes, "When it comes to toilet bowls, consumers everywhere, it seems, just want a product that cleans."[19] Armand De Malherbe of Ted Bates France also believes that certain products lend themselves more easily to pan-European campaigns than others. Because tastes in clothes and foods are more colored by nationality, he predicts that 30–40 percent of all products will continue to be advertised on national media. On the other hand, "Products such as cars, perfumes, wines and beers, detergents, and other household products are relatively easy to sell to consumers in Sweden or Spain because they are things linked to everyday consumer matters."[20] It should be noted that while very few brands currently share the same brand name, product formulation process, type of distribution outlet, or advertising message across borders, there may well be many more in the years to come.

Opinion is not unanimous as to whether a large number of advertisers will, in fact, employ a pan-European marketing approach. Pan-European promotion in particular raises several concerns. Consumers may well chafe at advertising messages that employ a homogenized, pan-European style. Some advertising executives predict a backlash of nationalism in response to such messages; others are concerned that pan-European ads, in attempting to avoid offending the sensibilities of any nation, will end up being bland and uninspired.

Differences in language, history, climate, religion, and work habits have resulted in life style and consumption patterns that vary greatly across Europe. The recent trend toward more open borders and reduced insularity has not automatically erased such differences among European countries. Only 28 percent of Europeans speak any second language, and even those who do prefer to speak their own language and to read or listen to both programming and commercial messages in their mother tongue. Statistics suggest that a product package printed only in English, for example, would be understood by at most two out of five consumers in the EU, and in other languages by even fewer. Product information would need to be printed in at least five languages to be of use to as many as nine out of ten Europeans.[21]

Beyond language differences, life styles and consumption patterns continue to vary greatly across Europe. Notes George Simko, president of D'Arcy Masius Benton & Bowles/Europe: "Too many people assume that the tastes and preferences of the European consumer will consolidate. Is it really likely? Will the Irish stop eating nearly 4 times as many potatoes as the Italians? Will the British abandon their vinegar, the Germans their schnapps, and the French their baguettes? I'm not holding my breath."[22] Over the past few years, a number of multinational liquor companies have poured money and time into launching global brands in Europe. Reports *ADWEEK:* "The result? France is still dominated by sales of its culturally beloved pastis; Germany, brandies; and Italy, its herb-filled bitters and aperitifs."[23] In short, national preferences still present powerful barriers to pan-European efforts. While foods and beverages may appear particularly culture-bound, even among durable products there are significant differences in consumption levels. For example, while over half the households in the United States and almost one-third of the households in the United Kingdom own a clothes dryer, ownership of this appliance is significantly lower in many other European countries, where hanging clothes out to dry is a long-standing tradition. Only 10 percent of Italian consumers own a clothes dryer, and fewer than 5 percent of Spanish consumers.[24] These statistics reinforce the claim that Europeans do not display homogeneous buying behavior and that national consumer preferences are unlikely to disappear quickly.

Given such differences in languages and life styles, instead of addressing Europe as one homogeneous mass market, many firms are looking for consumer clusters with similar geographic, demographic, or psychographic characteristics. One approach to European marketing breaks Western Europe into six "Euro-consumer clusters," as shown in Exhibit 11.1. Each cluster is ranked according to language, geography, age, and income. These clusters cut across both cultural and national boundaries, reinforcing the claim that consumers living in different countries share similar characteristics. Consumers in each cluster display similar needs and purchasing behavior.[25] In this system Cluster 1 consists of the United Kingdom and Ireland, where consumers share a common language. Cluster 2 includes central and northern France, southern Belgium, central Germany, and Luxembourg. This grouping has a small proportion of middle-aged people and a high proportion of elderly; French and German are the primary languages. Cluster 3 contains Spain and Portugal, with a young population and a lower-than-average per capita income. Cluster 4 includes southern Germany, northern Italy, southeastern France, and Austria. This grouping has a large proportion of middle-aged people and a higher-than-average per capita income. Cluster 5 contains Greece and southern Italy, with lower-than-average per capita income and a young population. Finally, Cluster 6, the northern catch-all, includes Denmark, northern Germany, the Netherlands, northern Belgium, Sweden, and Norway (and Switzerland, Iceland, and Finland, if and when they join the EU). This grouping has the highest per capita income and a large proportion of middle-aged people. It is also the most multilingual of all groupings, with people speaking various Scandinavian, French, Italian, and German dialects. Note that this model represents just one example of a market segmentation method. Given the challenge associated with reaching some 360 million consumers, agencies and advertisers alike probably will develop their own cluster systems—based on markets or products—for reaching European consumers.

EXHIBIT 11.1 Six Euro-Consumer Clusters (population in thousands)

SOURCE: World Bank and CartaGen DemoGraphics. Reprinted by permission of the American Marketing Assn.

Whether there really is a Euro-consumer—or whether one will evolve—is still open to debate. Currently, EU consumers continue to remain quite diverse and, above all, fiercely protective of their distinct history, unique cultural heritage, and national products. In a survey of 24,000 Europeans in six countries in which consumers were asked if they considered themselves "Euro-shoppers," almost every respondent noted a preference for buying from indigenous manufacturers.[26] It is possible that the tastes and preferences of European consumers will consolidate. It is equally possible, though, that this diversity will only continue to grow as the market expands. The one thing that can be said with some degree of certainty is that the changes to date, along with those likely to occur, will have profound effects on both firms already operating in Europe and those that intend to. They will impact how advertisers look at product development, production, pricing, distribution, and promotional efforts.

The Commonwealth of Independent States

Developments Influencing the Marketing and Advertising Environment

Several features characterized the Soviet system prior to the recent economic restructuring. First, the Soviet economy was centrally planned, and resource allocation was predominantly under administrative control. The result, writes Everett M. Jacobs, was that "central planners established rational consumption norms so that, according to official doctrine, private consumption reflected people's true wants rather than the interests of private sellers. Consequently, consumption was to be regulated so that demand was not stimulated beyond what was thought to be rational or desirable."[27] Second, enterprises in the former Soviet Union operated under an extreme production, and not market, orientation. Until quite recently, the success of an enterprise was determined mainly by whether it fulfilled production plans, not by whether it met unsatisfied demand. Lastly, the Soviet economy was characterized by scarcity rather than abundance. Many goods of interest to consumers—from leather shoes to cars to food items—were quite simply unavailable, and those available were generally of poor quality. Shortages were the norm, and prices were fixed by the state.

Both the political and economic situation impacted the role of advertising in the former Soviet Union. The traditional Soviet view of commercial advertising was that it was a parasitic activity, a drain on the economy. In accordance with Marxian principles, it was associated with "bourgeois decadence."[28] However, following the death of Stalin in 1953, communist leaders gradually concluded that advertising, used in *great moderation,* might help solve certain practical problems. According to Leslie Szeplaki, "One common use was the sale of unacceptably large inventories, sometimes in conjunction with hierarchically approved and highly selective price reductions. Another was in selling obsolescent goods, with obsolescence in certain cases being the reason for the unsatisfactorily large size of the inventory. Still another use was for goods that were seasonally produced, especially if perishable."[29]

In the 1980s the first years of *perestroika,* or economic restructuring, served to undermine the institutions and processes of the former Soviet command economy but failed to replace them with efficiently functioning markets. Prior to 1987, all foreign contracts came through the Ministry of Foreign Trade, which controlled the activity of about fifty specialized foreign trade organizations (FTOs). Each FTO was responsible for the export and import of a specific group of products and services; FTOs coordinated the actual purchasing from foreign vendors and the selling to foreign buyers. In 1987 a decree stipulated that for the first time firms could engage in joint ventures with foreign corporations but that the shares of foreign partners in any such ventures could not exceed 49 percent. Less than twelve months later, foreigners were allowed controlling interests in joint ventures. Despite the increased potential for private enterprise, both domestic and foreign firms seeking to conduct business in Russia or any of the republics faced many factors that complicated business transactions, including changing laws concerning corporate activity, price decontrols, and an unstable currency.

Republics in the Commonwealth of Independent States (CIS) lack consistent laws governing corporate activity. Western entrepreneurs are operating in an environment that Robert Hormats, an international investment banker at Goldman, Sachs, likens to "a Yukon–Wild West economy where investors don't know for sure if they have legal title to what they purchase or laws to back them."[30]

The recent lifting of price controls has resulted in the prices of consumer goods jumping from a minimum of 100 percent to several hundred percent. There is a strong belief that price decontrols will be the right medicine for the economy. However, increased prices have not always translated into increased availability; all too often, shelves remain nearly empty and lines remain long. Further, until the ruble is truly convertible, it will be difficult for trade to move beyond the barter situation currently used by many companies such as PepsiCo, which trades Pepsi for Russian vodka (Stoli) to sell in the West.[31]

Each of the republics is facing rampant inflation. For example, during the first quarter of 1993 alone, inflation in Russia threatened to top 50 percent, and Russian salaries have failed to keep pace with such inflation. When McDonald's first opened the doors of its Moscow restaurant in January 1990, a Big Mac, fries, and Coke cost 6 rubles; today, the same meal costs 1,100 rubles. An average Russian's monthly salary is approximately 10,000 rubles. As a consequence, reports Betsy McKay, "The three hour line, immortalized by the media, has all but disappeared, replaced by a brief 15 minute wait during some peak hours. Sales clerks are sometimes heard politely offering to cut back an order when their customers, embarrassed, find they don't have enough money."[32]

Profile of the Commonwealth Consumer Market

The population of the CIS exceeds 276 million, making it one of the largest markets in the world. The land area is slightly less than 2.5 times the size of the United States. The CIS consists of ten independent republics (Armenia, Belarus, Kazakhstan, Kyrgyzstan, Moldova, Russia, Tajikistan, Turkmenistan, Ukraine, and Uzbekistan); five additional republics (Azerbaijan, Estonia, Georgia, Latvia, and Lithuania) are not currently members of the CIS. The population is a heterogeneous one, and while the official language is Russian, there are more than two hundred languages and dialects (at least eighteen with more than 1 million speakers). Table 11.3 presents basic demographic information for all fifteen republics.[33] Note that Russia, with its nearly 149 million consumers, is by far the largest of the republics. As a result, many of the examples in the following pages reflect current developments in this republic.

The influx of Western investment along with the privatization of state enterprises is creating a rapidly growing middle class in many republics. For example, Russia's privatization program currently involves over half of the country's industry. Notes Paul Klebnikov: "In 1993, the government gave vouchers to 144 million Russian citizens. With a face value of 10,000 rubles, the vouchers can be tendered for shares in a company at one of the privatization auctions or sold on the secondary market."[34] Since the program began, over 48,000 enterprises of all sizes have been privatized. By 1995 the government hopes to have sold off nearly all state-owned enterprises.[35] While fully 99 percent of Russians were employed by the government during the final months of communist rule, Russians today are increasingly employed in the private sector and, as a result, beginning to earn more money. And, with more money in their pockets, consumers are demanding Western goods. Not only is the middle class expanding, but recent market surveys have revealed the growth of a new class of wealthy consumers called the "super-spenders." Russian super-spenders are in the top 5 percent income bracket, earn about $1,000 per month (ten times the income of the average Russian), and generally own their own business or work for an international firm. After covering essential expenses, such as household goods, education

TABLE 11.3   Demographic Profile of the Commonwealth of Independent States

REPUBLIC	POPULATION (IN MILLIONS)	PERCENT RUSSIAN	1992 PER CAPITA GNP
Armenia	3.5	1.6%	$2,955
Azerbaijan	7.2	5.6	2,870
Belarus	10.3	13.0	5,729
Estonia	1.6	30.0	5,390
Georgia	5.5	6.3	3,065
Kazakhstan	17.0	38.0	3,803
Kyrgyzstan	4.5	21.5	2,436
Latvia	2.7	34.0	5,689
Lithuania	3.7	9.4	4,034
Moldova	4.35	13.0	3,600
Russia	148.8	82.0	5,396
Tajikistan	5.5	7.6	1,613
Turkmenistan	3.8	9.5	2,682
Ukraine	51.9	22.0	4,397
Uzbekistan	21.1	8.3	2,321

SOURCE: Paul Kahan, "Russia—the Ultimate Emerging Market," *Time,* December 7, 1994, pp. 36–37.

costs, and auto maintenance, super-spenders typically still have about 40 percent of their income left. This newly emerging group with such a large discretionary income would spend more money—if only more quality products and services were available. These consumers tend to be very brand conscious, and Western brands top their list of favorite products. Smirnoff (the Western vodka with the Russian name), Coca-Cola, and Marlboro are their brands of choice.[36]

Opportunities for Advertisers and Agencies

Bruce MacDonald, general director of BBD&O Marketing in Moscow, notes that "the government now has a mandate to speed much faster ahead with radical programs to produce a market economy. If I were a Western company, I'd get on a plane and come here right now."[37] Indeed, a multitude of Western companies are doing just that. Johnson & Johnson, Eastman Kodak, Holiday Inns Worldwide, and Kellogg's are among the dozens of firms currently knocking on the Commonwealth's door. Procter & Gamble signed a joint venture agreement in August 1991 with Leningrad State University to start marketing and distributing consumer products such as Wash & Go shampoo (the European name used for Pert Plus). Since then, Camay soap, Head & Shoulders shampoo, and Oil of Olay moisturizers have been added to the firm's lineup. In addition, Philip Morris has signed agreements with the Russian republic to supply more than 20 billion cigarettes—the largest order in the company's history—but still only about 5 percent of the market for cigarettes in that country.[38] Further, in 1992 General Motors' Trinity Motors—a Russian, American, and British joint venture—opened its first dealership in downtown Moscow to sell autos to customers from all over the CIS. The Cadillac Seville ($50,000), the Chevrolet Caprice ($23,500), and the Chevrolet Corsica ($17,500) are among the eight models available at the new dealership. While such prices are far out of range for typical consumers, the dealership is appealing to the Commonwealth's elite as well as to corporations.[39] These examples reflect just the tip of the iceberg with regard to foreign corporate activity in the CIS.

In addition to increased opportunities, however, the breakup of the Soviet Union in 1991 has caused Western firms a variety of headaches. For example, in an intricate barter arrangement PepsiCo planned to build dozens of bottling plants and open several Pizza Hut restaurants in the former Soviet Union and convert the rubles generated from its operations by selling vodka and ships in the West. These well-laid plans began to unravel with the collapse of the Soviet Union. Explains Betsy McKay: "Instead of dealing with one country, Pepsi found itself enmeshed in an arrangement involving numerous former republics that were now countries in their own right, with their own laws and trade policies, and in some cases, resources essential to the company's success. To salvage the deal, Pepsi had to negotiate new contracts with myriad interests ranging from new governments to independent companies."[40]

Advertising agencies have followed their clients into the new Commonwealth. Ogilvy & Mather became the first officially registered Western advertising agency in the former Soviet Union when, in February 1989, it formed a three-way joint venture with the Soviet shop Soyuztorgreklama and Hungary's Mahir. Now independent of its joint venture, Ogilvy & Mather has seen its business skyrocket to $5 million.[41] Prior to the dismantling of the Soviet Union, an agency team from Young & Rubicam was sent to Moscow to build Young & Rubicam/Sovero—a joint venture between Y&R and Sovero, a former Soviet advertising agency. Gary Burandt, former head of Y&R's Moscow office, noted that the agency was three to five years ahead of the marketplace. Initially, the lack of product availability and competing brands meant that advertising was not yet necessary. Instead, Y&R offered a range of other services to its clients, including public relations, consumer testing, management consulting, and simple hand-holding, to help U.S. companies understand the market.[42] By the beginning of 1993, however, Y&R was doing $5 million in billings, boasted of a fully staffed creative department, and was busy creating messages for Sony, Jacobs Suchard, and Russia's privatization campaign. Promoting privatization is, in fact, one of Y&R/Sovero's major accounts. The goal of the $3-million account, which constitutes nearly two-thirds of the agency's business, is to explain privatization to Russians.[43]

Bozell SMG Moscow is also tied closely to the reform process. The agency has worked on behalf of the Russian government in a public education and information program that is credited with helping the cause of economic reform. In addition, the agency has taken major steps in obtaining desperately needed market information. As Alison Jones and Billy Rogers report, "To measure the results of its work, Bozell SMG created an unprecedented nationwide database of every newspaper, TV and radio station, local official, election result, and demographic, including population density and ethnic makeup. This system enabled the establishment of a nationwide media and trend monitoring system. Within days, the agency can monitor ads and tell clients what products are selling and what's not from Moscow to Magadan (on the Pacific Ocean)."[44]

Ogilvy & Mather, Young & Rubicam, and Bozell SMG are not the only Western advertising/public relations firms operating in the CIS. Rival organization D'Arcy Masius Benton & Bowles set up a full-service office in Moscow in mid-1990 in a partnership with the Promstroy Bank.[45] DMB&B International president John Ferries said the agency made its move there quickly "while there's a selection of joint venture partners . . . so that when a client begins to think about this market, you've got a stable partnership with someone who can really help them with the fundamental marketing questions."[46] In addition, McCann-Erickson and BBD&O have also opened offices in Moscow. McCann-Erickson had a mere $234,000 in billings in 1992 when it ended a joint-venture agreement with Novosti and began to operate independently. For 1994 the agency is estimating $15–$20 million in billings from blue-chip multinational clients such as Coca-Cola, General Motors, Opel Europe, Nabisco Foods Group, Gillette, and R. J. Reynolds International.[47] When BBD&O first hung out its shingle, the agency's three employees spent most of their time on public relations and marketing consulting. Today, the agency's twenty-five to thirty staffers devote at least 60 percent of their time to media and creative projects. Exhibit 11.2 shows ads for Lucky Strike, Sprint, and Pepsi created by BBD&O. While much progress has been made in just the past few years, the advertising business in the CIS is sufficiently new that there are still no figures available for overall advertising spending.

EXHIBIT 11.2 Russian Ads for Lucky Strike, Sprint, and Pepsi Created by BBD&O

The Evolving Commonwealth
Media Landscape

Many of the traditional media that U.S. marketers and advertisers are accustomed to are nonexistent or underutilized in the CIS, while many other, nontraditional media abound. Trade fairs, exhibitions, seminars, and symposia are considered the standard approaches to this market, while media advertising—print and broadcast—direct mail, and outdoor advertising are perceived as innovative.

Trade Fairs, Exhibitions, Seminars, and Symposia Edward Shevyrjov, deputy general director of the Association of Foreign Economic Cooperation for Medium and Small Business, suggests that marketers entering the CIS rely on trade fairs or exhibitions. Trade fairs and exhibitions provide both domestic and foreign firms an opportunity to present their products. Decades of faulty production and distribution systems under the communist regime have conditioned buyers in the CIS to believe only what they see, and as a result, trade fairs and exhibitions are perceived as a very effective way to communicate with both businesspeople and consumers.[48] Approximately twenty international fairs are organized each year by the Commonwealth's Chamber of Commerce and Industry, and hundreds of smaller specialized fairs are held in Moscow, Saint Petersburg, and other cities. It is not uncommon for trade fairs to attract as many as a half-million attendees. Another means of communicating with target audiences is advertising in exhibition catalogues. Fair catalogues (which list all participating firms according to product line) are kept on file by the foreign trade organizations and referred to when the FTO is looking for a new Western supplier.[49]

Beyond trade fairs and exhibitions, staging individual company seminars or symposia is seen as one of the fastest ways to establish an identity with potential customers.[50] Inoreklama, an organization operating under Vneshtorgreklama (the All-Union Foreign Trade Advertising Agency, which serves foreign clients desiring to promote goods in the CIS), has been the prime contact for foreign firms wishing to coordinate such seminars or symposia. Inoreklama is staffed with promotions experts closely connected with key decision makers in the industrial ministries, FTOs, research and development institutes, and individual enterprises. Inoreklama assists in assessing local organizations' interest in the proposed symposium theme and the product line for sale, compiling a list of attendees, printing and distributing invitations, renting symposium premises and equipment, providing interpreters, and distributing promotional literature. In addition, it assists with customs clearance for products shipped to the symposium as well as visas for personnel.

Print Media Over 5,400 magazines are published throughout the CIS.[51] However, the vast majority are targeted toward the trade—only one-fifth of these magazines are targeted to the general consumer. In addition to mass appeal magazines, there are national publications covering family life, health and sports, art, literature, humor, politics, and other areas. Several dozen magazines are published for children and teens. Each republic publishes a number of magazines, usually in the local language.

To date, consumer advertisements are still rather rare. While many publications have huge circulations, such as *Working Woman* and *Farm Woman*, each with circulations of more than 20 million, they do not carry advertising messages on a regular basis. Even *Argumenty i Fakti* (Argumentation and Facts), a weekly magazine that boasts a world-record circulation of more than 30 million copies, is noncommercial. Only in the past several years have a number of magazines begun to accept advertisements.

Recently, several Western magazines have begun publishing editions for the Commonwealth market. *Reader's Digest* introduced its Russian-language edition in July 1991, joining publications such as *Business Week*, *New Farmer, Omni,* and *PC World*.[52] Playboy Enterprises apparently is ready to move ahead with plans to introduce a Russian-language edition of *Playboy. Cosmopolitan* is also planning to enter the market.

Trade publications contain comparatively more ad messages than consumer magazines. About 60 percent of all Western and other European advertising in the CIS is placed in such specialized periodicals, as compared to 25 percent in daily and weekly newspapers and 15 percent in other media. In addition, the cost of advertising in these publications is much lower than in the West.[53] Because of the specialization of these journals—each periodical covers a specific field of industry or science and has a clearly defined function and readership—advertisers can pinpoint messages to audiences with an interest in a particular type of product. Circulation rates range from 3,200 for *Chemistry & Technology for Fuels & Oils* to 210,000 for *Horticulture*.[54]

Citizens in the CIS have access to over 8,600 newspapers, 10 of which are all-union papers.[55] Many are local papers put out by factories, universities, large collective farms, and other institutions. Most run only several pages in length. As recently as 1986, 95 percent did not run retail or wholesale advertising, although a minimal amount of classified advertising existed.[56] However, advertisements in newspapers have become increasingly common in the past few years.

Among the national newspapers *Pravda* and *Izvestia* are particularly important. Founded in 1912 by Lenin, *Pravda* was formerly the mouthpiece of the Communist party. The paper declared its independence after the coup and became an employee-owned and -operated publication. Once the largest daily newspaper in the Soviet Union, *Pravda* now struggles to attract readers and was even forced to shut down for a short time. Currently, the paper's circulation stands at 2.5 million—down 69 percent from 1990.[57] Although *Pravda* has operated an advertising department since early 1991, few ads have run. However, faced with paying its own bills, the paper realized its primary hope for survival was through running advertising. Most of the currently running ads (at a volume of four to six pages per month) are for financial institutions, small stock exchanges, and trading companies that are cropping up around the country.

Although Western advertising has been practically nonexistent in *Pravda*, this has also begun to change. In May 1991 the International Media Group formalized a deal with *Pravda* allowing the group to manage all ad sales in the United States and Canada. Ad rates are $50,000–$60,000 for a full-page ad, but prices are negotiable. IMG is in the process of working with *Pravda* to develop a demographic and psychographic analysis of its readers. "This is a whole new ball game for publications in this country—they've never previously been compelled to engage in sophisticated readership studies or demographic research," said a spokesperson for IMG. "Our short-term strategy is to market *Pravda* as an effective brand awareness establishing vehicle which will evolve into an equally effective consumer advertising vehicle as the consumer market develops."[58]

The trends are similar at *Izvestia*, which boasts a daily circulation of 4.7 million. Also newly independent, *Izvestia* was the official organ of the Soviet Parliament until just after the coup. *Izvestia* began soliciting Western advertising in 1989 and has sold ad space to General Electric, Siemens, Samsung, Matsushita, and the state of New Jersey, among others.[59] A recent eight-page issue contained two pages of advertising. The current advertising rate is $52,000 per page.

As fledgling advertising departments at the major papers are forced to support publications in the face of dwindling governmental monies, "hidden advertising" has become increasingly popular. Explains Genine Babakian: "With hidden advertising, businesses can buy the publicity of their choice. The newspaper sends a staff journalist to meet with the company and write a piece that is reviewed by the client before publication. Usually, the text does not indicate that the story is an ad."[60] Apparently, readers respond differently to hidden ads, in general paying greater attention to such messages than to "straight ads."

Other newspapers are designed for specific segments of the total market. The daily *Komosomolskaya Pravda* is youth oriented while the twice-weekly *Pionerskaya Pravda* is oriented toward children. *Ekonomicheskaya Gazeta,* a weekly, deals with business and economics. *Sovetskaya Kultura* and *Literaturnaya Gazeta* deal with communications, cultural matters, and literature. *Krasnaya Zvesda* handles military affairs, *Selskaya Zhian* covers agriculture, and *Uchitelskaya Gazeta* covers education.[61]

Much as Western magazines have invaded this new market, newspapers, too, are looking to the CIS. A Russian-language edition of *The New York Times* is now sold on the street corners of Moscow. It is the first foreign-language edition of the 141-year-old publication. The paper will eventually be distributed to sixty cities in the CIS, from Kaliningrad on the Baltic Sea coast to Uzlen in the northeast, a few miles across the Bering Strait from Alaska. Other Western newspapers likely will follow this lead.

Broadcast Media Information regarding radio in the former Soviet Union is quite limited and dated. The Commonwealth's radio network consists of 14 national channels, 2 of which are commercial—Radio Mayak and Radio Moscow—plus some 600 local stations.[62, 63] Estimates indicate that there are some 194 million radio receivers in the CIS.[64]

Television reaches at least 97 percent of the population; nearly all urban households have TVs, totaling some 90 million sets, and 90 percent of the rural households also own TVs.[65] Almost 40 percent of all sets are color, and about 6 million sets are produced in the CIS each year.[66] Currently, there are four channels in the CIS—two national channels, a regional channel, and an educational channel—although new satellite systems likely will result in additional channels in the near future. Channel 1 is received by about 92 percent of the Commonwealth's 276 million people, while Channel 2 is received by about 50 percent. Each major city also has a local station that transmits programs of local interest. Some of these shows are in the language native to the region.[67]

The State Tele-Radio Broadcasting Company, known as Gosteleradio, runs Channel 1 and is the Commonwealth's primary television network service. While television commercials actually appeared as early as 1958, they were a rarity until the 1980s.[68] PepsiCo was the first company from outside the CIS to buy commercial air time. In 1988, during a series of programs about the United States, two Pepsi ads featuring Michael Jackson ran. Yet, Pepsi is tentative about using TV, describing the purchase of air time as "pretty much of an experimental thing at this point."[69] Spots for Visa and Sony also aired. Although most citizens do not carry a Visa card and Sony products are not yet available, these marketers are preparing for changes that appear increasingly inevitable.[70] Victor Oskolkov, Gosteleradio programming director, notes that Western interest has grown in recent months, citing positive moves toward a market economy as possible incentives for Western companies.[71]

Previously, there were few pricing standards on state-run television. Rates varied drastically, depending on which unit of Gosteleradio was contacted about placement.[72] For example, the network was notorious for quoting rates of $60,000 per minute for some foreign companies while letting others pay just a few thousand rubles. Currently, proposed rates are between $5,000 and $10,000 for a thirty-second spot.

Gosteleradio monopolized broadcasting until the republics began setting up their own stations. As part of the concept of *perestroika* and of transferring some control to the individual republics, Gosteleradio supported the decentralization of broadcasting. Asked how long such privatization of television would take, Leonid Kravchenko, chairman of Gosteleradio, indicated "no less than eight to 10 years."[73] The Russian State Television & Radio Company was the first major network to operate independently from Gosteleradio. Currently, the station is funded by the Russian republic but hopes to be free of government ties within five to six years. Airing since May 1991, the network broadcasts six and a half hours of news, information, and talk programs daily. Notes general director Anatoly Lysenko: "I think advertisements should be on TV, not only to bring income but because . . . good ads are one of the strongest engines of a healthy economy."[74] To date, all ads on RTR have been for locally produced goods; however, the network is actively seeking Western advertising. Representatives from RTR visited studios and advertising agencies in the United States to spread the word of their democratic television network.[75] This represents the first step in the network's plan to put together a schedule of American programming designed to attract the caliber of Russian viewer that RTR hopes will interest Western advertisers. RTR has test-programmed a number of shows, including "Donahue," cartoons such as "Robocop," "Spiderman," and "Popeye," as well as classic American movies and music videos. Sixty-second spots on RTR range from $3,750 in the morning to $5,750 during prime time. Because RTR is unable to use the nonconvertible rubles to buy programming, the network is negotiating deals to give distributors free ad time as well as sponsorship possibilities.

Other Media Direct mail targeted to consumers is a relatively new medium in the CIS—and may well be effective because citizens are not used to receiving personalized communications. Direct mailings to date have tended to be unadorned and rather plain so they would not be stolen. The CIS does not yet have the type or volume of mailing lists common in other markets. Vneshtorgreklama is one of the limited number of sources of such lists; it charges about $500 for up to a thousand addresses. And while lists for business or trade mailings exist, there are remarkably few lists for consumers.[76] Although marketers cannot obtain specific labels or a list printout, they can use reply cards returnable to Vneshtorgreklama.[77]

Regarding direct mailing to the trade, until recently, industry decision makers in the CIS—a few key people at the top of various FTOs—were easy to locate and reach. The situation today is in a state of flux due to economic reforms and the fact that people change positions at a rate never dreamed of under the previous system of centralized controls.[78] However, Vneshtor-greklama attempts to provide updated lists of manufacturers, economic councils, ministries, committees, and other parties in research and design work. Direct mail campaigns may be particularly effective if timed for delivery prior to exhibitions or fairs. Foreign marketers, though, need to be forewarned of the inefficiency of the postal system.

Previously, outdoor advertising in the CIS consisted primarily of multi-colored posters two to three feet in size. Early on, the bulk of the signs were devoted to the rules of Soviet life: "Don't waste bread," "Be thoughtful towards the elderly, women with children and war veterans," and "Conserve natural resources." Other outdoor posters contained announcements on entertainment and cultural events or party slogans urging the population to work harder for the state.[79] More recently, posters have also been used to promote goods and services. Newer forms of outdoor advertising include billboards and illuminated signs, but these are limited mainly to major cities and international airports.[80] Only recently were billboards made available to Western firms. Indeed, for a period of time, a billboard promoting Coca-Cola graced Moscow's Red Square, and billboards for Eastern European and Japanese firms lined about sixteen kilometers of highway to Moscow's airport. Since 1988 the sides of buses and trolley cars have also carried ads.[81] Information on outdoor advertising forms, placement, and costs is available from Inoreklama, the Vneshtorgreklama unit handling this medium.

Guidelines for Creating Advertising

The official Soviet policy regarding the role of advertising in a centrally planned economy affected not only the degree to which advertising was employed but also the content of advertising messages. While the practice of advertising in the CIS has advanced significantly in the past few years, consumers in this market still see relatively few advertisements, and those they are exposed to are predominantly business-to-business messages with the accompanying information-oriented copy.[82] For example, during a typical week TV viewers may be exposed to trade advertisements for computer equipment, retail outlets selling office furniture, banks promoting industrial services, and fairs and seminars. Television messages targeted at the general consumer typically are considerably fewer in number. Citizens may be exposed to ads for food processors, cosmetics and perfumes, contact lenses, sporting events, and retail outlets selling spare auto parts.[83]

Those print media that do carry advertising typically carry only a few messages per publication. And, as is the case with television, these advertisements are targeted more toward businesspeople than to consumers. Print ads usually are relatively small in size—perhaps a quarter page or less—and messages are quite restrained from a copy standpoint. Overall, the copy tends to be informative rather than persuasive, and if graphics are employed, they're typically limited to line art.[84] However, a few messages are breaking away from the norm, utilizing creative techniques familiar in the West.

Given this environment, advertisers must exercise great caution in deciding whether to utilize the same or similar messages employed in their domestic markets or to adapt commercial messages. In making this decision, marketers should be aware that inhabitants of the CIS may be both fascinated by and resentful of Western advertising. "It opens their eyes to a wide variety of choices but also reminds them of their bleak lives," according to a report issued by J. Walter Thompson Europe.[85]

Utilizing the same campaign employed in the West may prove effective. For one thing, consumers may be somewhat enamored with that which is foreign. For another, Western-style ads using glossy visuals and persuasive copy will certainly elicit attention when compared with their current counterparts in the CIS. However, using standardized messages may be less than appropriate for communicating with this audience for a number of reasons. Current U.S. campaigns, for example, may have dropped or condensed product information for Western consumers already familiar with the brand or product category. Yet, such information is essential to consumers whose exposure to both product categories and a variety of brands is quite limited. Because consumers in this market are hungry for product information from the West, advertising copy should contain all relevant information—technical and otherwise. Advertisers in the CIS might also consider highlighting the company that stands behind the product, as a well-known firm in the Western world may indeed be a stranger to most consumers in the CIS. And, given that many consumer goods produced in the former Soviet Union were traditionally of rather poor quality, advertisements emphasizing product quality over image-oriented messages may be especially well received. Finally, because so few commercial messages are competing for the consumer's attention, it may not be necessary to utilize attention-grabbing techniques so common in Western advertising.

Michael Adams summarizes the dilemma of international advertisers and marketers: "As strangers in a strange land . . . we must recognize that, although the fundamental precepts will and should apply, the messages and the media may look radically different from what we're accustomed to seeing now, here and elsewhere in the world. We must continue to be sensitive to international campaigns that are irrelevant or inapplicable to the economic conditions and ethnic psychographics [of this market]."[86] The list of international advertising blunders is lengthy enough. Rather than determining irrelevant or inapplicable approaches via trial and error, international advertisers would be well advised to undertake research to determine how consumers in the Commonwealth's various republics will respond to Western models, appeals, and artifacts in commercial messages as well as when and where a standardized campaign can be employed and when and where an adapted message would be more appropriate.

China

Developments Influencing the Marketing and Advertising Environment

October 1, 1949, marked the formal birth of a new nation—the People's Republic of China. From this date onward China experienced full-scale socialist reconstruction—income leveling, guaranteed work, and subsidized necessities. Under Mao Zedong private ownership of land, houses, and automobiles was forbidden, and travel outside one's immediate area was, for the most part, not allowed.[87] By 1956 private businesses had been transformed to "whole-people enterprises," with ownership of all private properties liquidated and all properties confiscated. Further, the communists imposed strict controls on production, consumption, and prices. The upshot of all this was that the economic growth of China was effectively stunted. In 1979, after 30 years of "reconstruction," China's per capita GNP of $253 ranked 101st of 150 countries and territories in the world.[88] As James C. F. Wang explains, "The emphasis in China during this time was on selfless dedication and self sacrifice as well as willingness to forgo private material gain and personal comfort."[89] As a result of both the political and economic situations, Chinese citizens had little opportunity to engage in consumer behavior. Purchases were limited, for the most part, to essentials such as food and clothing. And, much as in the former Soviet Union, under Leninist-Maoist socialism, marketing and advertising were perceived as parasitic and exploitative activities. Censorship of advertising reached its peak during the Cultural Revolution of 1966–1976, when advertising was branded as a capitalist tool and all but eradicated.

The year 1976 signaled the beginning of a new historical period in China. Under Deng Xiaoping's "market socialism," agricultural communes were broken up in favor of individual-initiative farms. The "iron rice bowl" of total job security started to crumble, and monetary wage incentives began to be introduced. Small-scale free enterprise was established, and ownership of land, houses, and automobiles was once again permitted.[90] As part of this economic restructuring, Chinese citizens were not only allowed to want things but encouraged to consume. During Mao Zedong's rule the three major consumer aspirations had been a bicycle, wristwatch, and sewing machine.[91] These desires were rapidly replaced with a refrigerator, washing machine, and television set.[92] Today, a cassette player, VCR, and motorcycle have been added to the list. China was quickly moving from a *Wen Bao* (enough-to-eat) society to a *Xiao Kang* (well-to-do) society.[93]

Deng's goal was for China to reach a standard of living by the year 2000 roughly equivalent to that enjoyed by the French and Germans in the 1950s. In order to emerge from the Third World and follow in the more prosperous path of her Pacific Rim neighbors, China decided it needed four ingredients from abroad: advanced technology, enterprise management skills and know-how, capital, and experience in international markets. In the eyes of Chinese leaders, foreign direct investment in China constituted an excellent vehicle to obtain all four ingredients. In order to accomplish China's goal of quadrupling the country's GNP by the end of the century, Deng initiated an "Open Door" policy. Since 1979 a variety of efforts have been undertaken to attract multinational corporations to invest in China.[94]

No longer dismissed as incompatible with socialist ideals, advertising was reinstated as a legitimate business activity. The government began to use advertising as an institution of commercial information and mass persuasion for two broad purposes: (1) to sell Chinese goods abroad (such as heavily advertised Tsingtao beer in the United States) and (2) to sell both Chinese and foreign goods at home.[95] In addition, notes Michael H. Anderson, advertising was considered to have specific functions, such as to "provide business information; guide consumption and production; promote foreign trade; beautify the cityscape; make people feel proud of socialistic economy and culture; be instrumental to catching up and competing with more developed economies; and be a valuable source of hard currency from foreign advertisers."[96]

The invitation to invest in China has not been ignored by savvy marketers, who see within China's borders nearly one out of every four of the world's consumers. Experiencing saturated markets and cutthroat competition in most industrialized countries, a flood of businesses now seek to enter the Chinese market, perceived as the fastest-growing economy on the globe. Many—such as Unilever and Procter & Gamble—have already done so with a good deal of success. Most of the foreign consumer goods flooding Chinese stores are produced via joint ventures with local Chinese firms. This approach allows investors to take advantage of China's pool of cheap labor as well as avoid duties on consumer products, which usually range from 40 percent up to 120 percent. Procter & Gamble and Unilever, as well as S. C. Johnson, Nestlé, and Britain's United Biscuits, all operate in this fashion.[97] Table 11.4 lists the twenty largest joint ventures in China, with foreign partners also noted. The largest investor in China is Hong Kong, followed by Japan and the United States.

TABLE 11.4   Top 20 Joint Ventures in China by 1992 Sales Volume (in million yuan)

RANK	VENTURE PARTNERS	SALES	PROFIT
1	Shanghai Volkswagen (Volkswagen AG, Germany)	7,108	715
2	Beijing Jeep (Chrysler, U.S.)	3,490	422
3	Gold Cup Jinbei Vehicle (Brilliance China Automotive Holding, Bermuda; General Motors, U.S.)	3,415	320
4	Guangzhou Peugeot (PSA Peugeot–Citroen, France)	2,444	297
5	Shenzhen South Pharmaceutical (Chia Tai Group, Hong Kong)	1,636	217
6	Southseas Oil & Fats Industrial (Chiwan) (The Kuok Group, Malaysia; Top Glory Holdings, Hong Kong)	1,429	69
7	Huaqiang Sanyo Electronics (Sanyo Electric, Japan)	1,403	25
8	Shanghai-Bell Telephone Equipment Manufacturing (Alcatel Bell Telephone Manufacturing, Belgium)	1,318	409
9	Guangzhou Iron & Steel (Guangdong Enterprises Holdings, Hong Kong)	1,268	180
10	Shenzhen Kangjia Electronics Group (Kong Wah International, Hong Kong)	1,213	120
11	Shenzhen Zhonghua Bicycles Group (Link Bicycle, Hong Kong)	1,166	151
12	Beijing Matsushita Color CRT (Matsushita Electronics, Japan)	1,142	320
13	Beijing Light Automobile Vehicle (Shortridge, Hong Kong, A Subsidiary of China International Trust & Investment, Beijing)	1,116	203
14	Pingshuo Coal Industrial (Founded with Occidental Petroleum, U.S., which has sold its interest to Bank of China and others)	1,053	279
15	Guangdong Jianlibao Beverages (Nan Yue Group, Macao; Guang Xin Enterprises, Hong Kong)	1,012	162
16	No. 1 Autoworks Volkswagen (Volkswagen AG, Germany)	902	−41
17	Chunlan Group (Zhongshan, Hong Kong)	883	169
18	Fujian Hitachi TV (Hitachi, Japan)	848	47
19	Shanghai Erfangji No. 2 Textile Machinery (Various Owners of Public Shares)	744	149
20	Sanyo Electrical Machinery (Sanyo Electric, Japan)	675	7

SOURCE: Marcus Brauchlei, "When in Huangpu," *Wall Street Journal*, December 10, 1993, p. R15+. Reprinted by permission of *The Wall Street Journal*, © 1993 Dow Jones & Company, Inc. All rights reserved worldwide.

Since introducing elements of a market economy some fifteen years ago, China's economy has made tremendous progress and international trade has boomed. In the last ten years total foreign investment in China has grown dramatically. For example, with regard to U.S.–China trade, between 1983 and 1992 exports from the United States increased from $2.16 billion to $7.47 billion. In contrast, imports from China jumped from $2.24 billion to over $25 billion. During the past decade China's annual GNP growth has averaged 9–10 percent; at this rate the country creates the equivalent of a new market roughly the size of Argentina's each year.[98] Presently, the country's GNP stands at $603 billion (in current dollars), compared to a GNP of over $5 trillion for the United States.[99] Given the progress made since 1979, some experts predict that it will take China only ten years to accomplish what Taiwan did in twenty-five. Indeed, many economists predict that China will become Asia's largest consumer market after Japan by 2000.[100]

Profile of the Chinese Consumer Market

With almost 1.17 billion consumers, China is the world's largest single-country market. Another 22 million new consumers are added each year. Including Taiwan the country consists of thirty provinces, municipalities, and autonomous regions (Table 11.5). China is a land of youth—almost 50 percent of the population is under age 24. The average family size ranges from 3.7 individuals in the Beijing municipality to 5.2 in the Yunnan and Qinghai provinces. While China is a unified country, it is comprised of many different nationalities. In addition to Han, the largest national group, there are some fifty-five other nationalities. The Chinese language, also known as Hanyu, usually refers to the standard language and its various dialects. Most of the minority nationalities speak their own languages.[101]

In evaluating the Chinese consumer market, virtually all economists discount from one-quarter to up to one-third of the population because they live in areas designated as rural and are perceived to be simply too hard to reach. Laurence Zuckerman explains: "Many experts note that the bulk of the market lies in the 31 cities with populations of a million or more—which makes for a market of some 62 million consumers. Rather than employing the rural/urban distinction in evaluating the market, by examining per capita income, others argue that the country now contains as many as 100 million households which can be characterized as approaching middle class—a number roughly equal to the size of the U.S. market."[102]

Officially, the country's per capita income is estimated at the equivalent of about $470 annually. However, the current consumption boom suggests that this figure is a far cry from reality. When governmental subsidies, black market activity, purchasing parity, and a number of other factors are taken into account, income may well be several times that level.[103] This is due in

TABLE 11.5 Population and Size of China's Provinces

PROVINCE, MUNICIPALITY, OR AUTONOMOUS REGION	POPULATION (IN MILLIONS)	AREA (IN THOUSAND SQUARE KM)
Beijing Municipality	9.2	16.8
Tianjin Municipality	7.8	11.3
Hebei Province	53.0	187.7
Shanxi Province	25.3	156.3
Inner Mongolia Autonomous Region	19.3	1,183.0
Liaoning Province	35.7	145.7
Jilin Province	22.6	180.0
Heilongjiang Province	32.7	469.0
Shanghai Municipality	11.6	6.1
Jiangsu Province	60.5	102.6
Zhejiang Province	38.9	102.0
Anhui Province	49.7	139.9
Fujian Province	25.9	120.0
Jiangxi Province	33.2	166.6
Shandong Province	74.4	153.3
Henan Province	74.4	167.0
Hubei Province	47.8	187.0
Hunan Province	54.0	210.0
Guangdong Province	59.3	212.0
Guangxi Zhuang Autonomous Region	36.4	236.2
Sichuan Province	99.7	570.0
Guizhou Province	28.6	176.3
Yunnan Province	32.6	394.0
Tibet Autonomous Region	1.9	1,228.4
Shaanxi Province	28.9	206.0
Gansu Province	19.6	454.0
Qinghai Province	3.9	721.5
Ningxia Hui Autonomous Region	3.9	60.0
Xinjiang Uygur Autonomous Region	13.1	1,600.0
Taiwan Province	18.3	35.9

SOURCE: Xu Bai Yi, *Marketing to China: One Billion New Customers* (Lincolnwood, IL: NTC, 1990). Reprinted by permission of the publisher.

large part to the remnants of the socialist state, which still showers urban workers with huge subsidies. Rents, for example, are both controlled and heavily subsidized, so most Chinese spend only a few dollars per month on housing. As Exhibit 11.3 shows, the average urban household in China spends less than 1 percent of its income on housing, just 3 percent on utilities, and only 1 percent on transportation.

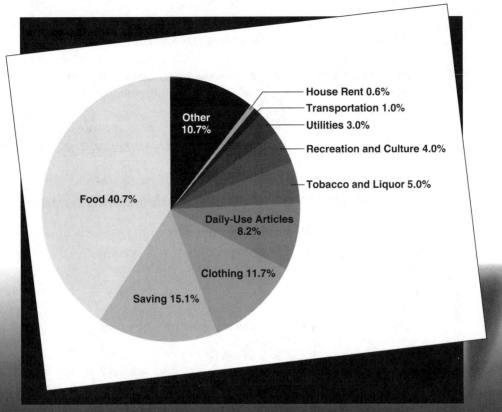

House Rent 0.6%
Transportation 1.0%
Utilities 3.0%
Recreation and Culture 4.0%
Tobacco and Liquor 5.0%
Other 10.7%
Food 40.7%
Daily-Use Articles 8.2%
Clothing 11.7%
Saving 15.1%

EXHIBIT 11.3 How the Average Urban Chinese Household Spends Its Income

SOURCE: Sally D. Goll and Yumiko Ono, "Consuming Passions," *Wall Street Journal,* December 10, 1993, p. R15+. Reprinted by permission of *The Wall Street Journal,* © 1993 Dow Jones & Company, Inc. All rights reserved worldwide.

Living arrangements, particularly among younger Chinese, also directly influence disposable income. Because most Chinese in their 20s live with parents or in apartments supplied by their employers or the government, they are able to save up to 50 percent of their income. In addition, as has been documented, very few Chinese pay any taxes.[104] China also has a vast and growing underground economy. According to Andrew Tanzer, "Urban residents report to their official jobs and knowing they can't be fired, quickly depart for second, or even third, jobs, either in the underground or in the new private sector."[105] Finally, Chinese consumers apparently have stashed away some $45 billion in savings in mattresses and the like.[106]

To come up with a more accurate figure than $470, writes Laurence Zuckerman, "the International Monetary Fund began estimating China's per-capita income based on purchasing power parity, or the equivalent in dollar terms of what the Chinese Yuan actually buys. The IMF pegged China's per-capita-income at $1,300 annually, catapulting the nation from the world's 11th-largest economy to No. 3. But the IMF estimate is still much lower than other estimates. According to estimates put forth by academics and the World Bank, China is the world's second-largest economy, smaller than the U.S., but larger than Japan."[107]

Marketing experts agree that once an economy breaks through an annual per capita income barrier of roughly $1,000, consumers move beyond buying staples and begin shopping for durables like TV sets, nonessential processed foods like ice cream, and packaged goods, including branded items such as Procter & Gamble's Oil of Olay skin cream.[108] Indeed, sales of cameras, refrigerators, color TV sets, and VCRs are brisk, as revealed in Exhibit 11.4.

Opportunities for Advertisers and Agencies

Chinese consumers have quickly become familiar with Western brands. Under Deng the Chinese were no longer discouraged from listening to overseas radio broadcasts, studying foreign languages, reading foreign literature and periodicals, or attending foreign films.[109] Travel to neighboring countries increased, and many Chinese have relatives in Hong Kong. Indeed, Hong Kong serves as a measuring stick in terms of quality of life in Mainland China.[110] Most influential in making Chinese consumers aware of foreign brands, of course, is the rapidly increasing number of Western advertisements appearing in Chinese media. "Newly affluent Chinese are very responsive to ads," notes J. Walter Thompson's Ron Cromie. "After the experience of shoddy domestic merchandise, they value the quality reassurance of foreign brand goods. They're looking to buy into a new international lifestyle."[111]

Economists note that, much as in the CIS, an affluent class of consumers is emerging in China with cravings for upscale products. In particular, affluent Chinese seek out foreign consumer goods. Consider the Shanghai Orient Shopping Center. From its appearance, writes Andrew Tanzer, "It could be in Hong Kong or Seattle. A piano tinkles in the lobby. On the first floor, fashionably dressed Shanghai women shop for Christian Dior cosmetics, Rado watches and gold jewelry. Downstairs, shoppers stock up on Unilever's Lux soap, Heinz infant cereal, Nestlé powdered milk and other Western brands. In the electric appliance section, newly married couples look over $1,000 Toshiba refrigerators and Panasonic color TV sets and $1,500 Pioneer stereo systems."[112] Indeed, report Sally Goll and Yumiko Ono, Chinese con-

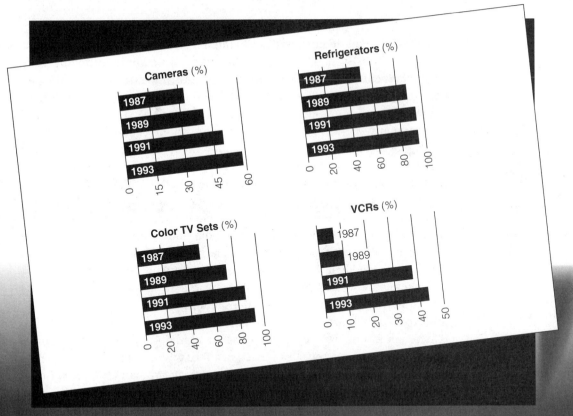

EXHIBIT 11.4 Percent Household Ownership of Cameras, Refrigerators, Color TV Sets, and VCRs in Shanghai

sumers are "accumulating the totems of Western and Japanese yuppiedom as fast as the merchandise can be stacked on store shelves."[113] Foreign brand goods—even those manufactured in China—generally cost two to three times as much as their local equivalents; nonetheless, they're snapped up by status-conscious Chinese. Notes James Wong, general manager of DDB Needham's Beijing office, "Consumers want to show off that they can afford to spend money. They leave the tags on sunglasses and labels on the sleeves of suits."[114] Such trends are only expected to increase.

Again, much as in the CIS, many advertisers are taking a long-term view of the Chinese market—investing now but realizing they won't be turning a profit for some years to come. For example, Shiseido, Japan's largest manufacturer of cosmetics, currently sells its products in many of China's state-run department stores but doesn't expect to turn a profit for five years. However, the company has plans to begin manufacturing its products locally via a joint venture. By the turn of the century, Shiseido hopes to post annual sales of about $95 million. Another cosmetics manufacturer, Avon, attempted to crack the Chinese market in the mid-1980s. The company spent five years negotiating with government authorities in Beijing for a venture in northern China but made little progress. Finally, the company contacted provincial officials in Guangdong and eventually hammered out an agreement after a year of negotiations. Today, Avon holds a 60 percent stake in a joint venture with Guangzhou Cosmetics Factory, its local partner. First-year sales of Avon cosmetics topped $4 million, and the company thinks sales could reach $50–$60 million within five years.[115]

Despite the potential noted above, marketers face steep hurdles as well. Valarie Reitman identifies several obstacles, including "an overheating economy choked by soaring inflation, difficulty in converting Chinese Yuan into foreign currency for importing supplies and repatriating profits, an abysmal infrastructure that can turn a rail shipment traveling from Canton to Beijing into a month-long odyssey, and the logistical nightmare of supplying thousands of tiny mom-&-pop stores that can afford to stock only a few bottles at a time."[116] Further, reports Louis Kraar, "American companies still find China, a country without a commercial code or independent courts for settling disputes, a tough endurance test. [One western diplomat in China notes:] 'There are tremendous risks in individual deals because the Chinese don't want to play by international rules and don't use standard accounting.' "[117]

Clearly, the events of June 4, 1989, have vastly increased the political risk perceived by many international executives. Marketers were unsettled by the brutal suppression of the prodemocracy demonstrators in Tiananmen Square. Investors around the globe had assumed that the gradual liberalization experienced during the previous decade would continue indefinitely and were lulled into believing that socialism in China was simply a way station on the road to capitalism.[118] There is an increased fear that the new economic freedoms in China could be curtailed—directly impacting international marketers.

Japan's Dentsu was the first agency to enter China, opening offices in Beijing and Shanghai soon after advertising was resumed in 1979. Other Japanese agencies, such as Hukuhodo, followed, and in the early years Japanese advertising occupied the bulk of foreign messages in China. By 1981, at least four major Western agencies (Young & Rubicam, McCann-Erickson, Ogilvy & Mather, and Leo Burnett) were actively negotiating with Chinese authorities. McCann-Erickson became the first American agency to actually station employees inside China as opposed to covering the country from headquarters or a nearby Asian office.

In just the past few years, there has been a dramatic increase in the number of international agencies that have opened shop or expanded offices in what is now a more than $1-billion advertising industry. For example, DDB Needham Worldwide officially opened its Beijing office in 1992, in a joint-venture operation with Beijing Advertising, a large government advertising unit. DDB Needham has majority control of the venture, which also offers public relations services. Clients include McDonald's, Fuji Photo Film, and Mobil Oil. At about the same time, Grey Advertising entered Beijing and Guangzhou. Grey is the majority partner in a joint venture with China International Trust and Investment; clients include B.A.T. Industries, Nike, and Procter & Gamble. Dentsu, Young & Rubicam, which has operated in China since 1986, formally opened a small office in Guangzhou as well and upgraded the DY&R Shanghai branch into a full-service agency. Gary Burandt, president and CEO of DY&R Partnerships, notes that the agency will make a profit for the first time thanks to the improving economy and the influx of new clients such as Colgate-Palmolive, which plans to produce toothpaste locally. Also during 1992, Saatchi & Saatchi Advertising Worldwide opened its new Beijing agency, formed as a joint venture with two local partners. While D'Arcy Masius Benton & Bowles established an office in Guangzhou in the mid-1980s, it plans to expand to Beijing as well. Roy Bostock, chairman and CEO of DMB&B, noted that the agency will be in the investment stage for up to three years: "We've made a commitment in order to build a very solid foundation." Looking ten years into the future, he expects China to develop into one of the agency's top 10 offices, with billings of perhaps $40–$50 million.[119] Numerous other foreign advertising firms have joined the ranks of the agencies just noted. Collectively, these advertising agencies have brought the advanced technology and modern advertising and marketing techniques needed to further develop China's advertising industry.[120]

One study asked foreign agencies to name the most important reasons for their entry into the Chinese market. "Service to clients" was expressed as the primary motive. Many agencies followed their clients into the People's Republic of China in hopes of keeping their existing customers satisfied. Apart from "service to clients" many agencies were attracted by the huge market potential present in China. Agencies were also asked to rate the importance of the Chinese business to their own company. While most agencies were rather conservative in rating the importance of the Chinese business to their current situation, the majority felt strongly that China would become "extremely" or "very" important to their companies in the near future. Moreover, long-term effects of a China presence were expected to be well worth the effort. Finally, when asked to name the major problems they encountered in conducting business activities in China, the agencies overwhelmingly named "the lack of professional advertising personnel" and the "lack of organized research data" as the major problems. The lack of organized information made it very difficult for foreign agencies that were unfamiliar with the vast Chinese market to carry out advertising effectively and to assess its results.[121] It is important to note that while international advertising activity has increased dramatically in China, foreign ads still account for a very small percentage of the Chinese advertising market. It is estimated that only about 10 percent of China's total revenue is attributable to foreign advertisers.

The Evolving Chinese Media Landscape

Print Media Newspapers are the most popular advertising medium in China, accounting for slightly less than 30 percent of total expenditures while running over $15 million worth of advertising each year. China has some 1,700 registered newspapers with a daily circulation of 202 million copies. All are published by central or provincial-level governments, and most carry advertisements. The largest paper, *Renmin Ribao* (People's Daily), has a reported circulation of nearly 5 million.[122] Often the first choice of advertisers wishing to reach top decision makers and a national audience, this paper, which is the official organ of the Communist party, is read by party members, government employees, and those who work in industrial and commercial organizations. The paper, which is printed in more than thirty cities, has an international readership as well.

Other popular papers favored by international advertisers include *Jeifang Ribao* (Liberation Daily), also read by decision makers; *Jingji Ribao* (Economic Daily), read in economic circles; and *Gongren Ribao* (Worker's Daily), read by over 1 million workers. At least a half dozen other papers also boast circulations of at least 1 million. In addition, there are a variety of regional publications as well as papers that attract audiences with specific interests, such as *Zhongguo Tiyi Bao* (China Sports) and *Zhongguo Qing Nian Bao* (China Youth Gazette).[123]

According to the State Administration for Industry and Commerce, more than 6,000 general interest magazines, periodicals, and publications targeting specific industrial sectors are printed in China, with an estimated circulation of 2.5 billion copies. This is a dramatic increase over the 930 magazines published in 1978. Generally, magazines with national circulations accept advertisements; however, magazines receive little more than 4 percent of advertising media dollars. The magazines with the largest circulation include *Red Flag* (9.7 million) and *Younger Generation* (5 million). Virtually all Chinese magazines are owned and controlled by the state, with just a few small regional publications owned by collectives or individuals.[124] Magazines dealing with the topics of natural science and technology are the most numerous, but publications dealing with philosophy, social science, culture, and education are also quite common.[125]

Broadcast Media China now has over seven hundred TV stations, and some 800 million Chinese have access to TV sets. Over 12 million color TV sets are sold annually, making China the world's largest market for this appliance. Expenditures for television advertising are considerably smaller than those for print—currently just above 18 percent—though the popularity of television advertising is increasing significantly as foreign marketers enter China. Indeed, the huge demand for TV time has created a seller's market in China, where some advertisers face rate hikes of more than 100 percent. Under a controversial three-tier system of media buying, local Chinese companies receive the lowest rates; joint ventures—foreign advertisers with a local manufacturing partner—get middle-range rates; and fully foreign-owned companies pay top dollar. Rates have been tiered for the few years foreign companies have been allowed to advertise in China. For example, the government network China Central Television hiked the rate of an average thirty-second spot for joint-venture advertisers to $6,175—an increase of over 100 percent. Similar increases are slated for local stations in Beijing and Shanghai, and in the booming southern province of Guangdong, rates will likely jump 45 percent. Foreign advertisers paying in U.S. dollars will pay up to $11,000 for a thirty-second spot, with an added 20 percent surcharge if the advertiser specifies a certain program. Despite the rate hikes TV advertising is still a bargain in China. When compared to the half million dollars a U.S. advertiser might pay to place an ad on a Super Bowl broadcast, in China a marketer can reach up to 600 million viewers for under $20,000.[126]

In addition to nationwide China Central Television, 746 municipal and provincial television stations have also begun accepting advertising. Typically, advertising time is not allowed to exceed 10 percent of total telecasting time. TV commercials are shown only during five- to fifteen-minute breaks between shows and range in length from ten to thirty seconds. The Chinese appear to enjoy television advertising—often, the fifteen-minute blocks of advertising receive higher marks than the programming. Quite surprisingly, messages for similar categories of products are aired together so that viewers may make claim comparisons. The most commonly advertised consumer products are cosmetics, medicines, and domestic electrical appliances, and social welfare announcements are also numerous. It is not uncommon, however, to see heavy machinery (tractors, industrial drill presses, and so on) advertised on prime-time TV. Program sponsorships are also increasing in popularity. Johnson & Johnson, for example, sponsored a prime-time baby-care series. Each of the four- to five-minute vignettes, featuring a couple puzzling over the care of their newborn infant, ended with a

Johnson & Johnson baby-care expert dispensing advice. The series both attracted a good deal of consumer attention and boosted product sales.[127]

The country's 1,211 local and national radio stations are listened to by 95 percent of the population on a regular basis. China has more than 300 million radios, which cover urban and rural areas. A major advantage of radio is that it is able to reach consumers unable to read newspapers. About 4 percent of advertising dollars are devoted to this medium.

Other Media There are nearly a quarter of a million billboards as well as thousands of neon signs, illuminated street signs (called "lighted boxes"), and window displays available to carry advertisers' messages at reasonable cost. In addition to glass bus shelters, buses, trolleys, pedestrian bridges, and sidewalk railings in major cities often carry advertising messages. The heavy traffic and bustling crowds typical of most Chinese cities guarantee large audiences for outdoor advertisements. For example, an estimated several million people pass through Shanghai's main thoroughfares every day.[128] Combined, outdoor and transit advertising receive almost 40 percent of all advertising dollars.

Direct mail advertising is still quite rare in China. Because Chinese consumers rarely receive commercial letters or fliers in the mail, they're likely to read and consider direct mail more carefully than do Westerners. Notes Xu Bai Yi: "The Chinese government appears open to the idea of direct mail; in 1991 the Shanghai post office launched a campaign to encourage firms to mail commercial messages. These messages can only be mailed at first class rates; they are not entitled to the cheaper bulk rates common in other countries. High international postage rates, moreover, generally make it uneconomical to send mass-mailings from overseas. Currently underused, direct mail is an area with strong potential for future advertising efforts."[129]

Guidelines for Creating Advertising

The Public Opinion Institute of People's University conducted a survey in Beijing and Tianjin in 1987 to gauge Chinese consumers' responses to advertising. Overall, consumer responses to marketing communications appear to be quite positive. Over 68 percent of survey respondents noted they preferred television advertisements, while only 31 percent preferred press, radio, and billboard messages. Nearly half of the respondents did claim, however, that there were too many television advertisements. Of these, 66 percent preferred domestic ads; only 33 percent preferred foreign commercials.[130]

A variety of factors may explain this preference for domestically produced advertisements. Overall, Chinese ads tend to be straightforward, showing illustrations of products without much embellishment.[131] Little attempt is made to persuade consumers to purchase the product being advertised. At the same time, Chinese messages tend to be rich with information. A content analysis of Chinese print messages revealed that magazine ads are characterized by relatively high levels of information. Two main factors appear to contribute to the high information content levels: (1) the limited experience of most Chinese citizens with consumer purchases, which leads to high-involvement decision making, and (2) government policy. Because consumer purchasing—particularly of durable items—is a relatively recent activity for most Chinese, many purchase decisions are characterized by an increased search for product or brand information, from both advertising and other sources, in order to reduce risks and maximize satisfaction. Chinese advertisers respond to this information-seeking behavior by providing information on performance, quality, and price. Further, the Chinese government stresses that advertising serves an important function in educating consumers and promoting market socialism.[132]

One explanation for the lagging popularity of foreign advertisements may be that Chinese consumers become frustrated with Western messages when advertised products aren't readily available. Foreign advertisements may also raise expectations, and given that many Chinese still cannot afford imported products that typically cost much more than locally produced goods, resentment may result. Often, foreign messages may quite simply not demonstrate cultural sensitivity. Xu Bai Yi gives an example:

> Recently an advertising lecturer came to Shanghai with a TV commercial he had designed for Ivory soap. In it a Chinese family—father, mother and children—all go to the paddy field to transplant rice shoots. Later they emerge covered with soil, and use Ivory soap to clean up. This TV commercial was completely off the mark. For one thing, this particular task is now done by machine. But—and this is most important—no one who is experienced in this work becomes so soiled. The image of dirtiness, which may be used with some appeal abroad, is simply insulting to the Chinese working consumer. Evidently, the commercial was made with a minimum of research.[133]

While some international advertisers have found success employing campaigns borrowed from their domestic markets (Tang, for example, has recycled old spots touting itself as the drink of American astronauts), others have chosen to tailor messages. Coca-Cola, often positioned as a global marketer, has localized its advertising operations for China. For the first time, in 1993 it produced a TV ad campaign entirely in China. Spots portrayed a montage of attractive, Coke-swigging Chinese, including smiling dockworkers heading home, a thirty-something entrepreneur who has just missed his bus, and a Chinese family celebrating at a Western-style wedding. In other instances advertisers may have little choice but to modify messages. In selling its instant coffee in this market, Nescafé was compelled to show the uninitiated Chinese consumer how to prepare a cup of coffee via a demonstration in TV spots.

Given the demand for consumer information, advertisers may benefit from creating messages specifically for Chinese audiences that provide detailed information on product attributes, performance, quality, and price rather than employ the symbolic advertising appeals common in the West.

Emerging from decades of quasi-isolation, operating under a socialist economic system—and one characterized by extreme scarcity at that—makes China a particular challenge for international marketers. Michael H. Anderson, among others, questions whether "China's people are really ready for an influx of foreign (or even domestic) advertising influences, no matter how culturally sensitive."[134] International marketers, however, are not likely to willingly step away from this, the world's largest marketplace. For China, says Xuejun Yu, the answer likely lies "between a total rejection or embrace of advertising and consumer culture. China needs to find a middle road in its advertising development in today's interdependent world."[135] In an opening address to the Third World Advertising Congress held in Beijing in 1987, Wai Li, China's acting premier, noted: "Advertising links production and consumption. It is an important part of the economic activities of modern society. It has become an indispensable element in the promotion of economic prosperity."[136] This is a remarkable statement given that a mere eight years earlier there was no evidence of advertising in this country.

The Pacific Rim

Much attention has been given to China as a booming market for both advertisers and agencies, yet the entire Pacific Rim region has, in fact, become synonymous with marketing opportunity. Indeed, says Mark Clifford, "Few ideas in the business world have changed more dramatically since the late 1980s than the image of Asia in the minds of U.S. and European corporations. After all, it was only a few years ago that . . . the only market worth thinking about was Japan. Now the rest of Asia is getting its due. Whether it is software or sewers, demand is growing more quickly in Asia than anywhere else in the world."[137] With the exception of recession-weary Japan, the Asia–Pacific Rim region is characterized by expanding economies, rising incomes, and emerging middle classes. Underlying these phenomena is the liberalization of economics and politics in the region. China and India (which between them account for 40 percent of the world's population) have embarked on far-reaching economic reforms, as have Vietnam and South Korea.[138] Multinational firms and agencies now have freer reign to sell their products and services—and to earn profits. As Clifford points out, "Companies now realize that it is no longer enough to treat Asia casually. The challenge for multinationals is to make Asia as important in 10 or 20 years as Europe is today."[139]

Marketers, however, face a complex region—one with some of the world's richest countries as well as some of its poorest. The region can be divided into four levels of consumer development: (1) affluent markets (Japan, Hong Kong, Singapore), (2) growth markets (Taiwan, South Korea), (3) emerging markets (Thailand, Malaysia, the Philippines, Indonesia), and (4) untapped markets (China, India, Vietnam).[140] Clifford explains:

> The more mature, affluent economies, with wealthy and well-educated consumers, are similar to those in the U.S., with their taste for Western goods and quality products. The "growth markets" of Taiwan and South Korea are spawning a middle class hungry for household items and leisure-time diversions; by the end of the decade, some 20–30 percent of their households should have incomes of more than US$30,000. Emerging countries still are held back by low spending power, but promise a significant future: they have large youth populations that are rapidly changing consumption behavior. (By the year 2000, the Asia/Pacific region will gain 80 million consumers aged 20–39, while the U.S. and Europe will show declines in that demographic.) The most long-term prospects are the giant landscapes of China and India, with hundreds of millions of poor, uneducated consumers—most of them aspiring to emulate their neighbors.[141]

International advertisers are recognizing the need to increase their firms' presence in Asia. Reports *ADWEEK:* "Companies that have been in the region for some time are reaping a rich harvest, much of which is being put back into further expansion. And a bevy of latecomers is trying to make up for lost time."[142] The leading foreign multinationals in Asia sell everything from soft drinks to cellular telephones. Long-established firms include Coca-Cola, which set up its first bottling plants in Asia in the 1920s; IBM, which opened in China in the 1930s; and Motorola, which manufactured black-and-white TVs in Asia after World War II. Hughes (the U.S.-based electronics firm), AT&T, Microsoft, Disney, and General Motors are among the newcomers.

As *ADWEEK* notes, "The demand for Western-quality goods is not in question; it's the ability of agencies to create and place ads that appeal to an endlessly varied market—from country to country, region to region, class to class—that will determine success or failure."[143] Table 11.6 shows the potential advertising gains now being realized. With the exception of Japan, the Pacific Rim region is expected to show 64 percent growth in advertising spending between 1992 and 1995. Seven of the ten fastest-growing advertising countries are from this region. This translates into increased profits for advertising agencies as well. For example, in 1993 J. Walter Thompson's

TABLE 11.6 Pacific Rim Advertising Spending (in U.S. million $)

COUNTRY	NEWSPAPER	MAGAZINE	TV	RADIO	CINEMA
Japan	$9,767	$2,964	$13,259	$1,888	—
South Korea	1,536	193	1,067	185	—
Australia	1,536	239	1,317	315	$58
Taiwan	1,102	173	901	108	—
China	405	43	514	50	19
Hong Kong	374	141	560	73	10
Thailand	223	71	393	87	1
India	482[b]	—	150	22	4
New Zealand	191	44	213	76	8
Indonesia	186	47	192	49	5
Singapore	231	38	148	18	4
Malaysia	188	44	175	11	2
Philippines	45[b]	—	160	35	—
Total	$16,266	$3,998	$19,051	$2,918	$111
Total excluding Japan	6,499	1,034	5,792	1,030	111

[a]Includes other advertising.
[b]Includes magazines.
SOURCE: *ADWEEK*, May 2, 1994, p. 26. Reprinted by permission of Zenith Media.

forty-three offices accounted for 17 percent of the agency network's $876 million in worldwide revenues. For 1994 that contribution is expected to grow 20 percent—with the region's offices boasting higher profit margins than their European counterparts."[144] For advertisers and agencies alike, operations in the Pacific Rim region translate into "money in the bank."

Latin America

As *ADWEEK* reports, "The nations of North, Central and South America are moving ahead economically, technologically and politically. And . . . these developments are being spurred by a variety of agreements designed to increase free-trade opportunities."[145] The North American Free Trade Agreement (NAFTA) is just one of several accords designed to improve market access in the Western Hemisphere. Advertisers and agen-

COUNTRY	OUTDOOR	1992 TOTAL	1995 ESTIMATE	% CHANGE
Japan	$5,163	$33,041	$35,151	6.4%
South Korea	698[a]	3,679	6,237	69.5
Australia	192	3,657	4,314	18.0
Taiwan	501[a]	2,786	4,019	44.3
China	200	1,231	4,394	256.9
Hong Kong	37	1,197	2,097	75.2
Thailand	27	802	1,461	82.2
India	68	727	1,114	53.2
New Zealand	38	570	660	15.8
Indonesia	30	509	783	53.8
Singapore	16	454	656	44.5
Malaysia	15	435	554	27.4
Philippines	2[a]	243	442	81.9
Total	$1,987	$49,331	$61,882	25.4%
Total excluding Japan	1,824	16,290	26,731	64.1

cies alike are anticipating Mercosur, the Southern Cone Common Market, which will unite the economies of Argentina, Brazil, Uruguay, and Paraguay. They also see a strengthening of ties among members of the Andean Pact—Venezuela, Colombia, Peru, Ecuador, and Bolivia—which plan to end tariff barriers sometime in 1995.[146] As Noreen O'Leary notes, "The ultimate ambitious goal of all this activity is to turn no less than half the world into a single free-trade zone."[147] Consumer products and services marketers are targeting Latin America in the 1990s. With more people living south than north of the Rio Grande (Latin America's population is expected to reach 512 million by 2000), growing consumer affluence, and economies emerging from decades of stagnation, marketers see Latin America as the region of opportunity.[148] Marketers find the region's age structure particularly appealing. Some 65 percent of Latin America's 450 million people are under 30, and a whopping 37 percent are in the crucial 10–29 age segment, considered prime consumers. This age structure offers many opportunities for companies marketing products such as disposable diapers, infant-care products, school supplies, and toys.[149] And just such advertisers have entered the Latin American market. Top advertisers in this region (in rank order) are Unilever, PepsiCo, Procter & Gamble, Colgate-Palmolive, Nestlé, Coca-Cola, and Philip Morris.

Agencies are not far behind. Writes Noreen O'Leary: "McCann-Erickson, with clients such as Exxon, has played a leading role in Latin American advertising for more than 50 years. So has J. Walter Thompson, which boasts clients such as Unilever and Nabisco. But now the scramble is on among other global networks to catch up. In 1994, Young & Rubicam acquired agency stakes in Guatemala, Costa Rica, El Salvador, Nicaragua and Panama."[150] In addition, D'Arcy Masius Benton & Bowles created its DMB&B Americas network in 1994, which features divisions in eight Latin American countries. Latin America, for many agencies, is the fastest-growing source of business.

"There are hiccups here and there, but the economies for the most part continue to burgeon. Democracy is now the norm in Latin America. You have a less polarized social strata, a growing middle class and higher consumer spending," notes Joe DeDeo, vice chairman/chairman of Young & Rubicam/Latin America.[151] Colombia, Chile, and Argentina, in particular, lead the reform pack and boast the most consistent economies. For example, Argentina reports a drastic dip in inflation, tariff reductions, improved consumer confidence, and an accompanying rise in consumption. The government's three-year-old economic recovery program is paying dividends, with record advertising spending levels. Billings among Argentina's top fifteen agencies climbed 29.6 percent—well in excess of the 7.4 percent inflation rate.[152]

However, things are not going quite so well in other Latin American nations. Venezuela's president imposed price and exchange controls in the summer of 1994 to "avert an almost certain financial meltdown." These controls served to freeze foreign investment, imports, privatization, and advertising spending. Reports Peter Wilson: "With growing unemployment combined with economists' predictions that inflation will hit 90 percent in 1994 and the GNP will dip 3 percent, marketers are holding off on ad spending waiting to see if price controls will rein in the runaway economy."[153] Similarly, it is hoped that Brazil's new inflation-fighting currency (the real) will curb the country's staggering inflation of 40 percent per month and restore some stability to the economy. "Stability in the Brazilian economy is important because we've been operating in the middle of complete uncertainty and nothing can be worse for a company that needs to do forward planning," notes an IBM spokesperson.[154]

Still and all, advertising spending is increasing in most Latin American countries, as Table 11.7 shows. And, while regional forecasts are hard to come by, agency executives estimate that billings have increased anywhere from 15 to 25 percent in 1994.

TABLE 11.7   Advertising Spending in the Americas (in U.S. million $)

COUNTRY	1992	1989	% CHANGE
Argentina	$1,071.4[a]	$556.8	92.4%
Brazil	1,919.0	2,051.0	−6.4
Canada	6,893.7	7,831.9	−12.0
Chile	344.4	157.7	117.7
Colombia	775.3	209.8	269.0
Costa Rica	97.0	64.5	50.4
Dominican Republic	3.1	3.8	−18.1
Ecuador	58.7	58.6[a]	0.1
El Salvador	31.8	20.0[a]	59.0
Guatemala	108.6	60.4	79.8
Honduras	18.4	13.8[b]	33.3
Mexico	2,896.1	907.6	219.1
Nicaragua	23.8	—	—
Panama	84.2	68.9[a]	22.2
Peru	237.1	251.6	−5.8
Puerto Rico	345.6	330.0	4.7
Uruguay	75.9	61.4	23.6
Venezuela	573.7	324.0	77.1
Total	$15,557.8	$12,971.8	19.8%

[a]1991 figure.
[b]1990 figure.
SOURCE: *ADWEEK*, July 18, 1994, p. 24.

Summary

The global marketplace is evolving before our very eyes. Individual markets are banding together to form regional economic pacts—such as the European Union—to facilitate trade between nations. Countries that were once not even considered by multinational firms are now perceived as "hot markets." The Soviet Union has evolved into the Commonwealth of Independent States and is slowly moving toward a free-market economy. China, which was once deemed one of the world's poorest countries, now boasts nearly 100 million households that can be designated as middle class. Indeed, the entire Pacific Rim region is characterized by expanding economies and rising incomes. And, the Latin American nations are also moving ahead economically as well as technologically and politically. International marketers are not limiting their attention to these countries. Many African countries, as well as the

Middle East, are perceived as virtually untapped markets. Literally every corner of the world is ripe with opportunity for the international marketer. In short, then, business will continue to become increasingly global as we move toward the year 2000.

Additional Readings

Arons, Rick. (1991). *EuroMarketing: A Strategic Planner for Selling into the New Europe.* Chicago: Probus Publishing.

Foster, Lawrence W., and Lisa Tosi. (May/June 1990). "Business in China: A Year After Tiananmen." *The Journal of Business Strategy,* pp. 22–27.

Rijkens, Rein. (1992). *European Advertising Strategies: The Profiles and Policies of Multinational Companies Operating in Europe.* London: Cassell.

Ryans, John K., Jr., and Pradeep A. Rau. (1990). *Marketing Strategies for the New Europe.* Chicago: American Marketing Association.

Swanson, Lauren A. (1990). "Advertising in China: Viability and Structure." *European Journal of Marketing,* 24(10).

Yi, Xu Bai. (1990). *Marketing to China: One Billion New Customers.* Lincolnwood, IL: NTC.

Notes

1. Toyne, Brian, and Peter Walters, *Global Marketing Management: A Strategic Perspective* (Boston: Allyn & Bacon, 1989), p. 95.

2. Young, Stephen, James Hamill, Colin Wheeler, and J. Richard Davies, *International Market Entry and Development* (Englewood Cliffs, NJ: Prentice-Hall, 1989), p. 280.

3. Danton de Rourrignac, Peter, *How to Sell to Europe* (London: Pitman, 1989), pp. 13–14.

4. Mariotta, George, "Europe Inc.," *San Diego Union,* August 20, 1989, p. C1.

5. Danton de Rourrignac, *How to Sell to Europe,* p. 17.

6. Antal, Vivienne, "Achieving Success in the Global Marketplace," *Europe,* November 1986, pp. 16–17.

7. Wolfe, Alan, "The Single European Market: National or Euro-brands," *International Journal of Advertising,* 10, pp. 49–58.

8. Ibid.

9. Vandermerwe, Sandra, and Marc-Andre L'Huillier, "Euro-Consumers in 1992," in John K. Ryans, Jr., and Pradeep A. Rau, eds., *Marketing Strategies for the New Europe* (Chicago: American Marketing Association, 1990), pp. 151–164.

10. Ibid.

11. U.S. Department of Commerce, Bureau of the Census, *Statistical Abstract of the United States, 1993,* 113th ed. (Washington, DC: GPO, 1993).

12. *ADWEEK,* June 1, 1987.

13. *Media & Marketing Europe,* March 1990.

14. "Data Watch," *Advertising Age,* October 26, 1992, p. I10.

15. Crumley, Bruce, "European Market Continues to Soar," *Advertising Age,* February 21, 1994, p. 22.

16. *American Demographics,* "Yves Franchet, Director General of Eurostat, Explains Why Good Data and a Democratic Europe Must Go Together," October 1990, p. 23.

17. Kesler, Linda, "Getting Post Position in Europe," *ADWEEK,* June 6, 1988, p. G24.

18. Stiansen, Sarah, "DDB Needham's Euromarketing Plan," *ADWEEK,* June 1, 1987, p. G.A. 14.

19. Resener, Madlyn, "Europe's New Mass Market Appeal," *ADWEEK,* June 1, 1987, p. G.A. 6.

20. Ibid., p. G.A. 10.

21. Wolfe, "The Single European Market."

22. Wagner, Jim, "A Brand Name Ball Game," *Food Processing,* September 1991.

23. *ADWEEK,* "Brands on the Run," February 14, 1994, pp. 38–40.

24. U.S. Department of Commerce, *Statistical Abstract of the United States, 1993.*

25. Vandermerwe and L'Huillier, "Euro-Consumers in 1992."

26. Wagner, "A Brand Name Ball Game."

27. Jacobs, Everett M., "New Developments in Soviet Advertising and Marketing Theory," *International Journal of Advertising,* 5(3), 1986, pp. 243–246.

28. Szeplaki, Leslie, "Advertising in the Soviet Bloc," *Journal of Advertising Research,* 14(3), June 1974, pp. 13–17.

29. Greer, Thomas V., *Marketing in the Soviet Union* (New York: Praeger, 1973), p. 96.

30. Uchitelle, Louis, "U.S. Firms Look to New Wild West for Profits," *San Diego Union,* December 27, 1991, p. 1.

31. Joseph, Charles, "International Profiles: Soviet Union," *Advertising Age,* November 9, 1988, p. 114.

32. McKay, Betsy, "Inflation Bites Russians Who Still Bite into Big Mac," *Advertising Age,* March 15, 1993, pp. I3+.

33. Kahan, John, "Holding Russia's Fate in His Hands," *Time,* December 7, 1992, pp. 36–39.

34. Klebnikov, Paul, "Russia—The Ultimate Emerging Market," *Forbes,* February 14, 1994, pp. 88–94.

35. McKay, Betsy, "Russian Reform Surviving Turmoil," *Advertising Age,* April 19, 1993, pp. 1+.

36. Moore, M. H., "Homing In on Russian Super Spenders," *ADWEEK,* February 28, 1994, p. 14.

37. Advertising Age Roundup, "New Marketing Era for U.S.S.R.," *Advertising Age,* August 26, 1991, p. 1.

38. "Is Soviet Rush On?" *Advertising Age,* September 2, 1991, pp. 3, 46.

39. McKay, Betsy, "Caddies Supplant Communism As GM Sells Cars in Moscow," *Advertising Age,* June 15, 1992, p. 10.

40. McKay, Betsy, "Soviet Collapse Sparks Upheaval in Capitalist Plans," *Advertising Age,* September 28, 1992, p. I3.

41. McKay, Betsy, and Steven Gutterman, "For Ads, Russian Revolution Lives," *Advertising Age,* March 7, 1994, p. 40.

42. Jay, Leslie, "Madison Avenue Lands in Moscow," *Management Review,* 79(3), 1990, pp. 54–56.

43. McKay, "Russian Reform Surviving Turmoil."

44. Jones, Alison, and Billy Rogers, "The New Russia," *Bozell Opinion,* 6(2), Fall 1993, pp. 3–7.

45. Wentz, Laurel, "Soviet Bargain Hunt," *Advertising Age,* August 20, 1990, p. 60.

46. Lafayette, Jon, "Agency Execs Bullish on China: Soviet Economy Stalling Ad Activity," *Advertising Age,* November 12, 1990, p. 64.

47. McKay and Gutterman, "For Ads, Russian Revolution Lives."

48. Jacobson, David, "Tapping the Soviet Market," *Business Marketing,* May, 1991, pp. 26–28.

49. *Doing Business with the USSR,* a Business International European Research Report, 1986, pp. 62–68.

50. Black, George, "Tactics for the Russian Front," *Business Marketing,* January, 1989, pp. 42–49.

51. *Europa World Year Book* (London: Europa Publications, 1989), p. 2686.

52. Donaton, Scott, "Chill on Russian Front: Turmoil Makes US Publishers More Cautious," *Advertising Age,* February 25, 1991, p. 46.

53. *Doing Business with the USSR.*

54. Trebus, Robert S., "How Advertising Can Help You Sell in Socialist Nations,"

Industrial Marketing, 62(4), 1977, pp. 72–87.

55. *Europa World Yearbook.*

56. Tinsley, Elisa, "Soviet Briefs," *Advertising Age,* January 6, 1986, pp. 38–39.

57. McKay, Betsy, "Pravda Struggles Post-Coup," *Advertising Age,* October 21, 1991, p. 20.

58. Sharkey, Betsy, "Russian? Nyet! ECHO Chief Negotiates International Pravda Deal in Spanish," *ADWEEK,* May 27, 1991, p. 4.

59. "Advertising in Russia: Look but Don't Touch," *The Economist,* 135, June 16, 1990, pp. 80–82.

60. Babakian, Genine, "Hidden Advertisers See Light in Russia," *ADWEEK,* November 15, 1993, p. 14.

61. Greer, *Marketing in the Soviet Union.*

62. "McCann-Erickson European Media Facts 1991," in-house resource, p. 43.

63. Ostlund, Lyman E., "Russian Advertising: A New Concept," *Journal of Advertising Research,* 13(1), February 1973, pp. 11–19.

64. *Europa World Yearbook.*

65. Ibid.

66. Brown, Kathy, "First Glasnost, Then Donahue: Soviets Try American Programs," *ADWEEK,* July 15, 1991, p. 1.

67. Tinsley, "Soviet Briefs."

68. Ostlund, "Russian Advertising."

69. Simurda, Stephen, "Soviet TV's U.S. Channel," *Nation's Business,* February 1989, pp. 18R–19R.

70. Joseph, "International Profiles."

71. McKay, Betsy, "Soviet TV Sets First Ad Guidelines," *Advertising Age,* December 2, 1991, p. 2.

72. Wentz, "Soviet Bargain Hunt."

73. Ostrow, Joel, "Soviet TV Head Puts Focus on Future," *Advertising Age,* July 29, 1991, p. 32.

74. Ostrow, Joel, "New TV now Competing in Russia," *Advertising Age,* July 6, 1991, p. 30.

75. Brown, "First Glasnost, Then Donahue."

76. McKay, Betsy, "Russian Revolution: Digest Brings Marketing Savvy to U.S.S.R.," *Advertising Age,* July 29, 1991, p. 3.

77. Black, "Tactics for the Russian Front."

78. Ibid.

79. Tinsley, Elisa, "The Soviet Promise of Expanded Markets," *Advertising Age,* January 6, 1986, pp. 38–39.

80. "McCann-Erickson European Media Facts 1991."

81. Babkin, Alexander, "Soviet Union Takes First Steps in Advertising," *Marketing,* September 10, 1990, p. 20.

82. Mueller, Barbara, "From the Cold War to a Hot Marketplace: The Role of Advertising in the Commonwealth of Independent States," *Proceedings of the 1993 Conference of the American Academy of Advertising,* Esther Thorson, ed., pp. 248–263.

83. Ibid.

84. Ibid.

85. Wentz, Laurel, "Push Quality in Ads to E. Europe: JWT," *Advertising Age,* July 8, 1991.

86. Adams, Michael, "Creative Revolution Next for Soviets," *Advertising Age,* September 16, 1991, p. 20.

87. Belk, Russell W., and Non Zhou, "Learning to Want Things," *Advances in Consumer Research,* 14, 1987, pp. 478–481.

88. Berney, Karen, "China's Growing Consumer Market," *China Business Review,* April 1981, pp. 18–20.

89. Wang, James C. F., "Values of the Cultural Revolution," *Journal of Communications,* 23(3), 1977, pp. 41–46.

90. Belk and Zhou, "Learning to Want Things."

91. Walder, Andrew, "Rice Bowl Reforms," *China Business Review,* November/December 1983, pp. 18–21.

92. Church, George, "Ching Deng Xiaoping Leads a Far-Reaching Audacious But Risky Second Revolution," *Time,* January 6, 1986, pp. 24–41.

93. Tong, Louis, "China Market—Fascinating and Ever Changing," research report published by the SRH Group, Hong Kong, 1987, pp. 10–11.

94. Thorelli, Hans B., and Joseph Y. Battat, "Marketing to China: Still the Silk Road," in Hans Thorelli and Helmut Becker, eds., *International Marketing Strategy* (New York: Pergamon Press, 1980), pp. 403–413.

95. Anderson, Michael H., "China's Great Leap Toward Madison Avenue," *Journal of Communication,* 31(1), Winter 1981, p. 10.

96. Yu, Xuejun, "Government Policies Toward Advertising in China (1979–1989)," *Gazette,* 48(1), 1991, pp. 17–30.

97. Tanzer, Andrew, "This Time It's for Real," *Forbes,* August 2, 1993, pp. 58–61.

98. Ibid.

99. U.S. Department of Commerce, *Statistical Abstract of the United States, 1993.*

100. Saporito, Bill, "Where the Global Action Is," *Fortune,* Autumn/Winter 1993, pp. 63–65.

101. Yi, Xu Bai, *Marketing to China: One Billion New Customers* (Lincolnwood, IL: NTC, 1990).

102. Zuckerman, Laurence, "Buying Power: The Market for Products Is Big—But Not Quite So Large As You Thought," *Wall Street Journal,* Eastern Edition, December 10, 1993, p. R15.

103. Tanzer, "This Time It's for Real."

104. Ibid.

105. Ibid., pp. 58–61.

106. Kilburn, David, "Japan's Retailers Travel to China," *Advertising Age,* March 15, 1993, p. I15.

107. Zuckerman, "Buying Power," p. R15.

108. Tanzer, "This Time It's for Real."

109. Anderson, "China's Great Leap."

110. Moore, M. H., "Affluent Consumers Stake Claim in China," *ADWEEK,* December 6, 1993, p. 16.

111. Tanzer, "This Time It's for Real," pp. 58–61.

112. Ibid.

113. Goll, Sally, and Yumiko Ono, "Consuming Passions: A Surge in Spending Money Has Created a Nation of Avid and Discriminating Shoppers," *Wall Street Journal,* Eastern Edition, December 10, 1993, pp. R15+.

114. Tanzer, "This Time It's for Real," pp. 58–61.

115. Tanzer, Andrew, "Ding-Dong, Capitalism Calling," *Fortune,* October 14, 1991, pp. 184–186.

116. Reitman, Valarie, "Enticed by Visions of Enormous Numbers, More Western Marketers Move into China," *Wall Street Journal,* July 12, 1993, pp. B1+.

117. Kraar, Louis, "Now Comes the Hard Part for China," *Fortune,* July 26, 1993, pp. 130–134.

118. Foster, Lawrence W., and Lisa Tosi, "Business in China: A Year After Tiananmen," *The Journal of Business Strategy,* May/June 1990, pp. 22–27.

119. Geddes, Andrew, and Laurel Wentz, "Agencies Flock to China as Market Explodes," *Advertising Age,* August 31, 1992, p. 12.

120. Yi, Xu Bai, "Reaching the Chinese Consumer," *China Business Review,* November/December 1992, pp. 36–42.

121. Lo, Thamis Wing-chun, and Amy Yung, "Multinational Service Firms in Centrally-Planned Economies: Foreign Advertising Agencies in the PRC," *MIR,* 28(1), 1988, pp. 26–33.

122. Rice, Marshall D., "China's Sleeping Market Wakes Up," *Marketing News,* September 25, 1987, p. 4.

123. Yi, "Reaching the Chinese Consumer."

124. Rice, Marshall D., and Zaiming Lu, "A Content Analysis of Chinese Magazine Advertisements," *Journal of Advertising,* 17(4), 1988, pp. 43–48.

125. Yi, *Marketing to China.*

126. Strasser, Steven, "Where the Admen Are," *Newsweek,* March 14, 1994, p. 39.

127. Yi, "Reaching the Chinese Consumer."

128. Ibid.

129. Ibid., pp. 36–42.

130. Yi, *Marketing to China.*

131. "China Bars Absurd Ads," *Marketing News,* December 4, 1987, p. 1, and "China's First Polling Company Finds Public Ready to Express Opinions," *Marketing News,* September 25, 1987, p. 4.

132. Rice and Lu, "A Content Analysis."

133. Yi, *Marketing to China,* p. 86.

134. Anderson, Michael H., *Madison Avenue in Asia* (Cranbury, NJ: Associated University Presses, 1984), p. 283.

135. Yu, "Government Policies Toward Advertising," pp. 17–30.

136. Rice, "China's Sleeping Market," p. 4.

137. Clifford, Mark, "Selling the World to Asia," *Far Eastern Economic Review,* December 30, 1993/January 6, 1994, pp. 37–38.

138. Ibid.

139. Ibid.

140. O'Leary, Noreen, "Playing the Asia Card," *ADWEEK,* May 2, 1994, pp. 28–38.

141. Clifford, "Selling the World," pp. 37–38.

142. "The World's Greatest Market Beckons: Global Quarterly Asia," *AD-WEEK,* May 2, 1994, p. 26.

143. Ibid.

144. O'Leary, "Playing the Asia Card."

145. "Latin Markets: Bloom or Bust," *ADWEEK,* July 18, 1994, p. 24.

146. Turner, Rik, and Delinda Karle, "Shops See Unity of Latin America," *Advertising Age,* April 27, 1992, p. 44.

147. O'Leary, Noreen, "Good Neighbors," *ADWEEK,* July 18, 1994, pp. 32–34.

148. Zbar, Jeffrey D., "Walls Abound, but Links to Latin America Grow," *Advertising Age,* January 24, 1994, p. S4.

149. Clarke, Frank, "Latin America: Accent on Youth," *Advertising Age,* September 7, 1992, p. S20.

150. O'Leary, "Good Neighbors."

151. Ibid.

152. Galetto, Mike, "Ad Boom Bust," *Advertising Age,* July 18, 1994, p. I21.

153. Wilson, Peter, "Venezuelan Price Controls Lead Marketers to Hesitate," *Advertising Age,* July 18, 1994, p. I3.

154. Penteado, Claudia, "Brazil Advertisers' Campaign Blitz Aims to Make Real Sense of New Currency," *Advertising Age,* July 18, 1994, p. I3.

Epilogue

As noted in Chapter 1, a variety of forces foster the internationalization of business. Firms that operate internationally must also communicate with consumers around the globe. Worldwide advertising expenditures are expected to more than double between 1990 and 2000. Moreover, international advertising expenditures will continue to surpass U.S. volume; preliminary forecasts indicate that almost 60 percent of the nearly $1 trillion to be spent on advertising by the turn of the century will be invested outside the United States. Opportunities for employment in international advertising—on the client side, within advertising agencies, and in media and research organizations—also will continue to grow as an ever-expanding number of firms become involved in marketing abroad. Increasingly, firms that operate globally are adopting a multicultural philosophy, hiring foreigners for both entry-level and top management positions. Individuals trained in the language, culture, politics, economics, and legal systems of markets around the world will be in particular demand in the coming decade.

Aggressive preparation is the key to a career in international advertising. Coursework in international advertising and marketing should provide the necessary grounding in the basic principles. Other relevant courses might include cross-cultural studies, comparative politics, anthropology, and international business as well as courses in consumer behavior. Those seriously interested in seeking career opportunities in the international arena should be prepared to learn a foreign language or, better yet, consider becoming proficient in several foreign languages.

Students should become avid readers of any and all materials related to international advertising and marketing. The "Additional Readings" listed at the end of each chapter in this text are a good starting point. Academic journals, such as the *International Journal of Advertising,* the *International Marketing Review,* the *Journal of International Business Studies,* and the *European Journal of Marketing,* among others, are excellent resources and should be scanned regularly. *ADWEEK, Marketing & Media Decisions, Business Marketing,* and, in particular, *Advertising Age* publish articles regarding international advertising, international agencies, and clients that operate multinationally.

The IAA Diploma in International Advertising, launched in 1974 by the International Advertising Association, is considered a "world-class credential" in many advertising circles. The IAA Diploma offers advanced advertising students and practicing professionals the opportunity to acquire the necessary skills and insights in managing advertising on an international basis. To obtain this diploma, students must pass an examination that is evaluated by advertising practitioners with in-depth experience in all aspects of international advertising. The examination consists of two parts. Part One tests a broad range of knowledge about how to advertise on a worldwide basis; Part Two is based on an advertising case study supplied to the candidate in advance of the examination date. Candidates may sit for the examination in their own country provided a local IAA chapter exists in that country. The examination is held once annually. Well over five thousand individuals hold this world-class credential to date.[1]

Advanced degrees also help to set candidates for international advertising positions apart. The pamphlet "Where Will I Go to Study Advertising and Public Relations" lists the institutions around the country offering degrees at the Master's and/or Ph.D. levels.[2] Personal experience in foreign markets is critical as well. Students can acquire familiarity with other cultures through travel, scholarships to study abroad—such as the Fulbright scholarships[3]—and actually working in foreign countries. While difficult to come by, foreign internships are available.

Norman Vale, director-general of the International Advertising Association, offers the following advice for those interested in a career in a foreign country:

1. "Acquire solid agency experience in either a large U.S. agency or its counterpart in another country, and plan to stay there for 3 to 5 years—less time may not sufficiently prepare you for that next international step.

2. Attempt to work your way into a multinational account. Many positions are available within agencies where products and services are similarly introduced and available in foreign markets.

3. Make your management aware of your interest, be diligent in your pursuit, and find an appropriate mentor within your organization.

4. Be open-minded about the country assignment offered. There is a world beyond London and Paris; besides, the talent pool in both England and France is sufficiently large. You may find similar challenges and satisfaction along with greater opportunity for advancement in other countries.

5. Don't view a career in international advertising as a free ticket to travel. It's hard work, and any other perception will not be appreciated by prospective employers.

6. Above all, have patience, patience and even more patience."[4]

Notes

1. For additional information on the IAA Diploma, contact the IAA Education Secretariat, Dellaertlaan 37, 1171 HE Badhoevedrop, Netherlands.

2. For a copy of "Where Will I Go to Study Advertising and Public Relations," edited by Billy I. Ross and Keith F. Johnson, write to: Advertising Education Publications, P.O. Box 4164, Lubbock, Texas 79409.

3. For information regarding Fulbright scholarships, write to: Council for International Exchange of Scholars, 3007 Tilden Street, N.W., Suite 5M, Box GPOS, Washington, DC 20008-3009.

4. Norman Vale, "Quo Vadis, World?" *Advertising Career Directory*.

ICC International Code of Advertising Practice

Introduction

This edition of the ICC International Code of Advertising Practice follows the well-established policy of the ICC of promoting high standards of ethics in marketing by self-regulation against the background of national and international law.

The Code, which was first issued in 1937, later revised in 1949, 1955, 1966 and 1973, demonstrates that industry and commerce, including all parties involved in advertising, recognize their social responsibilities towards the consumer and the community, and the need to establish a fair balance between the interests of business and of consumers.

The edition combines past experience with current thinking based on the concept of advertising as a means of communication between sellers and customers. In this respect the ICC considers freedom of communication (as embodied in article 19 of the United Nations International Covenant of civil and political rights) as a fundamental principle.

The Code is designed primarily as an instrument for self-discipline but it is also intended for use by the Courts as a reference document within the framework of the appropriate laws.

The ICC believes that this new edition of the Code, like its predecessors, by promoting a further harmonization of advertising standards, will facilitate the circulation of goods and services across frontiers to the benefit of consumers and the community throughout the world.

Scope of the Code

The Code applies to all advertisements for any goods, services and facilities, including corporate advertising. It should be read in conjunction with the other ICC Codes of Marketing Practice namely:

▶ Marketing Research Practice

▶ Sales Promotion Practice

▶ Direct Mail and Mail Order Sales Practice

▶ and Direct Sales Practice.

The Code sets standards of ethical conduct to be followed by all concerned with advertising, whether as advertisers, advertising practitioners or agencies, or media.

Interpretation

The Code, including the Guidelines for Advertising to Children (Sectorial Guidelines will be available separately), is to be applied in the spirit as well as in the letter.

Because of the different characteristics of the various media (press, television, radio and other electronic media, outdoor advertising, films, direct mail, etc.) an advertisement which is acceptable for one medium is not necessarily acceptable for another.

Advertisements should be judged by their likely impact on the consumer, bearing in mind the medium used.

The Code applies to the entire content of an advertisement, including all words and numbers (spoken and written), visual presentations, music and sound effects.

Definitions

For the purpose of this Code:

▶ the term "advertisement" is to be taken in its broadest sense to embrace any form of advertising for goods, services and facilities, irrespective of the medium used and including advertising claims on packs, labels and point of sale material.

▶ the term "product" includes services and facilities.

▶ the term "consumer" refers to any person to whom an advertisement is addressed or who is likely to be reached by it whether as a final consumer or as a trade customer or user.

Rules

Decency

Article 1 Advertisements should not contain statements or visual presentations which offend against prevailing standards of decency.

Honesty

Article 2 Advertisements should be so framed as not to abuse the trust of the consumer or exploit his lack of experience or knowledge.

Article 3

1. Advertisements should not without justifiable reason play on fear.
2. Advertisements should not play on superstition.
3. Advertisements should not contain anything which might lead to or lend support to acts of violence.
4. Advertisements should avoid endorsing discrimination based upon race, religion or sex.

Truthful Presentation

Article 4

1. Advertisements should not contain any statement or visual presentation which directly or by implication, omission, ambiguity or exaggerated claim is likely to mislead the consumer, in particular with regard to

   a. characteristics such as: nature, composition, method and date of manufacture, fitness for purpose, range of use, quantity, commercial or geographical origin;

   b. the value of the product and the total price actually to be paid;

    c. other terms of payment such as hire purchase, leasing, installment sales and credit sale (see Special Provision b);

    d. delivery, exchange, return, repair and maintenance;

    e. terms of guarantee (see Special Provision a);

    f. copyright and industrial property rights such as patents, trade marks, designs and models and trade names;

    g. official recognition or approval, awards of medals, prizes and diplomas;

    h. the extent of benefits for charitable causes.

2. Advertisements should not misuse research results or quotations from technical and scientific publications. Statistics should not be so presented as to imply a greater validity than they really have. Scientific terms should not be misused; scientific jargon and irrelevancies should not be used to make claims appear to have a scientific basis they do not possess.

Comparisons

Article 5 Advertisements containing comparisons should be so designed that the comparison itself is not likely to mislead, and should comply with the principles of fair competition. Points of comparison should be based on facts which can be substantiated and should not be unfairly selected.

Testimonials

Article 6 Advertisements should not contain or refer to any testimonial or endorsement unless it is genuine and related to the experience of the person giving it. Testimonials or endorsements which are obsolete or otherwise no longer applicable should not be used.

Denigration

Article 7 Advertisements should not denigrate any firm, industrial or commercial activity/profession or any product, directly or by implication, whether by bringing it into contempt or ridicule, or in any similar way.

Protection of Privacy

Article 8 Advertisements should not portray or refer to any persons, whether in a private or a public capacity, unless prior permission has been obtained;

nor should advertisements without prior permission depict or refer to any person's property in a way likely to convey the impression of a personal endorsement.

Exploitation of Goodwill

Article 9

1. Advertisements should not make unjustifiable use of the name or initials of another firm, company or institution.
2. Advertisements should not take undue advantage of the goodwill attached to the name of a person, the trade name and symbol of another firm or product, or of the goodwill acquired by an advertising campaign.

Imitation

Article 10

1. Advertisements should not imitate the general layout, text, slogan, visual presentation, music and sound effects etc., of other advertisements in a way that is likely to mislead or confuse.
2. Where an international advertiser has established a distinctive advertising campaign in one or more countries, other advertisers should not unduly imitate this campaign in the other countries where he operates, thus preventing him from extending his campaign within a reasonable period of time to such countries.

Identification of Advertisements

Article 11 Advertisements should be clearly distinguishable as such, whatever their form and whatever the medium used; when an advertisement appears in a medium which contains news or editorial matter, it should be so presented that it will be readily recognized as an advertisement.

Regard to Safety

Article 12 Advertisements should not without reason, justifiable on educational or social grounds, contain any visual presentation or any description of dangerous practices or of situations which show a disregard for safety. Special care should be taken in advertisements directed towards or depicting children or young people.

Children and Young People

Article 13

1. Advertisements should not exploit the natural credulity of children or the lack of experience of young people and should not strain their sense of loyalty.

2. Advertisements addressed to or likely to influence children or young people should not contain any statement or visual presentation which might result in harming them mentally, morally or physically.

Responsibility

Article 14

1. Responsibility for the observance of the rules of conduct laid down in the Code rests with the advertiser, the advertising practitioner or agency and the publisher, medium-owner or contractor.

   a. The advertiser should take the overall responsibility for his advertising.

   b. The advertising practitioner or agency should exercise every care in the preparation of the advertisement and should operate in such a way as to enable the advertiser to fulfill his responsibility.

   c. The publisher, medium-owner or contractor, who publishes, transmits or distributes the advertisement should exercise due care in the acceptance of advertisements and their presentation to the public.

2. Anyone employed within a firm, company or institution coming under the above three categories and who takes part in the planning, creation, publishing or transmitting of an advertisement, has a degree of responsibility commensurate with his position for ensuring that the rules of the Code are observed and should act accordingly.

Article 15 The responsibility for observance of the rules of the Code embraces the advertisement in its entire content and form, including testimonials and statements or visual presentations originating from other sources. The fact that the content or form originates wholly or in part from other sources is not an excuse for nonobservance of the rules.

Article 16 An advertisement contravening the Code cannot be defended on the grounds that the advertiser or someone acting on his behalf has subsequently provided the consumer with accurate information.

Article 17 Descriptions, claims or illustrations relating to verifiable facts should be capable of substantiation. Advertisers should have such substantiation available so that they can produce evidence without delay to the self-regulatory bodies responsible for the operation of the Code.

Article 18 No advertiser, advertising practitioner or agency, publisher, medium-owner or contractor should be party to the publication of any advertisement which has been found unacceptable by the appropriate self-regulatory body.

Implementation

Article 19 This Code of self-discipline is to be applied nationally by bodies set up for the purpose and internationally by the ICC's International Council on Marketing Practice as and when the need arises.

Special Provisions

The following provisions are intended to provide elaboration of relevant articles of the Code.

Guarantees

Provision a Advertisements should not contain any reference to a guarantee which does not improve the legal position of the purchaser. Advertisements may contain the word "guarantee," "guaranteed," "warranty" or "warranted" or words having the same meaning only if the full terms of the guarantee as well as the remedial action open to the purchaser are clearly set out in the advertisements, or are available to the purchaser in writing at the point of sale, or with the goods.

Consumer Credit, Loans, Savings and Investments

Provision b

1. Advertisements containing hire-purchase, credit sale or other consumer credit terms should be so presented that no misunderstand-

ing could arise as to the cash price, deposit, schedule of payment, rate of interest and total cost of the goods as advertised or to the other conditions of sale.

2. Advertisements offering loans should not contain any statement likely to mislead the public in respect of the type and duration of the loan, the securities required or other qualifications, the terms of repayment and the actual costs of interest and possible other charges.

3. Advertisements relating to savings or investments should not contain any statement likely to mislead the public on the commitments undertaken, on the actual or estimated yield, stating the factors affecting this, and on possible tax benefits.

Unsolicited Goods

Provision c Advertisements should not be used in connection with the unfair sales method of supplying unsolicited products to a person who is required to pay for them unless he refuses or returns them, or who is given the impression that he is obliged to accept them (inertia selling).

Franchise Schemes

Provision d Advertisements by franchisors seeking franchisees should not mislead, directly or by implication, as to the support provided and likely reward, or the investment and work required. The full name and permanent address of the franchisor should be stated.

Parallel Imports

Provision e Advertisements for goods imported in parallel should avoid creating any misunderstanding in the minds of consumers concerning the characteristics of the goods offered or the ancillary services provided, particularly when these differ significantly from the goods otherwise distributed.

Poisonous and Flammable Products

Provision f Advertisements for products which are potentially poisonous or flammable but which may not be readily recognized as such by consumers should indicate the potential danger of such products.

Guidelines for Advertising Addressed to Children

The following guidelines are intended to provide interpretation of relevant articles of the Code.

The guidelines apply to advertisements for products whether paid for or given free

1. addressed to children under 14 years of age or whatever age is considered appropriate at the national level;

2. in children's media (i.e. media specifically intended for children under 14 years of age or whatever age is considered appropriate at the national level).

Guidelines

Guideline 1: Identification Because of the particular vulnerability of children and in order to give special effect to Article 11 of the Code, if there is any likelihood of advertisements being confused with editorial or programme material, they should be clearly labelled "advertisement" or identified in an equally effective manner.

Guideline 2: Violence In giving effect to Article 13.2 of the Code it should be borne in mind that advertisements should not appear to condone violence in situations or actions which might contravene the law and/or generally accepted national standards of social behaviour.

Guideline 3: Social Values Advertisements should not undermine social values when suggesting that possession or use of a product alone will give the child a physical, social or psychological advantage over other children of the same age, or that non-possession of this product would have the opposite effect.

Advertisements should not undermine the authority, responsibility, judgment or tastes of parents, taking into account the current social values.

Guideline 4: Security To give effect to Articles 12 and 13.2 of the Code, advertisements should not contain any statement or visual presentation that could have the effect of bringing children into unsafe situations or of encouraging them to consort with strangers or to enter strange or hazardous places.

Guideline 5: Persuasion Advertisements should not include any direct appeal to children to persuade others to buy the advertised product for them.

Guideline 6: Truthful Presentation To give effect to Article 4 of the Code, special care should be taken to ensure that advertisements do not mislead children as to the true size, value, nature, durability and performance of the advertised product. If extra items are needed to use it (e.g. batteries) or to produce the result shown or described (e.g. paint), this should be made clear. A product which is part of a series should be clearly indicated as should the method of acquiring the series.

Advertisements should not understate the degree of skill required to use the product. Where results of product use are shown or described, the advertisement should represent what is reasonably attainable by the average child in the age range for which the product is intended.

Guideline 7: Price Price indication should not be such as to lead children to an unreal perception of the true value of the product, for instance by using the word "only." No advertisement should imply that the advertised product is immediately within reach of every family budget.

Index